THE I TATTI
RENAISSANCE LIBRARY

James Hankins, General Editor

SANNAZARO

LATIN POETRY

ITRL 38

JACOPO SANNAZARO
✦ ✦ ✦
LATIN POETRY

TRANSLATED BY

MICHAEL C. J. PUTNAM

THE I TATTI RENAISSANCE LIBRARY
HARVARD UNIVERSITY PRESS
CAMBRIDGE, MASSACHUSETTS
LONDON, ENGLAND
2009

Series design by Dean Bornstein

Library of Congress Cataloging-in-Publication Data

Sannazaro, Jacopo, 1458–1530.
[Poems. English & Latin. Selections]
Latin poetry / Jacopo Sannazaro ; translated by
Michael C. J. Putnam.
p.   cm. — (The I Tatti Renaissance library ; 38)
Includes bibliographical references and index.
ISBN 978-0-674-03406-8 (cloth : alk. paper)
1. Christian poetry, Latin (Medieval and modern) — Translations into English.
2. Latin poetry (Medieval and modern) — Translations into English.
3. Mary, Blessed Virgin, Saint — Poetry.   4. Jesus Christ — Poetry.
I. Putnam, Michael C. J.   II. Title.
PA8570.S3A2 2009
871'.04 — dc22   2009000602

Contents

☙❧

Introduction

❧❧❧

Jacopo Sannazaro, one of the luminaries among writers of Latin poetry in Renaissance Italy, was born and died in his beloved Naples (1458–1530).[1] His literary talent was early recognized, and he became the protégé of Giovanni Pontano, whose Accademia Pontaniana he had entered by 1478, taking the name Actius Sincerus. (He became the Academy's head after the death of Pietro Summonte in 1525.) In 1499 King Federico of Aragon gave him a villa at Mergellina, on the western outskirts of Naples, that figures in several of his poems.[2] He accompanied Federico into exile in France in 1501 but, after the king's death three years later, returned to Naples in 1505. He is buried in the church of Santa Maria del Parto that he had built near his villa, at a short distance below what was then considered to be the tomb of the Augustan poet Vergil, one of the most potent influences on Sannazaro's Latin writings.[3]

He gained early fame from his vernacular masterpiece, *Arcadia*, written largely during the 1480s but not published definitively until 1504. But otherwise his greatest achievements were written in Latin. The most well known are his epic *De partu Virginis*, which he worked on for several decades, and his five piscatory eclogues (*Piscatoria*), also the product of many years' labor. Both were published in 1526.[4] Over the course of his career he also wrote a number of elegies and a wide variety of poems in equally diverse meters. They ultimately formed three books each of *Elegiae* and of *Epigrammata* that were collected by the poet's friend Antonio Garlon and published posthumously in 1535.

In his late, autobiographical elegy to Cassandra Marchese (*el.* 3.2) Sannazaro lists his works in apparent order of composition.

vii

He begins with a précis of the work that made his initial reputation, the *Arcadia* (35–42):

> Tunc ego pastorum numero, silvestria primum
>   tentavi calamis sibila disparibus.
> Deductumque levi carmen modulatus in umbra,
>   innumeros pavi lata per arva greges.
> Androgeumque, Opicumque, et rustica sacra secutus,
>   commovi lacrimis mox pia saxa meis,
> dum tumulum carae, dum festinata parentis
>   fata cano, gemitus dum, Melisaee, tuos.

> Then, among the crowd of shepherds, for the first time I attempted sylvan whistlings on uneven reeds and, after I had sounded a fine-spun song in the slight shade, I fed countless sheep across the broad pastures. After being in thrall to Androgeos and Opicus and rural rites, I soon moved the holy rocks with my tears when I sing of the grave, the hurried doom, of my mother, when of your lamentations, Melisaeus.[5]

The *Arcadia* is an elaborate pastoral in twelve books, each combining prose and verse. It forms one of the most important links between the work of Petrarch, its inspiration, and that of Sir Philip Sidney.[6] Written in the vernacular as are the hundred or so surviving *Rime*, it is largely the product of the last decades of the fifteenth century.[7] It is important to mention the writings in Italian at the start of a brief overview of Sannazaro's career, not only because of their intrinsic importance, but because their early production points to one of the paradoxes of his poetic development. After writing an initial masterpiece in Italian he turned to Latin for all his subsequent major achievements, parts of which were already written, or at least contemplated, during the composition of the *Arcadia*. This linguistic reorientation perhaps serves as a confirmation in Sannazaro's intellectual development of his allegiance to Christian humanism. More particularly it may also be his devotion to Vergil (70–19 BCE) — the order of whose three great works, *Eclogues*, *Georgics*, and *Aeneid*, introduced an influential model for a poet's career in its progression from pastoral to didactic to epic — that provided him with a telling impetus for his own accomplishments in the earlier master's tongue.

The first of the Latin poems Sannazaro mentions in the elegy to Cassandra Marchese is his epic *De partu Virginis* (el. 3.2.45–52):[8]

> Mox maiora vocant me numina, scilicet alti
>   incessere animum sacra veranda Dei,
> sacra Dei Regisque hominum, Dominique Deorum,
>   primaevum sanctae religionis opus;
> nuncius aethereis ut venerit aliger astris,
>   dona ferens castae Virginis in gremium.
> Quid referam caulasque ovium, lususque canentum
>   pastorum, et reges, Arsacis ora, tuos?

> Soon greater Powers summon me. Nothing less than the awe-inspiring holiness of God on high entered my mind, the holiness of God, both the King of men and the Lord of Gods, our blessed religion's original achievement: how the winged messenger came from the ether's stars, carrying gifts for the lap of the chaste Virgin. Why should I tell of the sheepfolds, and the sporting of shepherds at song, and your kings, realm of Arsaces?

From the course of the narrative of Sannazaro's extraordinary three-book poem we can piece together the life of Christ: preaching to the elders, passion and ultimate triumph (book 1), birth (book 2), baptism and miracles (book 3), but, as the title of the poem makes clear, the central figure is Mary and the focal event in her life, the mystery that Sannazaro celebrates, is the virgin birth.

This doesn't mean that the poem is actionless. As Sannazaro parallels the course of the biblical story we do move from the Annunciation in book 1 to the Visitation in book 2 followed by the return home and the journey to Bethlehem. Book 3 picks up the narrative thread with the rejoicing of angelic choirs and earthly shepherds.

But the poem is as much a grand meditation as it is an historical chronicle. Part of the stability or fixedness that the reader senses arises from Sannazaro's careful structuring of the whole. We begin and end at Mergellina, which is to say at Naples, enjoying the poet's topography of inspiration. Speeches of God the Father begin both the first and third books, and two still longer prophecies — one put into the mouth of the Old Testament king and psalmist David, the other given to Proteus, shape-changing seer who is a literary figure in pagan antiquity from Homer's *Odyssey* on — receive extended treatment at the conclusions of the same books in such a way as to confirm the careful balances of the whole poem.[9] And at the middle of the poem, forming the essential topic of book 2, is the magical parturition around the telling of which the whole revolves.

This concern with proportional structure does not diminish the force of epic elements in *De partu Virginis*. As in the *Aeneid*, action moves both horizontally, as we follow the terrestrial lives of Mary and her son, and vertically, with heaven and hell making important appearances, especially in the figures of David and of God the Father. A river god plays an important role in each poem, the Tiber for Vergil, the Jordan for Sannazaro. And there are in common the usual elements in any epic composition, similes, for instance, of which Sannazaro has six that are richly inventive. The Neapolitan poet also follows Vergil in his love of ekphrasis, three examples of which dot the text.

But, as is also the case with the figure of ekphrasis, other elements enter into the mix that tend to give the poem as a whole a static nature, to replace the excitement of forward action with the charm of description. Sannazaro, for instance, delights in lists. In book 2 we have the brilliant overview of the Mediterranean world at the time of Augustus; in book three we learn in detail of the daughters of Jordan and of the miracles of Christ. The depiction of Christ's triumphal chariot near the end of book 1 is another case where the eye of the reader's mind is put to work in a slow examination of an artifact that decorates the story line, even as it brings action to a halt while looking at an event far into the future.

Most noteworthy by comparison with previous epics is the predominance of the spoken word.[10] The poem's many speeches may break the narrative flow but they also offer significant commentary on its major themes. And many are virtuoso performances in their own right. Sannazaro's paraphrases of the words of Gabriel's annunciation, or of the *Nunc dimittis* and *Magnificat*, function as important meditations on the biblical texts which served as their bases. Nor are pagan authors exempt from the poet's commentary. Lines 186–236 of book three offer a detailed dissertation on Vergil's fourth *eclogue*, a poem that from the time of Lactantius on had been considered by Christian authors as offering a prediction of the coming of the redeemer.

Mention of Vergil raises two further points, one specific, one general. In terms of detail the presence of the Roman poet is to be felt on every page. The New Testament, and the Old to a lesser degree, offered Sannazaro both story line and specific texts that he moulds, and melds, into his own. But Vergil is the classical author who, through all three of his works, looms large in the intellectual background of his brilliant successes. The *Eclogues* furnished the many pastoral elements of shepherding, woods and song that we find. The *Georgics* supplied a model for the didactic tone inherent in Sannazaro's presentation, and the *Aeneid*, Sannazaro's essential epic model, for the poem's core grandeur.

The presence of Vergil leads to a more general point. Like his great Italian predecessors Dante and Petrarch, not to speak of Classical authors who follow in Vergil's wake, Sannazaro would have been fully aware of the Vergilian career, that is to say the progress from pastoral to didactic to epic, as he pondered his own growth as poet. And, as noted above, all three of the Augustan poet's masterpieces play their parts as Sannazaro crafted his own most expansive work. The *Eclogues* in particular play a crucial role in serving as touchstone not only for the bucolic elements in *De partu Virginis* but also for the *Piscatoria* as a whole where the later poet challenges his master by moving the setting of pastoral from a generalized Arcadia, with touches of north Italy, to specific sites along the Neapolitan littoral. As we will shortly see, Sannazaro himself doesn't lay claim to any structured generic progress but speaks of working contemporaneously on both his epic and his pastorals.

Perhaps it is best, then, not to speak of an evolution in Sannazaro's career based on the Vergilian model but of an interpenetration of Vergil's masterpieces with Sannazaro's poetry as a whole. But one detail stands out, and it has to do with the carefully structured balances in *De partu Virginis* mentioned earlier. Vergil plays a part in this achievement and here it is the *Georgics*, not the *Eclogues* or the *Aeneid*, that gains special prominence. Lines 19–32 of book I of Sannazaro's poem, addressed to Mary as muse, are carefully modeled on lines 24–42 from the opening of Vergil's central masterpiece, where the future Augustus is apostrophized as patron and imminent divinity. And, just as the fourth and final *Georgic* ends with a lengthy appearance of the sea-god Proteus and an envoi which places the poet in Naples, so the central set piece of Sannazaro's concluding book is also given over to Proteus, and we conclude, as we began, with the beauties of the same bay and its Siren namesake.[11]

These parallels in turn suggest to the reader that, however important the *Eclogues* and the *Aeneid* are as elements to bear in mind as he evaluates Sannazaro's generic originality, it is the *Georgics* that has pride of place as a creative force on Sannazaro and not the more predictable Vergilian epic that had served as climax of the earlier poet's career. The lesson to draw seems to be that the Neapolitan master sees his poem as, on the deepest level, didactic.[12] That is to say, it stands primarily as a document that teaches us about something necessarily static, one of the central mysteries of the Christian faith, and that the pastoral elements that serve as appropriate decoration and the epic component that offers the central subject a narrative context take second place to the poet's primary goal as an educator.

In the elegy to Cassandra Marchese, Sannazaro mentions his collection of pastorals, the *Piscatoria*, immediately after summarizing *De partu Virginis* but, as we have noted, in a way that makes the composition of the two works seem contemporary (*el.* 3.2.53–8):[13]

> Nec minus haec inter piscandi concitus egit
>   ardor in aequoreos mittere lina sinus,
> fallacesque cibos vacuis includere nassis,
>   atque hamo undivagos sollicitare greges,
> quandoquidem salsas descendi ego primus ad undas,
>   ausus inexpertis reddere verba sonis.

> Likewise along with these matters an excited passion for fishing drove me to launch my nets into the sea's bays, to hide deceitful bait in weels, to tempt wave-wandering schools with the hook, since I was the first to make my way down to the salt waters, having dared to render words in untried melodies.

The language of the final two lines presents similarities to the way in which Sannazaro's speaker describes the collection in the fourth

Eclogue, also a late poem, dedicated to Ferdinando of Aragon, son of the exiled king of Naples, Federico (17–20):

> . . . nunc litoream ne despice Musam
> quam tibi post silvas, post horrida lustra Lycaei
> (si quid id est) salsas deduxi primus ad undas,
> ausus inexperta tentare pericula cymba.

> For now do not scorn the muse of the seashore whom, after the forests, after the rugged wilds of Lycaeus (if that counts for anything), I was the first to bring down to the salt waves for you, daring to risk their dangers in my untested bark.

In this instance Sannazaro places the composition of the *Piscatoria* later than that of the *Arcadia*, which is to say, to the subsequent time when his muse journeyed from woods to waves, from the romance of Mt. Lycaeus in a make-believe Arcadia to the realities of the Bay of Naples, and he himself turned from the vernacular to Latin as his primary vehicle for poetic expression. In both instances he also calls attention to his combination of daring and primacy, which is to say his courage in being the first to alter the received tradition of a major genre of classical poetry, the pastoral eclogue, by changing its setting from the pasture land of shepherds to the shore and sea of fishermen.[14]

Whatever the novelty and individual brilliance of the five completed *Piscatoria*, Sannazaro never loses sight of his classical heritage from Theocritus and especially Vergil. To move, as does his collection, from dialogue to monologue, contest, catalogue and refrain-based interchange is to survey many of the modes of presentation of his ancient models. Nevertheless, for all his dependence on his Latin master, Sannazaro's masterpiece has elements of great originality. In changing the venue of his poems from the world of shepherds to that of fishermen, Sannazaro adds an element of practicality to his poetry largely absent from Vergil's great poems. This novelty could be looked at in terms of place and of time. Though we have mentions of the river Mincio and of the cities of Mantua and Cremona in Vergil's *Eclogues*, and though Rome and the places to which it can send its victims into exile loom large in the extraordinary and programmatic introductory poem, neverthe-less Vergil's shepherds still regularly inhabit an Arcady of song, prominent in poems 4, 7 and 10. Sannazaro, by contrast, draws us constantly into the harsh realities of his characters' marine exis-tence and into the specifics of the Bay of Naples and its environs, to which we attend to some degree in every poem.

Occasionally, too, real people, like Asinius Pollio and Alfenus Varus, enter Vergil's verses as does the immediacy of late Republi-can Roman history, especially through reference, in *Eclogues* 1 and 9, to the harshness of the land proscriptions following upon the battle of Philippi in 42 BCE, proscriptions from which the ancient *vitae* tell us that Vergil himself suffered. And the speaking "I," whether or not we take its utterances as true for the poet in his own person, does enter the fourth, sixth and tenth of the poems, usually in connection with the creation of poetry itself. But the presence of Neapolitan history looms even larger for Sannazaro than does that of Rome for Vergil. Meliboeus, in Vergil's initial eclogue, may be preparing for distant relegation, and the ninth poem in Vergil's collection tells of trouble in the landscape caused by dispossession. But Chromis, in *Eclogue* 3 of Sannazaro—a stand-in for the poet himself—has already endured the exile that, from 1501 to 1505, took the poet from Naples to Tours and be-yond, in the suite of his king, Federico III. And the experience is given further prominence in the two poems that follow,[15] the first of which, *Eclogue* 4, is dedicated to Federico's son, Ferdinando III, likewise an exile from his kingdom, this time in Spain. What is novel for Vergil by contrast with Theocritus becomes even more pronounced for Sannazaro, as the actuality of a fisherman's life on the Bay of Naples, and of the realities faced himself by the poet who wrote about them, take center stage in his verse.[16]

Sannazaro limits his summary description of the *Elegiarum Libri* to two lines (59–60):

Quid referam mollesque elegos, miserabile carmen,
  et superis laudes non sine ture datas . . . ?

Why should I also tell of soft elegies, song of lament, and of praises, graced with incense, given to the gods?

The poet's brevity does scant justice to the variety to be found in these twenty-four fascinating poems. We have six elegies addressed to or concerning his scholarly circle of friends and poets. Pontano is singled out at 1.9 and a diatribe against Envy introduces the catalogue of Sannazaro's intellectual associates that concludes the first book (1.11).[17]

Four other poems are addressed to kings and statesmen, one to an unknown exile. We have two birthday poems (2.2 and 2.8), one on the actual occasion of parturition (1.4), one on the first of the year (2.3). There is a hymn to a pagan god (2.5) and a eulogy of a recently deceased Christian saint (1.7). We have a series of laments, as we would expect from the genre of elegy, some devoted to unhappy love, others to the relentless passage of time and to death or to their various combinations. Sannazaro gives us three examples of monologue: his widow Lucretia grieves for the passing of Sarro Brancaccio (1.6); the goddess Astraea, in language indebted to Vergil's fourth *Eclogue* and second *Georgic*, reminds Pierre de Rochefort of the nobility of his calling (1.8); and pomegranates sing their own virtues in the concluding poem of the second book (2.10). The poem on pomegranates joins another group centered on aetiology. The fourth poem of the first book tells, in Ovidian fashion, of the origin of the white mulberry, while

2.9 is a powerful meditation on the rise and passing of the town of Cumae. The initial poem of book 2, addressed to Alfonso II, is a *recusatio*, a "refusal" poem that is also a catalogue of the king's accomplishments.

The three poems that constitute the third book are also deeply concerned with time. The first, by far the longest in the collection, is dedicated to Federico of Aragon and is in essence an expansive catalogue of his deeds. Though the king is apostrophized several times, the poem ends by acknowledging the death that brought an end to his sufferings and the urn that possesses all that remains after the grand biography is finished. The second, parallel, poem, dedicated, as we have seen, to his patroness Cassandra Marchese, summarizes the legacy of the poet's imagination. It too ends in resignation, as he commits the arrangements for his funeral—for the disposition of his mortal remains—to his friend. Pride in the imagination's enterprise anticipates only the final acknowledgement of the speaker's humanity.

The third and concluding poem that rounds out the collection as well as the book brings a change of tone. We attend to the description of the building of a house, real, perhaps, but with equal likelihood hypothetical. Sylvan gods will bless the expansive dwelling that will contain statues of four kings within whose reigns Sannazaro had spent his life and will enjoy a vista sweeping over the poet's beautiful Naples. It is a hymn of thanksgiving for his safe return. It is also a poem about the creation of poetry and the setting that fosters it. It is not accidental that Sannazaro's references to his restored *otia* (leisure, l. 46) and to the siren Parthenopea herself in the elegy's concluding line (52) recall the final lines of another masterpiece associated with Naples that we have seen exert great influence on Sannazaro's Latin verse: Vergil's *Georgics*. Our poet's heroic Federico may be dead while Vergil's Augustus yet lives to thunder in the East, but for Vergil as well as for Sannazaro leisure (*oti, geo.* 4.564) nourished by his muse

Parthenope (564) is a crucial element as he continues to pursue his vocation as *vatis*.

As we would expect, the work of the Roman elegists, especially Tibullus and Propertius, is here a prominent, pervasive source of inspiration for the Neapolitan master. Poem 2.1, to Alfonso, for instance, draws upon the similarly placed *recusatio* to Propertius's patron Maecenas, and 2.7, to Bacchus, is a riff on Propertius's hymn to the same divinity. But Sannazaro's special touch is never absent and some of his most original poems, such as the reflection on time's passing that contemplation of the ruins of Cumae elicits, rise to the level of the greatest poetry.

Two lines also suffice for the poet's description to Cassandra Marchese of the three books of epigrams (*el.* 3.2.61–2):

Quaeque aliis lusi numeris, dum seria tracto,
    dum spargo varios per mea dicta sales . . .

And what I played in other meters, while I was dealing with serious matters, while I was strewing my words with assorted wit . . .

Sannazaro's brevity does only summary justice to the rich variety of subjects and of their presentation in these more than five score poems. We have compositions on the poet's kings and patrons, on friends and enemies, on places and dates. We move easily between hymn and invective, between love poetry and satire, eulogy and condemnation, and in such a way that juxtaposition often serves to elicit any poem's special essence.

The cast of characters has a full range. Among figures of note we have Neapolitan royalty (Alfonso II, Federico and Ferdinando of Aragon) and popes (Innocent VIII, Hadrian VI, Leo X), scholarly friends like Altilio, Cariteo, Acquaviva and Summonte, all members of the Neapolitan academy, as well as humanists of earlier generations such as Poggio, Platina and Fra Giocondo. The death of Petrus Compater (Piero Golino) is mourned, and the graves of King Ladislas, of Hannibal and of the young Veronese poet Cotta, among others, serve as sources for meditation on the challenge time's passage offers human achievement. These several poems on human mortality are counterbalanced by equally moving celebrations of birth and birthdays. (Birthdays, we know, were always occasions for poetic outpourings from members of the Academy.) Personages from classical antiquity, like Homer, Cato and Brutus, add to the diversity.

Places too are often Sannazaro's focus, whether he is dealing with his villa at Mergillina, the remains of a Campanian theatre or the city of Venice, for which he had a particular fondness. The town of Nola is singled out for its injudicious treatment of his mentor, Giovanni Gioviano Pontano.

Religious and secular elements easily cohabit in this miscellany. San Nazario, the family saint on whose feast day Sannazaro was born, receives three poems and is eulogized quietly in a fourth, and San Gaudioso two. But hymns are never far removed from satire and invective. (Elegiac couplet is by a large margin Sannazaro's meter of choice, but six other meters lend an element of contrast echoed in the evolution of the collection as a whole.) Five poems have Cesare Borgia as target and Politian is attacked in two. And lesser or unknown figures, like a certain Vetustinus with a fixation on his grave monument, a Phyllis whose buttocks are worthy of note, an unwisely argumentative "owl," along with miscellaneous drunkards and degenerates stand revealed through Sannazaro's graphic ribaldry.

An erotic component is also prominent in the epigrams, whether we count Nina's kisses, admire the beauty of Cassandra Marchese or move to Olympus and the amatory adventures of Jupiter, Juno, Venus, Ganymede and company.

Pagan and Christian themes and modes of presentation form regular neighbors. The poetry of Catullus and Martial on similar topics is often on Sannazaro's mind. But even within a genre like the hymn we learn from juxtaposition. The poems to San Gaudioso (2.58 and 59) are a case in point. The first is written in iambic dimeter, the meter that St. Ambrose had utilized more than a millennium earlier for his innovative works. For the second Sannazaro chose Sapphic stanza, the meter the Roman lyricist Horace preferred second only to Alcaics. Or we could look at such collocations in terms of subject matter. One of the odes to San Nazario (2.51) is preceded by a poem made up of two elegiac distichs, on Jupiter and Amor, and followed by another, also in elegiac couplets, on Amor the fugitive. A glorification of Cassandra Marchese's charms (2.57) precedes one of the hymns to San Gaudioso. A powerful duet of poems exposing the vices of Cesare Borgia (1.14–15) is followed by a moving vignette devoted to a gemstone and the piety its carving illustrates. And the pair of virulent poems attacking Politian (1.61–62) is preceded by a single distich on the poet as lover and followed by two brief epigrams on statues of Actaeon and Orpheus.[18]

Even within these two sets of examples, *variatio* is at work. Of the two poems against Cesare Borgia, the first is in elegiac couplets, the second in iambic dimeter; of those attacking Politian, a poem in hendecasyllabics is followed by another in iambic dimeter.

As usual the initial and concluding poems of each book have particular force. The final offering in the third (3.9) deserves special mention. As a lament for his departure into exile, it forms not only a moving conclusion in itself but also a balance with the last poem of the three books of elegies which ends with the speaker's pronouncement of gratitude for safe return to the charms and comforts of Naples.

Two shorter pieces complete the corpus of Sannazaro's Latin poetic writing. The first is *Salices (The Willows)*, a virtuoso recounting of the tale of Nymphs of the Neapolitan river Sarnus (Sarno) pursued by local Satyrs, Pans and Fauns, and changed into willows before rape could occur. Sannazaro's chief inspiration is the *Metamorphoses* of Ovid, a poem dotted with similar stories of chase followed by transformation of the hunted, usually into non-human form. (One of the most accomplished of the elegies, 2.4, relates the similar myth of the change of Morilla, a Naiad who captured the fancy of Pan, into a mulberry tree. Here also Sannazaro gives the story a distinctively Neapolitan setting.)

If the poem's narrative technique is indebted to Ovid, several details of setting and presentation also owe much to Vergil of the *Eclogues*, pastoral poetry against which Sannazaro regularly tested his originality. Two examples: First, the opening of the narrative proper (14–21), which places us in a woodland setting during the heat of the day, looks back to the initial thirteen lines of Vergil's *Eclogue* 2. There, after locating the lovelorn Corydon "among thick beeches" (*inter densas . . . fagos*, 3), like Sannazaro's protagonists "among thick alders" (*densas inter . . . alnos*, 21), the poet has him sing of his love for Alexis, accompanied in the noon-day heat only by the buzzing of the cicadas (the detail is in common between *Eclogue* 2.13 and *Salices* 17). Secondly, at line 43 Sannazaro offers a careful variation on a moment from the opening of Vergil's tenth *Eclogue* where the speaker announces that his song, far from falling on deaf ears, draws an echo from the nearby woods. The Neapolitan poet by contrast has his emboldened singers resort to physical force after their words fail to elicit a positive response. And at this point in Sannazaro's poem the language of pastoral lament, whether paralleled in the songs of Corydon in Vergil's *Eclogue* 2 or Gallus in his *Eclogue* 10, gives way to narrative action, and we enter more fully the world of Ovidian mutations for the poem's concluding segment.

If we were to seek a Christian analogue in the poetic career of Sannazaro to the pagan poetics of *Salices* it would be *De morte Christi Domini ad mortales lamentatio*, the second of his two shorter works to be considered. More a jeremiad than an elegy, the poem begins and ends with "you," which is to say sinful mankind, the subject of the speaker's lecture, first marveling at God's grand designing of the celestial universe, then being received into the same sky after final repentance. But the force of the speaker's authority directs us immediately after its start to the physicality of Christ on the cross, to the incarnate God's graphic suffering on behalf of lapsed mortals, a spectacle to which he returns two further times during the course of the poem. This earthly scene stands in contrast not only with heaven, in its present sorrow at the Son's affliction and as future residence of redeemed humanity, but also with the underworld of hell which harbors the souls of the guilty after death but before their salvation, to implement which is at the core of the preacher's teaching.

The modern reader may find in Sannazaro's juxtaposition of the pagan and Christian worlds an irony that the poet would no doubt have taken as a matter of course. The speaker exhorts decadent humans to give up "the inheritance of lying gods and abominable rituals," incense-filled rites taking place in temples that receive dead animals as offerings. Yet the intellectual frame of the poem is based as much upon the world of Roman religion, myth and intellectual history as it is upon dogmas that the medieval Church both practiced and illustrated so tellingly in Romanesque and Gothic art. If we look at Sannazaro's designations for heaven, earth and hell as he describes their interconnections in Christ's *vita*, we find God, a Thunderer like Jove, living on Olympus, seat of pagan divinities. The sea is the domain of Triton, the moon personified as Phoebe, the realm of the dead associated with Cocytus, Orcus and Avernus. Even in a poem as intellectually and emotionally concerned with one of the crucial moments for the history of Christian doctrine as is the *Lamentatio*, the world of Rome is not far distant, whether as a touchstone to highlight the higher morality of the new faith or as a continuing stimulus for the imagination. We have already watched in *De partu Virginis* a different, more elaborate variation of the same combination.

I owe particular thanks to Professor James Hankins, distinguished editor of the I Tatti Renaissance Library, for sharing his learning as well as for his meticulous eye. The manuscript was also greatly improved by the counsel of Julia Haig Gaisser. I dedicate the book to her — student, friend, guide.

NOTES

1. The most recent life of Sannazaro, and its first ample treatment in English, is by Kidwell, *Sannazaro* (for full references see Bibliography). It contains extensive notes and bibliography. The most detailed evaluation of his poetry in English is that of Kennedy, *Sannazaro*.

2. On the date of the gift see Kidwell, *Sannazaro*, 85 and 224, n. 70.

3. This proximity is the nub of Cardinal Pietro Bembo's epitaph engraved on Sannazaro's tomb: *Da sacro cineri flores. Hic ille Maroni / Sincerus musa proximus ut tumulo* (Give flowers to the holy ash. Here lies Sincerus, nearest to Maro [Vergil] in his genius as in his grave). Bembo is also the author of a second epitaph: *Quid moror? aeterni te suspicit umbra Maronis, / Et tibi vicinum donat habere locum* (Why do I wait? The shade of immortal Maro esteems you and grants you to have a place near him). For a record in poetry of Bembo's admiration for Sannazaro see Bembo's *Sarca* 590–604, in Pietro Bembo, *Lyric Poetry. Etna*, tr. Mary P. Chatfield (Cambridge, Mass., 2005), 170. Pontano's dialogue *Actius*, named after the young poet and written by June 1499 (see Kidwell *Pontano*, 285), presents him as already an authority on Vergil's poetry.

4. We hear of an outline of *De partu Virginis* from the 1490s (Kidwell, *Sannazaro*, 41, 143 and 236, n. 38), and it is likely that the first eclogue dates from 1499. The next three in the collection all refer to the poet's exile in France. The shorter *Salices* and *Lamentatio de morte Christi domini* were both also published in 1526.

5. For detailed references to this and the subsequent quotations from *elegy* 3.2 see the relevant notes in Notes to the Translation.

6. For the Arcadia and its nachleben see Sukanta Chaudhuri, *Renaissance Pastoral and Its English Developments* (Oxford, 1989); *Sidney's Arcadia. A Map of Arcadia: Sidney's Romance in Its Tradition*, by W. R. Davis, and *The Old Arcadia*, by R. A. Lanham (New Haven, 1965); M. S. Goldman, *Sir Philip Sidney and The Arcadia*, Illinois Studies in Language and Literature 17 (1934), nos. 1–2; M. McCanles, *The Text of Sidney's Arcadian World* (Durham, N.C., 1989); R. Stillman, *Sidney's Poetic Justice: The Old Arcadia, Its Eclogues, and Renaissance Pastoral Traditions* (Lewisburg, 1986); and especially D. Kalstone, "The Transformation of Arcadia: Sannazaro and Sir Philip Sidney," *Comparative Literature* 15 (1963): 234–49; and idem, *Sidney's Poetry: Contexts and Interpretations* (Cambridge, 1965). The first authorized publication of the *Arcadia* was in 1504, following a corrupt edition of 1502.

7. The *Rime* were first published posthumously in 1536. They are summarized at *el*. 2.3.63–4: *Multaque praeterea, dilectae grata puellae, / Adscisco antiquis rursus Etrusca modis* (Furthermore I adapt again to ancient meters many Tuscan matters, pleasing to my beloved mistress).

8. For significant appraisals of *De partu Virginis* see Greene, *Descent from Heaven*, 144–70; Kennedy, *Sannazaro*, 180–224; Quint, *Origin and Originality*, 43–80.

9. The list can be extended. The descent of Gabriel in book 1, for instance, is parallel to that of Laetitia in book 3. The combination of David and Proteus speaks broadly to Sannazaro's merger of the worlds of the Old Testament and of classical antiquity which were formative for his work.

10. The proportion of speech to narrative is considerably higher in *De partu Virginis* than in Vergil's *Aeneid* where (if only the speeches of Aeneas' narrative in books 2 and 3 are included) the spoken word accounts for 3666 hexameters out of some 9897.

11. In actuality the parallels between *Georgic* 4 and the third book of *De partu Virginis* are still more extensive. The catalogue of the daughters of Jordan (*DPV* 3.281–97), for example, is closely modeled on that of

Cyrene's sister nymphs at *geo.* 4.334–44, and the watery worlds of each are parallel. We should also note the triple iteration of the name Eurydice at *geo.* 4.525–27 and of Jordan at *DPV* 3.413–15. And at the end of *DPV* 1 (456–62) Sannazaro is clearly thinking of *geo.* 4.481–84.

12. The reader thus takes the place of Vergil's Aristaeus in the position of learner. It is scarcely accidental that the last line of Sannazaro's poem alludes to Lucretius *De Rerum Natura* (1.118), arguably the most extraordinary didactic poem remaining from antiquity.

13. For an important recent critique of the *Piscatoria* see Hubbard, "Exile from Arcadia."

14. Sannazaro would have found a classical model not in Vergil for his *Piscatoria* in Theocritus *Id.* 21. For poetic daring as a topic in Sannazaro's classical models see Vergil *geo.* 2.175; for primacy, Horace *epi.* 1.19.23, and compare *c.* 3.30.13–14, where Horace also uses the verb *deduco*. In *ecl.* 2.42–45 Sannazaro receives the blessing of Melisaeus, i.e., Pontano himself, for his pastoral undertaking.

15. See *ecl.* 4.81–6 and 5.113–15.

16. The nocturnal setting of *Eclogue* 2 is another departure from the tradition of Vergil, whose parallel poem is set during the heat of the day.

17. Compare the tone and content of the penultimate poem in Horace's first collection of epistles (*epi.* 1.19).

18. That the arrangement of these poems was probably made by Garlon in no way detracts from their rich diversity.

LATIN POETRY

DE PARTU VIRGINIS
LIBRI TRES

Clementi VII pontifici maximo Actius Syncerus

Magne parens custosque hominum, cui ius datur uni
    claudere coelestes et reserare fores,
occurrent siqua in nostris male firma libellis,
    deleat errores aequa litura meos:
5 imperiis, venerande, tuis submittimus illos,
    nam sine te recta non licet ire via.
Ipse manu sacrisque potens Podalirius herbis
    ulcera paeonia nostra levabis ope,
quippe mihi toto nullus te praeter in orbe
10 triste salutifera leniet arte malum.
Rarus honos summo se praeside posse tueri,
    rarior a summo praeside posse legi.

THE VIRGIN BIRTH
IN THREE BOOKS

Actius Syncerus to Clement VII, Supreme Pontiff

Great father and warden of mankind, to whom alone is granted
the right to seal and to unbar the gates of heaven: if anything un-
sound in my little books comes to your attention, let your good
judgment's cancellation expunge my mistakes. I submit them, your
worship, to your commands, for without you no one may walk a   5
straight path. A Podalirius yourself, through the power of hands
and holy herbs, you will relieve my cankers with Paeon's resource,
since in my view no one in the whole world except you will as-
suage sad misfortune with restorative skill. It is a rare honor to fall   10
under the protection of the supreme guardian, rarer still is to be
able to be read by the supreme guardian.

Liber Primus

Virginei partus magnoque aequaeva parenti
progenies, superas coeli quae missa per auras
antiquam generis labem mortalibus aegris
abluit obstructique viam patefecit Olympi,
5   sit mihi, coelicolae, primus labor, hoc mihi primum
surgat opus: vos auditas ab origine causas
et tanti seriem, si fas, evolvite facti.
Nec minus, o Musae, vatum decus, hic ego vestros
optarim fonteis, vestras nemora ardua rupes,
10 quandoquidem genus e coelo deducitis et vos
virginitas sanctaeque iuvat reverentia famae:
vos igitur, seu cura poli seu virginis huius
tangit honos, monstrate viam, qua nubila vincam,
et mecum immensi portas recludite coeli;
15 magna quidem, magna, Aonides, sed debita posco,
nec vobis ignota: etenim potuistis et antrum
aspicere et choreas, nec vos orientia coelo
signa nec eoos reges latuisse putandum est.
Tuque adeo, spes fida hominum, spes fida deorum.
20 alma parens, quam mille acies quaeque aetheris alti
militia est, totidem currus, tot signa tubaeque,
tot litui comitantur ovantique agmina gyro
adglomerant: niveis tibi si solennia templis
serta damus, si mansuras tibi ponimus aras
25 exciso in scopulo, fluctus unde aurea canos
despiciens celso se culmine Mergilline
attollit nautisque procul venientibus offert,
si laudes de more tuas, si sacra diemque
ac coetus late insignes ritusque dicamus,
30 annua felicis colimus dum gaudia partus:

Book I

Born of a virgin, offspring coeval with his mighty Father who, sent
through the lofty breezes of heaven, washed away from ailing mor-
tals the ancient taint of their race and thrust open the blocked
path to Olympus: you dwellers in heaven, let this be my first toil,
let my first task take this as start. If it is proper, unfold from the   5
beginning causes that you have heard and the sequence of such a
great event.

You Muses, grace of bards, here as well I would yearn for your
fountains, your crags with their lofty groves, since you trace your
ancestry from heaven, and since virginity pleases you and respect   10
for your sacred fame. Therefore, whether care for the realm above
or esteem for the virgin of my poem affects you, reveal the path by
which I might vanquish the clouds and, together with me, unbar
the gates of the boundless sky. Great indeed are my requests,
Aonian sisters, great, but they are my due, and not outside your   15
understanding. For you were able to behold both the cave and the
dances, nor must it be thought that either the stars rising in the
sky or the eastern kings escaped your notice.

So it is that you also, fostering mother, trusted hope for men,
trusted hope for gods, whom a thousand battle lines attend, and
all the soldiery of the lofty sky — so many chariots, so many ban-   20
ners and trumpets, so many clarions! — and around whom squad-
rons swarm with encircling celebration: if we offer to you ceremo-
nial garlands in gleaming shrines, if we dedicate to you enduring
altars in the rock we have hollowed out, from which golden   25
Mergellina, gazing from above on the whitening waves, rises with
lofty peak and is visible to sailors approaching from afar, if we duly
sing your praises, sing your worship and holy day, your gatherings
and rites widely renowned, when we observe the annual rejoicing
at the blessed moment when you gave birth: do you, goddess, aid   30

tu vatem ignarumque viae insuetumque labori,
diva, mone, et pavidis iam laeta adlabere coeptis.
  Viderat aetherea superum regnator ab arce
undique collectas vectari in Tartara praedas
35 Tisiphonemque imo conantem cuncta profundo
vertere et immanes stimulantem ad dira sorores,
nec iam homini prodesse alto quod semina coelo
duceret aut varios animum excoluisset ad usus:
tantum letiferae poterant contagia culpae!
40 Tum pectus pater aeterno succensus amore
sic secum: 'Ecquis erit finis? tantis ne parentum
prisca luent poenis seri commissa nepotes,
ut quos victuros semper superisque crearam
pene pares, tristi patiar succumbere leto
45 informesque domos obscuraque regna subire?
Non ita, sed divum potius revocentur ad oras,
ut decet, et manuum poscunt opera alta mearum,
desertosque foros vacuique sedilia coeli
actutum complere parent, legio unde nefandis
50 acta odiis trepidas ruit exturbata per auras;
cumque caput fuerit tantorumque una malorum
foemina principium lacrimasque et funera terris
intulerit, nunc auxilium ferat ipsa modumque
qua licet afflictis imponat foemina rebus'.
55 Haec ait, et celerem stellata in veste ministrum
qui castae divina ferat mandata puellae,
alloquitur, facie insignem et fulgentibus alis:
'Te, quem certa vocant magnarum exordia rerum,
fide vigil, pars militiae fortissima nostrae,
60 te decet ire novumque in saecula iungere foedus:
nunc animum huc adverte atque haec sub pectore serva.
Est urbes Phoenicum inter lateque fluentem
Iordanem regio nostris sat cognita sacris:

the memory of your bard who is both unsure of the path, and un-
used to the toil. Already joyous, abet his anxious undertaking.

The Ruler of the gods had observed from his celestial citadel
that booty drawn together from every side was being carried into
Tartarus, that Tisiphone in her lowest deep was attempting to
confound all things as she goaded her savage sisters toward dread   35
deeds, and that it was now no help to man that he traced his an-
cestry from the lofty heavens or that he had improved his skill for
sundry purposes. So great was the force of infections from the sin
that brought death! Then the Father, his heart on fire with ever
enduring love, spoke thus to Himself: "Will there be any end?   40
Will the late-born offspring pay such great punishments for the
ancient transgressions of their forebears, so that I might suffer
those whom I begot to live forever and to be nearly the equal of
the angels to succumb to bitter death and to enter featureless
dwellings and realms without light? Not at all. Rather let them be   45
called back to the regions of the gods, as is fitting, and let them
seek out my exalted handiwork. Let them without delay prepare to
fill up the abandoned seats and vacant benches of heaven, from
which the army, driven by heinous hatred, fell headlong, swirled
through the quivering breezes. Since the source of such great mis-   50
fortune, which had brought tears and death to the earth, origi-
nated in a single woman, now let a woman herself bring help and
place whatever end she may to their troubled affairs."

After these words, he addresses his swift attendant — glorious   55
his features and gleaming wings, his garb adorned with stars — to
convey God's command to the chaste girl: "My faithful guardian,
most valiant member of our soldiery, whom the sure beginnings of
great affairs summon, it is fitting for you to venture forth to forge
a new covenant for the ages. Devote your attention to me, and   60
lodge this now in your breast. Between the cities of the Phoeni-
cians and the broad flow of the Jordan lies a land well known for
our worship. Men call it Judaea, strong in might and in law. Here

Iudaeam appellant armisque et lege potentem.
65 Hic claris exorta atavis vatumque ducumque
antiquum genus et dignis licet aucta hymenaeis,
pectoris inlaesum virgo mihi casta pudorem
servat adhuc, nullos non servatura per annos —
mirus amor! — seniumque sui venerata mariti
70 exiguis degit thalamis et paupere tecto,
digna polo regnare altoque effulgere divum
concilio et nostros aeternum habitare penates.
Hanc mihi virginibus iam pridem ex omnibus unam
delegi prudensque animo interiore locavi,
75 ut foret intacta sanctum quae numen in alvo
conciperet ferretque pios sine semine partus.
Ergo age, nubivagos molire per aëra gressus,
deveniensque locum, castas haec iussus ad aures
effare et pulcris cunctantem hortatibus imple,
80 quandoquidem genus e stygiis mortale tenebris
eripere est animus saevosque arcere labores'.
    Dixerat. Ille altum Zephyris per inane vocatis
carpit iter, scindit nebulas atque aëra tranat,
ima petens pronusque leves vix commovet alas.
85 Qualis, ubi ex alto notis maeandria ripis
prospexit vada seu placidi stagna ampla Caystri,
praecipitem sese candenti corpore cycnus
mittit agens, iamque implumis segnisque videtur
ipse sibi, donec tandem potiatur amatis
90 victor aquis: sic ille auras nubesque secabat.
Ast ubi palmiferae tractu stetit altus Idumes,
reginam haud humiles volventem pectore curas
aspicit; atque illi veteres de more Sibyllae
in manibus, tum siqua aevo reseranda nepotum
95 fatidici casto cecinerunt pectore vates.
Ipsam autem securam animi laetamque videres

8

a chaste virgin, sprung from famous ancestors of prophets and princes, an ancient race, though she has been blessed with a wor- 65 thy marriage, still preserves for me, and will preserve as the many years pass, her heart's modesty untainted. Astonishing devotion! While worthy to reign in heaven and to illuminate the lofty council of the saints and to abide forever in our dwelling, honoring the old age of her husband she passes her life in the meager quarters of a poor man's abode. In my wisdom I have long since chosen her 70 alone from all virgins, and have sequestered the notion deep in my thoughts that she should be the virgin who would conceive in her womb the sanctity of God, and bear her holy offspring from no 75 seed. So on your way! Depart on your cloud-wandering passage through the air. When you reach the spot, speak these things to her chaste ears, as you have been ordered. However hesitant she be, flood her with noble encouragement, since it is my purpose to snatch the race of mortals from the darkness of the Styx and to 80 deliver it from its harsh suffering."

He had spoken. The other, once the Zephyrs were summoned, pursues his lofty path through the void, cleaving the clouds and sailing through the air. He scarcely moves his nimble wings, aiming downward for the world below. Just as when a swan with gleaming form from on high has beheld the waters of the Meander with its familiar banks, or the spreading pools of the languid 85 Cayster, it sends itself plunging on a headlong course. Now it seems to itself featherless, with motion stilled, until, having at last won its way, it lays claim to its beloved waters. Thus he sheared the breezes and clouds. But when he has taken his lofty stand in 90 the territory of pine-rich Idume, he beholds the queen giving thought to her heart's grave worries. As was her custom, she held in her hands the ancient Sibyls, if once upon a time the prophetic bards in purity of heart had chanted anything to be disclosed in the era of their descendants. But you would observe that she her- 95 self at least, in joyful assurance of mind, was awaiting her Creator.

authorem sperare suum: nanque affore tempus,
quo sacer aethereis delapsus spiritus astris
incorrupta piae compleret viscera matris,
100 audierat. Pro quanta alti reverentia coeli
virgineo in vultu est! Oculos deiecta modestos
suspirat matremque dei venientis adorat,
felicemque illam humana nec lege creatam
saepe vocat, nec dum ipsa suos iam sentit honores,
105 cum subito ex alto iuvenis demissus Olympo
purpureos retegit vultus, numenque professus
incessuque habituque, ingentes explicat alas
ac tectis late insuetum diffundit odorem.
  Mox prior haec: 'Oculis salve lux debita nostris,
110 iam pridem notum coelo iubar, optima virgo,
cui sese tot dona, tot explicuere merenti
divitiae superum, quicquid rectique probique
aeterna de mente fluit, purissima quicquid
ad terras summo veniens sapientia coelo
115 fert secum et plenis exundans gratia rivis.
Te genitor stabili firmam sibi lege sacravit,
perpetuos genitor cursus qui dirigit astris,
mansuramque tuo fixit sub pectore sedem;
idcirco coetus inter veneranda pudicos
120 una es, quam latis coeli in regionibus olim
tot divum celebrent voces. Pro gaudia terris
quanta dabis, quantis hominum succurrere votis
incipies!' Stupuit confestim exterrita virgo,
demisitque oculos totosque expalluit artus:
125 non secus ac conchis siquando intenta legendis
seu Micone parva scopulis seu forte Seriphi
nuda pedem virgo, laetae nova gloria matris,
veliferam advertit vicina ad litora puppim
adventare, timet, nec iam subducere vestem

She had heard that the time was at hand when the Holy Spirit, gliding down from the celestial stars, would fill the untainted womb of a saintly mother. Ah, what adoration of lofty heaven lies in the virgin's glance! She sighs, her eyes lowered in modesty, and 100 worships the mother of the god to come. She often calls her blessed and not created as subject to human law. Nor does she herself yet perceive that the honor was already hers, when of a sudden the youth dispatched from lofty Olympus reveals his radiant features. Proclaiming his divinity by gait and garb, he stretches 105 his mighty wings and with a remarkable fragrance suffuses the house's breadth.

He starts quickly thus: "Hail, light owed to our eyes, O brilliance long since known to heaven, finest of virgins, who deserve 110 the abundance of gifts, the abundance of riches that the gods have proffered — whatever both upright and noble flows from the everlasting mind, whatever quintessential wisdom, proceeding from heaven's height earthwards, conveys with it, and grace brimming in full streams. The Father has dedicated you steadfastly to him by 115 fixed decree, the Father who guides the everlasting pathways of the stars, and he has established his enduring abode beneath your heart. So it is that you alone are to be adored among the chaste choirs, you whom someday so many angel voices might exalt in the broad reaches of heaven. What great rejoicing you will bring to the 120 earth! How many prayers of mankind you will begin to support!"

Straightway the virgin grew numb with fright. She lowered her eyes and turned pale throughout her whole being: just as when a barefoot maiden, the fresh pride of her happy mother, is engrossed 125 with the harvesting of pearl-oysters on tiny Micon or, should it chance, on craggy Seriphos. Noticing a full-sailed ship gain the shore nearby, she grows fearful and dares not now raise her dress

130 audet nec tuto ad socias se reddere cursu,
sed trepidans silet obtutuque immobilis haeret;
illa Arabum merces et fortunata Canopi
dona ferens, nullis bellum mortalibus infert,
sed pelago innocuis circum nitet armamentis.

135   Tum rutilus coeli alipotens, cui lactea fandi
copia divinique fluunt e pectore rores
ambrosiae, quibus ille acres mulcere procellas
possit et iratos pelago depellere ventos:
'Exue, dia, metus animo, paritura verendum

140 coelitibus numen sperataque gaudia terris
aeternamque datura venis per saecula pacem.
Haec ego siderea missus tibi nuntius arce,
sublimis celeres vexit quem penna per auras,
vaticinor, non insidias, non nectere fraudes

145 edoctus: longe a nostris fraus exulat oris.
Quippe tui magnum magna incrementa per orbem
ipsa olim partus, virgo, sobolisque beatae
aspicies: vincet proavos proavitaque longo
extendet iura imperio populisque vocatis

150 ad solium late ingentes moderabitur urbes,
nec sceptri iam finis erit nec terminus aevi;
quin iustis paulatim animis pulcherrima surget
relligio: non monstra, piis sed numina templis
placabunt castae diris sine caedibus arae'.

155   Dixerat. Illa, animum sedato pectore firmans,
substitit, et placido breviter sic ore locuta est:
'Conceptus ne mihi tandem partusque futuros,
sancte, refers? me ne attactus perferre viriles
posse putas, cui vel nitenti matris ab alvo

160 protinus inconcussum et ineluctabile votum
virginitas fuit una, nec est cur solvere amatae
iura pudicitiae cupiam aut haec foedera rumpam?'

or hurry herself on a course of safety to her comrades, but trem- 130
bling she grows speechless, and stands fast with her gaze mesmer-
ized. The vessel, laden with the goods of Arabia and the rich gifts
of the Canopus, portends no war for humankind, but with inno-
cent equipage shimmers on the ambient sea.

Then heaven's crimsoned strong-of-wing, from whose breast 135
pours ample milkiness of speech and ambrosia's celestial dew—his
means for soothing harsh breezes and for sweeping angry winds
from off the sea: "Shed your mind's worries, Goddess, destined
to give birth to a divinity revered by the saints, and to bestow 140
the joys for which it had hoped upon the earth, and unceasing
peace through the ages. Sent as your messenger from the starry
citadel, I, whose towering wings have carried me through the swift
breezes, taught to weave no wiles, no deceit—deceit is banished
far off from our world—make this prediction. Indeed you your- 145
self, Virgin, will one day witness great fruitfulness pervading the
great earth through your childbearing and through your blessed
offspring. He will excel his forebears, and will spread his forebears'
rights over extended dominion, and, with their peoples summoned
to his throne, will guide mighty cities far and wide. There will 150
never be an end to his rule, or a boundary of his age. So it is that
in the minds of the just the most beautiful form of worship will
gradually arise. Not monsters but chaste altars in holy shrines will
appease divinities, without abominable bloodshed."

These were his words. She paused, bracing her mind, with
heart now at ease, and spoke thus briefly from her calm lips: "Are 155
you in fact forewarning me of conception and childbirth to follow,
blessed creature? Do you believe that I can endure the touch of a
man, I, whose unshakeable, unalterable vow, even from the mo- 160
ment that I emerged from my mother's radiant womb, was for vir-
ginity alone, and who have no reason to wish to annul the obliga-

'Immo istas (quod tu minime iam rere) per aures'
excipit interpres 'foecundam spiritus alvum
165 influet implebitque potenti viscera partu,
flammifero veniens coelo atque micantibus astris.
At tu, virgineum mirata tumescere ventrem,
haerebis pavitans; demum, formidine pulsa,
gaudia servati capies inopina pudoris.
170 Neve haec vana putes dictis aut territa nostris
indubites, serae dudum concessa senectae
dona oculos pone ante tuos; nam sanguine avito
iuncta tibi mulier (sterilis licet illa gravique
pressa aevo) haud quaquam speratum hoc tempore pignus
175 fert utero et felix sexto sub mense laborat:
usque adeo magno nil non superabile coelo est!'
His dictis, regina oculos ad sidera tollens
coelestumque domos superas atque aurea tecta,
annuit et tales emisit pectore voces:
180 'Iam iam vince, fides, vince, obsequiosa voluntas!
en adsum: accipio venerans tua iussa tuumque
dulce sacrum, pater omnipotens; nec fallere vestrum est,
coelicolae: nosco crines, nosco ora manusque
verbaque et aligerum coeli haud variantis alumnum'.
185   Tantum effata, repente nova micuisse penates
luce videt: nitor ecce domum complerat; ibi illa,
ardentum haud patiens radiorum ignisque corusci,
extimuit magis. At venter (mirabile dictu!
non ignota cano) sine vi, sine labe pudoris,
190 arcano intumuit verbo: vigor actus ab alto
irradians, vigor omnipotens, vigor omnia complens
descendit — deus ille, deus! — totosque per artus
dat sese miscetque utero. Quo tacta repente
viscera contremuere; silet natura pavetque

tion to my beloved chastity or to break this compact?" "Rather,"
responds the messenger, "the Holy Spirit, descending from flame-
bearing heaven and from the glittering stars, will flow into your
fertile womb through your very ears (a thing you now scarcely
imagine) and will fill your belly with a mighty birth. As you mar-   165
vel at the swelling of your virgin's womb, you will stand transfixed
with terror. At last, with fear rejected, you will experience the un-
expected joys of your chastity preserved. But, lest you consider
this delusive or hesitate in fright over our words, set before your   170
eyes the gifts already bestowed on venerable old age. For a woman
joined to you by ancestral blood, though she is barren, and bur-
dened with the weight of time, at this hour carries in her womb a
child she had not at all hoped for, and happily endures the trials of
her sixth month. To such an extent is nothing insurmountable by   175
the greatness of heaven!" After these words the queen raised her
eyes to the stars, and to the abodes of the saints above and their
golden dwellings. She gave a nod and spoke thus from her heart:
"Now be victorious, my faith, now be victorious, my compliant
will! See, I stand ready. In worship I accept your commands, al-   180
mighty Father, and your joyous ritual. Inhabitants of heaven, de-
ception is not your part. I recognize the locks, I recognize the fea-
tures, hands, words, and the winged offspring of an unchanging
heaven."

That was all she spoke. Suddenly she sees her home glow with
a strange light. Watch how the brilliance had filled her house!   185
Then her fear became greater as she barely withstood the blazing
rays and shimmering fire. But her womb (I tell a marvel, though
my song is not unknown!) swelled with the hidden Word. There
was no force; her chastity was untainted. A luminous strength   190
conveyed from on high, an all-powerful strength, a strength that
permeates all, makes its descent — a God he is, a God! — and lends
itself to all her limbs and mingles in her womb. Under its touch
her inner being suddenly trembled. Nature, as if thunderstruck,

15

195 attonitae similis, confusaque turbine rerum
    insolito occultas conatur quaerere causas,
    sed longe vires alias maioraque sentit
    numina: succutitur tellus laevumque sereno
    intonuit coelo rerum cui summa potestas,
200 adventum nati genitor testatus, ut omnes
    audirent late populi, quos maximus ambit
    Oceanus Tethysque et raucisona Amphitrite.
      Hos inter medios coeli terraeque fragores,
    aequatis properans volucer pulcherrimus alis,
205 omnia dum trepidant, discesserat altaque nabat
    per loca, cum virgo celsis in nubibus illum
    alternantem humeros videt atque immensa secantem
    ventorum spatia et iam versicolore per auras
    fulgentem pluma ac coeli convexa petentem.
210 Quem demum tali aspectans sermone secuta est:
    'Magne ales, celsi decus aetheris, invia rerum
    qui penetras longeque et nubila linquis et Euros
    antevolans: laeto seu te felicia tractu
    sidera quaeque suos volvuntur signa per orbes
215 expectant redeuntem, alti seu certa reposcit
    crystalli domus et vitrei plaga lucida regni,
    seu propiora vocant supremo tecta Tonanti,
    qua patet in summum regio flammantis Olympi
    teque amor et liquidis flagrans alit ignibus aura:
220 i, precor, i, nostrum testis defende pudorem'.
    Nec plura his. Tum vero aciem deflectit et omnes,
    haud mora, sollicito percurrit lumine montes
    agnatamque animo conceptaque pignora versat,
    multa putans serumque uteri miratur honorem.
225   Interea Manes descendit Fama sub imos
    pallentesque domos veris rumoribus implet:

grows silent and afraid. Confounded by the strange cataclysm, it   195
attempts to seek out its hidden origins, but feels the extraordinary
forcefulness and expanded presence of divinity. The earth is
shaken, and the Father, whose power is utmost, thundered on the
left in a cloudless sky as He bore witness to the coming of his Son,
so that all peoples far and wide, whom mightiest Oceanus, and   200
Tethys, and gravelly-voiced Amphitrite embrace, might hear.

    In the midst of these crashes of sound in heaven and earth,
while the universe trembled, the winged creature had made his de-
parture, hastening with stunning beauty on balanced wings and   205
swimming through the spaces above. Then the virgin beholds him
amid the towering clouds, shoulders moving in rhythm as he
shears the vast territory of the winds, and now gleams with varie-
gated plumage through the breezes on his way toward the sphere
of heaven. As she watched she followed him at last with these   210
words: "Mighty winged creature, glory of the lofty sky, who in sur-
passing flight voyage into matter's pathless ways and leave far be-
hind both the clouds and the Euri: whether the happy stars in
their joyous sweep and the constellations revolving through their
rounds await your return, or a sure palace of soaring crystal, or the   215
brilliant expanse of the glassy realm craves you, or dwellings nearer
to the highest Thunderer summon you, where the domain of fiery
Olympus opens out at its peak, where love and a breeze aflame
with transparent fires nourishes you: make your way, I beseech
you, and, as you make your way, bear witness in defense of my
chastity." She added nothing more. Then she turns her eyes else-   220
where and, with no delay, runs her worried glance along the
mountains, and ponders in her mind her cousin and the child that
she had conceived. In thought after thought she marvels at the
honor come late to her womb.

    Meanwhile Rumor makes her way down to the lowest Shades
and fills their wan dwellings with true reports: the day for which   225
they yearned was approaching when, victorious over darkness,

optatum adventare diem, quo tristia linquant
Tartara et evictis fugiant Acheronta tenebris,
immanemque ululatum et non laetabile murmur
230 tergemini canis, adverso qui carceris antro
excubat insomnis semper rictuque trifauci
horrendum, stimulante fame, sub nocte profunda
personat et morsu venienteis appetit umbras.
Tum vero heroes laetati animaeque piorum
235 ad coelum erectas coeperunt tendere palmas;
atque hic insignis funda citharaque decorus,
insignis sceptro senior, per opaca locorum
dum graditur nectitque sacros diademate crines,
dum legit effoetos lethaeo in gramine flores,
240 qua tacitae labuntur aquae mutaeque volucres
ducunt per steriles aeterna silentia ramos,
attonita subitos concepit mente furores
divinamque animam et consueto numine plenus,
intorquens oculos venientia fata recenset:
245 'Nascere, magne puer, nostros quem solvere nexus
et tantos genitor voluit perferre labores;
magne puer, cui se haec tandem spolianda reservant
regna, tot heu miseris hominum ditata ruinis,
nascere, venturum si te mortalibus olim
250 pectore veridico promisimus, igneus ut nos
viribus afflatos coelestibus ardor agebat
insinuans, si sacra peregimus et tua late
iussa per immensum fama vulgavimus orbem.
En ridet pax alma tibi: simul ecce potentes,
255 impulsi coelo divisque authoribus acti,
orbe alio properant reges. Salvete, beati
Aethiopes, hominum sanctum genus, astra secuti
scilicet huc vestris affertis munera regnis.
Accipe dona, puer, tuque, o sanctissima mater,

they would depart from gloomy Tartarus and flee Acheron, its vast
wailing and the ugly howls of the three-headed hound, ever bed-
ded sleepless in a cave facing the prison. As hunger goads him on,   230
in the depths of night he roars dreadfully from his triple-throated
maw and seeks to gnaw the shades as they arrive. Then indeed the
rejoicing heroes and the souls of the pious begin to stretch their
raised hands toward heaven. At this point an elder, distinguished   235
by a sling, graced with a lyre and distinguished also by a scepter,
strides through the places of dark and interweaves his blessed
locks with a diadem. While he plucks sterile blossoms on Lethe's
grass, where the waters silently glide and songless birds keep ever-   240
lasting silence among the barren boughs, he conceives a flashing
wildness and the breath of God in his rapt imagination. Filled
with his accustomed inspiration and rolling his eyes he predicts
the tale to come: "Be born, great child, whom the Creator or-
dained to undo our bonds and to endure such great sufferings.   245
Great child, for whom these realms save themselves to be har-
rowed at last, enriched, alas, by so many sad human catastrophes,
be born, if once long ago we promised with truth-telling heart that
you would come on behalf of mortals, at the time when burning   250
passion, working its way in, urged us on under the inspiration of
heaven's strength—if we fulfilled your worship and published your
orders in fame far and wide through the globe's extent. Look,
nourishing peace smiles for you. Behold, too, powerful kings has-
ten from a world elsewhere, impelled by heaven and by divine au-
thority. Hail, blessed Ethiopians, holy race of men. We see for   255
sure how, following the stars, you carry offerings here from your
kingdoms. Receive the gifts, young child, and you, holiest of
mothers, gather your strength. Already both nations and leaders

260 sume animos: iam te populique ducesque frequentant
litore ab extremo et odoriferis Nabathaeis.
    Ille autem aurata fulgens in veste sacerdos
iam canus, iam maturo venerabilis aevo,
quid sibi vult, sacras puerum qui sistit ad aras,
265 sic venerans laetoque inspectans aethera vultu?
Seque dehinc facili clausurum lumina fato
exclamat, quod speratum per saecula munus
promissamque diu pacem certamque salutem
terrarum exorta liceat sibi luce tueri
270 optanti seniumque ideo Parcasque trahenti.
    Sed quid ego, heu, dira conspersos caede penates
infantum et subito currenteis sanguine rivos
aspicio tristisque meas vagitus ad aures
fertur? io, scelus est partus iugulare recentes!
275 Crudelis, quid agis? nihil hi meruere neque illum
quem petis insano dabitur tibi perdere ferro.
Nunc nunc, o matres, scelerata abscedite terra,
dum licet, inque sinu pueros abscondite vestros,
nam ferus hostis adest; propera iam, regia virgo,
280 inque paretonias transfer tua pignora terras:
admonet hoc magnum genitor qui temperat orbem;
tuta domus tutique illic tibi, dia, recessus.
    Verum ubi bissenas hyemes bissenaque nati
solstitia et tantos superaveris anxia casus,
285 ingentes imo duces de pectore questus
aureaque assiduis pulsabis sidera votis.
Nam puerum, quanvis per compita saepe vocatum,
saepe expectatum consuetae ad gaudia mensae,
perquires nequicquam amens, nec cara petentem
290 oscula nec sera redeuntem nocte videbis.
Tresque illum totos moerenti pectore soles
et totidem trepidas somni sine munere noctes

throng about you from the farthest shore and from the incense- 260
bearing Nabathaeans.

"But the priest there, glowing in cloth-of-gold, already white-
haired, already venerable in the ripeness of age, what does he, rev-
erent and scanning the heavens with joyous features, have in his
mind when he places the boy at the holy altars? His cry is that 265
henceforth he will close his eyes in an easy death because at day-
break he is allowed to see the gift hoped for through the ages,
peace long promised, and the sure salvation of this world—yearn-
ing and dragging out the fated allotment of his old age just for
this. 270

"But why, alas, do I behold as well homes spattered dreadfully
by slaughter of infants, and streams suddenly running with blood?
Why is sad wailing carried to my ears? Ah, what a crime it is to
murder the newly born! What are you doing, cruel man? These 275
deserved nothing. Nor will you be allowed to destroy with a mad-
man's sword the one you seek. Now depart from this criminal
land, now, mothers, while it is possible. Hide your children in
your bosom, for your savage enemy is at hand. Hasten now, royal
virgin, and convey your charge into the Paretonian land. The Fa- 280
ther who regulates the mighty universe sends this warning. There,
goddess, your dwelling, your sanctuary will be safe.

"But when in anxiety you will have survived twelve winters and
twelve summers along with such perils for your son, you will draw
protracted groans from the depth of your breast, and buffet the 285
golden stars with prayer after prayer. At your wit's end, you will
keep searching in vain for your boy, though you have often
shouted for him at cross-streets, often awaited him at the dining
table's usual pleasures. You won't see him seeking your affectionate
kisses or returning late into the night. For three whole days and 290
three anxious nights you and your ancient husband, with sorrow-
ing breast and lacking the gift of sleep, will weep for him, your

omnia lustrantes, questu omnia confundentes,
flebitis indigno perculsi corda dolore
295 tuque senexque tuus; quarto sed Lucifer ortu
purpureos tremulo cum tollet ab aequore vultus,
inventum dabit et quaerentibus offeret ultro.
O quas tunc lacrimas, o quae tunc oscula, mater,
quos dabis amplexus, misto inter gaudia fletu,
300 cum natum ante aras patris et delubra sedentem
mulcentemque senes dictis animosque trahentem
aspicies gavisa, ipso admirante senatu
primitias pueri ingentes, nec inane sagacis
pectoris indicium nataeque ad grandia mentis!
305   Tu vero quid in arma ruis, scelerata iuventus?
quid galeas ensesque virum et fulgentia cerno
agmina scutatasque procul sub nocte cohortes
obscura et crebris radiantes ignibus hastas?
tot ne unum telis petitur caput? heu furor, heu mens
310 caeca hominum semperque odiis accincta nefandis!
Iamque oleas montemque sacrum circumque supraque
cinxere et longa lucum obsedere corona.
Quo feror? Ecce trahunt manibus post terga revinctis
insontem, modo quem latas mira illa per urbes
315 edentem patrisque palam praecepta docentem
attoniti stupuere, illum regemque deumque
humanaeque ducem vitae fontemque salutis
haud veriti, populo circum plaudente, fateri.
Heu facinus! mortem ne etiam et crudele minantur
320 supplicium? Saevos stringunt in vulnera fasces
horrenteisque parant paliuro intexere dumos,
tormenti genus, et capiti premere inde coronam
vulnificam: viden alternos ut arundinis ictus
incutiunt geminantque truci convicia lingua?
325   Parte alia ingentes video de stirpibus imis

hearts stricken with sorrow not your due, as you cast your eyes ev-
erywhere about and roil the world with grief. But at the fourth   295
dawn, when Lucifer raises his brilliant features from the shimmer-
ing sea, he will allow his discovery, and of his own accord will ap-
pear before his searchers. O what tears then, mother, O what
kisses, what embraces will you then bestow, weeping amid your
gladness. Filled with joy you will behold your son sitting before
the altars and shrines of his Father, winning over the elders with   300
his sayings and molding their minds, as the group of old men
marvels at the boy's powerful debut, the impressive sign of a wise
heart and of a mind born to greatness.

"But why do you rush to arms, criminal young men? Why, in   305
the distance through the haze of night, do I behold men in hel-
mets, swords, gleaming battle-lines, squadrons with shields, and
spears glittering from the clusters of fires? Is one life the object of
so many weapons? Woe, O woe—the madness, the thoughts of
heedless men, ever girt with unspeakable hatreds! Now around   310
and above they have enclosed the olives and the holy mount. They
have besieged the grove in an extended circle. (Where am I carried
off?) See! They drag along the guiltless man, hands bound behind
his back, the man at whom a moment ago they stood in awe,
amazed as he performed miracles through broad cities and
preached to all the teachings of his Father. As the surrounding   315
throng voiced its approval, they fearlessly proclaimed him king,
God, prince of human life, and fountain of salvation. Woe the
crime! Do they even threaten cruel punishment and death? They
bare their savage rods to scourge him and—gruesome torture!—   320
they prepare to mesh sheaves of bristling Christ's-thorn with
brambles, and then to press the wounding crown on his head. Do
you see how they strike rhythmic blows of the rod and intensify
their abuse with cruel tongues? Elsewhere I view enormous palm
trees, palms as lofty as the stars, overturned from the base of their   325

everti palmas, altas ad sidera palmas,
infelix opus, unde hominum lux illa decorque
pendeat. Ah, trepidis dirum et miserabile terris,
cum patri aethereo moriens liventia pandet
330 brachia turpatosque atra de morte capillos
oraque demissosque oculos frontemque cruore
iam madidam et lato patefactum pectus hiatu!
   At mater, non iam mater sed flentis et orbae
infelix simulacrum, aegra ac sine viribus umbra,
335 ante crucem demissa genas, effusa capillum,
stat lacrimans tristique irrorat pectora fletu.
Ac si iam comperta mihi licet ore profari
omnia, defessi spectans morientia nati
lumina, crudeles terras, crudelia dicit
340 sidera, crudelem se se, quod talia cernat
vulnera, saepe vocat; tum luctisono ululatu
cuncta replens, singultanti sic incipit ore,
incipit et duro figit simul oscula ligno,
exclamans: «Quis me miseram, quis culmine tanto
345 deiectam subitis involvit, nate, procellis?
Nate, patris vires, sanguis meus, unde repente
haec fera tempestas? quis te mihi fluctus ademit?
quae manus indignos foedavit sanguine vultus?
cui tantum in superos licuit? bella impia coelo
350 quis parat? hunc ego te post tot male tuta labores
postque tot infelix elapsae incommoda vitae
aspicio? tu ne illa tuae lux unica matris,
tu ne animae pax et requies spesque ultima nostrae
sic raperis? sic me solam exanimemque relinquis?
355 O dolor, extincto iam te pro fratre sorores,
pro natis toties exoravere parentes:
ast ego pro nato, pro te dominoque deoque
quem misera exorem? quo tristia pectora vertam?

24

trunks, from which that brilliance and beauty of mankind might hang, a dreadful deed. Ah, wretched and ill-boding for the terror-stricken earth when, dying, he extends to his heavenly Father bruised arms, hair and features befouled by black death, lowered 330 eyes, brow now sodden with gore and chest rent open, wide and gaping.

"But his mother, no longer mother but wretched specter, weeping and bereft, a sickened, feeble shadow, stands in tears before the cross. Her face is lowered, her hair outspread. She dampens her 335 breast with a flood of sadness. And, if I can now give voice to all that I have discovered, as she gazes at the dying eyes of her exhausted son, she calls the earth cruel, the stars cruel. Over and over she calls herself cruel because she bears witness to wounds such as these. Then, filling the world with grief-shrieked wailing, 340 she takes her start from sobbing lips, she takes her start, crying out at the same time, as she plants her kisses on the unyielding wood: 'Who embroiled me, my son, in a sudden whirlwind—me, piteous and cast down from so great a height? Son, strength of his 345 Father, blood of my blood, whence this fierce storm, without warning? What cataclysm has snatched you from me? What hand unworthily defiled your face with blood? Who was allowed such license against the dwellers above? Who fashions criminal war against heaven? Do I, hardly safe after so many toils and unfortu- 350 nate after so many tribulations of a life that has slipped away, do I see you like this? Are you thus torn away, you, your mother's only life-light, my mind's final peace, and rest, and hope? Are you abandoning me thus to loneliness and exhaustion? O the sorrow! Sisters once beseeched you on behalf of their dead brother, parents so 355 many times on behalf of children, but in my sadness whom should I beseech on behalf of my son, on your behalf, my lord, my god? Where will I turn my joyless heart? To whom utter my com-

cui querar? O tandem dirae me perdite dextrae,
360 me potius, siqua est pietas, immanibus armis
obruite, in me omnes effundite pectoris iras!
vel tu (si tanti est hominum genus) eripe matrem
quae rogat et stygias tecum duc, nate, sub umbras;
ipsa ego te per dura locorum inamoenaque vivis
365 regna sequar: liceat rumpentem cernere portas
aeratas, liceat pulcro sudore madentem
eversorem Erebi materna abstergere dextra».
    Hos illa et plures fundet de pectore questus.
Quod scelus eois ut primum cernet ab undis
370 sol, indignantes retro convertere currus
optabit frustraque suis luctatus habenis,
quod poterit tandem, auratos ferrugine crines
inficiet moestamque diu sine lumine frontem
ostendet terris, ut qui iam ploret ademptum
375 authorem regemque suum; quin ipsa nigranti
fratris ab ore timens et tanto concita casu
Cynthia caeruleo vultus obnubet amictu
avertetque oculos lacrimasque effundet inanes.
At contra horrisono tellus concussa tremore
380 cum gemitu fremet et ruptis excita sepulcris
emittet simulacra. Quid, o, quid abire paratis,
illustres animae? Non omnibus haec data rerum
conditio: paucis remeare ad lumina vitae
concessum; sed tempus erit cum martia rauco
385 mugitu coelum quatiet tuba cumque repente
corpora per terras omneis late omnia surgent.
Nunc autem sat tartarei si claustra tyranni
effringat rex ille et caligantia pandat
atria: diffugiant immisso lumine dirae
390 Eumenidum facies, iactis in terga colubris,
quas atro vix in limo Phlegethontis adustum

plaints? O furious hands, bring me death at last. If there is any pi- 360
ety, overwhelm me in his stead with your savage weapons. Vent
against me your heart's every anger! Or, if you place such value on
humankind, snatch away your mother as she prays and, my son,
lead her as your companion beneath the shades of Styx. I will fol-
low you through the hard landscape and realms hateful to the liv-
ing. May I watch you dash in the doors of bronze. May I with a 365
mother's hand wipe clean of beautiful sweat the harrower of
Erebus.'

"These laments and more she will pour from her heart. When
the sun first beholds that crime from the waves at dawn, he will
wish to turn back his reluctant chariot. And, after struggling 370
ineffectually with the reins, he will do what at least he can and dye
his golden locks rust-dark, and for a length of time display to the
earth his sad face without light, since he now laments the loss of
his creator and his king. Likewise Cynthia, frightened by her 375
brother's blackening features and stirred by such a disaster, will
cloak her face with a sea-green shroud, turn her eyes away, and
pour forth useless tears. In response the earth, stricken with
screaking quake, will roar with a groan, and send forth ghosts
awakened from their broken tombs. Why, O why, eminent spirits, 380
do you make ready to depart? These terms are not given to every-
one. It is allowed to a few to make their way back toward the lights
of life, but there will be a time when Mars's trumpet will shake the
heavens with piercing roar and when all bodies scattered through- 385
out every land will suddenly arise. For now it must suffice if that
very king breaks through the barriers of Tartarus's tyrant, and lays
bare the dwellings of darkness: the dreadful forms of the
Eumenides flee in different directions when the light is let in, their
snakes tossed against their backs. The scorched woods scarcely re- 390
ceive them in Phlegethon's black mud and bury them in its smoul-

accipiat nemus et fumanti condat in ulva;
tum variae pestes et monstra horrentia Ditis
ima petant, trepident briareia turba Cerastae
395 semiferumque genus Centauri et Gorgones atrae
Scyllaeque Sphingesque ardentesque ora Chimaerae
atque Hydrae atque canes et terribiles Harpyiae;
ipse catenato fessus per Tartara collo
ducetur Pluton, tristi quem murmure circum
400 inferni fractis moerebunt cornibus amnes.
      At nos, virginea praecincti tempora lauru,
signa per extentos coeli victricia campos
tollemus laetoque ducem clamore sequemur:
«Victor, io; bellator, io: tu regna profunda,
405 tu Manes Erebumque potestatesque coerces
aërias letumque tuo sub numine torques».
Ille alto temone sedens levibusque quadrigis
lora dabit volucresque reget placido ore iugales,
non iam cornipedum ductos de semine equorum
410 nec qui consuetas carpant praesepibus herbas.
Primus enim valido subnixus eburnea collo
fert iuga formosi pecoris custodia taurus,
stellatus minio taurus, cui cornua fronti
aurea et auratis horrent palearia setis,
415 perque pedes bifidae radiant nova sidera gemmae;
torva bovi facies, sed qua non altera coelo
dignior imbriferum quae cornibus inchoet annum,
nec quae tam claris mugitibus astra lacessat.
Et iuxta nemorum terror rexque ipse ferarum
420 magnanimus nitet ore leo, quem fusa per armos
convestit iuba, pectoribus generosa superbit
maiestas, non iam ut caedes aut praelia saevus
appetat (innocuis armatur dentibus ora
grataque tranquillo ridet clementia vultu),

dering sedge. Then let manifold diseases and dreadful monsters
seek the depths of Dis, then let the Cerastae—Briarean throng—
the half-beast race of Centaurs, black Gorgons, and Scyllas,   395
Sphinxes and Chimaeras with faces ablaze, Hydras, and Hounds,
and fearful Harpies. Pluto himself, exhausted, his neck in chains,
will be led through Tartarus. Around him in saddened roar the
rivers below will lament with their horns broken.   400

   "But, after we have girded our brows with virgin laurel, we will
raise aloft the standards of victory through heaven's broad plains.
We will follow our leader with joyous acclaim: 'Hail, champion;
hail warrior. You control the deep realms, you the Manes, Erebus,
and the demons of the air. You bend death to your godhead.' He,   405
sitting on his lofty chariot, will give rein to its four nimble steeds.
With serene features he will master his swift teams, not now de-
scended from the seed of horn-hoofed steeds or champing ordi-
nary fodder in their steadings. For first the bull, warden of a hand-   410
some herd, bears the ivory yoke which he supports on sturdy neck,
the bull, star-bright with vermilion. The horns on his brow are
golden and his dewlaps are thick with gilded bristle. Through his
feet cloven jewels gleam forth like fresh stars. The face of the ox is   415
fierce, but there is no other in the heavens worthy to initiate the
rain-bearing year with his horns or to challenge the stars with
such clear lowing. Next to him gleams the face of the stout-
hearted lion himself, terror of forests and king of beasts. A spread-   420
ing mane clothes his shoulders, the majesty of his noble race is re-
splendent in his breast, not so that he might search savagely for
slaughter or battle—his mouth is armed with harmless teeth and a
welcome forbearance smiles on his calm features—but so that he

425 sed coelo ut spatietur et alta ad sidera tendat.
     Hos post insequitur pulcros pennata per artus
     alituum regina, sacrae cui vertice plumae
     assurgunt flavoque caput diademate fulget;
     ipsa ingens alis, ingentis fulminis instar,
430 supra hominum tecta ac montes supraque volucres
     fertur et obstantes cursu petit obvia nubes.
     Ultimus humana sociat cervice laborem
     alatus tergo iuvenis, cui luthea laevo
     ex humero chlamys eois inspersa lapillis
435 pendet: eam variant centum longo ordine reges,
     antiquum genus et solymae primordia gentis,
     ostro intertexti; veros cognoscere vultus
     est illic, veros montes et flumina credas
     et vera extremo Babylon nitet aurea limbo.
440   Tali sidereas curru subvectus in auras,
     indutos referens spoliis pallentibus axes,
     perveniet, recto qua panditur orbita tractu
     lactea et ad sedes ducit candentis Olympi.
     Illic auratae muros mirabimur urbis
445 auratasque domos et gemmea tecta viasque
     stelliferas vitreosque altis cum montibus amnes.
     Atque ibi, seu magni celsum penetrale Tonantis
     sive alios habitare lares ac tecta minorum
     coelicolum dabitur, stellas numerare licebit
450 surgentemque diem pariter pariterque cadentem
     sub pedibus spectare et longos ducere soles
     longaque venturis protendere nomina saeclis'.
         Haec ubi dicta, patres plausu excepere frequentes
     fatidicum vatem sublatumque aggere ripae
455 attollunt humeris laetumque per avia ducunt.
     Intremuere Erebi sedes obscuraque Ditis
     limina; suspirans imo de corde Megaera

might range the sky and wend toward the lofty stars. After these 425
follows the queen of winged creatures with body beautifully feath-
ered. On her crest blessed plumage arises and her head gleams
with a golden diadem. She herself, like a mighty lightening-bolt, is
borne on mighty wings above the dwellings of mankind, above
mountains and birds. She pursues the clouds that she meets across 430
her path. The last, who shares the effort with human neck, is a
youth with wings on his back. A saffron cloak besprinkled with
eastern gems hangs from his left shoulder. Interwoven in purple, a
hundred kings adorn it in a long rank, an ancient race, the founda- 435
tion of the people of Jerusalem. There one can recognize real faces.
You would believe that the mountains and streams are real. A real
Babylon gleams in gold on the outermost border.

   "He will bring back a wagon caparisoned in the wan world's
spoils. Borne to the starry breezes on such a chariot, he will arrive 440
where the Milky Way opens out its forward sweep and leads to
the dwellings of gleaming Olympus. There we will marvel at the
walls of the gilded city, the gilded homes and bejeweled abodes,
the paths that carry the stars, crystalline streams that companion 445
their lofty hills. There too, whether it will be granted to reside in
the exalted shrine of the great Thunderer or in dwellings else-
where, the homes of lesser divinities, it will be allowed to count
the stars and to gaze under your feet, equally as the day rises,
equally as it sets, and to pass drawn out suns, and to extend your 450
repute at length to future generations."

   When he had uttered these words, the throng of fathers greeted
the prophetic seer with applause. They raise him up on their
shoulders from the ridge of the bank and carry him rejoicing
through the wasteland. The dwellings of Erebus and the dim 455
thresholds of Dis trembled. Megaera groans, sighing from her

dat gemitum et torvas spectat sine mente sorores;
tum caudam exululans sub ventre recondidit atram
460 Cerberus et sontes latratu terruit umbras,
commotisque niger Cocytus inhorruit antris
et vaga sisyphiis haeserunt saxa lacertis.

Liber Secundus

Regina ut subitos imo sub pectore motus
sensit et afflatu divini numinis aucta est,
haud mora, digressu volucris suspensa ministri,
exurgit monteisque procul contendit in altos
5 festinans: ea cura animo vel prima recursat,
matronam defessam aevo, cui nulla fuissent
dona uteri, mirum dictu, iam segnibus annis
foecundam sextique gravem sub pondere mensis
protinus affari vocemque audire loquentis
10 et spectare oculis sterili data pignora matri.
Ergo accincta viae, nullos studiosa paratus
induitur, nullo disponit pectora cultu,
tantum albo crines iniectu vestis inumbrans:
qualis stella nitet, tardam quae circuit Arcton
15 hiberna sub nocte aut matutina resurgens
Aurora aut ubi iam Oceano sol aureus exit.
Quaque pedes movet, hac casiam terra alma ministrat
pubenteisque rosas nec iam moestos hiacynthos
narcissumque crocumque et quicquid purpureum ver
20 spirat hians, quicquid florum per gramina passim
suggerit, immiscens varios natura colores.
Parte alia celeres sistunt vaga flumina cursus,
exultant vallesque cavae collesque supini

heart's depth, and gazes stupefied at her fierce sisters. Then Cerberus with a howl hid his black tail beneath his belly, and frightened the guilty shades with his bark. Murky Cocytus shuddered as   460
its caverns trembled. His wandering boulder clung to Sisyphus's arms.

Book II

The queen experienced the sudden motion in the depths of her heart, and gloried in the inspiration of God's power. In her anxiety at the departure of the winged messenger she rises up with no delay, and hastens to make her way toward the lofty mountains afar. The principal desire that ever returns to her mind is to converse at   5
once with the matron worn out with age, her womb never gifted with offspring, who now—a marvel to tell!—is fertile, though her age is feeble and heavy with her six months burden, and to listen to her words as she speaks, and to cast her eyes upon child pledged to barren mother. So, girded for the journey, she clothes   10
herself with scant interest in her attire. She decorates her bosom with no adornment, only shrouding her hair with the covering of a white shawl: like the gleam of a star which, on a winter's night, circles sluggish Arctos, or like the rising of the morning's Aurora, or   15
when the golden sun now makes its way out of Ocean. Wherever she moves her feet, there the nourishing earth furnishes marjoram and burgeoning roses, hyacinths no longer mournful, narcissus and crocus—whatever the breath of purple spring uncloses, whatever flowers nature everywhere heaps up throughout the fields as   20
she mingles her dappled hues. Elsewhere meandering streams halt their swift passage, hollow valleys and sloping hills take delight,

et circumstantes submittunt culmina pinus
25   crebraque palmiferis erumpunt germina silvis.
Omnia laetantur: cessant Eurique Notique,
cessat atrox Boreas; tantum per florea rura
regna tenent Zephyri coelumque tepentibus auris
mulcent, quaque datur gradientem voce salutant.
30   Ut ventum ad sedes, vultu longaeva verendo
occurrit coniux iusti senis atque repente
plena deo subitoque uteri concussa tumultu,
excipit amplexu venientem ac talibus infit:
'O decus, o laudis mulier dux praevia nostrae,
35   coelitibus sola humanum quae digna reperta es
conciliare genus coetusque attollere ad astra
foemineos, gremium cuius divinus obumbrat
palmes inexhaustis terras qui compleat uvis:
quis me, quis tanto superum dignatur honore?
40   Tu ne procul visura humiles, regina, penates
venisti? tu ne illa mei pulcherrima regis
mater ades? viden ut nostra puer excitus alvo,
cum mihi vix primas vocis sonus ambiat aures,
iam salit et dominum ceu praecursurus adorat?
45   Felix virgo animi, felix, cui tanta mereri
credulitas dedit una: in te nam plena videbis
omnia, quae magni verax tibi dixit Olympi
aliger, arcano delapsus ab aethere cursu'.
      Illa sub haec: 'Miranda alti quis facta Tonantis,
50   o mater, meritas coelo quae tollere laudes
vox queat? Exultant dulci mea pectora motu
authori tantorum operum, qui me ima tenentem
indignamque humilemque suis respexit ab astris;
munere quo gentes felix ecce una per omnes
55   iam dicar. Nec vana fides, ingentia quando
ipse mihi ingenti cumulavit munera dextra

the encompassing pines bow their crests, and many a bud bursts
forth in the palm-bearing groves. Everything rejoices. Euri and   25
Noti give way. Savage Boreas yields place. Zephyrs alone hold
sway through the blossoming countryside and soothe the heavens
with warm breezes. As she makes her way they greet her with
whatever voice is given to them.

When she arrived at the dwelling, the noble old man's aged wife   30
greets her with worshipping countenance. All at once, filled with
God as her womb is startled by the sudden stir, she clasps her in
her embrace as she approaches, and speaks thus: "O glory, O
woman, harbinger of our praise to come, you who alone have been
found worthy to commend the race of men to the dwellers in
heaven and to raise womankind to the stars, whose womb is over-   35
shadowed by a holy vine-branch to fill the earth with limitless
grapes: who, in heaven, who considers me worthy of so great an
honor? O queen, did you come from a distance to visit our lowly
abode? Is it you, that most beauteous mother of my king, who are   40
here? Do you see how the child in my belly now leaps spiritedly
when the sound of your voice scarcely reaches my ears for the first
time, and, ready to be his herald, reverences his master? O virgin,
blessed of soul, blessed, whose faith alone granted you to deserve   45
so much: in you you will see consummated everything that the
winged truth-teller of great Olympus told you, after he slipped
down from on high along his secret path."

She in reply: "O mother, who could glorify the marvelous
deeds of the Thunderer on high, what voice raise their deserved
praise in heaven? My heart throbs with throes of delight for the   50
fashioner of such great works, who from the stars above has taken
notice of me, lowly, unworthy and humble. Because of his favor—
behold!—I alone will now be called happy throughout all nations.
Nor is my trust vain since the Almighty himself has amassed   55
bounteous gifts for me with bounteous right hand, and holy is his

omnipotens sanctumque eius per saecula nomen,
et quae per magnas clementia didita terras
exundat, qua passim omnes sua iussa verentes
60 usque fovens nullo neglectos deserit aevo.
Tum fortem exertans humerum dextramque coruscam
insanos longe fastus menteisque superbas
dispulit afflixitque super solioque potentes
deturbans dedit in praeceps et ad ima repressit,
65 extollensque humiles aliena in sede locavit,
pauperiemque famemque fugans implevit egenos
divitiis; vacuos contra nudosque reliquit
qui nullas opibus metas posuere parandis.
Postremo sobolem (neque enim dare maius habebat),
70 aeternam genitor sobolem saeclisque priorem
omnibus aequalemque sibi de sanguine fidi
suscepit pueri (tantis quod honoribus unum
deerat adhuc), non ille animi morumque suorum
oblitus, quippe id meditans promiserat olim
75 sacrificis proavorum atavis stirpique nepotum'.
    Haec virgo. At senior, nullus cui vocis ademptae
usus erat, supplex nunc gressum observat euntis
virgineosque pedes tactaeque dat oscula terrae;
nunc laetus tollit duplices ad sidera palmas,
80 quoque potest solo testatur gaudia nutu,
ostenditque manu vatum tot scripta priorum,
quae quis, agente deo, quondam, dum vita manebat,
edidit et populis liquit celebranda futuris:
scilicet effusum tacitis de nubibus imbrem
85 lanigerum in tergus germenque e stirpe vetustae
arboris exurgens incombustumque sonoro
igne rubum et priscis stellam de patribus ortam.
Quae dum cuncta gravi, venturi haud inscia, visu
percurrit relegens, alto cum corde volutat

name through the ages, and his mercy spreads in abundance
through the reaches of the earth by which he ever cherishes all
who respect his commands and at no time abandons them to ne-
glect. Then, baring his brave shoulder and his brandishing right   60
hand, he also smote and routed afar those crazed with haughtiness
and the prideful of mind. Toppling the mighty from their throne,
he hurled them headlong and confined them to the depths. He
raised up the lowly and placed them in the others' seat. Exiling   65
poverty and hunger, he filled the needy with riches. On the other
hand he abandoned penniless and naked those who had placed no
limits to their amassing of wealth. Finally — for what greater did
he have to offer! — the Father took up his everlasting offspring,
offspring earlier than all the ages, his own contemporary, from the   70
blood of his faithful servant, because this alone was yet lacking
among his due honors. He was not forgetful of his plan and of his
habit; indeed with this in mind, he had long ago made a promise
to the priestly ancestors of ancestors and to the offspring of their
descendants."   75

These were the virgin's words. But the old man makes humble
obeisance to the virgin's steps as she walks, and to her feet, since
the use of his voice had been taken away, and offers kisses to the
ground that she touched. Now in joy he raises both his hands to
the stars and bears witness to his happiness the only way he can —
by a nod. With his hand he displays the numerous writings of ear-   80
lier prophets which each, under the sway of God, once pro-
claimed, while life remained, and left for commemoration by peo-
ples to come: that we would know him as rain poured from silent
clouds on a fleecy back, as a shoot springing from the stem of an
ancient tree, as a bush unconsumed within a roar of fire, as a star   85
risen from the fathers of old. While the virgin reads anew, scan-
ning these matters with serious countenance in full awareness of
the future, in the depths of her heart she ponders her novel con-

90   conceptus virgo insolitos et ab aethere lapsam
progeniem pluviae in morem, quae vellere molli
excepta haud ullos sonitus nec murmura reddit,
seque rubum virgamque, alto se denique missam
sidus grande mari prorsum agnoscitque videtque:
95   non tamen ausa loqui tanto aut se ducere dignam
munere, sed tacito affectu tibi, maxime divum,
grates, rector, agit mentemque ad sidera tollit.
    Et iam luna cavum ter luce repleverat orbem,
ter solitas de more intrarat caeca latebras,
100 cum virgo in patriam reditum parat, omnia quando
certa videt: subeunt dilectae grata parentis
alloquia assuetaeque piis sermonibus aedes
quaeque salutantis voces ac verba ministri
audiit et primos excepit cella volatus,
105 cella choris superum lustrata et cognita coelo.
Ergo iter inceptum, caris digressa propinquis,
accelerat relegitque viam per nota locorum;
nec mora nec requies usquam nec lumina flectit,
coelicolum quanvis sacro circundata coetu,
110 donec ad optatum pervenit sedula limen;
atque ibi, dum consueta suo cum pectore versat
gaudia, paulatim maturi tempora ventris
adventare videt: scires iam numen in illa
grande tegi; nullos adeo sentire dolores
115 dat superum genitor nullaque ex parte gravari.
    Interea terra parta iam pace marique
Augustus pater aeratis bella impia portis
clauserat et validis arctarat vincta catenis;
dumque suas regnator opes viresque potentis
120 imperii exhaustasque armis civilibus urbes
nosse cupit, magnum censeri iusserat orbem,

ceiving, and her offspring gliding from heaven like a rain-shower 90
which gives back no sound or noise at all as it lands on a soft
fleece. She sees and recognizes that she is the bush and the
branch, and, finally, that she has been sent from on high exactly
like a stately star upon the sea. Nevertheless she dared not utter a
word or consider herself worthy of such a gift but, keeping her 95
feelings to herself, she offers thanks to you, our Ruler, greatest
among the divine, and raises her thoughts to the stars.

By now the moon had thrice filled out her crescent orb with
light, and thrice as usual in darkness had entered her accustomed
seclusion, when the virgin prepares her return to the land of her
fathers, now that she sees all matters assured. She remembers 100
pleasant exchanges with her beloved mother, and her home, used
to noble conversation, and the room that listened to the messen-
ger's speech and words of greeting and that received him after his
initial flight, the room ringed by choirs of angels and sanctioned
by heaven. So, departing from her dear kin, she hastens on the 105
way that she had set out and retraces her route through the famil-
iar landscape. In her eagerness she neither paused nor rested at
all. She doesn't turn aside her gaze, though thronged about by
holy angels, until she eagerly reaches the threshold for which she
longed. There, while she continues in her heart to meditate upon 110
the joys to which she is now accustomed, she observes that the
moment of her womb's fullness is gradually drawing near. You
would now recognize that a mighty divinity was sheltered within
her. For the Creator of the angels grants her to feel no pangs and
to be in no way cumbered. 115

Meanwhile, with peace won on land and on sea, father Augus-
tus had imprisoned immoral wars within doors of bronze and had
tautened their bonds with stout chains. While as ruler he desires
to know his resources, the strength of his powerful empire and the
cities worn out by civil strife, he had commanded that a census be 120
taken of the whole world, that peoples over its extent be recorded

describi populos late numerumque referri
cunctorum ad se se capitum, quae maxima tellus
sustinet et rapido complectitur aequore Nereus.
125 Ergo omnes lex una movet: sua nomina mittunt
qui monteis, Aurora, tuos, regna illa feracis
Armeniae, qui convalles atque alta Niphatae
saxa tenent, longe pictis gens nota pharetris,
gens fines lustrare suos non segnis et arcu,
130 qua vagus Euphrates, qua devius exit Araxes,
felices tractus et late munere divum
concessos defendere agros bene olentis amomi.
Censetur Tauri passim, censetur Amani
incola praedatorque Cilix et isaurica quisquis
135 rura domat quicunque tuas, Pamphylia, silvas
quique Lycaoniam, felicia iugera, quique
flaventem curvis Lyciam perrumpit aratris.
Iam clari bello Leleges populique propinqui
iussa obeunt, gens quaeque suo dat nomina ritu:
140 qui Ceramon bimaremque Gnidon quique alta tuentur
moenia, dispositis ubi circumsepta columnis
tollit se nivei moles operosa sepulcri,
barbara quam rapto posuit regina marito;
et quos Maeandri toties ludente recursu
145 unda rigat, rigat ipse suo mox amne Cayster,
herboso niveos dum margine pascit olores,
quosque metalliferis veniens Pactolus ab antris
circuit et rutila non parcior Hermus arena;
Misorum manus omnis apollineaeque Celenae
150 Idaque rhoetaeaeque arces celebrataque Musis
Pergama sigaeumque iugum, priameia quondam
regna armis ducibusque ducum nunc nota sepulcris,
quae nauta, angustum dum praeterit Hellespontum,
ostendens sociis 'hoc' inquit 'litore flentes

40

and that a count be brought to him of all individuals whom the
earth's full span supports and Nereus embraces with his rushing
sea. One law thus sets all in motion. Aurora, names are submitted   125
by those who possess your mountains, the kingdom of fruitful Ar-
menia, the glens and lofty crags of Niphata, a race known abroad
for variegated quivers, a race not slow to patrol its boundaries and
to protect with the bow the fertile plains and fields of sweet-
scented spice, broadly bestowed by the gift of the gods, where the
wandering Euphrates, where the remote Araxes rises. Every   130
dweller of the Taurus, of the Amanus, the Cilician pirate and
whoever tames the land of the Isauri, and your forests, Pamphylia,
whoever with curved ploughs furrows the prosperous acreage of   135
Lycaonia, whoever grain-yellow Lycia. Now the Leleges, famed in
battle, and nearby tribes obey the order. Each race presents its
names according to its own manner: those who guard Ceramus,
and Gnidos of the two seas, and the lofty bastions where, sur-   140
rounded with ordered columns, rises the elaborate pile of the
snow-white tomb which a barbarian queen had built for her de-
parted husband; those whom the wave of the Meander supplies
with water, as its playful channel again and again doubles back,
soon those whom the Cayster waters with its stream, while it feeds   145
snowy swans on its grassy verge, and whom the Pactolus, sprung
from ore-rich caves, surrounds, and the Hermus, equally unspar-
ing of its red-gold sand, the whole band of Misians, and Apollo's
Celenae, and Ida, the peaks of Rhoetaeum, Pergama made famous   150
by the Muses, the ridge of Sigaeum, Priam's kingdom, once re-
nown for arms and warriors, now for warriors' tombs. When the
sailor passes through the narrow Hellespont he shows them to his
comrades with the words: "On this shore the Nereids stood weep-

41

155 Nereides steterant, passis cum moesta capillis
ipsa suum de more Thetis clamaret Achillem'.
His et bitynae classes et pontica late
accedit regio, paret scopulosa Carambis,
parendi studio fervet simul alta Sinope,
160 fervet Halys quique immensis procul amnibus auctus
Cappadocum medios populos discriminat Iris,
Thermodonque Halybesque attritaque saxa Prometheo.
Praeterea qua se Thracum mavortia tellus
pandit et algentem Rhodope procurrit in Aemum,
165 qua Macetum per saxa ruit torrentibus undis
Axius umbrosaeque tegunt Halyachmona ripae
quaque iacet diris omen Pharsalia bellis
et bis romana ferales clade Philippi:
conveniunt populi certatim et iussa facessunt.
170 Vos etiam vestros his adiunxistis alumnos,
vicinae passim vacuis iam moenibus urbes,
antiquae Graiorum urbes, gens optima morum
formatrix, clara ingeniis et fortibus ausis,
seu quae litoreos tractus montesque tenetis
175 seu quae per medias dispersae exurgitis undas.
Tum latus Epiri, qua formidabile nautis
attollunt summo caput Acroceraunia coelo,
urget opus, iamque Alcinoi dat regia censum,
illyricaeque manus impacatique Liburni
180 litoraque Ionio passim pulsata profundo.
Nec tu, cui late imperium terraeque marisque
bellatrix peperit virtus et martius ardor,
non populos, non ipsa tuas, terra inclyta, gentes
describis, terra una armis et foeta triumphis,
185 una viris longe pollens atque aemula coelo,
nubiferae quam praeruptis anfractibus Alpes
praecingunt mediamque pater secat Apenninus

ing when with loosened hair grieving Thetis herself gave the tradi-   155
tional cry for her Achilles." The Bithynian citizenry is added to
these and the wide region of Pontus. Rocky Carambis obeys, and
lofty Sinope likewise is excited with eagerness to obey. The Halys
is afire, and the Iris, swollen by huge, distant rivers, that divides   160
the peoples of Cappadocia in two, and the Thermodon and the
Halybes, and the cliffs worn down by Prometheus. Moreover
where the land of Mars's Thracians extends and Rhodope runs
into chill Aemus, where the Axius courses with its swirling waves
through the rocks of the Macetae, and where shady banks shroud   165
the Halyacmon, and where Pharsalia lies, omen of dread war, and
Philippi, twice death-stricken with Roman slaughter: their peoples
race to assemble and carry out the order. You also added your
offspring to these, O neighboring cities with their walls now ev-
erywhere deserted, ancient cities of Greece, a race the finest fash-   170
ioner of our culture, renowned for imagination and daring bravery,
whether you who claim the sweeping shore land and mountains or
you who rise up, scattered through the midst of the waves. Then   175
the coast of Epirus, where Acroceraunia rears to heaven's heights
its peak dreaded by sailors, presses on with the task, and now the
palace of Alcinous gives its account, and the Illyrian throng, and
the untamed Liburni, and the shores everywhere pounded by the
Ionian deep. Nor did you yourself, land of glory, for whom cour-   180
age in battle and passion for Mars gave rise to a vast empire over
land and sea, fail to list your peoples and your races—land unique
for strength of arms and teeming with triumphs, unique for your
heroes' spacious sway, rival of heaven whom the cloud-bearing   185
Alps gird with their sheer windings, whose midst father
Apenninus cleaves and around whom the twin water thunders

et geminum rapido fluctu circumtonat aequor.
Descripsere suos, quanvis non axe sub uno,
190 hinc Rhenus pater indigenas, hinc latior undis
Danubius, qui silvarum per vasta volutus
pascere non populos, non lambere desinit urbes,
donec ad optatam rapido venit agmine Peucen.
Quin et proceras scrutatur Gallia silvas,
195 Gallia caesareis Latio dignata triumphis,
quam Rhodanus, quam findit Arar, quam permeat ingens
Sequana piscosoque interluit amne Garumna.
Tum quas piniferis gentes praerupta Pyrene
rupibus herculeas prospectat adusque columnas
200 cogit Anas, cogit ripa formosus utraque
Duria et albenti Baetis praecinctus oliva
auratamque Tagus volvens sub gurgite arenam
quique suo terras insignit nomine Iberus.
Parte alia vastas circunvocat Africa vires:
205 getuli maurique duces rimantur opaci
Atlantis nemora et dispersa mapalia silvis;
scribitur et vacuis ut quisque inventus arenis
seu pastor seu succinctis venator in armis
observans saevos latebrosa ad tesqua leones,
210 Massylum quicunque domos, quicunque repostos
Hesperidum lucos munitaque montibus arva
incolit et ramis nativum decutit aurum,
et qui vertentes immania saxa iuvencos
flectit arans, qua devictae Carthaginis arces
215 procubuere iacentque infausto in litore turres
eversae. Quantum illa metus, quantum illa laborum
urbs dedit insultans Latio et laurentibus arvis!
nunc passim vix relliquias, vix nomina servans,
obruitur propriis non agnoscenda ruinis:
220 et querimur genus infelix humana labare

44

with its fierce flood. They registered their peoples, though not un-
der a single sky, here father Rhine and next the Danube, wider   190
with his waves, which as it rolls through vast forests never ceases
to feed his people, never ceases to lap his cities in hurrying course
until he reaches his beloved Peuce. Even Gaul also surveys her
soaring woods, Gaul, glorified in Latium for the triumphs of
Caesar, which the Rhône, which the Saône divides, through which   195
the mighty Seine makes its way, and the Garonne passes with its
fish-filled waters. Then the Guadiana musters the races the sheer
Pyrenees scan with their pine-bearing crags, all the way to the Pil-   200
lars of Hercules, and the Duria, beautiful on either bank, musters
them, and the Baetis, girded with shimmering olives, and the
Tagus, rolling golden sands beneath its flood, and Ebro that
stamps the land with its name. Elsewhere Africa summons its vast
strength: Gaetulian and Moorish leaders scour the forests of shad-
owy Atlas and the huts scattered through the woods. Anyone dis-   205
covered in the empty desert is also enrolled, whether shepherd or
hunter, girdled with weapons as he tracks fierce lions to their co-
vert thickets, and whoever dwells in the homes of the Massyli,
whoever in the remote groves of the Hesperides and in their fields   210
protected by mountains, shaking native gold from their branches,
and the plowman who directs his oxen as they upturn huge boul-
ders where the vanquished citadels of Carthage stretched in ruins
and the razed towers lie on the cursed shore. How much terror,   215
how much tribulation that disdaining city gave Latium and the
Laurentian fields! Now, everywhere about, it lies buried, scarcely
preserving its remains, scarcely its name, not even to be recognized
in its own wreckage. And we, unfortunate race, complain that
human limbs crumble over time, when kingdoms and cities die   220

membra aevo, cum regna palam moriantur et urbes!
Iamque Macas idem ardor habet; venere volentes
Barcaei, venere suis Nasamones ab arvis,
navifragas qui per Syrtes infidaque circum
225 litora moerentum spoliis onerantur et altos
insiliunt nudi cumulos extantis arenae
inque suas vertunt aliena pericula praedas.
Postremo Psylli garamanticaque arva tenentes
quique cyrenaeas suspendunt vomere glebas
230 laudatasque legunt succis praestantibus herbas
quique Iovis palmeta Hasbytarumque recessus,
marmaricas qui late oras, qui pascua servant
Aegypti Meroesque, sacer quos Nilus inundat,
Nilus ab aethereo ducens cunabula coelo.
235 Nec minus et casta senior cum virgine custos
ibat, ut in patria nomen de more genusque
ederet et iussum non segnis penderet aurum.
Ille domum antiquam et regnata parentibus arva
invisens, secum proavos ex ordine reges
240 claraque facta ducum pulcramque ab origine gentem
mente recensebat tacita numerumque suorum,
quanvis tunc pauper, quanvis incognitus ipsis
agnatis, longe adveniens explere parabat.
Iam fines, Galilaea, tuos emensus et imas
245 Carmeli valles quaeque altus vertice opacat
rura Thabor sparsamque iugis samaritida terram
palmiferis, solymas a leva liquerat arces,
cum simul e tumulo muros ac tecta domorum
prospexit patriaeque agnovit moenia terrae:
250 continuo lacrimis urbem veneratur obortis
intenditque manus et ab imo pectore fatur:
'Bethlemiae turres et non obscura meorum
regna patrum magnique olim salvete penates,

46

before our eyes! Now the same eagerness possesses the Macae.
Willingly the Barcaei came, the Nasamones came from their fields
who amid the shipwrecking Syrtes and around their treacherous
shores load themselves with the booty of those who have come to
grief. They leap naked onto the lofty mounds of protruding sand, 225
and turn other people's danger into pillage for themselves. Finally
the Psylli and those claiming the fields of the Garamantes and
those who raise with their plough-share the turf of Cyrene and
pluck the plants praised for the quality of their juice, and the 230
Egyptians and Meroes, who watch over Jupiter's palm groves and
the retreats of the Hasbytae, over the extensive shores and pas-
tureland of Marmarica, whom the holy Nile floods, the Nile that
draws its origin from heaven's sky.

Likewise her aged guardian with his chaste virgin also made his
way so that, as was the custom, in the land of his fathers he might 235
furnish his name and race, and not be slow in rendering the gold
as commanded. As he beheld his hereditary dwelling and the fields
ruled over by his forbears, in the quiet of his mind he catalogued
in order the kings who were his ancestors, the glorious accom-
plishments of his chiefs, his handsome race back to its start. 240
Though now poor, though unknown to his relatives and arriving
from afar, he yet was preparing to complete the listing of his folk.
After he had traversed your bounds, Galilaea, and the deep valleys
of Carmel and the countryside which soaring Thabor overshadows 245
with its crest, and the land of the Samaritans, dotted with palm-
bearing ridges, he had now left the heights of Jerusalem on his left.
Then and there from a hillock he caught sight of walls and the
roofs of houses, and recognized the ramparts of the land of his fa-
thers. Immediately with up-welling tears he offers homage to the
city. He stretches forth his hands and speaks from the depths of 250
his heart: "Hail, towers of Bethlehem and famous kingdoms of
my forefathers, once mighty dwellings, and hail to you again, land,

tuque o terra, parens regum visuraque regem,
255 cui sol et gemini famulantur cardinis axes,
salve iterum: te vana Iovis cunabula Crete
horrescet ponetque suos temeraria fastus,
moenia te dircaea trement ipsamque pudebit
Ortygiam geminos Latonae extollere partus.
260 Parva loquor: prono veniet diademate supplex
illa potens rerum terrarumque inclyta Roma
et septemgeminos submittet ad oscula montes'.
Dixit et extrema movit vestigia voce
maturatque viam senior tardumque fatigat
265 vectorem et visas gressum molitur ad oras.
    Et iam prona dies fluctus urgebat iberos
purpureas pelago nubes aurumque relinquens,
ecce autem magnis plenam conventibus urbem
protinus, ut venere, extremo e limine portae
270 aspiciunt. Mixtum confluxerat undique vulgus,
turba ingens: credas longinquo ex aequore vectas
ad merces properasse aut devastantibus arva
hostibus in tutum trepidos fugisse colonos.
Cernere erat perque anfractus perque arcta viarum
275 cuncta replesse viros confusoque ordine matres,
permixtos pecori agricolas: hos iungere plaustra,
hos intendere vela, alios discumbere apertis
porticibus, resono compleri cuncta tumultu,
accensos variis lucere in partibus ignes.
280 Quae pater admirans, tacito dum singula visu
percurrit circumque domos et limina lustrat
nec superesse locum tecto videt, 'ibimus' inquit,
'quo deus et quo sancta vocant oracula patrum'.
    Est specus haud ingens parvae sub moenibus urbis,
285 incertum manibus ne hominum genio ne potentis
naturae formatus, ut haec spectacula terris

the parent of kings and soon to see a king whom the sun and the
sky's twin poles serve. Reckless Crete, false cradle of Jupiter, will   255
be in awe of you and will forgo its haughtiness, the walls of Dirce
will fear you, and Ortygia herself will be ashamed to boast of the
twin offspring of Latona. I tell of small matters: even glorious   260
Rome, powerful over the world's affairs, will come, a suppliant
with crown bowed downward, and will lower her seven-twinned
hills to proffer kisses." The old man spoke and, his words ended,
he presses forward and hastens on his way. He urges on his weary
beast of burden, and wends his course toward the sites in his view.   265

Now the sloping day was pressing toward the Iberian sea, leav-
ing in the ocean its clouds of purple and its gold, when imme-
diately upon their arrival at the outer threshold of the gate —
watch! — they view the city congested with throngs of arrivals. A
motley throng had come together from everywhere, a huge multi-
tude. You would believe that they had hurried for wares brought   270
from a distant sea, or were fearful settlers in flight to safety from
foes laying waste their fields. Through the winding narrow streets
one could see men and women in jumbled array, farmers mingled
with their flocks, filling every inch. Some yoke their wagons, oth-   275
ers stretch tents, others sprawl in the open walkways. A noisy hub-
bub pervades all. Fires lit here and there give off a gleam. Taken
aback by the sight, the father runs his eyes over everything in si-
lence, and, surveying the dwellings and their entrances round   280
about, observes that no house had a place left. He says: "We will
make our way where God and where the holy prophecies of the fa-
thers beckon."

There was a cave of no great size under the walls of the tiny
city. It was uncertain whether it had been fashioned by the hand
of man or by the intelligence of powerful nature so that it might   285
present these sights to the world and, set aside long ago for such a

49

praeberet tantosque diu servatus in usus
hospitio coelum acciperet, cui plurima dorso
incumbit rupes, pendentibus undique saxis
290 aspera, et exesae cingunt latera ardua cautes,
defunctis operum domus haud ingrata colonis.
Huc heros tandem, superata ambage viarum,
sic monitus, ducente deo, cum coniuge sancta
devenit multaque senex se nocte recepit.
295 Ac primum siccis ramalibus excitat ignem
stramineoque toro comitem locat, aegra cubantis
membra super vestem involvens; mox alligat ipsos
permulcens iam non duros, iam sponte sequentes
quadrupedes, ut forte aderat foenile saligna
300 suffultum crate et palmarum vimine textum.
      Nunc age castaliis quae nunquam audita sub antris
Musarum ve choris celebrata aut cognita Phoebo
expediam: vos secretos per devia calleis,
coelicolae, vos, si merui, monstrate recessus
305 intactos. Ventum ad cunas et gaudia coeli
mirandosque ortus et tecta sonantia sacro
vagitu: stat ferre pedem, qua nulla priorum
obvia sint oculis vatum vestigia nostris.
      Tempus erat, quo nox tardis invecta quadrigis
310 nondum stelliferi mediam pervenit Olympi
ad metam et tacito scintillant sidera motu,
cum silvaeque urbesque silent, cum fessa labore
accipiunt placidos mortalia pectora somnos;
non fera, non volucris, non picto corpore serpens
315 dat sonitum, iamque in cineres consederat ignis
ultimus et sera perfusus membra quiete
scruposo senior caput acclinaverat antro:
ecce autem nitor ex alto novus emicat omnemque
exuperat veniens atrae caliginis umbram

grand purpose, receive heaven as its guest. Many a crag, rough
throughout with hanging rock, broods over its ridge, and boulders
eroded away gird its sheer sides—a not unwelcome refuge for   290
landsmen tired from their labors. Here the heroic old man, already
forewarned and under God's guidance, after he had made his way
out of the maze of streets, arrived at last with his holy wife and in
the dead of night found entrance. First he sparks fire from dry
branches and rests his companion on a bed of straw, wrapping her   295
exhausted limbs in a cloth as she lay. Then he tethers and strokes
his four-footed creatures, not now recalcitrant but following of
their own accord, as there chanced to be a manger supported by
willow wickerwork and woven from withes of palm.   300

Attend now! I will unfold subjects never heard in the grottoes
of Castalia or extolled by the choirs of Muses or fathomed by
Apollo. You, heaven-dwellers, if I have earned the honor, show me
byways off the trodden path, show havens yet unspoiled. We have   305
reached the cradle, the jubilation of heaven, the marvelous birth,
the roof resounding with the blessed cry. It is time to take my step
where no traces of earlier bards will meet my eyes.

It was the moment when night, riding on its slow chariot, had
not yet reached the midway turning-post of star-bearing Olympus
and the constellations sparkled on their quiet course, when forests   310
and cities as well are hushed, when mortal breasts, fatigued from
their efforts, receive sleep's calm. No wild creature, no bird, no
dappled snake makes a sound. Now the last of the fire had sunk
down into ashes, and in the scraggy cave the old man, his limbs   315
steeped in the late hour's stillness, had nodded his head. Behold, a
fresh splendor shines out from on high and in its coming overpow-
ers the shadow of black darkness. Choirs of angels and heaven's

320 auditique chori superum et coelestia curvas
agmina pulsantum citharas ac voce canentum.
Agnovit sonitum partusque instare propinquos
haud dubiis virgo sensit laetissima signis.
Protinus erigitur stratis coeloque nitentes
325 attollit venerans oculos ac talia fatur:
'Omnipotens genitor, magno qui sidera nutu
aëreosque regis tractus terrasque fretumque,
ecquid adest tempus, quo se sine labe serenam
efferat in lucem soboles tua? quo mihi tellus
330 rideat et teneris depingat floribus arva?
En tibi maturos fructus, en reddimus ingens
depositum: tu, nequa pio iactura pudori
obrepat, summo defende et consule coelo.
Ergo ego te gremio reptantem et nota petentem
335 hubera, care puer, molli studiosa fovebo
amplexu; tu blanda tuae dabis oscula matri
arridens colloque manum et puerilia nectes
brachia et optatam capies per membra quietem'.
Sic memorat fruiturque deo comitumque micanti
340 agmine divinisque animum concentibus explet.
Atque olli interea, revoluto sidere, felix
hora propinquabat. Quis me rapit? Accipe vatem,
diva, tuum; rege, diva, tuum: feror arduus altas
in nubes, video totum descendere coelum
345 spectandi excitum studio; da pandere factum
mirum, indictum, insuetum, ingens: absistite, curae
degeneres, dum sacra cano. Iam laeta laborum,
iam non tacta metu saecli regina futuri
stabat adhuc, nihil ipsa suo cum corde caducum,
350 nil mortale putans: illam natusque paterque
quique prius quam sol coelo, quam luna niteret,
spiritus obscuras ibat super igneus undas,

52

throngs are heard, strumming curved lyres and giving voice to 320
song. The virgin in her utmost joy recognized the sound and from
the palpable tokens realized that the time of birth was near. Im-
mediately she rises from her bed and, lifting up her gleaming eyes
to heaven in prayer, says: "Almighty Father, who with your great 325
nod rule the stars, the sweep of the sky, the lands and the seas, am
I to believe that the moment is at hand when your offspring con-
veys himself without taint into the tranquil light, when the earth
smiles on me and stipples her fields with tender flowers? See how 330
we pay back your profit come to full return! See how we pay back
your prodigious trust! Be my guardian and my counsel on heaven's
peak, lest any loss steal upon my chaste holiness. So it is that I am
the one who will eagerly cherish you, dear child, in soft embrace
as you snuggle in my lap and reach for the familiar teats. Smiling 335
you will bestow gentle kisses on your mother, and entwine your
child's hands and arms around my neck and take longed-for sleep
throughout your limbs."

Thus she speaks, and delights in God and in the gleaming
squadron of angels. She fills her mind with the celestial harmo-
nies. Meanwhile, as the constellations turn, her blessed hour came 340
near. Who grips me? Receive your bard, goddess. Goddess, direct
your bard. I am borne aloft into the clouds on high. I see the
whole of heaven descending, stirred with eagerness to see. Grant 345
me to make known a deed, wondrous, never before told, huge. Ig-
noble concerns, be off, while I sing of holy matters. Happy now in
her birth-struggle, now stricken by no fear, the queen of the age to
come still stood there, meditating within her heart on nothing
fleeting, nothing mortal. The Son, the Father, and the fiery Spirit, 350
who brooded over the dark waves before the sun, before the moon
shone in heaven, stand around and soothe her heart with great

stant circum et magnis permulcent pectora curis.
Praeterea redeunt animo quaecunque verendus
355 dixerat interpres, acti sine pondere menses
servatusque pudor, clausa cum protinus alvo
(o noctem superis laetam et mortalibus aegris!),
sicut erat foliis stipulaque innixa rigenti,
divinum, spectante polo spectantibus astris,
360 edit onus: qualis rorem cum vere tepenti
per tacitum matutinus desudat Eous
et passim teretes lucent per gramina guttae;
terra madet, madet aspersa sub veste viator
horridus et pluviae vim non sensisse cadentis
365 admirans gelidas hudo pede proterit herbas.
Mira fides! puer aethereas iam lucis in auras
prodierat foenoque latus male fultus agresti
impulerat primis resonum vagitibus antrum.
Alma parens nullos intra praecordia motus
370 aut incursantes devexi ponderis ictus
senserat; haerebant immotis viscera claustris:
haud aliter quam cum purum specularia solem
admittunt; lux ipsa quidem pertransit et omnes
irrumpens laxat tenebras et discutit umbras;
375 illa manent inlaesa, haud ulli pervia vento,
non hyemi, radiis sed tantum obnoxia Phoebi.
    Tunc puerum tepido genitrix involvit amictu
exceptumque sinu blandeque ad pectora pressum
detulit in praesepe. Hic illum mitia anhelo
380 ore fovent iumenta. O rerum occulta potestas!
Protinus agnoscens dominum procumbit humi bos
cernuus, et mora nulla simul procumbit asellus
submittens caput et trepidanti poplite adorat.
Fortunati ambo! non vos aut fabula Cretae
385 polluet antiqui referens mendacia furti

thoughts. Everything the esteemed messenger had said now also returns to her mind: the course of the months without burden, the preservation of her chastity. Then of a sudden, as she sup- 355 ported herself on the leaves and on the stiff straw, from her closed womb — O night joyous for those in heaven and for suffering mortals! — she brings forth her holy burden, while the heavens, while the stars watch: as when, in the warmth of spring's morning, Eous 360 silently distills its dew, and smooth droplets gleam everywhere amid the grass. The earth grows damp, the unkempt wayfarer grows damp under his moistened garments. Astonished that he doesn't feel the force of the falling rain, he treads the chill grass with sodden foot. Promise marvelously fulfilled! A child had now 365 come forth into the airy breezes of light. With his side barely supported on the rustic straw he made the cave echo with his first wails. His nourishing mother had felt no stirring within her vitals or assaulting blows of a weight in descent. Her innards clung tight 370 with bonds unmoved, much as when panels of glass receive the limpid sun. Indeed the light itself passes through and in a burst dissolves the blanketing darkness and scatters the shadows. The panes remain unscathed, permeable by no blast of wind or storm, but vulnerable only to Phoebus's rays. 375

Now the mother wrapped her child in warm clothes. Receiving him in her lap and clasping him tenderly to her bosom, she laid him in the manger. Here the gentle animals cherish him with their warm breath. O the mysterious force in things! Suddenly recog- 380 nizing his master, the ox falls to the ground with his brow bowed. With no delay the donkey also falls, head lowered, and makes obeisance on trembling knee. Blessed by fortune, both! Neither will a Cretan tale defame you, reporting lies about a theft of old 385

sidoniam mare per medium vexisse puellam,
aut sua dum madidus celebrat portenta Cithaeron
infames inter thyasos vinosaque sacra
arguet obsequio senis insudasse profani;
390 solis quippe deum vobis et pignora coeli
nosse datum, solis cunabula tanta tueri.
Ergo dum refugo stabit circundata fluctu
terra parens, dum praecipiti vertigine coelum
volvetur, romana pius dum templa sacerdos
395 rite colet, vestri semper referentur honores,
semper vestra fides nostris celebrabitur aris.
Quis tibi tunc animus, quae sancto in corde voluptas,
o genitrix, cum muta tuis famulantia cunis
ac circum de more sacros referentia ritus
400 aspiceres domino genua inclinare potenti,
et sua commotum trahere ad spectacula coelum?
Magne pater, quae tanta rudes prudentia sensus
leniit? informi tantos quis pectore motus
excivit calor et pecudum in praecordia venit,
405 ut quem non reges, non accepere tot urbes,
non populi, quibus una aras et sacra tueri
cura fuit, iam bos torpens, iam segnis asellus
authorem late possessoremque salutent?
   Vocibus interea sensim puerilibus heros
410 excitus somnum expulerat noctemque fugarat
ex oculis, iamque infantem videt et videt ipsam
maiorem aspectu maiori et lumine matrem
fulgentem, nec quoquam oculos aut ora moventem
sublimemque solo, superum cingente caterva
415 aligera: qualis nostrum cum tendit in orbem
purpureis rutilat pennis nitidissima phoenix,
quam variae circum volucres comitantur euntem;
illa volans solem nativo provocat auro

and that you carried the girl of Sidon through the midst of the
sea. Nor will drunken Cithaeron, in the course of advertising her
fables, accuse you of sweating at the command of a vulgar old man
during obscene routs and vinous rites. To you alone we know that
it was granted to recognize God and heaven's pledge, to you alone   390
to stand guard by so grand a cradle. As long as mother earth re-
mains firm, enclosed by the retreating tide, as long as the heavens
turn in their rushing cycle, as long as a holy priest duly worships
at the temples of Rome, your praises will ever be told, your trust   395
will ever be glorified on our altars. What were your thoughts,
mother, what pleasure was in your holy heart, at the moment
when you beheld dumb creatures offering adoration at your cra-
dle? Carrying out the blessed ritual nearby, they bent their knees   400
to their almighty Lord and drew astonished heaven to see them.
Great Father, what grand instinct tamed their rough emotions?
What warmth aroused such grand feelings in shaggy breasts and
reached the hearts of beasts, that He whom kings or cities in
number or peoples whose only charge was the protection of altars   405
and rites did not accept, now a sluggish ox, now an indolent don-
key should earnestly greet as their lord and master?

Meanwhile the hero, gradually awakened by the child's sounds,
had cast off sleep and put night to flight from his eyes. He now   410
sees the baby, then sees the mother herself, more impressive to be-
hold and radiating a more impressive glow. She moves neither her
eyes nor her features anywhere, surrounded by a winged gathering
of angels, but rises above the ground like a phoenix in full bril-
liance, with red-resplendent plumage, as it glides into our realm.   415
Varied birds roundabout accompany it in its course. Soaring it
challenges the sun—its head nature's golden amber, its sapphire-
blue tail spangled with roseate specks. Its very entourage is awe-

fulva caput, caudam et roseis interlita punctis
420 caeruleam; stupet ipsa cohors plausuque sonoro
per sudum strepit innumeris exercitus alis.
Miratur lucem insolitam, miratur ovanteis
coelicolum cantus senior; tum victus et amens
attonitusque animi tantisque ardoribus impar
425 corruit et geminas vultum demisit in ulnas,
adfususque diu telluri immobilis haesit.
Hic illum superi iuxta videre iacentem,
vidit dia parens, nec longum passa seniles
obduci tenebris oculos dat surgere et aegrum
430 substentare genu tremulisque insistere plantis
divinosque pati vultus superique nitorem
ignis et aethereas vibrantia lumina flammas.
Ille, ubi paulatim vires animumque resumpsit,
nodoso incumbens baculo modulantia primum
435 agmina reginamque deum de more salutat;
mox ipsum accedens praesepe ulvaque palustri
impositum spectans dominum terraeque marisque,
(o timor, o mentis pietas!) puerilia membra
non ausus tractare manu, cunctatur. Ibi auram,
440 insperatam auram divino efflantis ab ore
ore trahens, subito correptus numinis haustu
afflatusque deo, sic tandem voce quieta
incipit et lacrimis oculos suffundit obortis:
    'Sancte puer, non te Pariis operosa columnis
445 atria, non variata Phrygum velamina textu
excepere (iaces nullo spectabilis auro),
angustum sed vix stabulum, male commoda sedes
et fragiles calami lectaeque paludibus herbae
fortuitum dant ecce torum. Laqueata tyrannos
450 tecta et regifico capiant aulaea paratu:
te pater aeterno superum ditavit honore

struck, and in array sends the echoing beat of countless wings re-
sounding through the clear sky. The old man marvels at the un-   420
usual light, astonished at the angelic concert of praise. Then, over-
come, his mind and wits in turmoil, unequal to such radiance, he
collapsed and lowered his face into both his arms. Stretched out   425
on the ground, for a while he remained motionless. At this mo-
ment the angels nearby saw, the godlike mother saw him lying
there. Not allowing his aged eyes to be clothed for long in dark-
ness, she helps him to rise, to support his faltering knees, and to
stand on trembling feet. He endures the holy faces, the glistening   430
of the celestial fire and the light aquiver with heaven-sent flames.
When bit by bit he has recovered his strength and energy, as he
leans on his gnarled staff he first greets the singing choirs and, fol-
lowing his custom, the queen of the gods. Soon, approaching the   435
cradle itself and gazing upon the lord of land and sea lying on
marsh-reed, he hesitates — what concern, what reverence of
mind! — not daring with his hand to caress the child's limbs. Then
drawing in breath from his mouth, the unexpected breath issuing
from the mouth of God, and rapt suddenly by a draught of the su-   440
pernatural and of god-sped inspiration, he thus at last in a soft
voice begins, bathing his eyes with up-welling tears:

"Blessed child, no palaces elaborate with columns from Paros,
no coverlets embroidered with Phrygian weave gave you welcome.
No gold greets our eye as you lie there. Look, instead, scarcely a   445
small stable as an ill-furnished resting place and brittle straw and
swamp-culled reeds provide a haphazard bed. Coffered ceilings
and tapestries receive tyrants with regal display. The Father of the   450
gods has adorned you with the brilliance of everlasting glory. The

illustrans, tibi siderei domus aurea coeli
plaudit inextinctosque parat natura triumphos.
Et tamen hanc sedem reges, haec undique magni
455 antra petent populi, longe quos caerula Calpe
litore ab occiduo nigrisque impellet ab Indis
sol oriens, quos et Boreas et fervidus Auster
diverso inter se certantes cardine mittent.
Tu pastor, tu dispersas revocare per agros
460 missus oves late pectusque offerre periclis,
prodigus ah nimium vitae, per tela, per hostes
obscurum nemus irrumpens, rabida ora luporum
compesces saturumque gregem sub tecta reduces.
O mihi certa fides superum, decus addite terris,
465 nate deo, deus ipse, aeterno e lumine lumen:
te te ego, te circum genitrix laetique ministri
concinimus primique tuos celebramus honores
longaque perpetuis indicimus orgia fastis'.

Liber Tertius

Auratum interea culmen bipatentis Olympi
conscendit genitor, rerum inviolata potestas,
laeta fovens tacito sub pectore. Mox iubet omneis
ad se se acciri superos, quique atria longe
5 observant, quique arcanis penetralibus adstant,
praeterea quos eoos Aurora per ortus
et quos occiduae propior videt Hesperus orae;
nanque ferunt olim leges cum conderet aequas
rex superum et valido mundum suspenderet axe,
10 diversas statuisse domos diversaque divis
hospitia et dignos meritis tribuisse penates

golden dwelling of the starry heavens sounds its praise for you, and nature readies triumphs never to be dimmed. And yet kings will seek out this spot, and mighty peoples the world over this cave—those whom sea-blue Calpe will urge on from the western   455 shore afar, and the rising sun from the dark-hued Indi, those whom both Boreas and scorching Auster, vying with each other, will send from opposite poles. You it was, you, who were sent as shepherd to call back your sheep widely scattered through the fields and to offer your heart to danger. Too generous, yes,   460 with your life, through weapons, through enemies you will burst through the forest of darkness. You will muzzle the wolves' frenzied jaws, and guide back your sated flock within the fold. O my trust in heaven now assured, O grace added to the world, child of God and very God, Light from everlasting Light, around you I   465 and your mother, around you the rejoicing retinue, join in song as we initiate the proclamation of your glory and extend the celebration of your timeless rituals through ever-enduring ceremony."

Book III

Meanwhile the Father, the unchallenged power over the universe, climbs to the gilded crest of twin-gated Olympus, cherishing happiness in his silent heart. Soon he commands all the angels to be summoned before him—angels who watch over distant palaces, who keep guard at hearths hidden to view as well as those whom   5 Aurora beholds at her eastern risings and Hesperus nearing the western shore. For they say that, once, when the King of the heavens was hanging the world on its sturdy axis and promulgating its laws of balance, he established a variety of homes and a variety of lodgings for the angels. He gave them housing consistent with   10 their deserts, to each by rank. They frequent the dwellings be-

ordine cuique suos: illi data tecta frequentant
armaque et aeratis affigunt nomina valvis.
Haud mora fit: celerant iussi, volat aethere toto
15 coelicolum glomerata manus, pars igne corusco
tota rubens, pars stelliferis innexa coronis.
Ipse sedens humeris chlamydem fulgentibus aptat
ingentem et coelum pariter terrasque tegentem,
quam quondam, ut perhibent, vigilans noctesque diesque
20 ipsa suo nevit rerum natura Tonanti,
adiecitque sacrae decus admirabile telae
per medium perque extremas subtegminis oras
immortale aurum intexens grandesque smaragdos.
Illic nam varia mundum distinxerat arte
25 gnara operum mater certisque elementa figuris
et rerum species animasque et quicquid ab alta
fundit mente pater. Generis primordia nostri
cernere erat limum informem; iam praepete penna
deferri volucres liquidum per inane videres,
30 iam silvis errare feras pontumque natari
piscibus et vero credas spumescere fluctu.
    Hic postquam aligeros gemmata sedilia coetus
accepere, pater solio sic infit ab alto:
'Aetherei proceres (neque enim ignoratis et ausus
35 infandos dirumque acies super astra frementes),
si mecum iuvat antiquos ab origine motus
inspicere et veterum pariter meminisse laborum,
quandoquidem haec vobis peperit victoria laudem,
huc animos, huc pacatas advertite mentes.
40 Vos, cum omne arderet coelum servilibus armis
arctoumque furor pertenderet impius axem
scandere et in gelidos regnum transferre Triones,
fida manus mecum mansistis et ultima tandem
experti coelo victricia signa tulistis

stowed on them and attach their weapons and titles to the bronze-
clad doors. With no delay they hasten as bidden. The massed bat-
talion of angels takes flight throughout the sky, some all reddened   15
with the flash of fire, some encircled by starry crowns. Himself
taking his seat, he fits to his gleaming shoulders a cloak, huge and
covering the heavens and as well as the earth. Tradition has it that
the Nature of things herself, working without sleep day and night,
once wove it for her Thunderer. She added astonishing beauty to   20
the holy cloth, embroidering the center of the web and its outer
edges with deathless gold and massive emeralds. There with mani-
fold artistry, wise in her work, the mother had marked off the uni-
verse and the elements with defining symbols, and the appearance   25
and the inner essence of matter and whatever the Father pours
forth from the depths of his thoughts. On view were the begin-
nings of our race in shapeless mud. Now you would notice birds
borne on headlong wing through the clear void, now you would
believe that beasts were wandering in the woods, and that the sea
was swimming with fish and frothing with real billows.   30

Here, after the jewelled chairs had received the winged bands,
the Father begins thus from his lofty throne: "Princes of heaven
(for you remain aware both of the vile daring and of the battle-
lines that roared dreadfully beyond the stars), if it is your pleasure   35
to review with me the ancient turmoil from its start and to recol-
lect together our troubles of old, since this victory has provided
your praise, here turn your thoughts, here turn your minds, now
at peace. When all the heavens were afire with ignoble arms, and   40
immoral Madness made aim to scale the axis of Arctos and shift
the seat of rule to the chill Triones, you remained for me a trusted
band and, after enduring everything to the end, you carried in
heaven the standards of victory and established an immortal tro-

45 aeternumque alta fixistis in arce trophaeum.
Quos ego pro meritis insigni munere palmae
donavi regnique in partem operumque recepi
praecipuosque habui lectosque ad iussa ministros:
usque adeo fixa antiqui stat gratia facti!

50 Nec minus et nostras audistis saepe querelas
vidistisque graves flammati pectoris aestus,
tunc cum prima novas egit dementia gentes
arboris auricomae coelestia carpere poma,
poma gravi seros gustu laesura nepotes:

55 munere quin superum indignas spoliastis et umbra
sacrorum late nemorum assiduoque labore
multastis miseras vitae et brevioribus annis.
Quid repetam veteri sumptas de crimine poenas
exiliumque informe Erebi tenebrasque repostas,

60 quae tacito mecum spectastis lumine et iidem
terrarum sortem moesti indoluistis acerbam?
aut etiam ut nostri longo post tempore tandem
pectoris indomitas clementia vicerit iras,
visque arcana leves sensim demissa per auras

65 foecundam intactae complerit virginis alvum?
an temere hoc nullaque actum ratione putatis?
Quippe ita mansuras decuit me ponere leges,
quo terraeque polusque, homines divique vicissim
foederibus starent certis et pignore tanto

70 servarent memorem cognatae stirpis amorem.
Quare agite et iam nunc humana capessite fata;
ac primum duris parvi sub cautibus antri
gramineos lustrate toros, lustrate beatam
pauperibus sedem calamis, cunctique recentes

75 submissi cunas accedite, dum pia mater
complexu in molli natum fovet, hubera pernox
indulgens teneris pueri rorantia labris.

phy on the citadel's peak. For your services I have presented you   45
with the palm's glorious gift and received you into a share of my
kingdom and of my works, and considered you my special atten-
dants, chosen to do my bidding. To such an extent remain assured
our thanks for your past enterprise! Moreover, you have often
heard our complaints, and observed the depth of worry that fired   50
our heart, at the time when folly first impelled the new race of
men to pluck the ambrosial fruit of the golden-tressed tree, fruit
destined to harm their later generations with its grievous taste. In-
deed you deprived them in their unworthiness of heaven's gift and   55
of the spacious shade of the holy groves. You punished their
wretchedness with unceasing toil and with shorter years of life.
Why shall I retell the punishments extracted for the ancient
crime, the shapeless exile and remote darkness of Erebus which
you beheld, as did I, with silent glance and along with me grieved   60
in sadness for earth's bitter lot? Or, furthermore, how at last, after
long lapse of time, mercy has overcome the unbridled wrath in our
breast, and a hidden force, eased gently downward through the
nimble breezes, has filled the fertile womb of a chaste virgin? Do   65
you imagine that this was done capriciously and without consider-
ation? Indeed it thus was fitting for me to establish ever-enduring
laws whereby both earth and sky, both men and gods, might in
turn be steadied by assured principles and, through so great a
guarantee, maintain a love mindful of their kindred beginning. So   70
take heed and even now attend to the destiny of humankind. First
of all, bring radiance to the bed of straw beneath the flinty rocks
of the tiny cave, search out the blessed spot with its simple reeds.
In a mass humbly approach the new cradle while the holy mother
warms her son in her soft embrace, all night long offering her   75
flowing breasts to the boy's tender lips. Nearby lie the silent ani-
mals, with their bodies resting low upon the hay. They lick the

Nec procul in stipula demisso pectore mutum
procumbit pecus et domini vestigia lambens
80 pervigilat, longos fundit dum tibia cantus.
Hic faustos ortus pueri noctemque verendam
discursu per inane levi passimque canoris
laudibus excipite et plausu celebrate faventes
omnia felicem ventura in saecula pacem
85 certatimque renascentis cunabula mundi,
victum anguem victumque anguis furiale venenum.
Sic placitum, sic aversos coniungere terris
coelicolas, sic ferre homines ad sidera certum est'.
    Haec ubi dicta, novum superis inspirat amorem,
90 quo subito veteres deponant pectoris iras,
obliti scelerum patrisque exempla secuti,
terrarum flagrent studio et mortalia curent.
Nec mora, Laetitiam choreis tum forte vacantem
advocat (haec magni motusque animosque Tonantis
95 temperat et vultum discussa nube serenat),
Laetitiam, quae coelicolum per limina semper
discursat raroque imas petit hospita terras,
curarumque expers lacrimasque exosa virago
exultat totoque abigit suspiria coelo.
100 Ut stetit ante patrem terrasque accedere iussa est,
mobilibus pictas humeris accomodat alas
lenimenque viae comites vocat. Ilicet adsunt,
iucundae visu facies, Cantusque Chorique
Gaudiaque Plaususque et honestis ignibus ardens
105 rectus Amor, quem nuda Fides Spesque inscia luctus
vadentem mira unanimes pietate sorores
observant; sequitur mox inculpata Voluptas
Gratiaque et niveam suadens Concordia pacem.
Cumque propinquasset portae, quae maxima coelo
110 dicitur aeternumque micat radiata coruscis

66

feet of their master as they keep watch, while the flute lets flow a
stream of song. Here everywhere share with hymn's acclaim in the   80
propitious birth of the boy and in the awe-inspiring night, after
nimble descent through the void. Vie in celebrating with applause,
and praise the auspicious peace for all generations to come and the
cradle of the newborn world. The serpent is subdued, subdued the   85
serpent's frenzied poison. Thus I have decreed, thus I have de-
cided to join earth with indifferent angels in harmony, thus to
bring mankind to the stars."

   After speaking these things he breathes into the angels new
love, so that in a flash they lay aside their hearts' long-standing an-
ger, forgetting man's crimes and imitating their Father's lead, and   90
burn with enthusiasm for the earth, and attend to the affairs of
mortals. With no delay he summons Happiness, then by chance
at leisure from her dances (she calms the passionate outbursts of
the mighty Thunderer, she clears his features by dispersing the
clouds). Happiness ever sweeps across the thresholds of heaven's   95
dwellers, and only on occasion seeks out the earth below in her
travels. No party to worry and loathing tears, the heroine lives for
joy and relegates sighs from the whole of heaven. When she has
stood before the Father and received her orders to approach the
earth, she fits variegated wings to her supple shoulders and sum-   100
mons comrades as solace for her journey. Immediately they appear,
their faces a pleasure to see: Songs and Dances, Rejoicings and
Applause, true Love, burning with a noble flame, whom naked
Faith and Hope, ignorant of grief, whose passage her like-minded   105
sisters honor with wondrous deference. Blameless Pleasure soon
follows, and Grace, and Concord, urging on snow-white Peace.
When she approached the gate, which in heaven is named greatest
and forever shimmers, gleaming with the signs of the stars—the   110

astrorum signis, quando mortalibus aegris
dant nimbos aliae et damnant caligine terras,
succinctae occurrunt Horae properantibus alis,
insomnes Horae, nanque his fulgentia divum
115 limina et ingentis custodia credita coeli.
Protinus aeratos impulso cardine posteis
cum sonitu magnoque polos quassante fragore
praepandunt obnixae humeris. Volat illa per auras
obscura sub nocte nitens; gratantur eunti
120 sidera, iam festas meditatur luna choreas,
exultant Hyades, gaudet mutata Bootes
plaustra auro totosque auro fulgere iuvencos;
tunc primum visa est miseri post fata parentis
risisse Erigone et longum posuisse dolorem,
125 armatoque ensis subducitur Orioni.
Ut vero umbrosis posuit vestigia silvis,
culmina conscendit pastorum, atque omnia late
perlustrans tacitis oculis loca concutit alas
applaudens, pictosque sinus sub nocte coruscans
130 subrisit laetum puraque in luce refulsit.
Primi illam sensere canes, sensere iacentes
haedorum passim per dura cubilia matres,
balatuque ovium valles sonuere propinquae
saxaque et attoniti caput erexere magistri.
135 Tunc ait: 'O parvi vigiles gregis, o bona pubes
silvarum, superis gratum genus, ite, beati
pastores, ite, antra novis intendite sertis:
reginam ad cunas positumque in stramine regem
(certa fides) alti iam iam moderator Olympi
140 cernere dat; properate, novique tepentia lactis
munera cumque suo date condita subere mella,
insuetum et silvis stipula deducite carmen'.
Nec plura effata, in nubes taciturna recessit

others bestow clouds on anxious mortals and consign the earth to darkness—the Hours run up, girded with rushing wings, the sleepless Hours. To them the glittering thresholds of the angels and of the mighty heavens are entrusted in charge. Immediately, 115 pushing with their shoulders, they apply force to the hinges and throw open the gates of bronze with a huge crash that shakes the poles. She flies through the breezes, flashing amid the dimness of night. The stars are gladdened as she makes her way. Now the moon gives thought to festive dances. The Hyades are jubilant. 120 Boötes rejoices that his wagon has been changed to gold and that his bullocks are completely resplendent in gold. Then, for the first time since the demise of her hapless father, Erigone seemed to smile and to lay aside her deep-seated sorrow, and armed Orion is relieved of his sword. But when she set foot in the shady woods, 125 she climbed the roofs of the shepherds and, surveying the whole area far and wide with silent eyes, she flapped her wings in approval, and, shaking her variegated garments in the darkness, she beamed in happiness and glowed in clear light. First the dogs felt 130 her presence, then the she-goats felt it, lying here and there in their stony lairs. The nearby valleys and crags echoed with the bleating of sheep, and the amazed shepherds raised their heads. Then she speaks: "O guardians of a small flock, O virtuous offspring of the woods, race dear to the gods, make your way, blessed 135 shepherds, make your way. Clothe the cave with fresh garlands. Now, even now—assurance of your faith!—the Master of lofty Olympus allows you to behold your queen at the cradle and your king placed upon straw. Make haste and offer the warming gift of 140 fresh milk and of honey preserved with its bark. Spin forth on your reed pipe a song new even to the woods." With no further words she silently withdrew into the clouds, and buried herself deeply in the black shadow of night.

et penitus nigra noctis se condidit umbra.

145 Olli inter se se vario sermone volutant
quid superum mandata velint, quas quaerere cunas,
quos iubeant reges, quae cingere frondibus antra.
Continuo variis innectunt tempora ramis;
nectitur et lentiscus opacaeque arbutus umbrae
150 rosque maris buxusque et densa comas terebinthus,
cunctaque frondenti redimitur turba corona.
Mox silvam exquirunt omnem saltusque repostos
flammiferis lustrant tedis: ardere putares
arva procul totumque incendi lumine montem.
155 Tandem inter dumos fessi sub rupe cavata
speluncam aspiciunt vocemque rudentis aselli
auribus accepere, vident ipsumque bovemque
longaevumque senem stantemque ad lumina matrem
insomnem et pressis refoventem pignus in ulnis.
160 Ergo insperatae gavisi munere sortis,
ocyus ingentem procero stipite laurum
avulsamque solo palmam ab radicibus imis
attollunt humeris perque intervalla canentes
cum plausu choreisque et multisono modulatu
165 vestibuli ante aditum statuunt, omnemque coronant
fronde locum, grandes oleas cedrosque comanteis
affigunt longisque advelant limina sertis
et late idaliam spargunt cum baccare myrtum.
Quos bonus ex antro dictis ingressus amicis
170 compellat senior placidaque haec voce profatur:
'Dicite, pastores (neque enim sine numine credo
tam certum tenuistis iter), cui tanta paratis
munera, cui virides ramis frondentibus umbras
texitis? an ne aliquis superum patre missus ab alto
175 has docuit sedes locaque haec accedere iussit?'
Sic memorans se se laetum venientibus offert.

In the give and take of conversation they talk over among themselves the meaning of the divine commands: what cradle, what 145 royalty they order them to seek out, what cave to wreathe with leaves. Immediately they bind their brows with particolored sprigs. Mastic is part of the weave and dark-shaded arbute, rosemary and box, terebinth with its thick foliage. The whole crowd is festooned 150 with leafy crowns. They hasten to explore all the woods, and they scan the hidden glades with flaming torches. You would imagine from a distance that the fields were on fire and that the whole hillside was blazing with light. At last in their weariness they see a cave amid the thickets under a hollow rock, and their ears pick up 155 the sound of a donkey braying. They spy it, as well as an ox, an aged old man and a wakeful mother standing before the light, warming a child enclosed in her arms. So, rejoicing in fortune's unexpected gift, they quickly raise on their shoulders the huge 160 trunk of a lofty laurel and a palm tree, torn from the ground by the bottom of its roots. With intervals of singing, applause, dances and many a melodious tune, they place them before the front of the entranceway, and bedeck the whole area with foliage. They 165 plant huge olive trees and leafy cedars, and swathe the threshold with a sweep of garlands while roundabout they scatter Idalian myrtle together with foxglove. Making his way out from the cave the noble ancient addresses them with friendly words and with gentle voice speaks thus: "Tell me, shepherds: For whom do you 170 make ready such gifts, for whom do you weave greening shade from leafy branches? Indeed I don't believe that you held to so sure a route without divine aid. Or did one of the angels sent from the exalted Father teach you of this spot and order you to make your way right here?" With these words he presents himself hap- 175 pily to the arrivals. They in their turn: "O father, a new vision of

Illi autem: 'Nova per tenebras, nova lucis imago,
o genitor, media visa est modo lumina silva
spargere et in nostras diffundere gaudia mentes,
180 sive deus coelo veniens seu forte deorum
nuntius, in dubio est: nos vultum habitumque loquentis
vidimus et motas per noctem audivimus alas'.
Sic fati iungunt dextras; mox ordine longo
antrum introgressi, calathis silvestria plenis
185 dona ferunt, matrem et laeto simul ore salutant.
      Tum puero adstantes Lycidas et maximus Aegon —
Aegon, getulis centum cui pascua campis,
centeni per rura greges massyla vagantur:
ipse caput late, qua Bagrada, qua vagus errat
190 Triton, cinyphiae qua devolvuntur arenae,
ingens agricolis, ingens pastoribus Aegon;
at Lycidas vix urbe sua, vix colle propinquo
cognitus, aequoreas carmen deflexit ad undas —
et tamen hi non voce pares, non viribus aequis,
195 inter adorantum choreas plaususque deorum,
rustica septena modulantur carmina canna:
'Hoc erat, alme puer, patriis quod noster in antris
Tityrus attritae sprevit rude carmen avenae,
et cecinit dignas romano consule silvas.
200 Ultima cumaei venit iam carminis aetas,
magna per exactos renovantur saecula cursus;
scilicet haec virgo, haec sunt saturnia regna,
haec nova progenies coelo descendit ab alto,
progenies per quam toto gens aurea mundo
205 surget et in mediis palmes florebit aristis.
Qua duce, siqua manent sceleris vestigia nostri
irrita perpetua solvent formidine terras
et vetitum magni pandetur limen Olympi;
occidet et serpens, miseros quae prima parentes

light, new through the darkness, seemed just now to scatter its
brilliance in the midst of the wood and to suffuse our minds with
joy. Whether it was God coming from heaven or by chance a mes-
senger from the divinities remains in doubt. We ourselves saw   180
the features and dress of the speaker, and heard wings flapping
through the night." After these words they join hand in hand. In a
moment they enter the cave in a long line, bringing peasant gifts in
heaping baskets and at the same time greeting the mother with
faces of gladness.   185

Then Lycidas and mightiest Aegon standing by the boy—
Aegon, who possesses a hundred pastures in the plains of the
Gaetuli, whose hundred flocks roam the countryside of the
Massyli, himself chieftain of an expanse where the Bagrada, where
the roving Triton wanders, where the sands of the Cinyps roll
along, Aegon, remarkable among farmers, remarkable among   190
shepherds. Lycidas, however, scarcely known in his own city,
scarcely on the neighboring hill, bent his song to the waves of the
sea. These, though unequal in voice as unequal in power, perform
their uncouth song on seven-fold reed, as they share in the dance
and applause of the worshipping angels: "This was the reason,   195
gracious child, that our Tityrus in his homeland grottoes scorned
the unpolished song of the well-worn pipe of reeds and sang of
woods worthy of a Roman consul. 'Now the last age of the song of
Cumae has come, the great ages start anew, as they fulfill their   200
course. This for certain is the Virgin, this the kingdom of Saturn.
This new offspring descends from the lofty heavens, offspring be-
cause of whom a golden race will arise throughout the whole
world and a vine will flourish in the midst of grain. If any traces of   205
our guilt remain, under his leadership they will become void, re-
leasing the earth from her abiding fear. The once forbidden
threshold of great Olympus will lie open. The serpent, too, will
perish which, steeped in monstrous poisons, first deceived our

210 elusit portentificis imbuta venenis.
Tu ne deum vitam accipies divisque videbis
permistos heroas et ipse videberis illis
pacatumque reges patriis virtutibus orbem?
Aspice felici diffusum lumine coelum
215 camposque fluviosque ipsasque in montibus herbas;
aspice, venturo laetentur ut omnia saeclo.
Ipsae lacte domum referent distenta capellae
hubera nec magnos metuent armenta leones,
agnaque per gladios ibit secura nocentes
220 bisque superfusos servabit tincta rubores.
Interea tibi, parve puer, munuscula prima
contingent ederaeque intermixtique corymbi;
ipsa tibi blandos fundent cunabula flores
et durae quercus sudabunt roscida mella;
225 mella dabunt quercus, omnis feret omnia tellus.
At postquam firmata virum te fecerit aetas
et tua iam totum notescent facta per orbem,
alter erit tum Tiphys et altera quae vehat Argo
delectos heroas; erunt etiam altera bella
230 atque ingens stygias ibis praedator ad undas.
Incipe, parve puer, risu cognoscere matrem,
cara dei soboles, magnum coeli incrementum'.
Talia dum referunt pastores, avia longe
responsant nemora et voces ad sidera iactant
235 intonsi montes; ipsae per confraga rupes,
ipsa sonant arbusta: 'Deus, deus ille, Menalca'.
  Hic subito magnum visi per inane volatus
coelestum cursusque alacres alacresque recursus,
auditaeque procul voces sonitusque rotarum.
240 Scilicet innocuis per sudum exercitus armis
ibat ovans: divisae acies, terna agmina ternis
instructa ordinibus belli simulacra ciebant.

wretched parents. Will you take on the life of the gods and will   210
you behold heroes and immortals mingled, and will you yourself
be seen by them? Will you rule over a world brought to peace by
the virtues of your father? See the heavens, the fields and streams,
the very grasses on the mountainsides, covered with a propitious
glow. See how all things rejoice in the coming age. Of their own   215
accord goats will bring home udders swollen with milk, and the
herds will not fear mighty lions. Without concern the lamb will
make its way through swords meant to harm and, dyed once and
again, will preserve the red on red poured over it. Meanwhile ivy   220
mixed with its berries will form the first modest gifts for you,
small child. The cradle itself will pour forth for you delightful
flowers, and hard oaks will ooze with the dew of honey. Oaks will
offer honey, every land will produce everything. But, after time has   225
given you the strength of manhood, and your accomplishments
are now famous through the whole world, then there will be an-
other Tiphys and another Argo to carry chosen heroes. There will
also be other wars, and you will make your way, a mighty
Harrower, to the waters of the Styx. Begin, small child, cherished   230
scion of God, great offspring of heaven, to acknowledge your
mother with a smile.'" While the shepherds tender such words,
the pathless woods reecho from afar and unshorn mountains fling
their voices toward the stars. The very crags amid their thickets,
the very copses resound: "A god, he is a god, Menalcas."   235

At this, flights of angels appeared of a sudden through the great
void, with swift advances and swift withdrawals. Voices and the
noise of wheels are heard from afar. A triumphant army was there,
making its way through the clear sky with harmless weaponry. The   240
lines of battle are parted: three squadrons arrayed in triple ranks
were setting in motion a semblance of war. You might see them

Ter clypeis iam cedentes invadere nubes
aspiceres, vacuas ter mittere tela per auras,
245 ter clamare ducem; mox dissita cogere signa
atque unam laetae faciem praeferre phalangis;
rursus et aërios percurrere milite campos,
semotosque alios constanti incedere passu
nubila per latasque vias et iungere nexu
250 brachia, perpetuis quatientes motibus alas
gestantesque manu nostrae argumenta salutis:
spinasque clavosque horrenti et vimine fasces
haesuramque hastam lateri medicataque felle
pocula sublimemque crucem immanemque columnam.
255 Ibant et dulci mulcebant aethera cantu.
Innumeras alii laudes et magna parentis
facta canunt: ut prima novi fundaverit orbis
moenia telluremque vagis discluserit undis;
ut passim varios coelo suspenderit ignes
260 lunamque stellasque; ut magni lumina solis,
iam late extremo tenebris oriente fugatis,
protulerit. 'Tu belligeras, metuende, cohortes
deiicis exturbasque polo; tu fulmine quassas
cum duce signa suo nigroque involvis Averno
265 Cocytumque iubes tristesque habitare lacunas.
Te gemini cecinere axes, te maxima tellus
victorem, cecinit vastis cum fluctibus aequor;
nec te hominum fraudes, non avertere nefanda
crimina, sed laeto spectas mortalia vultu
270 dignatasque tuo solaris numine terras.
Salve, magne opifex coeli, rex maxime divum
terrarumque hominumque salus, quem sidera, quem sol,
quem metuunt reges tenebrarum et Tartarus ingens,
cui late humanum servit genus, omnia solus
275 qui regis, omnia amas pariter; tibi nomina mille,

now three times assault the yielding clouds with their shields,
three times launch their spears through the empty breezes, three
times call upon their leader. Soon they gather their scattered stan- 245
dards and present their buoyant phalanx in a single front. Then
once more they traverse the fields of air with soldiery. Others at a
distance march forward with steady pace through clouds and
broad avenues. They intertwine their arms, flapping their wings in 250
continuous movement and carrying in their hands the symbols of
our salvation: the thorns, nails, scourges of bristling withes, a
spear soon to pierce his side, goblets anointed with gall, the tower-
ing cross and brutal pillar. As they went their way they soothed
the air with their sweet song. Others chant the infinite praises and 255
great deeds of the Father: how he first established ramparts for the
new world, and sequestered the earth from the meandering waters;
how everywhere in the heavens he hung motley fires, along with
both moon and stars; how he created the light of the mighty sun 260
in the farthest east, with darkness now thoroughly routed. "O
dreaded one, you hurl down the warring legions and expel them
from the sky. You it is who with the thunderbolt convulse both
their standards and their leader. You engulf them in dark Avernus
and command that Cocytus and its dismal pools be their dwelling.
The twin poles have sung of you as victor, you, the mightiest 265
earth, the sea with its capacious floods, have sung. You do not
turn yourself away from man's deceits and unspeakable wrongs.
Rather you gaze at the affairs of mortals with a face of joy and
bring comfort to an earth deserving of your divinity. Hail, great 270
Craftsman of heaven, greatest King of the gods, Salvation of earth
and of mankind, whom the stars, whom the sun, whom the rulers
of the world of darkness and vast Tartarus fear, whom the human
race everywhere serves. You alone equally rule all, love all. Yours 275

mille potestatum, regnorum insignia mille!
Salve author, salve immensi dominator Olympi,
et nobis felix terrisque labantibus adsis!'
Ingeminant plausum nubes lateque per auras
280   discursat vox et coeli convexa resultant.
      Herboso tum forte toro undisonisque sub antris
venturas tacito volvebat pectore sortes
caeruleus rex, humentum generator aquarum
Iordanes, quem iuxta hilari famulantia vultu
285   agmina densentur natae, pulcherrima Glauce
Dotoque Protoque Galenaque Lamprothoëque,
nudae humero, nudis discincta veste papillis;
Callyroë Bryoque Pherusaque Dinameneque
Asphaltisque assueta leves fluitare per undas,
290   ipsaque odoratis perfusa liquoribus Anthis,
Anthis, qua non ulla novos miscere colores
doctior aut pictis caput exornare coronis;
mox Hyale atque Thoë et vultu nitidissima Crene
Gongisteque Rhoëque et candida Limnoria
295   et Dryope et virides Botane resoluta capillos,
ore omnes formosae, albis in vestibus omnes,
omnes puniceis evinctae crura cothurnis.
Ipse antro medius pronaque acclinis in urna
fundit aquas: nitet urna novis variata figuris
300   crystallo ex alba et puro perlucida vitro,
egregium decus et superum mirabile donum.
Umbrosis hic silva comis densisque virebat
arboribus; cervi passim capreaeque fugaces
aestivum viridi captabant frigus in umbra.
305   In medio, effulgens fluctibus, amnis
errabat campo et cursu laeta arva secabat.
Hic iuvenis, fulvis velatus corpora setis,
stans celso in scopulo regem dominumque deorum

are a thousand names, a thousand emblems of power and of sovereignty. Hail, Creator, hail Master of boundless Olympus: may you remain kindly even to us and to the stumbling earth." The clouds redouble the applause. The sound sweeps soaring through the breezes and the vault of heaven reverberates.   280

At that time it happened that Jordan, the sea-blue king, begetter of moistening waters, on his grassy couch beneath his wave-resounding cave was pondering in his silent heart what was fated to occur. In attendance next to him his daughters throng in bands, with cheerful features — most beautiful Glauce, Doto and Proto,   285 Galena and Lamprothoë, their shoulders bare, their breasts bare with garments ungirdled, Callyroë and Bryo, Pherusa and Dinamene, and Asphaltis, who liked to drift through the delicate waves, and Anthis herself, Anthis, bathed in fragrant perfumes (there was none more skilled at mingling fresh hues or at adorning   290 her head with variegated wreaths); next Hyale and Thoë, Crene with richly gleaming features, Gongiste and Rhoë, and bright Limnoria, Dryope and Botane, her green hair loosened, all with   295 lovely faces, all in white garments, all with their legs bound with crimson buskins. He himself in the midst of the cave pours forth his waters as he leans against a sloping urn. The transparent urn of clear crystal and limpid glass gleams with ornaments of recondite shape. It was a magnificent object of beauty, an astonishing   300 gift of the gods. Here a forest flourished, shady with foliage and thick with trees. Everywhere deer and skittish roebucks were in quest of summer's coolness in the verdant shade. At its center a river with gilded shimmering waves roamed through the plain and   305 cleaved the fertile fields with its course. Here a young man, his body clothed in tawny bristles, as he stood on a lofty rock was

vorticibus rapidis medioque in fonte lavabat;
310 at viridi in ripa lecti de more ministri
succincti exspectant pronisque in flumina palmis
protendunt niveas, coelestia lintea, vestes.
Ipse pater coelo late manifesta sereno
signa dabat natoque levem per inane columbam
315 insignem radiis mittebat et igne corusco;
attonitae circum venerantur numina nymphae,
et fluvius refugas ad fontem convocat undas.
Talia caelata genitor dum spectat in urna
fatorum ignarus oculosque ad singula volvit
320 admirans, videt insolitos erumpere fonteis
ingentemque undare domum cavaque antra repleri
fluctibus atque novum latices sumpsisse saporem;
dumque haeret pavitatque simul, dum sublevat undis
muscosum caput et taurino cornua vultu,
325 aspicit insuetas late florescere ripas
claraque per densas discurrere lumina silvas
pastorum ludo, et laetos ad sidera cantus
divinasque audit voces et numina passim
advenisse deum testantia. Protinus ambas
330 ad coelum palmas hilaris cum voce tetendit:
    'O maris, o terrae, divumque hominumque repertor,
quis tua vel magno decreta incognita coelo
detulit huc audax mediisque abscondit in undis?
Ipse mihi haec quondam, memini, dum talia mecum
335 saepe agitat repetitque volens, narrare solebat
caeruleus Proteus; mendax si caetera Proteus,
non tamen hoc vanas effudit carmine voces:
«Adveniet tibi, Iordanes, properantibus annis,
adveniet, mihi crede», inquit «—certissima coelum
340 signa dedit nec me delusum oracula fallunt—
qui te olim Nili supra septemplicis ortus,

80

bathing the king and master of the gods in the rushing swirls at
the middle of the stream. But on the green bank chosen atten-
dants, high girt as was their custom, are waiting. From their hands   310
sloping toward the water they stretch snow-white towels of linen,
fit for a god. The Father himself gave clear signs far and wide in
the cloudless heavens. For his Son he sent through the void a nim-
ble dove, striking for its rays and shimmering fire. The astonished   315
nymphs roundabout worship the godhead, and the river recalls to
their source his receding waves. While their father, ignorant of the
future, was scrutinizing such scenes on the engraved urn and was
casting his eyes in awe at the details, he sees an unusual torrent
burst forth and overflow his expansive dwelling. The hollows of   320
the cave fill up with the flood while the liquid has taken on a novel
taste. Hesitant and afraid at the same time, when he raises out of
the waves his mossy head and the horns on his bull-like face he
beholds for a distance an unprecedented flowering of his banks
and bright lights darting through the thick woods from the shep-   325
herds at play. He also hears the joyous songs directed to the stars,
the god-like voice and the divine presences everywhere, bearing
witness to the arrival of God. In his happiness he immediately
stretched his hands to heaven and said: 330

"O Creator of the sea, of the land, of gods and of men, who in
boldness brought hither your decrees, unrevealed even in mighty
heaven, and hid them in the midst of my waves? I recall that once
upon a time sea-blue Proteus himself used to tell me the history of
these matters when in my presence he regularly touched on such
things and was willing to pass them in review. If in other things   335
Proteus spoke lies, in this prophecy nevertheless he has not
poured forth empty words: 'Believe me, O Jordan, someone will
come to you, someone will come, as the years rush past,' he said,
'—for heaven has given the most certain of signs nor do false ora-
cles deceive me—who someday will raise your reputation above   340
the rising of the seven-fold Nile, above the Indus and the Ganges

supra Indum et Gangen fontemque binominis Istri
attollet fama, qui te Tyberique Padoque
praeferet atque tuos astris aequabit honores.
345 Cuius in adventu tristes discedere morbi
corporibus passim incipient; iam victa repente
cessabit, turpeis squamas maculasque remittet
dira lues lacerosque elephas effusus in artus
ulcera sanguineo sistet manantia tabo.
350 Quin et letales (dictu mirabile!) febres
diffugient iussae possessaque membra relinquent;
cedet et infestae violentior ira Dianae,
ira nocens, quae fulminea velut icta ruina
corpora cum gemitu ad terram prosternit et igni
355 interdum, nunc perdere aqua (miserabile visu!)
festinat: stygio nimirum armata veneno
exuperat vis et spumas agit ore tumenteis.
Nec iam ultra, longo vires minuente veterno,
tabificus per operta impune vagabitur hydrops,
360 exitio obrepens miserorum atque omnia late
viscera per varios perdet tumefacta dolores.
Non alias vinctae tam crebra silentia linguae
abrumpent noctem aut toties tenebrasque priores
excutient oculi, qui nunquam sidera, nunquam
365 ardentem magni viderunt lampada solis.
Multa quidem maiora fide, sed vera, sed ipsos
quae teneant spectantum oculos, possum ore referre,
sed propero: ventura tamen mirabitur aetas.
   Cernere erit claudos passim genua aegra trahentes
370 firmato subitos extendere poplite gressus;
tum nervis labefacta diuque trementia membra
(quis credat nisi certa meus mihi cantet Apollo?)
restringi et validas cum robore sumere vires;
atque alius, rapto iussus consurgere lecto,

and the source of the Hister with its double name, who will ex-
alt you beyond the Tiber and the Po, who will match your glory
with the stars. At his arrival grim diseases will everywhere begin
to depart from bodies. Grievous contagion will suddenly give way   345
in defeat and shed its ugly scale and blotches. Leprosy, spread
through mangled members, will check its ulcers oozing with
bloody gore. Even deadly fevers—marvel at the telling!—will flee
upon command and abandon the limbs that they had claimed.   350
The furious wrath of hostile Diana will also recoil, destructive
wrath that fells bodies with a groan onto the ground as if stricken
by a thunderbolt's onrush and—piteous to see—hastens their
doom at times with fire, now with water. Its violence, bolstered   355
with Stygian poison, claims certain victory and flings bloated froth
from the mouth. Nor will infectious dropsy, with its drawn-out,
wasting torpor, now thereafter covertly roam invulnerable, as it
steals ruinously upon the miserable and completes the destruction   360
of all their innards through an array of torments. Not at any other
time will mute tongues so frequently shatter the silence, or eyes,
which never saw the stars, never the burning light of the great sun,
so often shake off night and their former darkness. Indeed I am   365
able to tell of many things, far beyond belief, but true, which
might rivet the very eyes of beholders. But I hasten on. The age to
come will stand amazed.

"'One will see everywhere the lame, dragging their feeble knees
along, suddenly tighten their pace after their joint regains power.
At that time limbs, trembling for long with muscles collapsed, are   370
tautened and assume the solidity of full strength. (Who would be-
lieve, except that there is no disputing the songs of my Apollo!)
Another, ordered to arise and take up his bed, will without any

375   haud mora, prosiliet, passuque in templa citato
contendens, onus ipse humeris portabit: ibi ingens
clamor et innumerae circum donaria voces
spectantis populi et rerum novitate paventis.
Parte alia extinctam penitus sensuque carentem
380   ad sua iam cernes revocari munera dextram,
nec minus et tacta compesci veste cruorem
foemineum exanguesque artus pallentiaque ora
ilicet obstructis calefacta rubescere venis;
ipsas quin etiam Furias sub Tartara pelli,
385   immanes Erebi Furias, tum fessa levari
pectora vexatosque malis cruciatibus artus;
hinc vacuas late impleri stridoribus auras
dirarum frustra clamantum ac saeva trementum
verbera perque cavas conantum evadere nubes.
390   Iam deploratis vitam post funera reddi
corporibus video, iam moestam incedere pompam
feralemque anteire tubam; mox gaudia matrum
insperata patrumque hilares verso ordine fletus
et circumfusam populis laetantibus urbem.
395   Huic tu nutanteis quoties assurgere montes
et, mirum, insuetas curvare cacumina silvas
aspicies, quoties humenti in gramine ripae
aut solantem aestus aut lenes pectore somnos
carpentem tenui assuesces mulcere susurro!
400   Macte tuis merito ripis, macte omnibus undis;
ad te deposito properabunt numina fastu
nudabuntque sacros artus et carmina dicent
ad numerum, cum tu felix iam flumine sancto
authorem rerum divumque hominumque parentem
405   (tantus honos, laus tanta tuo, rex maxime, fonti)
exutum veste accipies atque hospite tanto
attonitus trepidas hortabere voce Napaeas:

delay leap forth and, walking toward the temple with quickened 375
step, will carry the weight on his own shoulders. There will be a
huge roar and around the treasure chamber countless voices from
the crowd of on-lookers, frightened at the unfamiliar. Elsewhere
you will behold a hand, completely useless and lacking sensation,
now brought back to its full competence. In addition a woman's 380
flow of blood is controlled by the touch of his garment, and her
bloodless limbs and pale face on the spot grew warm and rosy
when her veins were stopped up. In fact even the Furies them-
selves, the savage Furies of Erebus, will be driven down to
Tartarus. Then worn out hearts and limbs tortured by wracking 385
pain find relief. As a result the empty breezes are filled through
with the shrieks of the Dread Ones as they cry out in vain, and
cower before the savage lash and attempt to escape through the
hollow clouds. Now I see life restored after death to bodies already
mourned: the sad procession already making its way, preceded by 390
the funereal trumpet, but soon the unexpected rejoicing of the
mothers, the fathers' weeping changed to delight, the city brim-
ming with people in celebration. How often you will watch rising
mountains bow to him and—a marvel!—unaccustomed forests 395
bend their tree-tops. How often, on the dewy grass of your river-
bank, will you grow used to soothing him with gentle hum, as he
seeks relief from the heat or embraces soft sleep to his heart. Justly
hail to your banks! Hail to all your waves! Haughtiness cast aside, 400
the gods will hasten to you. They will bare their holy limbs and
chant rhythmic songs, when you in your good fortune will then re-
ceive unclothed in your holy stream the creator of things, the fa-
ther of gods and men. Your waters, greatest king, will have such
praise, such glory! In awe of such a guest you will encourage the 405
anxious Napaeans with a word: "Go quickly, sea-blue companions.

«Ite citae, date thura pias adolenda per aras,
caeruleae comites, viridique sedilia musco
410 instruite et vitreis suspendite serta columnis;
purpureas miscete rosas, miscete hiacynthos
liliaque et pulcro regem conspergite nimbo».
Tunc nomen late clarum Iordanis ad auras
attollent montes, Iordanem maxima circum
415 aequora, Iordanem silvaeque amnesque sonabunt.
       Illa autem humanis quanvis latura ruinis
auxilium finemque dies, gratissima quanvis
urbibus adveniat totumque optanda per orbem,
fluminibus tamen et nostris felicior undis
420 (siqua fides, siqua est veri prudentia Proteo)
ostendet roseos stellis ridentibus ortus,
quandoquidem non divitias, non quaeret honores
ille patris decus ac virtus, mortalia postquam
membra sibi et fragiles iam sponte induxerit artus.
425 Non sceptrum invadet Cyri, non caspia regna
diripiet, non exuviis Babylona superbam
eruet aut alto scandet Capitolia curru
militibus circum et laeto comitante senatu,
sed maris undisoni tractus et litora longe
430 curva secans, media socios sibi quaeret in acta
dispersosque mari nautas nudosque colonos
undarum, sinuosa fretis iactare parantes
retia vexatas aut iam reparare sagenas
sollicitos, patris ad solium ac sua tecta vocabit.
435 Atque ollis ius omne potestatemque medendi
adiiciet: pellent morbos denteisque retundent
vipereos Orcique acies ac monstra fugabunt.
Quin et custodes foribus radiantis Olympi
praeficiet, servare aditus et claustra iubebit
440 aurea; queis non ulla queat vis saeva nocere

Offer incense for us to burn on holy altars. Deck out the benches
with green moss and hang garlands from the columns of glass.
Mix red-bright roses, mix hyacinths and lilies, and shower your 410
king with a rain of beauty." Then will the mountains raise to the
breezes the far-famed name of Jordan. Jordan! the mightiest seas
roundabout will resound, Jordan! the woods and streams. 415

"'But that day, although it will bring help and an end to man-
kind's fallen state, although its arrival will be greeted most joyously
by cities and yearned for throughout all the earth, nevertheless — if
any trust, if any prevision of the truth rests with Proteus — will 420
flaunt its roseate rising to the smiling stars still more felicitously
for our streams and waves. The reason is that he, though the grace
and strength of his Father, will not seek riches, not glory, after he
has been clothed, now of his own will, in a mortal body with its
frail limbs. He will not pursue the scepter of Cyrus nor plunder 425
Caspian realms. He will not destroy Babylon, proud with its
spoils, nor will he climb the Capitol in his lofty chariot, sur-
rounded with soldiery and accompanied by the senate's ovation.
Instead, traversing for a distance the reaches of the wave-resound-
ing sea and the bending shores, he will seek disciples for himself
right there on its beaches. He will call to the throne and palace of 430
his Father sailors scattered on the sea and naked cultivators of its
waves, who are preparing to cast bellying nets upon the waters or
are now busy with mending their battered seines. He will bestow
on them every authority and power of healing. They will drive out 435
diseases and blunt the viper's tooth. They will put to flight Orcus's
battle lines and monsters. Indeed, he will also put them in charge
of guarding the entrances of gleaming Olympus; he will command
them to watch over its access ways and gates of gold. No savage vi-
olence of the Eumenides can do them harm nor can the shades' 440

Eumenidum durique umbrarum obsistere postes.
Tum sedes passim emeritis duodena per astra
instituet: distincta suos de more sequetur
turba duces; illi leges et sancta vocatis
445 iura dabunt, plausu sociorum atque agmine laeti.
Felices, qui iam cymba remisque relictis
alta serenati conscendent culmina coeli!
Praeterea (si certa fides nec vana futuri
gaudia) cognatas etiam spectabimus undas
450 lenaeos verti in latices: ea prima deum rex
arcana, hos primos per signa ostendet honores
accepti late imperii; mirabitur auctus
lympha suos, iussa insuetum spumare capaces
per pateras largeque novum diffundere nectar
455 et mensas hilarare et felices hymenaeos.
Nec semel ille altum remis evectus in aequor,
cum iam frustrato socios rediisse labore
accipiet, praeda ingenti ditabit et hudos
squamigerum strata cumulos exponet in alga.
460 Iratos etiam fluctus tumidasque procellas,
miscentesque imo turbatam gurgite arenam
iamque superiecto mersuras aequore puppim,
imperio premet increpitans: cadet arduus undae
impetus atque audisse minantis iussa putares
465 Eurosque Zephyrosque et ovanteis turbine Coros.
Quid loquar, ut gemino numerosas pisce catervas
munere et exiguo Cereris, miserabile vulgus
matres atque viros pariter per gramina pascet,
ut iam bissenis redeant fragmenta canistris?
470 aut intempesta gradiens ut nocte per altum
libera substrato ponet vestigia ponto
vixque undas sicco tanget pede? scilicet olli
adnabunt blandae Nereides; humida passim

stout doors withstand them. Then, when they have completed
their service, he will set up twelve thrones scattered amid the stars.
A separate assemblage as usual will follow each of its leaders.
They will give laws and holy rights to those called, happy with the
applause and with the mass of their disciples. Blessed by fortune,   445
with skiff and oars left behind, they will climb the lofty peaks of a
heaven now at peace. Moreover, if trust is assured and the joys to
come not empty, we will even see our kindred waters turn into
Lenaeus's nectar. The King of the gods will present those first   450
mysteries, these first honors, to exemplify the wide authority he
has received. Water will marvel at its ennoblement, given the ex-
ceptional command to froth in generous bowls, to pour out un-
stintingly the new nectar, and to bring joy both to banquets and to
happy wedding ceremonies. Often, after he has rowed out into   455
deep water, when he sees his followers now returning empty-
handed from their efforts, he will enrich them with an enormous
catch, and will set out dripping piles of scaly creatures on the scat-
tered seaweed. He will also keep under his sway, and censure, all
the wrathful billows and presumptuous gusts, as they churn the   460
swirling sand at the flood's depth and even now aim to sink a ship
with a deluge of water. The wave's towering broadside will yield
place. You would think that the Euri, and the Zephyrs, and the
Cori, delighting in their whirl, had heeded his chiding commands.
Why tell how, with two fish and Ceres's small offering, he will feed   465
thronging crowds, a pitiable company dispersed throughout the
grass, women and men alike, so that the remnants come back in
twelve baskets? Or how, walking across the deep in the dead of
night, he will place his feet at will on the sea spread beneath him   470
and, dry-shod, will scarcely touch the waves? Know that the gentle
Nereids will swim toward him. Everywhere the wet ways will sub-

sternent se freta, tum fundo Neptunus ab imo
475 excitus, agnoscet dominum positoque tridente
cum Phorco Glaucoque et semifero comitatu
prosiliet trepidusque sacris dabit oscula plantis.
Sed quid ego exili vectus super alta phaselo
cuncta sequor memorans? Non si parnasia Musae
480 antra mihi sacrosque aditus atque aurea pandant
limina, sufficiam; non si mihi ferrea centum
ora sonent centumque aerato e gutture linguae
vocibus expument agitantem pectora Phoebum,
laudatos valeam venturi principis actus
485 enumerare novoque amplecti singula cantu».
    Haec senior quondam felici pectore Proteus
vaticinans, ut forte meo diverterat antro,
praemonuit: nunc eventus stat signa futuri
expectare. Nitor roseo sed fulsit ab ortu
490 clarior et radiis dux praevia matutinis
Oceani procul extremo se litore tollit
exoriens Aurora, sinusque induta rubenteis
ante diem citat auricomos ad frena iugales;
et iam consuetis tempus me currere ripis
495 undantem magnosque lacus et prata secantem
vorticibus. Viden ut nostros agit impetus amnes
Iordanemque vocat tumidarum murmur aquarum?'
Sic fatus, confestim humeris circundat amictus
insolitos, quos pulcrae hudis nevere sub antris
500 Naiades molli ducentes stamina musco,
sidonioque rudes saturantes murice telas
aurea consperso variarunt sidera limbo.
Atque ita se tandem currenti reddidit alveo
spumeus et motas aspergine miscuit undas.
505   Hactenus, o superi, partus tentasse verendos
sit satis; optatum poscit me dulcis ad umbram

side. Then Neptune, roused from the lowest depth, will acknowl-
edge his Lord and, setting aside his trident, will rush forward in   475
the company of Phorcus, Glaucus and their brutish entourage,
and timidly press kisses on the blessed feet.

"'But why, as I sail over the main in my tiny bark, do I pursue
everything in my memory? Not if the Muses were to open for me
the grottoes of Parnassus, its holy approaches and golden thresh-   480
olds, would I have the strength. Not if I had a hundred iron
mouths to give me voice and a hundred tongues to pour forth
from my throat of brass the Phoebus stirring my breast, would I
have the strength to catalogue the praiseworthy deeds of the fu-
ture prince and to encompass their detail in fresh song.'   485

"This is the prophecy that once upon a time, when he had
chanced to visit my cave, the aged Proteus foretold from his in-
spired heart. Now it remains to await the signs of what is yet to
come. But a brighter gleam has begun to glisten from the roseate
east, and rising Aurora, who leads the way with her morning rays,
in the distance lifts herself from Ocean's farthest shore. Swathed   490
in her reddening billows, she stirs with the reins her golden-
maned team in anticipation of the day. Now it is time for me to
run past my accustomed bank with my waves, as their crests slice
through great pools and meadows. Don't you see how our streams   495
rush onwards and how the roar of their swollen waters calls out
Jordan?"

Speaking thus, he quickly shrouds his shoulders in the novel
cloak that the lovely Nereids had woven in their dewy caves.
Spinning the thread from soft moss and soaking the rough weave   500
with Sidonian purple, they scattered gilded stars to adorn its bor-
der. At last he returned in froth to the course of his stream-bed,
and churned up the swirling waters with spray.

Let what we have done so far suffice, O gods — to have had as   505
our endeavor the awesome birth. Sweet Posillipo beckons me, for

Pausilypus, poscunt neptunia litora et hudi
Tritones Nereusque senex Panopeque Ephyreque
et Melite quaeque in primis mihi grata ministrat
510 ocia Musarumque cavas per saxa latebras,
Mergillina, novos fundunt ubi citria flores,
citria Medorum sacros referentia lucos,
et mihi non solita nectit de fronde coronam.

whom she has yearned, into her shade. Neptune's shores, the drip-
ping Tritons, the old man Nereus, Panope, Ephyre and Melite
beckon, and, foremost, Mergillina who bestows pleasant leisure
and the Muses' lairs hollowed amid the rocks, Mergillina, where   510
the citrus orchards pour forth fresh flowers, orchards that bring to
mind the sacred groves of the Persians. She crowns me with a gar-
land woven from foliage new.

DE MORTE CHRISTI DOMINI AD MORTALES LAMENTATIO

Si quando magnum mirati surgere solem
oceano et toto flammas diffundere coelo,
certatimque suo terras ambire meatu
noctivagam Phoeben praecinctam cornibus aureis,
5   aeternosque astrorum ignes coelique micantes
scintillare oculos, aliquem dare iura putastis
atque polo regnare hominum rerumque parentem,
cui mare, cui tellus, cui pareat arduus aether,
cuncta supercilio qui temperet: hunc simul, aegri
10 mortales, si vestra dolor praecordia tangit,
adspicite immiti traiectum pectora ferro,
pectora foedatasque manus, perfusaque tabo
ora, cruentatumque caput, crinesque revulsos,
adspicite, et plenos lacrimarum fundite rivos.
15 Heu scelus, heu crudele nefas, iacet altus Olympi
Rector, et amisso torpent elementa magistro.
Quinetiam vacuum adsueto sine pondere coelum
nutat, et ipsa suum quaerunt solia aurea regem.
Quem diversa procul saevo cum crimine tellus
20 ignotum populis caput et miserabile corpus
sustinet, exsanguesque sinu complectitur artus,
et tremefacta graves testatur murmure questus.
Testatur sol ipse suum sub nube dolorem
iam latitans, atraque notans ferrugine frontem.
25 Tu quoque deformesque genas pallentiaque ora
contegis, inferiasque tuo das, luna, Tonanti,
auratum flavo tondens de vertice crinem,
et lacrimas uda fundens in nocte tepentes.

LAMENTATION TO MORTALS
ON THE DEATH OF CHRIST
OUR LORD

If ever you marveled that the mighty sun rises from the ocean and spreads his flames over the whole sky, and that in competition night-wandering Phoebe, encircled with horns of gold, embraces the world in her course, and that the stars' undying fires and the gleaming eyes in heaven shimmer, and you thought that someone, the father of men and nature, was in power and ruling in the sky, 5 whom the sea, the earth, the towering ether obey, who controls all things with his nod: look at him at the same time, wretched mortals, if grief touches your hearts, his breast pierced through by the 10 pitiless sword, his breast and hands befouled, his face smeared with gore, his head bloodied, his hair torn out, behold, and pour forth full floods of tears. Alas the wickedness, alas the cruel sacrilege. The exalted ruler of Olympus lies dead, and the elements 15 grow numb at the loss of their master. Yes, even the empty heaven nods, lacking its accustomed weight, and the very thrones of gold search for their king. Through a savage act of villainy the distant earth holds him far away, his head unrecognized by his peoples and his pitiable body, and embraces his bloodless limbs in her lap. 20 Trembling she bears witness to the depth of her sorrowing with a groan. The sun himself, lurking now beneath a cloud, bears witness to his grief, branding his brow with rust's darkness. You also, O moon, cover over your disfigured cheeks and wan features, and 25 offer funeral homage to your Thunderer, trimming a gilded lock from your tawny crown, and pouring forth warm tears during the

Nec minus abruptis fama est exisse sepulcris,
30　perque vias errasse novis simulacra figuris,
excitasque umbras medias ululasse per urbes
sub noctem, et notos questu implevisse penates.
Quid? Non et pelagi rabies adtollere fluctus
immanes visa est, montesque evolvere aquarum,
35　deiectura urbes terrasque haustura profundo
cum simul et caput undisonis emersus ab antris
caeruleus Triton rauco super aequora cornu
constreperet, nautasque horrenda voce moneret
naturae cecidisse patrem, regemque, deumque?
40　Haene manus vasti iunxerunt foedera mundi?
Harum opus est quodcunque iacet, quodcunque movetur,
quicquid ubique parens rerum natura gubernat,
frugiferens tellus, foetumque animantibus aequor,
vitalisque aer, atque ignibus aethra coruscis?
45　Et nunc, proh facinus!, quantum potuere nocentum
flagitia, immissis dant pervia vulnera clavis,
liventesque atro foedant squallore lacertos.
Heu caput indignum spinis venerandaque coelo,
et toties clara stellarum implexa corona
50　caesaries. Heu pectus hians, convulsaque dira
barba manu, tunsique artus, et frigida membra.
Vosne pedes, coelum premere et vaga sidera sueti,
fulgentesque domos superum, sublimia tecta,
tam saevae immanes perpessi cuspidis ictus,
55　et terram et duras sparsistis sanguine cautes?
Nec trepidat mens caeca hominum? Quae tanta tenaci
durities in corde riget? Num nigra videtis
Tartara tot claris hominum viduata trophaeis,
desertasque in nocte domos, et tristia regna,
60　felicesque animas laetum paeana canentes
pone sequi regem et coelo insedisse sereno?

dewy night. Moreover there is also a story that ghosts in strange
shapes came forth from their shattered tombs and roamed the   30
streets, and that shades, summoned up, howled at night in the
midst of cities, and filled their familiar homes with lamentation.
What? Wasn't the raging sea seen to raise up huge billows, and to
roll mountains of water, so as to overthrow cities and swallow the
earth in the deep, when at the same time sea-blue Triton, putting   35
out his head from his wave-resounding caves, roared over the wa-
ters with his shrill trumpet, and with dread voice warned sailors
that the father, king and god of nature had fallen? Had not these
hands joined the compacts of the huge universe? Is not their work   40
whatever lies still, whatever moves, whatever nature, mother of
things, everywhere governs, the productive earth and the sea teem-
ing with living creatures, the life-giving air, the ether with its
shimmering fires? And now—oh, how great a crime of which the
outrages of the guilty are capable!—his wounds offer passage to   45
nails hammered in and befoul his bruised arms with black filth.
Alas, the head, undeserving of thorns, the luxuriant hair to be
worshipped so often in heaven, intertwined with a bright crown of
stars. Alas, the gaping breast, the beard wrenched by fearful hand,
the pummeled joints and chill limbs. And you, feet wont to tread   50
the heavens and the wandering stars and the shining homes, lofty
dwellings, of the gods, after you endured the monstrous blows of
the savage spear, did you spatter the earth and the hard boulders
with blood? And does the blind mind of man not tremble? What   55
great hardness grips his stubborn heart? Do you not see black
Tartara bereft of so many glorious trophies of men, her houses
abandoned in darkness, her realm gloomy, the souls of the blessed,
singing a happy Paean, following behind their king, and taking   60
seats in the calm of heaven? What if he, the creator of things and

97

Quid si non tantos subiisset sponte labores,
humanamque sua pensasset morte salutem
ille sator rerum et summi mens certa parentis,
65 qui nutu ingentes mundi moderatur habenas
ut tandem intactos picea Phlegetontis ab unda
post obitum aeternae donaret munere lucis,
in partemque suorum operum regnique vocaret?
Tantus amor generis servandi et gloria nostri!
70 Quare agite, ex animis mortales pellite vestris,
siquid adhuc manet antiqua de sorde relictum,
mendacesque deos et detestanda priorum
sacra prophanatis tandem detrudite ab aris.
Imbuat effuso terram nec sanguine taurus,
75 nec miser ille suae divulsus ab ubere matris
ignotos agnus balet super hostia cultros.
Vivat ovis, vivat quicquid sub sole creatum est.
Mentem animumque deo, non tura aut exta parate:
has illi pecudum fibras, haec reddite dona.
80 Cernitis ut pronum flectat caput, ut pia pandat
brachia, et ingratas vocet ad sua vulnera gentes,
oblitasque viae moneat meminisse relictae,
scilicet amplexus non reiecturus amicos?
At vos obtusas ignari avertitis aures,
85 infelix genus, et saevae ludibria mortis,
nec, quanta a tergo iam instent tormenta, videtis.
Tempus erit, cum vestra illum commissa notantem,
multantemque reos, altaque in nube sedentem
adspicietis et horrentes tremor opprimet artus.
90 Nec iam ferre oculos flammarum ardore coruscos,
aut tumidos acie vultus contendere contra
audebit quisquam sibi conscius. Ibit in ignes
turba nocens sontesque exsolvet corpore poenas,
pallentesque aeternum amnes vastasque lacunas

sure mind of the supreme Father, who with a nod guides the
mighty reins of the world, had not of his own will undergone such
suffering and ransomed man's salvation by his own death, so that
at last he might give us, untouched by the pitch-black wave of
Phlegethon, the gift of eternal light after death, and bid us share   65
in his works and in his kingdom? So great is his love and pride in
preserving our race! So come now, mortals: if anything yet remains
of the ancient stain, drive it from your hearts. Thrust away at last   70
from your polluted altars lying gods and abominable rituals. Let
not the bull dye the ground with a stream of blood, nor let the
pitiable lamb bleat, torn from its mother's udder, a victim over the   75
unfamiliar knife. Let the sheep live, let live whatever is born under
the sun. Ready your mind and soul for god, not incense or in-
nards. Present these as animal entrails, these as gifts, to him. Do
you behold how he bends down his head, how he extends his holy   80
arms, how he, certainly not about to scorn their friendly embraces,
calls ungrateful humans to his wounds, and reminds them in their
forgetfulness to recall the way that they abandoned? But you in
your ignorance turn your deadened ears away, unfortunate race,
playthings of savage death, nor do you see what great torments   85
now loom from behind. There will be a time when you will behold
him recording your misdeeds and punishing the guilty as he sits
on a lofty cloud, and like an earthquake overpowers your shudder-
ing limbs. Nor will anyone, aware of his true self, now dare to
withstand the eyes glistening with the burning of flames or to   90
meet his angry look with his gaze. The miscreant throng will go
into the fire and will pay with their bodies the penalty for their
crimes. It will forever tenant the wan streams and the desolate

95   Cocyti colet, et furias horrescet hiantes,
      atque animum monitis non intendisse pigebit.
      Tunc vos exactae capient mala taedia vitae,
      expertes coeli atque aurae sub nocte profunda,
      inque caput trifidos nequicquam optabitis ignes,
100 et frustra erectas tolletis ad aethera palmas.
      Quos superum coetus et fortunata piorum
      agmina vix lacrimis poterunt spectare retentis,
      invidiae stimulis dirisque ultricibus actos.
      Ergo vitales miseri dum carpitis auras,
105 dum compos mens ipsa sui est, dum certa facultas,
      dum ratio tempusque sinunt, simul ite frequentes.
      Ite pii, veniam factis exposcite vestris,
      ite, animos purgate, Orcique inhibete rapinas,
      et tandem patrio mentem convertite coelo.
110 Sic rex ille hominum, vacui spoliator Averni,
      oblitus scelerum cognatae stirpis amore,
      promissique memor, mentes intrabit amicas
      vestraque posthabitis recolet praecordia templis.
      Postque tot exhaustos vitaeque obitusque labores,
115 illo quo pluvias, quo pellit nubila vultu,
      ablutos labe excipiet, laetusque reponet
      sidereos inter proceres sanctumque senatum,
      sub pedibusque dabit stellantia cernere claustra.

pools of Cocytus, and tremble before the gaping furies. It will re- 95
gret that it paid no heed to his warnings. And then, bereft of the
air of heaven in the depths of night, ugly loathing of your past life
will take hold of you. In vain you will wish the triple fires upon
your head and without avail you will raise outstretched hands to
the sky. The bands of angels and blessed companies of the holy 100
will scarcely be able to hold back their tears as they watch you
driven by goads of envy and by avenging furies. Therefore, poor
creatures, while you breathe the air of life, while your mind is
sound in itself, while your undiminished capability, your reason 105
and the passage of time allow: go together as a multitude. Go,
holy ones. Beg forgiveness for your deeds. Go, cleanse your souls
and thwart Orcus's plundering, and at last turn your mind to the
heaven of your father. Thus that king of men, plunderer of aban-
doned Avernus, forgetful of your sins, from love of kindred stock 110
and mindful of his promise, will enter your willing minds, and oc-
cupy again your hearts in preference to temples. And when he has
put behind him the toils of life and of death, he will receive you,
purged of taint, with that countenance that drives off the rain,
drives off the clouds, and in joy will place you among the princes 115
of the sky and the blessed senate. He will grant you to behold the
starry bastions beneath your feet.

PISCATORIAE ECLOGAE

: I :

Phyllis

Lycidas, Mycon

Lycidas

Mirabar, vicina, Mycon, per litora nuper
dum vagor exspectoque leves ad pabula thynnos,
quid tantum insuetus streperet mihi corvus et udae
per scopulos passim fulicae perque antra repostae
5 tristia flebilibus complerent saxa querelis,
cum iam nec curvus resiliret ab aequore delphin
nec solitos de more choros induceret undis.
Ecce dies aderat caram qua Phyllida terrae
condidimus tumuloque pias deflevimus umbras,
10 ah miseri; et posthac nec tristes linquimus auras
nec dubitat saevus solatia ferre Pylemon.

Mycon

Scilicet id fuerat tota quod nocte vaganti
huc illuc, dum Pausilypi latus omne pererro
piscosamque lego celeri Nesida phaselo,
15 nescio quid queruli gemerent lacrimabile mergi.
Phyllis ad inferias, Phyllis (si credimus) illos
ad gemitum, o Lycida, tumulique ad sacra vocabat.

PISCATORY ECLOGUES

Phyllis

Lycidas, Mycon

Lycidas

While I was roaming recently along the nearby shore and was awaiting the nimble tunnies to come feed, I kept wondering, Mycon, why the raven cawed at me so very strangely, and why the soaking coots, perched everywhere through the cliffs and through the caves, were filling the saddened rocks with sorrowful laments. It was a time when the curved dolphin neither bounded forth 5 from the waters nor, as usual, performed his accustomed dances in the waves. Yes, the day was at hand on which we entrusted our beloved Phyllis to the earth and wept at the grave for her holy shade. Alas for us! And even afterwards we neither take our leave from the sad breezes, nor does uncouth Pylemon hesitate to proffer his 10 words of comfort.

Mycon

Surely that was the reason why the mourning gulls groaned some lamentation as I was wandering the night through, hither and thither roaming past the whole slope of Posillipo and skirting fish- 15 filled Nesis in my speedy skiff. Phyllis, if we can believe it, O Lycidas, Phyllis was inviting them to her obsequies, was inviting them to grieve at her grave's ceremonies.

Lycidas

Eheu, care Mycon, qualis spectacula pompae
(nunc recolo) quas ipse manus quaeve ora notavi
20 his oculis; his, inquam, oculis quae funera vidi
infelix; nec me tandem dolor improbus egit
in scopulos, in saxa, rogove absumpsit eodem
ignea vis, vel saltem aliquis deus aequore mersit.

Mycon

O Lycida, Lycida, nonne hoc felicius illi
25 evenisse putas quam si fumosa Lycotae
antra vel hirsuti tegetem subiisset Amyntae,
et nunc heu viles hamo sibi quaereret escas
aut tenui laceras sarciret vimine nassas?
Sed tu, si quid habes veteres quod lugeat ignes,
30 quod manes cineresque diu testetur amatos,
incipe, quandoquidem molles tibi litus harenas
sternit et insani posuerunt murmura fluctus.

Lycidas

Immo haec quae cineri nuper properata parabam
carmina, ab extremo cum iam cava litora portu
35 prospicerem et nivei venerarer saxa sepulcri,
incipiam; tu coniferas ad busta cupressus
sparge manu et viridi tumulum super intege myrto.

Mycon

En tibi caerulei muscum aequoris, en tibi conchas
purpureas, nec non toto quaesita profundo
40 et vix ex imis evulsa corallia saxis

Lycidas

Alas, dear Mycon, the sights of such a cortège (I recall them now):
what hands, what features did I myself observe with these eyes.
With these eyes, I say, what a funeral I saw, unlucky me. But fi- 20
nally my relentless sorrow did not drive me against the cliffs,
against the rocks, nor did the force of fire consume me on the
same pyre, nor did any god even plunge me into the water.

Mycon

O Lycidas, Lycidas, don't you consider that this has turned out
more luckily for her than if she had endured the smoky caves of
Lycotas or the hovel of shaggy Amyntas, or now — sad thought! — 25
were foraging for paltry bait for her fishhook, or mending torn
weels with thin osier? But, if you have anything that might keen
for old flames, that might bear witness to ghosts and ashes long
beloved, begin. For the shore spreads out its soft sands for you, 30
and the wild surge has smothered its roar.

Lycidas

Rather I will begin with these verses that I rushed of late to ready
for her funeral, when I was looking out on the curved seashore
from the harbor's end and worshipping the stones of her snow-
white tomb. With your hand scatter cone-bearing boughs of cy- 35
press at the grave, and cover over the mound with green myrtle.

Mycon

See, we are bringing you moss from the green-blue sea, we are
bringing you purple conches, and coral for which we scoured
throughout the deep and scarcely wrenched from rocks in the
abyss. Begin now the appointed songs. Begin, while Milcon from 40

afferimus; tu sollemnes nunc incipe cantus.
Incipe, dum ad solem Baianus retia Milcon
explicat et madidos componit in orbe rudentes.

Lycidas

    Quos mihi nunc, Divae, scopulos, quae panditis antra,
45 Nereides? Quas tu secreti litoris herbas,
    Glauce pater, quae monstriferis mihi gramina sucis
    ostendes nunc, Glauce, quibus tellure relicta,
    ah miser, et liquidi factus novus incola ponti
    te sequar in medios mutato corpore fluctus
50 et feriam bifida spumantia marmora cauda?
    Nam quid ego heu solis vitam sine Phyllide terris
    exoptem miser? Aut quidnam rapta mihi luce
    dulce putem? Quidve hic sperem? quid iam morer ultra
    infelix? An ut hac vili proiectus in alga
55 arentes tantum frutices desertaque cernam
    litora et ingrato iactem mea verba sepulcro?
    Scilicet hos thalamos, hos felices hymenaeos
    concelebrem? Sic speratae mihi gaudia taedae
    dat Venus? Ambiguos sic dat Lucina timores?
60 Quis mihi, quis tete rapuit, dulcissima Phylli,
    Phylli meae quondam requies spesque unica vitae,
    nunc dolor aeternusque imo sub pectore luctus?
    Non licuit tecum optatos coniungere somnos
    dulcia nec primae decerpere dona iuventae
65 aut simul extremos vitam producere in annos.
    Nunc te (quis credat?) lapis hic habet et mihi nusquam es;
    nusquam terrarum Phyllis, sed fabula et umbrae
    frustrantur miseras per dira insomnia noctes.
    Me miserum, qua te tandem regione requiram?
70 Quave sequar? Per te quondam mihi terra placebat

Baiae unfolds his nets to the sun and brings a circle's order to his dripping lines.

Lycidas

Goddess Nereides, what rocks, what caves are you now throwing open for me? What plants from a sequestered shore, father 45 Glaucus, what herbs with miraculous juices, Glaucus, will you now show me, by which—poor me!—I will leave the land behind and, become a new denizen of the bright sea, with my body altered, will follow you into the midst of the flood, and with my forked tail strike its foaming surface? For why, alas, in my misery 50 should I yearn for life on the lonely land without Phyllis? Or what could I consider sweet, now that my light is snatched from me? What can I hope for here? Why, with my ill-luck, should I now make further delay? Stretched out on this tawdry seaweed, to gaze only upon dry shrubbery and desolate shores, and to toss out my 55 words to an unresponsive tomb? Is this the wedlock, are these the fortunate nuptials, that I am set to celebrate? Is this the way that Venus grants the joys of the wedding ceremony for which I had hoped? Does Lucina thus grant double-edged fears? Who, who snatched you from me, sweetest Phyllis, once the unique solace 60 and hope of my life, now an anguish and everlasting sorrow in the depths of my heart? I was not allowed to share with you the nights I had yearned for, or to pluck the sweet gifts of our first youth, or together to extend our lives to their final years. Now 65 (who can believe it?) this stone possesses you, and for me you are nowhere. Phyllis exists nowhere on earth, but the fictive and the ghostly baffle my lovesick nights with dreams of dread. Woe is me! Where will I finally seek you out? Where will I follow you? Because of you the land, its peoples, its joyous cities with their 70

et populi laetaeque suis cum moenibus urbes;
nunc iuvat immensi fines lustrare profundi
perque procellosas errare licentius undas
Tritonum immistum turbis scopulosaque cete
75   inter et informes horrenti corpore phocas,
quo numquam terras videam. Iam iam illa tot annis
culta mihi tellus, populique urbesque valete,
litora cara valete, vale simul optima Phylli.
Nos tibi, nos liquidis septem pro fluctibus aras
80   ponemus septemque tibi de more quotannis
monstra maris magni vitulos mactabimus hirtos,
et tibi septenis pendebunt ostrea sertis,
ostrea muricibus variata albisque lapillis.
Hic tibi Nisaee et flavos resoluta capillos
85   Cymodoce mitisque pia cum matre Palaemon
et Panope et Siculi custos Galatea profundi
sollemnes nectent choreas et carmina dicent
quae Proteus quondam divino pectore vates
edocuit, magni cum funera fleret Achillis
90   et Thetidis luctus consolaretur amaros.
At tu, sive altum felix colis aethera, seu iam
Elysios inter manes coetusque verendos
Lethaeos sequeris per stagna liquentia pisces,
seu legis aeternos formoso pollice flores,
95   narcissumque crocumque et vivaces amaranthos,
et violis teneras misces pallentibus algas,
aspice nos mitisque veni; tu numen aquarum
semper eris, semper laetum piscantibus omen.
Ut Nymphis Nereoque, ut flavicomae Amphitritae,
100   sic tibi victrices fundent libamina cymbae.
Interea tumulo supremum hoc accipe carmen,
carmen quod, tenui dum nectit arundine linum,
piscator legat et scopulo suspiret ab alto:

walls, once gave me pleasure. Now my happiness comes from tra-
versing the extent of the deep's abyss, and from wandering at my
will through the windswept waves, mingling with the throngs of
Tritons in the company of rock-haunting beasts of the sea and the
unkempt shapes of ugly seals. There I would never see the land.   75
Now, farewell, land in which I dwelt for so many years, farewell
now, peoples and cities, farewell, dear shores, and so farewell, no-
blest Phyllis. We ourselves will construct for you seven altars by
the clear waters, and by yearly custom sacrifice seven shaggy calves,
the great sea's monsters. Sevenfold swags of oysters will drape for   80
you, oysters interspersed with murex and white pearls. Here
Nisaee and Cymodoce, her blond hair unbound, and kindly
Palaemon with his pious mother, and Panope, and Galatea, war-   85
den of the Sicilian deep, will weave for you their annual dances,
and will sing songs that the seer Proteus once taught from his
godlike breast, when he mourned the death of mighty Achilles
and gave Thetis comfort for her bitter grief. But whether in your   90
good fortune you dwell in the heavens above or, amid the shades
of Elysium and its honored throngs, you now stalk the fish in
Lethe's crystal pools, or whether with your lovely thumb you pick
ever-enduring flowers, narcissus and crocus and long-lived
amaranthus, and commingle fragile seaweed with pale violets: keep   95
watch over us and come with kindness. You will always be a spirit
of the waters, always be a joyful omen to fishermen. Just as to the
Nymphs and to Nereus, just as to blond-haired Amphitrite, so
successful vessels will pour libations to you. Meanwhile, receive   100
this final song for your tomb, a song which, while he ties the line
to his slender rod, the fisherman might read, sighing from his lofty
crag:

IN. GREMIO. PHYLLIS. RECVBAT. SIRENIS. AMATAE
105   CONSVRGIS. GEMINO. FELIX. SEBETHE. SEPVLCRO

Mycon

Dulce sonant, Lycida, tua carmina, nec mihi malim
Alcyonum lamenta aut udo in gramine ripae
propter aquam dulces cycnorum audire querelas.
Sed tu (sic faciles vicina Megaria semper
110   sufficiat conchas, sic proxima Mergilline
ostrea saxosaeque ferat tibi rupis echinos)
quandoquidem nox obscuras iam distulit umbras
necdum permensus caelum Sol, incipe rursus
atque itera mihi carmen; habent iterata leporem.

Lycidas

115   Ne miserum, ne coge, Mycon; sat lumina, sat iam
exhaustae maduere genae; dolor (aspice) siccas
obduxit fauces quatit et singultibus imum
pectus, anhelantemque animam vox aegra relinquit.
Et tamen haec alias tibi nos et plura canemus,
120   fortasse et meliora, aderit si Musa canenti.
Quin et veliferis olim haec spectanda carinis,
seu Prochytae, seu Miseni sub rupe patenti,
inscribam grandesque notas ferrugine ducam
praeteriens quas nauta mari percurrat ab alto
125   et dicat: 'Lycidas, Lycidas haec carmina fecit'.
Sed quoniam socii passim per litus ovantes
exspectant poscuntque tuas ad retia vires,
eia age iam surgamus. Ego haec ad busta sedebo;
tu socios invise, escas nam quaerere tempus
130   et tibi nunc vacuae fluitant sine pondere nassae.

PHYLLIS RECLINES IN THE BOSOM OF HER BELOVED SIREN.
YOU RISE, SEBETO, BLESSED FOR YOUR DOUBLE TOMB. 105

Mycon

Lycidas, sweet sound your songs. I would not rather hear the laments of the halcyons or the sweet mourning of swans in the wet grass of the bank beside the water. But you—so may nearby Megaria ever readily supply you with conches, so may neighboring Mergelline from her rocky cliff produce for you oysters and sea-urchins—since now night has postponed her darkening shadows and the Sun has not yet taken the full measure of the sky, begin again. Sing your song for me once more. Charm comes with repetition. 110

Lycidas

Do not, Mycon, do not urge me on in my sadness. Enough already have my eyes, enough have my drained cheeks been drenched. See how grief has clogged my dry throat and shakes my inmost breast with sobs. My anxious voice abandons my panting soul. Yet these and more, perhaps even better, we will sing for you some other time, if the Muse attends my singing. One day I will even write these out to be seen by sailing ships, whether at Prochyta or under Miseno's spreading cliff. I will trace large letters in rust-black that the sailor, passing by from the deep sea, might scan and say: "Lycidas, Lycidas composed these songs." But since your joyous comrades everywhere along the shore are awaiting you and crave your strength at the net, come then, let's now be up. I myself will sit by this grave. Go see your comrades. It is time to search for bait. At the moment your empty weels are bobbing weightless. 115 120 125 130

: II :

Galatea

Forte Lycon vacuo fessus consederat antro
piscator qua se scopuli de vertice lato
ostentat pelago pulcherrima Mergilline.
Dumque alii notosque sinus piscosaque circum
5   aequora collustrant flammis aut linea longe
retia captivosque trahunt ad litora pisces,
ipse per obscuram meditatur carmina noctem:
   'Immitis Galatea, nihil te munera tandem,
nil nostrae movere preces? Verba irrita ventis
10   fudimus et vanas scopulis impegimus undas?
Aspice, cuncta silent, orcas et maxima cete
somnus habet, tacitae recubant per litora phocae,
non Zephyri strepit aura, sopor suus umida mulcet
aequora, sopito conivent sidera caelo;
15   solus ego (ei misero) dum tristi pectore questus
nocte itero, somnum tota de mente fugavi,
nec tamen ulla meae tangit te cura salutis.
At non Praxinoe me quondam, non Polybotae
filia despexit, non divitis uxor Amyntae,
20   quamvis culta sinu, quamvis foret alba papillis.
Quin etiam Aenaria (si quicquam credis) ab alta
saepe vocor; solet ipsa meas laudare Camenas
in primis formosa Hyale cui sanguis Iberis
clarus avis, cui tot terrae, tot litora parent
25   quaeque vel in mediis Neptunum torreat undis.
Sed mihi quid prosunt haec omnia, si tibi tantum
(quis credat, Galatea?) tibi si denique tantum
displiceo? si tu nostram crudelis avenam

: II :

Galatea

The weary fisherman Lycon had chanced to take his seat in an empty cave where from the crest of the cliff fairest Mergilline is on display to the broad sea. While the others with their lantern fires are illuminating the well-known bays round about and the fish-rich waters, or at a distance are tugging to shore their linen nets 5 and the fish that they have caught, he is rehearsing songs in the gloaming of the night:

"Pitiless Galatea, have our gifts not moved you, have our prayers not moved you at all? Have we poured forth our words in vain to the winds and dashed our useless waves against the cliffs? See how everything is quiet. Sleep claims the orcas and huge 10 whales. The seals lie silently at rest along the shore. No breath of Zephyr whispers. Their own repose soothes the sodden seas, and the stars shut their eyes as heaven slumbers. While during the night I rehearse my sorrows in my sad heart, alone (woe is me!), I 15 have exiled sleep completely from my mind. Yet no concern for my welfare touches you. Once upon a time Praxinoe didn't scorn me, nor the daughter of Polybotas, nor the wife of wealthy Amyntas, though her bosom was elegant, though her breasts were white. In- 20 deed, I am even regularly summoned — if you can believe it — from lofty Aenaria. Beautiful Hyale especially, whose blood was famous from her Spanish ancestors, whom so many lands, so many sea-shores obey, and who might even set Neptune afire in the midst of his waves, liked to praise my Camenae. But what good does all 25 this do me, if to you alone (who would believe it, Galatea?), if only to you in the end I give displeasure — if you alone in your cru-

sola fugis, sola et nostros contemnis amores?
30 Ostrea Miseni pendentibus eruta saxis
mille tibi misi, totidem sub gurgite vasto
Pausilypus, totidem vitreis Euploea sub undis
servat adhuc; plures Nesis mihi servat echinos
quos nec vere novo foliis lentiscus amaris
35 inficit aut vacuae tenuant dispendia Lunae.
Praeterea mihi sub pelago manus apta legendis
muricibus; didici Tyrios cognoscere sucos
quoque modo plena durent conchylia testa.
Quid refugis? Tingenda tibi iam lana paratur
40 qua niteas superesque alias, Galatea, puellas,
lana maris spumis quae mollior. Hanc mihi pastor
ipse olim dedit, hanc pastor Melisaeus, ab alta
cum me forte senex audisset rupe canentem,
et dixit, "Puer, ista tuae sint praemia Musae,
45 quandoquidem nostra cecinisti primus in acta".
Ex illo in calathis servavi, ut mittere possem.
Sed tu (ne qua mihi superet spes, ne qua futuri
condicio, Galatea) manum mihi dura negasti.
Hoc est, hoc, miserum quod perdidit. Ite Camenae,
50 ite procul; sprevit nostras Galatea querelas.
Scilicet (exiguae videor quod navita cymbae,
quodque leves hamos nodosaque retia tracto)
despicis. An patrio non hoc quoque litore Glaucus
fecerat, aequoreae Glaucus scrutator harenae?
55 Et nunc ille quidem tumidarum numen aquarum.
Sed nec (quae nimium vel me sic falsa fatigat)
fabula te moveat Lydae, licet illa puellis
iactet nescio quas mihi se misisse corollas;
non me Lyda tamen, non impulit, aequora testor
60 Nereidasque omnes. Si fallo, naufragus illas
experiar salsosque bibam sub gurgite fluctus.

elty shun my reed pipe, if you alone despise my love? I have sent
you a thousand oysters wrested from the hanging rocks of Miseno.
Posillipo yet harbors the same number under her broad flood, the   30
same, Euploea under her shimmering waves. Nesis harbors for me
a multitude of sea-urchins which in the freshness of spring mastic
doesn't taint with its bitter leaves nor the losses of the moon in
eclipse cause to wither. Furthermore my hand is skilled at plucking   35
murex under the water. I have learned to recognize Tyrian dyes
and how mollusks harden as their shells fill out. Why do you flee
away from me? I have wool ready to be dyed for you, Galatea,
wool softer than froth from the sea, in which you may gleam and
excel the other girls. This the shepherd Melisaeus, the shepherd   40
himself, once gave me, when the old man chanced to hear me as I
sang from my lofty rock. He said: 'Boy, let these be the rewards
for your Muse, since you were the first to sing along our shore.'
From that moment I saved baskets-full, that I could send it. But,   45
so that no hope remain for me, hard-hearted Galatea, no covenant
for the future, you have denied me your hand. This, this is what
destroyed pitiable me. Off with you, Camenae, off, afar. Galatea
has scorned my laments. I am certain that you scorn me because I   50
am the skipper of a tiny skiff and because I work with thin hooks
and knotty nets. Did not Glaucus also do this on his native shore,
Glaucus, explorer of the sands of the sea? He is now for certain a
divinity of the swelling waters. But let not Lyda's story disturb you   55
(it may be false, yet it brings upon me more than my share of trou-
ble), even though she keeps boasting to the girls that she sent me
some garlands. I call the seas and all the Nereids to witness that
Lyda has not tempted me at all. If I swear falsely, may I experience   60
them in shipwreck, and under the sea may I swallow their salt wa-

Heu quid agam? Externas trans pontum quaerere terras
iam pridem est animus, quo numquam navita, numquam
piscator veniat; fors illic nostra licebit
65 fata queri. Boreae extremo damnata sub axe
stagna petam et rigidis numquam non cana pruinis
an Libyae rapidas Austrique tepentis harenas,
et videam nigros populos Solemque propinquum?
Quid loquor infelix? An non per saxa, per ignes,
70 quo me cumque pedes ducent, mens aegra sequetur?
Vitantur venti, pluviae vitantur et aestus,
non vitatur amor; mecum tumuletur oportet.
Iam saxo meme ex illo demittere in undas
praecipitem iubet ipse furor. Vos o mihi, Nymphae,
75 vos maris undisoni, Nymphae, praestate cadenti
non duros obitus saevasque exstinguite flammas.
Scilicet haec olim, veniens seu litore curvo
Caietae, seu Cumarum navalibus altis,
dum loca transibit, raucus de puppe magister
80 hortatus socios "Dextrum deflectite," dicet,
"in latus, o socii, dextras deflectite in undas;
vitemus scopulos infames morte Lyconis."'
    Talia nequiquam surdas iactabat ad auras
infelix piscator et irrita vota fovebat,
85 cum tandem extremo veniens effulsit ab ortu
lucifer et roseo perfudit lumine pontum.

ters. Alas, what shall I do? It has long since been my thought to seek out foreign lands across the sea, never reached by a sailor, never by a fisherman. There chance will allow me to lament my fate. Shall I go in search of sluggish waters, consigned beneath the farthest pole of Boreas, eternally white with stiffening chill, or shall I view the scorching sands of Libya and of the searing Auster, and dark-skinned races and the nearby Sun? What am I saying, in my misfortune? Through rocks, through flames — wherever my feet take me — won't my troubled mind follow? Winds can be avoided, rains and sweltering heat avoided, but love is not avoidable. It should go to my grave with me. Now its very madness commands me to plunge headlong into the waves from the rock there. O you Nymphs, you Nymphs of the wave-resounding sea, grant me as I fall an easy passing and quench my savage flames. You may be sure that the time will come that the hoarse helmsman, when he is travelling through this area, whether he is journeying from Caieta's curved shore or from the tall dockyards of Cumae, will say, as he urges on his comrades from the poop: 'Veer to the right side, O comrades, veer to waters on the right. Let us avoid the cliffs notorious for the death of Lycon.'"

The unlucky fisherman was hurling such words in vain to the deaf breezes and was cherishing his bootless desires when at its far distant rising Lucifer glistened at last, and spread upon the sea a rosy glow.

: III :

Mopsus

Celadon, Mopsus, Chromis, Iolas

Celadon

Dic mihi (nam Baulis, verum si rettulit Aegon,
bis senos vos, Mopse, dies tenuere procellae)
quid tu, quid Chromis interea, quid vester Iolas,
dum Notus insultat pelago, dum murmurat unda?
5 Ecquid desertis vacui lusistis in antris?

Mopsus

Quid nostrae facerent ingrata per otia Musae,
o Celadon? Neque tum conchas impune licebat
per scopulos, non octipedes tentare paguros;
iam fragilem in sicco munibant saxa phaselum
10 raraque per longos pendebant retia remos;
ante pedes cistaeque leves hamique iacebant
et calami nassaeque et viminei labyrinthi.
Tum Chromis Inarimen spectans, 'His', inquit, 'ab oris
(ah dirum exsilium) nostrae solvere carinae,
15 cum regem post bella suum comitata iuventus
ignotis pelagi vitam committeret undis.
Quae tamen (ut fama est) Ligurum per saxa, per altas
Stoechadas emicuit Rhodanique invecta per amnem
(nam bene si memini, Rhodanum referebat Amilcon)
20 Oceani madidas vidit refluentis harenas
et quae caeruleos procul aspicit ora Britannos,
qua (nisi vana ferunt) quoties maris unda recedit,
indigenae captant nudos per litora pisces'.

: III :

Mopsus

Celadon, Mopsus, Chromis, Iolas

Celadon

Tell me, Mopsus—for if Aegon related the truth, the winds con-
fined you at Bauli for twelve days—what did you, what did
Chromis and your Iolas do during that time, while Notus played
havoc with the sea, while the wave rumbled? What was your sport
while you were at leisure in the empty caves?   5

Mopsus

O Celadon, what could our Muses do for the time of our unwel-
come leisure? We couldn't then go through the rocks in search of
either conchs or eight-footed crabs without coming to harm. Boul-
ders were now protecting our vulnerable skiff up on the land, and
our thin nets were hanging upon the long oars. Before our feet lay   10
our delicate baskets and hooks, our rods, weels, and osier traps.
Then, looking out at Inarime, Chromis says: "From this coast our
fleet set sail—yes, dreadful exile—when, the war over, our young
men, escorting their king, entrusted their lives to the sea's un-   15
known waves. After they had sped sailing, such is the report, past
the rocky coast of the Ligurians, past the lofty Stoechadae, past
the Rhône's stream (for if I remember well, Amilcon mentioned
the Rhône), they saw the dripping sands of Ocean's tides and the   20
shore that looks at the blue-eyed Britons from afar. There, unless
the report is groundless, whenever the tide goes out, the natives
rush to catch fish stranded on the shore."

'Ne, Chromi, ne luctus renova', respondit Iolas.
25 'Sat tuus haec nobis Lucrini nuper ad undam
narravit Lycabas: Solem se scilicet illic
trans fluctus trans et nubes vidisse cadentem
haud aliter quam si nostris e montibus illum
Caietae aspiceret longe post litora ferri,
30 et strepitum sensisse ruentis ab aethere currus.
Praeterea mores populorum urbesque locosque
exposuit quernasque domos et lignea tecta.
Addidit et varias (heu barbara nomina) gentes,
Bellovacos Morinosque et (quos quis dicere possit?)
35 Tarbellos; latis errare et flumina campis,
nescio quem Ligerim tectis se innasse carinis.
Sed mea nunc aliae poscunt sibi pectora curae.
Tu modo, si quid habes (et te quoque Chloridis ardor
excruciat) scopulo hoc mecum meditare vicissim.
40 Audiet et gracilem percurret Mopsus avenam'.
    Sic illi; ast ego nil contra, sed quae mihi collo
garrula pendebat manibus tunc sumpta cicuta est.
Scilicet alternos conabar arundine versus
excipere, alternis nam dicere uterque parabat.
45 Nec mora; iam Chromis hos, hos et referebat Iolas.

Chromis

Nereides, pelagi sacrum genus, aut mihi vestris
munera ferte vadis duram queis Chlorida placem,
aut, si muneribus flecti nequit, aequore toto
quaerite quae nostrum sanet medicina furorem.

Iolas

50   Sirenes, mea cura, audite haec ultima vota.
Aut revocet iam Nisa suum nec spernat Iolam,

Iolas answers: "Please, Chromis, please do not bring back my sorrow. Recently by the waters of the Lucrine your Lycabas told us enough about this: that there he had assuredly seen the sun falling   25 beyond the waves and beyond the clouds, just as if from our mountains he were seeing it carried far off past the shores of Caieta, and that he heard the noise of a chariot careening from the heavens. Furthermore he described the peoples' customs, their cit-   30 ies and neighborhoods, oaken houses and roofs of wood. He also added that there were different tribes (alas, the uncouth names), the Bellovaci, the Morini, and (who could mention them?) the Tarbelli, that rivers meandered through broad plains, and that he   35 himself had sailed on a certain Loire in covered vessels. But now different trials lay claim to my heart. Only do you, if you have any songs, rehearse them with me in turn on this crag—passion for Chloris tortures you also. Mopsus will listen and will pass his lips over the slender reed."   40

So they spoke. I said nothing in response, but then and there grasped in my hands the chattering pipe that was hanging from my neck. I was clearly attempting to capture their alternating verses on my reed, for each was getting ready to sing alternating verses. No delay: now Chromis uttered these, then Iolas these.   45

Chromis

Nereids, holy offspring of the sea, either bring me gifts from your waters with which I might please hard-hearted Chloris or, if she cannot be swayed by gifts, look in the whole sea for a remedy to cure my madness.

Iolas

Sirens, my love, give ear to these prayers, my last. Either let Nisa   50 now summon her Iolas back and not scorn him, or let her behold

aut videat morientem; haec saxa impulsa marinis
fluctibus, haec misero vilis dabit alga sepulcrum.

Chromis

Qualis tranquillo quae labitur aequore cymba,
55 cum Zephyris summae crispantur leniter undae,
tuta volat luditque hilaris per transtra iuventus,
talis vita mihi, mea dum me Chloris amabat.

Iolas

Aspicis iratae feriant ut saxa procellae,
ut validis imae Coris turbentur harenae?
60 Iam scopulis furit unda, tremit iam terra tumultu;
fallor, an haec ipsa est Nisae indignantis imago?

Chromis

O Proteu, pastor liquidi maris, o pater, o rex,
(quandoquidem insanos odistis, numina, fastus)
quaere Pithecusas tu, cui licet, atque superbae
65 dic Hyalae salsum te pascere monstra per aequor.

Iolas

Ille habet, ille meos scopulus mihi servat amores
qui propior terrae est; illum pete, Glauce, natatu,
neve manus duri contemnat Nisa mariti,
dic te squamigeras traxisse ad litora praedas.

Chromis

70 Est Veneri Cypros gratissima, Creta Tonanti
Iunonique Samos, Vulcano maxima Lemnos;

him nearing death. These stones, lashed by the sea's surge, this wretched seaweed, will furnish the poor fellow a tomb.

Chromis

Like a bark that glides upon a calm sea, when the crests of the waves gently ripple in the Zephyrs (it flies along in safety and 55 among the thwarts the happy youth make merry): such was my life when my Chloris was in love with me.

Iolas

Do you notice how the angry gusts strike the rocks, how the sands of the deep are churned by the blasts of the Cori? Now the wave rages against the cliffs, now the earth shakes in turmoil. Am I mis- 60 taken or is this the very semblance of Nisa when she is aggrieved?

Chromis

O Proteus, shepherd of the clear sea, O father, O king, since you divinities loathe outrageous pride, make your way to Pithacusae — such is your ability — and say to haughty Hyale that even you pas- 65 ture your beasts through the salt sea.

Iolas

That crag, the one nearer to land, possesses my love, that crag keeps watch over her. Swim out to it, Glaucus, and, so that Nisa may not despise her husband's calloused hands, tell her that you have dragged scaly prey to shore.

Chromis

Cyprus is most pleasing to Venus, Crete to the Thunderer, Samos 70 to Juno, greatest Lemnos to Vulcan. As long as beautiful Hyale

Aenariae portus Hyale dum pulchra tenebit,
nec Samos Aenariam vincet nec maxima Lemnos.

Iolas

Gradivus Rhodopen et Mercurius Cyllenen,
75 Ortygiam Phoebe, Tritonia iactat Hymetton;
Nisa colit Prochyten; Prochytes si commoda norint,
Ortygiam Phoebe, Tritonia linquat Hymetton.

Chromis

Hic specus, hic rupes texendisque optima nassis
vimina sunt, iunci densaeque per avia myrtus;
80 si mihi nunc Pholoe vel tantum Chloris adesset,
quam bene pugnaces possem contemnere ventos.

Iolas

Nulla mihi sine te rident loca, displicet aequor,
sordet terra, leves odi cum retibus hamos;
at si aderis tu, Nisa, placebunt omnia, laetus
85 tunc ego vel Libycis degam piscator harenis.

Chromis

Dat rhombos Sinuessa, Dicarchi litora pagros,
Herculeae mullum rupes, synodontas Amalphis;
Parthenope teneris scatet ambitiosa puellis.
Quis mihi nunc alias scrutari suadeat algas?

Iolas

90 In fluviis mugil versatur, sargus in herbis,
Polypus in scopulis, mediis melanurus in undis;

lays claims to the harbors of Aenaria, neither Samos nor greatest Lemnos will surpass Aenaria.

Iolas

Gradivus boasts of Rhodope and Mercury of Cyllene, Phoebe of Ortygia, Tritonia of Hymettus. Nisa dwells on Prochyte. Were   75
they to know the advantages of Prochyte, Phoebe would abandon Ortygia, Tritonia Hymettus.

Chromis

Here is a cave, here cliffs, and the best osiers for plaiting weels, here rushes, and by-ways thick with myrtle. If only Pholoe or Chloris were with me now, how easily I could disdain the combat-   80
ive winds.

Iolas

No places smile upon me without you. The sea gives no pleasure. I abhor the earth. I hate supple fishhooks and nets. But if you are near, Nisa, everything will give pleasure. I will then gladly pass my life as a fisherman even at the sands of Libya.   85

Chromis

Sinuessa yields flounder, the shores of Dicarchus crab, the cliffs of Hercules mullet, Amalphis bream. Parthenope shows off her swarms of delicate girls. Who could convince me now to explore seaweed elsewhere?

Iolas

The mullet dwells in streams, the sar in grass, the octopus around   90
rocks, the black-tail in the midst of the waves. I am always linger-

ante tuas, mea Nisa, fores ego semper oberro;
quae mihi det tales iucundior insula portus?

Mopsus

    Hactenus, o Celadon, resonis sub rupibus illos
95   inter se vario memini contendere cantu
horrida ventosi ridentes murmura ponti.
Qui tamen et laudes et munera digna tulere
carminibus, sed quae nequeat contemnere Triton:
hic, quam Circeio nudus sub gurgite cepi
100 nativis concham maculis et murice pictam,
ille, recurvato nodosa corallia trunco.

: IV :

Proteus

Ferdinando Frederici
Regis filio Aragonio, Calabriae duci

    Nunc primum notas velis maioribus undas
currimus, o Nymphae Craterides, ordine quando
suadet amor carae primos telluris honores
dicere; caeruleae magni Crateris alumnae,
5   telluris primos carae dicamus honores,
dum radiis fervens medium Sol excoquit aequor.
    Tu vero, patriae iuvenis decus, edite caelo,
spes generis tanti, seu te nimbosa Pyrene
pro dulci Latio, pro nostris detinet arvis,
10 seu vagus obiecto munimine claudit Iberus,
rumpe moras, nec te latis Hispania regnis

ing before your doors, my Nisa. What happier island could grant
me such harbors?

Mopsus

This is as far as I remember, O Celadon, of their vying with each
other in contrasting song beneath the echoing cliffs, as they　95
laughed at the blustery rumblings of the gusty sea. Yet they carried
off both praise and prizes worthy of their songs which even Triton
couldn't despise: this one a conch — purple, dappled with natural
specks, which I caught while swimming naked in Circeio's wa-
ters — that one knotty coral with its core curled back upon itself.　100

: IV :

Proteus

To Ferdinando of Aragon, Duke of Calabria
Son of King Federico

O nymphs of Crater, now for the first time we speed through our
familiar waves with larger sails since love of our dear land urges us
to sing in sequence its chief glories. Sea-blue offspring of great
Crater, let us sing the chief glories of our dear land, while the rays　5
of the broiling Sun are parching the sea's midst.

But you, young pride of your fatherland, descended from
heaven, hope of so great a nation, whether the rainy Pyrenees keep
you instead of sweet Latium, instead of our own fields, or the
wandering Ebro hems you in, with the river's bulwark thrown
across your path: break through delays. Let not Spain seduce you　10
with the expanse of its realm, nor the origins of your house nor

alliciat stirpisve tuae primordia et ille
gentis honos, licet effuso Tagus impleat auro
et pater Oceanus spumanti perluat unda.
15 Nam mihi, nam tempus veniet cum reddita sceptra
Parthenopes fractosque tua sub cuspide reges
ipse canam; nunc litoream ne despice Musam
quam tibi post silvas, post horrida lustra Lycaei
(si quid id est) salsas deduxi primus ad undas
20 ausus inexperta tentare pericula cymba.
        Quae vada non norunt, quis nescit Protea portus?
Illum olim veteris pascentem ad saxa Minervae
mulcentemque suas divino carmine phocas
e puppi sensere Melanthius et Phrasidamus,
25 ut forte a Capreis obscura nocte redibant.
Sensere et vario delphinas ludere cursu
tritonumque choris longe freta pulsa sonare.
Ipse autem haudquaquam mortali digna referri
verba sono vacuas laetus cantabat ad auras;
30 terrigena ut quondam matris de ventre Typhoeus
exsiliens infanda deos ad bella vocasset;
ut fratrum primus furiis et hiantibus hydris
instructus densas ductaverit ipse catervas;
ut nisu ingenti partes de monte revulsas
35 Aenariam Prochytenque altis immiserit astris
ac totum subito caelum tremefecerit ictu;
tum Pater haud segni molitus fulmina dextra
immanes acies deiecerit atque tropaeum
iusserit ardentes testari sulphure Baias,
40 quod gens victa illis lavisset vulnera lymphis.
        Hinc magni Alcidae tauros stratumque profundum
aggeribus memorat ductamque per oppida pompam.
        His veteres addit Cumas, loca cognita Phoebo,
vatis et horrendae lucos Triviaeque recessus

the well-known glory of your race, though the Tagus fill it to the
brim with outpouring of gold, and father Ocean bathe it with his
frothing wave. For the time will come for me, the time will come,
when I myself will sing of the scepters of Parthenope returned and   15
of the kings broken beneath your lance. For now do not scorn the
Muse of the seashore whom, after the forests, after the rugged
wilds of Lycaeus (if that counts for anything), I was the first to
bring down to the salt waves for you, daring to risk their dangers
in my untested bark.   20

What waters do not know, what harbor is ignorant of Proteus?
Melanthius and Phrasidamus, when chance had it that they were
returning from Capri in the night's darkness, awhile ago noticed
him from their ship feeding his seals by the rocks of ancient Mi-
nerva and soothing them with godlike song. They also noticed   25
dolphins cavorting this way and that, and the straits reechoing afar
as they were struck by the caroling of the Tritons. As for himself,
he was joyfully singing to the empty breezes words that can
scarcely find worthy utterance through human tones: how once
upon a time earthborn Typhoeus, bounding from his mother's   30
womb, provoked the gods into impious war; how, equipped with
furies and gaping hydras, he himself first led his brothers' close-
knit ranks; how with a mighty effort he hurled to the lofty stars
Aenaria and Prochyte, masses wrenched from a mountainside, and   35
made the whole heavens tremble with the sudden blow. Then the
Father, wielding thunderbolts in his vigorous right hand, demol-
ished their brutish ranks and commanded that Baiae, flaming with
sulfur, stand as a trophy in witness that the routed enemy had
bathed its wounds in her waters.   40

After this he recalls the bulls of great Hercules, the deep paved
with rubble, the parade marched through the towns.

To this he adds ancient Cumae, a spot well known to Phoebus,
and the groves of the dread priestess and Trivia's retreats, the

45 Cimmeriumque domos et opaca in vallibus antra.
   Te quoque formosae captum Nesidos amore,
   Pausilype, irato compellat ab aequore questu.
   'Ah miser, ah male caute, tuae quid fata puellae
   acceleras? Cupit in medios evadere fluctus
50 infelix, cupit insuetum finire dolorem.
   At tibi nec curae est quod eam Neptunia monstra
   circumstent, mare nec rapido quod sorbeat aestu.
   Ah miser, ah male caute, ultra quid bracchia tendis?
   Siste gradum; riget illa iugis assueta nivosis
55 venatrix, quam mille ferae timuere sequentem
   per saltus. Vos hanc, Panope, vos, candida Drymo
   Cymothoeque Rhoeque Pherusaque Dinameneque,
   accipite et vestris sociam lustrate choreis.'
   Tum canit antiquas sedes opulentaque regna
60 Auricomae Sirenis et altum in monte sepulcrum,
   sacraque Chalcidicosque deos magnisque per aequor
   auspiciis vectas haec ipsa ad litora classes.
   Tum liquidos fontes subter cava moenia ducit
   attollitque arces et culmina montibus aequat
65 tectorum, vastas protendit in aequora moles
   Euploeamque procul trepidis dat cernere nautis
   atque Pharon; vincit scopulos praeruptaque saxa
   Teleboum Sarnique amnes et pinguia culta.
   Tum canit ut Corydona sacro Melisaeus in antro
70 viderit et calamos labris admoverit audax
   formosum quibus ille olim cantarat Alexin,
   dixerat et musam Damonis et Alphesiboei.
   Queis fretus, dictante Dea, tot sidera nobis
   prodiderit, tantas caeli patefecerit oras.
75 Quid referam aut Stabias aut quae tenuisse canoris
   virginibus fama est abeuntes saxa carinas,

dwellings of the Cimmerii and caves overshadowed in their valleys.   45

  You also, Posillipo, enthralled by love for beautiful Nesis, he
addresses with angry outcry from the sea: "Ah, poor creature, ah,
incautious soul, why do you hasten the death of your girl? In her
misfortune she yearns to escape into the midst of the sea, she
yearns to put an end to her novel grief. But you do not worry that   50
Neptune's monsters might surround her or that the sea swallow
her in its grasping swirl! Ah, poor creature, ah, incautious soul,
why do you yet stretch forth your arms? Stay your step. She lies
stiff, the huntress accustomed to snow-covered ridges, she whom a
thousand wild beasts feared as she stalked them through the   55
glades. Do you take her to yourselves, Panope, you, fair Drymo
and Cymothoe, Rhoë, and Pherusa, and Dinamene. Circle round
her as companion in your dances."

  Then he sings of the ancient seat and wealthy kingdom of the
golden-tressed Siren, and of her tomb high on the mountainside,   60
the rites and gods of Chalkis, and the fleet that sailed the sea to
these very shores under grand auspices.

  Then he leads clear waters beneath the hollow walls, and raises
citadels, and makes the crests of houses at a level with the moun-
tains. He stretches vast piers into the sea, and allows fearful sailors   65
to catch sight of Euploea and Pharos from a distance. He subdues
the cliffs and sheer rocks of the Teleboans, and the streams of
Sarnus, and the fertile farmlands.

  Then he sings how Melisaeus saw Corydon in the sacred cave
and dared to move to his lips the reed-pipe by which that man had   70
once sung of beautiful Alexis and the muse of Damon and
Alphesiboeus. With their support, and following the words of the
goddess, he brought into our ken so many stars and revealed the
vast reaches of the sky.

  Why should I tell either of Stabiae or of the rocks which, it is
said, laid hold of passing vessels for the singing maidens, or how   75

aut ut terrifici sonitus ignemque Vesevi
et desolatas passim defleverit urbes?
 Postremo reges regumque ex ordine pugnas
80 enumerat, bellique artes et praemia narrat.
Addit tristia fata, et te quem luget ademptum
Italia infelix (sive id gravis ira deorum,
seu fors dura tulit) trans altas evehit Alpes,
mox agit Oceani prope litora, denique sistit
85 spumantem ad Ligerim parvaque includit in urna.
Heu sortem miserandam, heu pectora caeca futuri!
Haecine te fessum tellus extrema manebat
hospitiis post tot terraeque marisque labores?
Pone tamen gemitus, nec te monumenta parentum
90 aut moveant sperata tuis tibi funera regnis.
Grata quies patriae, sed et omnis terra sepulcrum.
 Haec ille et quae vix audita prioribus annis
heroum longaeva queat meminisse vetustas
commemorat (socio respondent aequora plausu)
95 luna suam donec paulatim fundere lucem
coepit et ad vitreas redierunt numina sedes.

: V :

Herpylis pharmaceutria

*Cassandrae Marchesiae
mulieri praestantissimae*

Dorylas, Thelgon

Sed iam vulgatos et nos referamus amores
quos pariter grata scopuli pendentis in umbra

he wept for the noise and fire of frightening Vesuvius and the cities everywhere laid waste.

In conclusion he catalogues kings and the battles of kings in order, and explains the arts and prizes of war. He adds the sad turns 80 of fate, and carries across the lofty Alps you whose loss ill-starred Italy mourns, whether the weighty anger of the gods or unyielding chance brought it about. Soon he propels you near the shores of Oceanus. Finally he settles you by the frothing Loire and encloses you in a tiny urn. Alas for his pitiable lot, alas, hearts blind to the 85 future. Did this farthest land await you with its shelter, exhausted after so many trials on land and on sea? Yet forego lamentation. Let not the tombs of your ancestors disturb you or the burial that you had expected in your own realm. To be at peace in one's fa- 90 therland is welcome, but earth is everyone's grave.

These matters he recalls to mind, and tales of heroes, given ear in years past, which long-lived age could scarcely remember — the waters give answer with communal applause — until bit by bit the moon began to pour forth her light, and the heavenly presences re- 95 turned to their shimmering thrones.

: V :

Herpylis the Witch

To the most excellent lady
Cassandra Marchese

Dorylas, Thelgon

But let us also tell of the now well-known loves which on this side Dorylas, on this side Thelgon, who dwells near the Teleboean sea,

hinc Dorylas, hinc Teleboi maris accola Thelgon
certantes docuere, quibus cava litora et ipse
5   aequoreus Platamon sacrumque Serapidis antrum
cum fonte et Nymphis assultavere marinis.
     Tu mihi, seu doctas percurris Palladis artes
Maeoniaeque aurum et subtegmina vincis Arachnes,
seu Dryadum choreis coetuque immista Dianae
10 haud minor incedis pictaque accincta pharetra
venatu Prochyten maternaque regna fatigas,
sive Dicarcheis qua molibus assilit aequor
ludentes spectas Nereidas, en age nostros
(si quis honos pelagi) Cassandra, en aspice lusus.
15 Non ingrata cano penitusque iniussa, neque umquam
arguerint ventura meis te saecula chartis
praeteritam; faveat modo non invitus Apollo
et quae me facili vexere per aequora remo
Pierides, queis longa dies et nomina curae.
20 Interea Dorylan iuvet hic audire canentem.

Dorylas

     Sebethi ad liquidas descenderat Herpylis undas,
Herpylis Euboidum non ultima, quam pater Alcon
erudiit, Musis et Phoebo cognitus Alcon.
Venerat et socii partem subitura laboris
25 unanimis soror et calathum de more ferebat.
Ipsa comas effusa pedemque exuta sinistrum
cum philtris longum submurmurat atque ita fatur:
     'Pone aram et vivos hauri de flumine rores
canaque vicino decerpe absinthia campo;
30 illum illum magicis conabor adurere sacris
qui miseram tota spoliatam mente reliquit.
Volvite praecipitem iam nunc, mea licia, rhombum.

heralded, as they competed together in the pleasant shade of the
hanging cliff. At this the curved seashore frolicked, and marine
Platamon himself, and the holy grotto of Serapis with its fountain 5
and sea nymphs.

Whether you are surveying the learned arts of Pallas and sur-
passing the golden weaving of Maeonian Arachne, or whether you
are making your way — no lesser a figure — mingled in the Dryads'
dances and the entourage of Diana, girded with a painted quiver,
and exhaust Prochyte and the realm of your mother with hunting, 10
or whether you watch the Nereids at play where the sea dashes
against the piers of Dicarchus, come now, Cassandra, attend to my
own play, if any glory comes from the sea. I sing songs not dis-
pleasing and entirely unasked for. Never might future generations 15
charge that you were passed by in my pages. Only may a willing
Apollo and the Pierian maidens look with kindness, who have
borne me across the waters with easy oar. Length of days and en-
during repute is their province. Meanwhile may you find pleasure
here in listening to the song of Dorylas. 20

Dorylas

Herpylis had gone down to the clear waves of the Sebeto, Herpylis
not least of the Euboids whom father Alcon taught, Alcon known
to the Muses and to Phoebus. Her like-minded sister had also
come to take a share in the common effort and carried the custom-
ary basket. Herpylis herself, with hair flung wide and left foot 25
shoeless, mumbles some time over her potions. Then she speaks:

"Set up an altar. Draw fresh moisture from the stream. Pluck
pale wormwood from the nearby field. I will try to set him aflame
with my magic spells, him who left me, lovesick, bereft of my 30
whole mind. Whirl now, my strings, whirl now the rushing wheel.

135

Rhombus ad Haemonias revocetur aeneus artes,
sistere qui pluvias, qui pellere nubila caelo,
35 qui potis est trepidos undis abducere pisces.
Volvite praecipitem, mea licia, volvite rhombum.
    Alga tibi haec primum tumidi purgamina ponti
spargitur et rapidis absumitur arida flammis;
sic mihi, sic, Maeon, uraris adusque medullas.
40 Volvite praecipitem iam nunc, mea licia, rhombum.
    Ter muscum, Clearista, ter hunc sine forcipe cancrum
ure simul "cum" que "his" dic "viscera Maeonis uro".
Volvite praecipitem, mea licia, volvite rhombum.
    Spongia nunc lacrimis perfunditur. Heus bona magno
45 spongia nata mari, lacrimas bibe sedula nostras,
utque rapis sitiens illas sic Maeonis omnem,
Maeonis ingrati, rapias de pectore sensum.
Volvite praecipitem iam nunc, mea licia, rhombum.
    Ut pumex, pinguescat, ut aequoris unda, quiescat,
50 quae ventis agitata huc illuc concita fertur.
Sed quid ego heu tristi pectus concussa dolore
imprecer et vanis iactem convicia ventis?
Maeon tot mihi damna, ego Maeoni verba rependam?
Volvite praecipitem, mea licia, volvite rhombum.
55 Huc, huc, qui rigida meditaris vulnera cauda,
saeve trigon, et tu proprium cui sistere naves
veliferas, echeneis, adeste et Maeonis acres
tu retinere pedes, tu figere corda labora.
Volvite praecipitem iam nunc, mea licia, rhombum.
60 Tunde iecur spumamque simul torpedinis atrae.
Haec ego cras illi lethalia pocula mittam;
ebibat et subito pallentes torpeat artus.
Volvite praecipitem, mea licia, volvite rhombum.

Let the brass wheel be summoned again to the arts of Haemonia, the wheel which can make rain cease, drive clouds from the sky, entice trembling fish out of the waves. Whirl, my 35
strings, whirl the rushing wheel.

First this seaweed, scum of the surging deep, is spread out for you and, when it is dry, it is caught up in the scorching flames and scattered as purification. Thus, Maeon, thus may you be burned for me even to your marrow. Whirl now, my strings, now the rushing wheel. 40

Three times, Clearista, burn this moss, three times this crab wanting a pincer, and say at the same time 'With these I burn the vitals of Maeon.' Whirl, my strings, whirl the rushing wheel.

Now the sponge is saturated with my tears. Alas, good sponge, born of the great sea, eagerly swallow my tears. And just as you 45
devour them in your thirst, so may you devour all feeling from the heart of Maeon, ungrateful Maeon. Whirl now, my strings, now the rushing wheel.

Let him grow fat, like pumice, let him grow calm, like a wave of the sea that is stirred and driven hither and thither by the blasts of the winds. But why should I utter curses, when my heart, alas, is 50
stricken by the sadness of grief? Why should I throw my rebukes to the empty winds? Will I pay back Maeon with as many words as Maeon's injuries to me? Whirl, my strings, whirl the rushing wheel.

Here, here, be at hand, savage sting-ray, devising wounds with your hard tail, and you, remora, whose power it is to halt sailing 55
vessels; make it your task, you, to hold back his feet, you, to pierce his heart. Whirl now my strings, now the rushing wheel.

Pound together the liver and saliva of the black cramp-fish. To- 60
morrow I will send him this deadly drink. Let him drink deep and let him suddenly grow numb in his pale limbs. Whirl, my strings, whirl the rushing wheel.

Scinde manu leporem; leporis penetrabile virus.
65 Nascitur Eois hic fluctibus; attulit Aegle,
docta Aegle, iussitque inimicum tangere limen.
Curre age, tange simul, simul obline; cras mihi poenas
perfidus ille dabit, gemet ipso in limine Maeon.
Sistite praecipitem iam nunc, mea licia, rhombum.
70 Contere et alcyonis nidum mihi; pellere ventos
dicitur et saevas pelagi mulcere procellas.
Forsitan hic nostros sedabit pectoris aestus.
Sistite praecipitem, iam sistite, licia, rhombum'.
Hactenus ille; quid hinc subiunxerit ordine Thelgon
75 accipe; non omnes unus dolor angit amantes.

Thelgon

Rupe sub hac mecum sedit Galatea; videbam
et Capreas et quae Sirenum nomina servant
rura procul; veteres alia de parte ruinas
Herculis ambusta signabat ab arce Vesevus.
80 Exsere caeruleos, Triton, de gurgite vultus.
Ipse meas, Triton, Nereo deferre querelas,
ipse potes curva resonans super aequora concha
et scopulis narrare et fluctivagis ballaenis.
Exsere caeruleos, Triton pater, exsere vultus.
85 Hic primos mihi congressus dedit illa roganti,
hic niveam formosa manum porrexit et (eheu,
quid recolo?) tacitos in me defixit ocellos.
Exsere caeruleos, Triton, de gurgite vultus.
Huc ades, o mea cura, quid, o quid lenta moraris?
90 Ipse ego te propter socios cymbamque reliqui.
Exsere caeruleos, Triton pater, exsere vultus.

Tear apart a sea-slug with your hand. The slug's poison pierces
through. This one comes from Eoan waters. Aegle brought it,   65
skillful Aegle. She told me to daub his hateful threshold. Get busy
and hurry: hurry and daub it, hurry, smear it. Tomorrow faithless
Maeon will pay me the penalty. He will groan on the very thresh-
old. Now, my strings, now stop the rushing wheel.

Also crush me a halcyon's nest. It is said to banish the winds   70
and to soften the sea's fierce blasts. Perhaps this will calm the tu-
mult in my breast. Stop now, strings, now stop the rushing wheel."

This far his words. Listen to what Thelgon then added to it.
No single pain afflicts all lovers.   75

Thelgon

Galatea was sitting with me under this rock. I was looking afar at
both Capri and the countryside that keeps the names of the Si-
rens. In the other direction Vesuvius from his charred crest pin-
pointed the ancient ruins of Hercules. Raise from the deep, Tri-
ton, your sea-blue features.   80

You yourself, Triton, can bear my laments to Nereus. You your-
self, as you make the seas above echo with your curved conch, can
tell both the cliffs and the wave-roaming whales. Raise, father Tri-
ton, raise your sea-blue features.

Here she allowed our first meetings at my pleading. Here,   85
beautiful as she was, she stretched forth her snowy hand (alas,
why am I thinking back on it?) and pierced me with her silent
eyes. Raise from the deep, Triton, your sea-blue features.

Come hither, dearly beloved. Why, O why, are you lingering
slowly? On account of you I have left behind my comrades and
skiff. Raise, father Triton, raise your sea-blue features.   90

Hic tibi consuetas formosior explicat umbras
populus; amplector saepe hanc atque oscula figo
corticibus, saepe ipsa pedum vestigia quaero
95 et, si quid manibus tetigisti, floribus orno.
Exsere caeruleos, Triton, de gurgite vultus.

Quem mihi nunc praefers? Si te iuga frondea, si te
arbuta pascentesque iuvant per rura capellae,
nos quoque non graciles nunc primum iungere avenas
100 discimus; incisas implent mea carmina fagos
et mea Maenaliis pendet iam fistula silvis.
Exsere caeruleos, Triton pater, exsere vultus.

Sin magis arrident haec litora, sin magis alti
divitiae pelagi, sparsos quis cogere pisces
105 doctior aut rigidum dextra iactare tridentem?
Exsere caeruleos, Triton, de gurgite vultus.

Non ego delphinis, te iudice, non ego thynnis
aequore vel medio dubitem certare natando.
Quid tibi me iactem, cui vix numerare vel hamos
110 nunc vacat aut restes onerataque retia plumbo
et Sinuessano textas de vimine nassas?
Exsere caeruleos, Triton pater, exsere vultus.

Me Ligurum durae rupes, me Gallica norunt
litora, piscantem pariter me Varus et ingens
115 sensit Arar, sensere maris fera monstra Britanni.
Obrue caeruleos, Triton, sub gurgite vultus.

Et post haec heu dura fugis; non te mihi tellus
extera, non venti rapuere. Sed accipe munus,
accipe; non ultra tecum, Galatea, sedentem
120 aspicies. I, laeta novas meditare choreas.
Obrue caeruleos, Triton pater, obrue vultus.

Here for you the handsome poplar unfolds its familiar shade. I often embrace it and plant kisses on its bark. Often I search for the very traces of your feet and, if you touched anything with your hands, I decorate it with flowers. Raise from the deep, Triton, 95 your sea-blue features.

Whom do you now prefer to me? If wooded ridges, if arbutus and goats at pasture through the countryside give you delight, we also are not now for the first time learning to link slender reeds. My songs fill the beech trees on which I have carved, and my pipe 100 already hangs in the woods of Maenalus. Raise, father Triton, raise your sea-blue features.

But if these shores, if the riches of the deep sea delight you more, who is more skilled at herding scattered fish or at hurling the sturdy trident with his right hand? Raise from the deep, Tri- 105 ton, your sea-blue features.

With you as judge I would have no hesitation, no hesitation at all, even in the middle of the sea, to vie in swimming either with dolphins or with tunnies. But why should I boast of myself to you when I now have scarcely the time to count either my hooks or my ropes, my nets weighted with lead and my weels woven from osier 110 of Sinuessa? Raise, father Triton, raise your sea-blue features.

The hard cliffs of the Ligurians know me, the shores of Gaul, the Var likewise has experienced my fishing and the mighty Saône, the wild monsters of the sea off Britain have experienced it. Sub- 115 merge, Triton, your sea-blue features under the swell.

Even after this, alas, you run away, hard-hearted. No foreign land, no winds have snatched you from me. But take this gift, take it. Never more will you watch me as I sit with you, Galatea. Off with you: take joy in pondering new dances. Submerge, father Tri- 120 ton, submerge your sea-blue features.

FRAGMENTUM

Zephyraeus, Eutycus

Optatos iam Euploea mihi circumspice portus,
quo passim uacuas liceat disponere nassas,
quo liceat trepidas nassis includere praedas
et Zephyris relevare graves spirantibus aestus,
5   siqua movet cupidam velocis gratia cymbae.
    Tuque ades, o nostri merces non parva laboris,
quam Phoebus mihi, quam doctae, mea turba, sorores
conciliant, dumque ipse ratem de litore pello
da vela insinuans pelagoque excurre patenti,
10 pars animae, Puderice, meae, te nam sua Nereus
per vada, te liquido Doris vocat aemula fundo,
dum late undisonum campus strepit omnis aquarum.
    Lucrinae ad Veneris scopulos convenerat omnis
Aenariae Prochytaeque manus. Zephyraeus opaca
15 scilicet Aenaria, Prochyta venit Eutychus alta,
insignes ambo calamis, et versibus ambo,
aptus uterque fretis, piscatibus aptus uterque,
ille hamos versare, hic retia solvere in aequor.

Zephyraeus

Tum prior haec Zephyre‹us›: Adeste o litore ab omni,
20 piscatorum artes, liquidas exquirite sedes,
vertite Tritonum latebras, penetrate recessus
Nereidum. Nunquam nostros sedabitis ignes,
nunquam me Pholoe, nunquam me Chloris amabit.
Ede tuos mecum tandem, cava buccina, fletus.

142

FRAGMENT OF AN ECLOGUE

Zephyraeus, Eutycus

Seek out for me now, Euploea, beloved harbors where one can dis-
tribute empty weels everywhere, where one can net trembling prey
in the weels, and the breezes of the West wind alleviate the in-
tense heat, if any love of a swift skiff rouse your desire.   5

   You come also, generous reward for my efforts, which Phoebus,
which the learned maidens, my troop, win over to me. And while
I myself launch my bark from shore, help billow out my sails, and
set forth over the open sea, Poderico, part of my soul. For
Nereus summons you through his flood, Doris his rival summons   10
you from the midst of her waves, while roars the whole sweep of
wide-thundering waves.

   All the inhabitants of Aenaria and of Prochyta had come to-
gether at the rocks of Lucrine Venus. Everyone knows that
Zephyraeus came from shady Aenaria, Eutycus from lofty
Prochyta. Both were famous for their reed-pipes, and both for   15
their verses, each trained for the sea, each trained in fishing, the
former in plying his hooks, the latter in spreading his nets into the
water.

Zephyraeus

Zephyraeus then sang this first: "Come here from all along the
shore, o artful fishermen. Seek out the sea-clear dwellings, aim for   20
the Tritons' lairs, enter the hideaways of the Nereids. You will
never quench my passion: Pholoe will never love me, me never
Chloris. Sound forth at last your laments with me, hollow conch.

Eutycus

25 Omnia tentavi, terras, mare, nubila, coelum
    ventorumque domos
    Omnia sed nocuere simul. Nunc ite, puellae,
    ite deae pelagi, furiis arcessite nostris
    nunc alios succos aliasque Melampodis herbas.
30 Ede tuos mecum tandem, cava buccina, fletus.

Zephyraeus

    Non magicos versus ignotaque nomina rerum
    dissimilesque deos Herebumque Chaosque reliqui,
    ipsos quin etiam filo convolvere rhombos
    edidici, parteisque meas de litore echinos,
35 de scopulis muscum, de fluctibus hausimus undas.
    Ede tuos mecum tandem, cava buccina, fletus.

Eutycus

    Testis Cymothoe, testis mihi caerula Cloto
    optavi quoties mediis in fluctibus aegram
    proiicere hanc animam, quoties ego gurgite in alto
40 occurri monstris immanibus. Ipsa fatentur
    aequora

42 Ede tuos mecum tandem, cava buccina, fletus.

Eutycus

I've tried everything—lands, sea, clouds, the heavens, and the   25
homes of the winds . . . but all alike have done me harm. Make
your way all you goddesses, make your way, goddesses of the sea:
now summon to cure our madness other potions and other herbs
of Melampus. Sound forth at last your laments with me, hollow
conch.   30

Zephyraeus

I have not abandoned incantations and strange names, and weird
gods, Erebus and Chaos. Indeed I have even learned to whirl the
very wheels with a string. As my province I have drawn sea-ur-
chins off the shore, moss from rocks, waves out of the sea. Sound   35
forth at last your laments with me, hollow conch.

Eutycus

Cymothoe bears witness for me, sea-blue Clotho bears witness,
how often I have yearned to cast this ailing spirit into the midst of
the waves, how often in the flood's depth I have confronted enor-
mous monsters. The waters themselves admit . . . [lacuna]. Sound   40
forth at last your laments with me, hollow conch.   42

SALICES

Traiano Cabanilio
Troiae ac Montellae domino

Si vacat, et blandos etiamnum ventilat ignes
quae dea caerulea vehitur super aequora concha,
turrigeramque Paphon, ditemque Amathuntha tuetur,
accipe flumineas properatum carmen ad undas,
5 o mihi non dubia, Cabanili, cognite fama,
sed longe varios rerum spectate per usus.
Nam tibi me doctae sic devinxere sorores,
sic mea felici permulcent pectora cura,
ut vix ulla queam melioris tempora vitae
10 te sine, vix placidos per noctem ducere somnos.
En agedum, Traiane, tuis haec praevia iussis
tractanti, iam iamque animo maiora paranti
da veniam, et tenues ne dedignare Camoenas.
    Forte inter virides, si vera est fama, genistas
15 capripedes Satyri, passimque agrestia Panes
numina cum Faunis, et montivagis Silvanis,
exercet dum Sol raucas per rura cicadas,
vitabant aestus, qua pinguia culta vadosus
irrigat, et placido cursu petit aequora Sarnus.
20 Grata quies nemorum manantibus undique rivis,
et Zephyris densas inter crepitantibus alnos.
Dumque leves aptant calamos, dum sibila pressis
explorant digitis, tenuique foramina cera
obducunt, vario modulantes carmina cantu,
25 auricomae viridi speculantur ab ilice Nymphae

THE WILLOWS

*To Traiano Cavaniglia,
Lord of Troia and Montella*

If you are at leisure and still now the goddess who rides above the waves in a sea-blue conch and protects turreted Paphos and rich Amathus is fanning her charming flames, receive, O Cavaniglia, a song brought in haste to the stream's waters. You are known to me through assured reputation and esteemed for the great variety of 5 your accomplishments. For the learned sisters have so linked me to you, so beguile my heart with happy yearning, that without you I can scarcely enjoy the stretches of my life's happiness, scarcely enjoy the quiet of nighttime's sleep. Come now, Traiano: grant me 10 pardon as I make ready this harbinger of what you ordered and now, even now, fashion greater things in my mind. Do not scorn my slender Camenae.

By chance, if the report is true, the divinities of the country-side — goat-footed Satyrs and Pans along with Fauns and moun- 15 tain-roaming Silvanuses — far and wide amid the green broom-plants were shunning the heat, while the sun was prompting the shrill cicadas through the landscape, where the shallow Sarnus waters its fruitful fields and seeks the sea in gentle course. The hush of the woods is welcome as rivulets glide everywhere about and 20 Zephyrs rustle among the copse of alders.

While they are tuning their delicate reeds and testing their piping at a finger's touch, plugging up slits with pliant wax and practicing their songs with various melodies, the golden-haired Nymphs, as they watch the scene from a green ilex, let fling re- 25

dulcia clarisonis solventes ora cachinnis.
Sed prope ferre pedem metuunt; nam saepe labores
audierant, Peneia, tuos, et qualibus olim
infelix eheu virgo Nonacria fatis,
30 infelix virgo (quid enim non illa moveret?)
Pana metu fugiens e vertice Cylleneo,
Pana deum Arcadiae, quamvis pulcherrima, quamvis
Dianae sacros inter lectissima coetus,
nodosa tenerum mutarit arundine pectus.
35 Quas simul ac nemorum petulans, effrenaque pubes
semiferi videre per herbida prata vagantes,
occultamque imis flammam traxere medullis;
sic timidas blandis hortantur vocibus ultro:
  'Huc huc o tenerae, placidissima turba, puellae:
40 quid procul adstatis? potius succedite ripae,
et viridi in prato molles de more choreas
ducite, quandoquidem calamos inflamus inertes,
et frustra ad surdas iactamus carmina silvas.'
Illae nil contra: celeri sed nuda parabant
45 crura fugae, tutosque agitabant mente receptus,
siqua forte viam per saxa irrumpere, et altis
evasisse iugis, deus aut sua fata dedissent.
Tum iuvenes: 'Procul o, clamant, procul iste, puellae,
sit timor, ignavas animo depellite curas:
50 nullae hic insidiae, nullae per aperta latebrae:
cuncta patent: nullas abscondunt haec loca fraudes.
Nos quoque non Lernae monstris, non igne Chimaerae,
Scyllaeisve lupis geniti, aut latrante Charybdi,
qui vestra immani laceremus viscera morsu;
55 sed divum genus, et qui semper rupibus altis
vobiscum crebris venatibus insultemus.'
His dictis permulsi animi, securaque tristem
corda metum eiiciunt, gressuque per uda citato

sounding peals of laughter from their sweet mouths. But they are
fearful of drawing near. They had heard of your tribulations,
daughter of Peneus, and the misfortune, alas, through which the
ill-starred Nonacrian maiden, the ill-starred maiden — (for what
did she not try?) fleeing Pan in fearful flight from the crest of Mt.   30
Cyllene, Pan the god of Arcadia, though she was the most beauti-
ful, though she was preeminent among Diana's holy bands — had
once changed her tender breast into a knotty reed. As soon as the
half-wild creatures, the unruly, lawless offspring of the woods,
caught sight of them roaming through the grassy meadows, they   35
conceived a hidden fire in their inmost marrow. Thus of their own
accord they encourage the shy creatures with coaxing words:

"Here, over here, gracious maidens, kindliest crowd: why are
you standing way off there? Come up to the riverbank instead.   40
Lead as usual your gentle dances in the green meadow, since we
play on ineffectual pipes and hurl our songs in vain to deaf
woods."

The nymphs made no response, but readied their bare legs for
swift flight and kept pondering their means for safe retreat, if per-   45
chance a god or their destiny had granted them to force a pathway
among the rocks or to escape over the lofty ridges.

Then the youths cry out: "Far off, far off, maidens, be that fear
of yours. Dismiss such idle worries from your mind. Here in the
open there are no snares, no hiding-places. Everything lies plain.   50
This spot conceals no deceit. And we're not sprung from the mon-
sters of Lerna, from the fire of the Chimaera, or from Scylla's
wolves or barking Charybdis, to rend your vitals with our enor-
mous bite. No, we are a race of gods who in your company might
ever leap over tall rocks in hunt after hunt."   55

Their minds were put at ease by these words. Their trusting
hearts thrust away bitter fear, and with hastening step through the
moist meadows they at last approach the lustful gods and the riv-

prata, deis tandem cupidis, ripaeque propinquant.
60 Tum manibus simul implicitis per gramina festas
exercent choreas; aliosque, aliosque reflexus
inter se laetae repetunt; nunc corpora librant
in saltus, nunc molle latus, nunc candida iactant
brachia, et alterna quatiunt vestigia planta.
65 Hic Satyri, quamquam voces audire canentum
crudeles, quamquam niveas spectare papillas
exsultant, oculisque bibunt sitientibus ignem,
tanta tamen saevi gliscit vis effera morbi
pectoribus, praecepsque amor, et malesana libido,
70 ut calamis sensim eiectis, ruptoque repente
foedere, surgentes ab humo, vento ocius omnes
exsiliant; spretaque deum pietate, fideque,
ah pavidas Nymphas, subitoque horrore rigentes
invadant avidi, saevorum more luporum,
75 qui laetas mediis proturbant lusibus agnas,
oblitasque sui passim rapiuntque, trahuntque,
dum viridi in campo cursant, aut valle sub alta,
et custos ignarus abest, et amica canum vis.
Sic illi; at miserae discisso pectore Nymphae
80 frondiferam moestis silvam clamoribus implent.
Atque huc, atque illuc fugiunt; non saxa, neque altis
tuta putant loca senta rubis: hinc ardua montis
praerupti iuga, diffusos hinc stagna per agros
adtonitae circumspiciunt, via nulla salutis,
85 et iam spes praerepta fugae. Tum denique ad undas
consistunt trepidae, flavosque a vertice crines
cum lacrimis, gemituque, et flebilibus lamentis
abscindunt, Sarnumque vocant, liquidasque sorores:
dumque vocant, fundo properat chorus omnis ab imo
90 Naiadum; properat vitreae rex caerulus undae
Sarnus, inexhaustumque vadis ciet agmen aquarum

150

erbank. Then, with hands intertwined together, they perform
their festive dances through the grass. Joyously as a group they un- 60
dertake turns and returns, first these, then those. Now they poise
their bodies for a leap, now they thrust forward a soft flank, now
white arms. They shake their feet with alternating step. At this
point, though the savage Satyrs rejoice in hearing the voices of the
singers, as they gaze at their snowy teats, and drink in fire though 65
thirsty eyes, nevertheless such a bestial force of fierce disease — im-
petuous passion and wild lust — swells in their breasts that, gradu-
ally tossing aside their pipes, of a sudden they break their word,
and all rise up from the ground, swifter than the wind, and leap 70
forward. Scorning respect toward the gods and good faith, eagerly
they rush toward the Nymphs, afraid, yes, and frozen with sudden
terror. Their behavior was like that of vicious wolves who throw
into turmoil carefree lambs in the middle of their play: everywhere 75
they snatch and drag them, as they rush about dumbfounded on
the greensward or beneath a lofty valley, when their unwitting
guardian and their dogs' friendly marshalling is elsewhere.

Thus the men, but the pitiable Nymphs, rending their breasts,
fill the leafy forest with sad wails. They flee hither, they flee 80
thither. They consider safe neither rocks nor rough stretches deep
with briars. Stunned, they cast their eyes on this side at the steep
ridges of the sheer mountain slope, on that side at the swamp-sod-
den fields. There is no road to safety; all hope of flight is snatched
away. Then at last they fearfully come to a stop at the mere's edge. 85
With tears, groans and grief-stricken weeping they tear their
blond hair from their heads. They call upon Sarnus and their sis-
ters of the stream. When they call, the whole band of Naiads has-
tens from the lowest depth. Sarnus, sea-blue lord of the glassy
wave, makes haste and, with strident roar, summons from the 90
shallows a boundless squadron of waters. But what could Sarnus

rauca sonans, sed quid Sarnusve, aut illa natantum
agmina Naiadum possint, ubi ferrea contra
stant fata, et duro leges adamante rigescunt?
95 Ergo defectae cura, auxilioque deorum,
ac coelum pariter Nymphae, lucemque perosae,
unum illud, rebus tandem quod restat in arctis,
finem optant, iamque in fluvium se mergere adortae
membra reclinabant, et aquas prono ore petebant:
100 cum subito obriguere pedes; lateque per imos
exspatiata ungues radix, fugientia tardat,
adfigitque solo vestigia. Tum vagus ipsis
spiritus emoritur venis, indignaque pallor
occupat ora, tegit trepidantia pectora cortex.
105 Nec mora: pro digitis ramos exire videres,
auratasque comas glauca canescere fronde,
et iam vitalis nusquam calor, ipsaque cedunt
viscera paullatim venienti frigida ligno.
Sed quamvis totos duratae corporis artus,
110 caudicibusque latus, virgultisque undique septae,
ac penitus Salices, sensus tamen unicus illis:
silvicolas vitare deos, et margine ripae
haerentes, medio procumbere fluminis alveo.

or those squadrons of swimming Naiads do when iron fate stands opposed and the laws of hard adamant remain unbending?

So the Nymphs, undone by worry and with the help of the gods, hating equally the heavens and its light, yearn to make an end—the one thing that finally remains when crisis looms. Attempting to sink into the stream, now they were bending their limbs forward and with down-turned faces were reaching out for the water when suddenly their feet grew stiff. A root spreads throughout the length of their toes that slows their fleeing feet and fastens them to the ground. Then shifting breath dies away in their veins, paleness seizes their undeserving features, bark clothes their trembling breasts. In a short while, you would see branches protruding where once were fingers, and golden hair grow hoary with leaves of gray. No heat of life now remains. Their cold vitals now yield slowly to the intruding wood. But, though they have grown hard in all their body's limbs, and though their flank is everywhere hedged with bark and with shoots, and they are completely Willows, nevertheless one emotion remains theirs: to elude the woodland gods and, clinging to the edge of the bank, to lean out over the mid-channel of the stream.

ELEGIARUM

Liber Primus

I. Ad Lucium Crassum

Te foecunda tenent saxosi rura Petrini,
　　rura olim proavis facta superba meis.
Et Sinuessanas spectas, mea gaudia, Nymphas,
　　quique novo semper sulfure fumat ager.
5　Et modo miraris veteres in litore portus,
　　nunc Liris gelida qua fluit amnis aqua.
Cunctaque felici figis vestigia cura,
　　observas Latiae dum monumenta viae.
At mihi paganae dictant silvestria Musae
10　　carmina, quae tenui gutture cantat Amor.
Fidaque secretis respondet silva querelis,
　　et percussa meis vocibus antra sonant.
Nec tantum populos, nec tantum horrescimus urbes,
　　quantum non iustae saevitiam dominae.
15　Hoc vitae genus, hoc studium mihi fata ministrant;
　　hinc opto cineres nomen habere meos.
Me probet umbrosis pastorum turba sub antris,
　　dum rogat agrestem lacte tepente Palem.
Me rudis indocta moduletur arundine Thyrsis;
20　　et tam constanti laudet amasse fide.
Inde super tumulumque meum, Manesque sepultos
　　Tityrus ex hedera serta virente ferat.
Hic mihi saltabit Corydon, et pulcher Alexis,
　　Damoetas flores sparget utraque manu.
25　Fluminibusque sacris umbras inducet Iolas,
　　dum coget saturas Alphesiboeus oves.

154

ELEGIES

Book I

I. To Lucio Crasso

The fertile countryside of rocky Petrinum holds you, countryside once made proud by my ancestors. And you gaze upon my delight, the nymphs of Sinuessa, and the field that ever smokes with fresh sulfur. And now you marvel at the ancient harbors along the shore, now at the chill water with which the Liris river flows. You 5 plant your every footstep with happy attention while you survey the monuments of the Latian road.

But my rural Muses recite rustic songs which Love sings with slender throat. The trusty woods make answer to my covert laments, and the grottoes re-echo, struck by my words. I dread not 10 so much the throngs, not so much cities, as the cruelty of my unfair mistress. The fates furnish me with this mode of living, this inclination. From this I want my ashes to have renown. May the 15 troop of shepherds within their shady grottoes grant me approval, when with warm milk they pray to Pales of the Fields. Let untrained Thyrsis sing of me on his rude reed, and praise my having loved with faith so true. Then over the grave that buries my re- 20 mains may Tityrus spread garlands of fresh ivy. Here Corydon and beautiful Alexis will dance for me, with each hand Damoetas will scatter flowers. Iolas will shroud the sacred streams with shade while Alphesiboeus will gather the full-fed flock. 25

Non mihi Maeoniden, Luci, non cura Maronem
    vincere: si fiam notus amore, sat est.
Quid feret Aeacides nobis, quid cautus Ulysses?
30   Quid pius Aeneas, Ascaniusve puer?
Ista canant alii, quorum stipata triumphis
    Musa vagum e tumulis nomen in astra ferat.
At mihi tete avidis liceat vincire lacertis,
    osculaque optata sumere longa mora.
35 Et liceat posita mirari membra lucerna,
    noctis et insolitas nectere blanditias:
atque manus, atque ora tuis componere in ulnis,
    teque meo lassam saepe fovere sinu.
Sed quid ego, hei misero, ventosus inania fingo
40   somnia, quae forsan non feret ulla dies?
Felix, qui potuit duram exorare puellam,
    et capere optati gaudia coniugii.
Ille dies, noctesque suos decantat amores,
    et recolit Veneris dulcia furta suae.
45 Ille etiam liquido perfusus odore capillos,
    exercet tenerum nocte iuvante latus:
inque sinu dominae primos reminiscitur ignes,
    quos leviter pennis aureus afflat Amor.
Nec cupit, Aethiopum quae canent vellera silvis,
50   nec quae Sidonio lana cruore rubet.
Solus habet, fuscis quicquid portatur ab Indis,
    solus habet ripas, aurifer Herme, tuas,
et quascumque metit segetes fragrantibus arvis
    Medus, et assiduo sole perustus Arabs.
55 Non auro, aut gemmis miseri torquemur amantes.
    Qui dominam poterit flectere, dives erit.
Dives ero ante alios, si te, mea vita, volentem
    sustineam ignota pauper, et exul humo.
Nam quid rubra iuvant fulgentibus aequora conchis?

Lucio, I have no ambition to best Maeonides, to best Maro. It is enough if I gain my repute from love. What will Aeacides profit me, what wary Ulysses, what pious Aeneas, or the boy Ascanius? Those matters let others sing whose Muse, glutted with triumphs, bears their wide-ranging reputation from their tomb to the stars. 30

Let me but enclose you with eager arms, and seize lingering kisses with hoped for slowness. With the lamp near, let me admire your limbs and weave the exquisite blandishments of night, let me cradle my hands and my face in your arms, and often warm your weariness in my embrace. But why do I, poor fickle creature, fashion empty dreams which perhaps no day will bring? Happy the man who has been able to prevail upon his pitiless girl, and to grasp the joys of yearned-for union. Day and night he croons of his loves, and recalls the stolen pleasures of his Venus. His hair drenched in a flood of perfume, he strokes her tender flank as night lends help. In his mistress's embrace he recalls the first flames of their passion that golden Love lightly fans with his wings. He desires no fleeces that whiten in the forests of the Ethiopians, no wool bloodied with Sidonian red. Within himself he owns whatever is brought from the dusky Indians, himself owns your banks, gold-bearing Hermus, and whatever harvest the Mede reaps from his redolent fields, and the Arabian, scorched by the unrelenting Sun. 35 40 45 50

We wretched lovers are not tormented for gold or for jewels. 55 He who can persuade his mistress will be rich. I will be rich beyond others if, my life, though impoverished and an exile in an unknown land, I lay claim to your good will. For of what avail are seas red with glittering shells, or the many acres that the dark-

60   Aut quae multa niger rura Sabaeus arat?
       Quidve torus prodest, pluma spectandus et ostro,
         si non est gremio cara puella meo?
       Si trahere infelix inter suspiria noctem
         cogor, et aeternos esse, negare, Deos?
65   Num me neglectis devovit saga sepulcris?
         Num rumpunt somnos carmen, et herba meos?
       Carmen inaccessa traducit ab ilice glandes.
         Carmen nocturnae supprimit ora canis.
       Carmen et informi pallentem sanguine Solem
70   inficit, et Lunae sistit euntis equos.
       Quid queror infelix? utinam mihi sola nocerent
         carmina, nec nostro pectore inesset Amor.
       Ille vel Aeaeae superat cantamina Circes,
         ille vel Aemoniis nata venena iugis.
75   Parce, puer; non vana queror: tu vulnere nostro
         crescis, et exsultas, saeve, cruore meo.
       Quod si te nostrae ceperunt taedia vitae,
         ne cesset, quaeso, funeris atra dies.

II. Ad Joannem Pardum Hispanum

Parde, decus patriae, spes maxima, Parde, tuorum,
       atque idem Hispani gloria rara soli,
quem iuvat immensi causas exquirere mundi,
       primaque constanti corpora iuncta fide:
5   an magnum aeterno volvatur numine caelum,
       an propria hoc ingens mole laboret opus;
cur salsi fluctus, cur ignibus aestuet Aetna,
       cur vomat epotas vasta Charybdis aquas;
unde nitor stellis, cur nox maiorve, minorve:
10   cur non ipsa suo lumine Luna micet.
Felix, caelestes cui fas nunc scandere sedes:

skinned Sabaean ploughs? What use a couch remarkable for its 60
down or for its purple, unless a dear girl rests in my lap, if, ill-
fated, I am compelled to draw out the night amid sighs, and to
deny the gods their immortality?

Surely a hag hasn't cursed me, has she? Does a magic song or 65
potion break my sleep? Song draws down acorns from the remote
oak, song stifles the howling of the dog at night. Song also dyes
the pallid Sun with unsightly blood and halts the horses of the
Moon in her course. Why do I complain in my misfortune? 70
Would that only song did me harm, and that Love wasn't housed
in my breast! He surpasses the incantations of Aeaean Circe, he
surpasses the poisons grown on the ridges of Haemonia. Spare
me, boy. My laments are not empty. You grow through my wound-
ing and, savage creature, you glory in my blood. But if weariness of 75
my life has gripped you, I pray, may the black day of my death not
come slowly.

II. To Giovanni Pardo of Spain

Pardo, ornament of your fatherland, Pardo, highest hope of your
people, and also unique glory of the country of Spain, you whom
it delights to investigate the principles of our boundless universe
and the first bodies joined in enduring trust, or whether heaven's
grandeur turns through an immortal Power, or this enormous 5
edifice toils by its own mass, why the seas are of salt, why Etna
blazes with fire, why huge Charybdis spews forth her swallowed
waters, whence the stars' brilliance, why the night is longer or
shorter, why the Moon doesn't shine with her own light. Happy, 10
since you are allowed now to scale the dwellings of heaven: may

in queis post obitum fata manere sinant.
At nos per silvas, et sordida rura capellas
versamus, quando Phyllis amare iubet.
15 Et teneris nostros ulmis incidimus ignes,
quos legat errantum coetus Hamadryadum.
Et nunc capreolos, et nunc venamur onagros,
interdum saevas fallimus arte feras.
Saepe iuvat pictas visco captare volucres;
20 nec Satyris ipso cedimus aucupio.
Quod mihi si liceat tenui revocare cicuta
Trinacrii niveas upilionis oves,
rura colam semper: populi valeatis, et urbes;
rura dabunt oculis grata theatra meis.
25 Illic gramineas, pastorum bella, palaestras
adspiciam, et celeri praemia parta pede.
Nec me poeniteat sudibus certare colurnis,
aut armare cavis pectora corticibus.
Pugnabunt tauri, pugnabunt cornibus hirci;
30 victores molli cespite serta ferent.
Plenaque pellitus lustrabit ovilia pastor,
ponet et agricolis rustica liba Deis.
Stabunt capripedes abiegno robore Fauni,
stabit et indocta falce dolata Pales.
35 Quorum solemnes ictus cadet agnus ad aras,
ictus ut innumeras expiet agnus oves.
Tum milium, et niveo statuet fumantia lacte
pocula, votivas concipietque preces.
Et ter transiliet flammantes potus aristas,
40 ter quoque non tardo rustica turba pede.
Dii facite, inter oves, interque armenta canendo
deficiam, et silvis me premat atra dies,
ut me non docta deploret pastor avena,
utque sub umbrosa contumuler platano.

the fates grant you to lodge among them after your death. But we maneuver our goats through woods and ugly fields, since Phyllis commands our love. And we carve our ardors on tender elms for the band of roaming Hamadryads to read. And now we hunt roe deer, now onagers, and on occasion we deceive wild beasts by our skill. Often it is our pleasure to catch speckled birds with lime, and in the art of fowling we do not yield to the Satyrs. But if on my slender reed I could conjure up the snow-white sheep of the Trinacrian herdsman, I would always dwell in the countryside. Farewell, peoples and cities. The countryside will offer delightful displays for my eyes.

There I will gaze at wrestling on the grass—the wars of shepherds—and prizes won by swiftness of foot. Nor should I object to vying with hazel stakes or arming my chest with hollow cork. Bulls will clash, goats will clash with their horns. On the soft grass the winners will wear garlands. The fleece-clad shepherd will survey his folds packed to the full and will set out crude cakes to the country gods. Goat-footed Fauns of fir will keep watch, Pales will watch, carved with unskilled knife. A lamb will fall, struck before customary altars, a lamb struck to purify sheep without number. Then he will put out millet and beakers brimming with snowy milk, and he will pronounce votive prayers. Drunk, he will leap three times through the burning stalks, three times, too, will the rustic throng with speeding foot.

Gods, see to it that I reach my end while singing among sheep and cattle, and that the black day overwhelm me in the woods, so that the shepherd laments me on untaught reed and that I may be buried beneath the shady plane-tree. May grazing goats pay hom-

45 Ossaque pascentes venerentur nostra capellae:
    nec procul a tumulo candida balet ovis.
Exsultent alii Panchaeo munere Manes,
    et quaerant Pariis marmora caesa iugis.
Mi sat erit, veteres recolat si Phyllis amores,
50   conserat et vernas ante sepulcra rosas.

III. Ad amicam

Nulla meos poterit mulier praevertere sensus,
    ipsa licet caelum linquat, et astra Venus.
Tu puero teneris ignis mihi primus ab annis:
    ultima tu tremulo flamma futura seni.
5 Iam sanxere semel nos inter foedera divi,
    foedera ad extremos non solvenda rogos,
ut si nostra tuo superesset funere vita,
    (dii tamen in ventos omen abire sinant)
ipse ego composito venerarer operta sepulcro
10   ossa, ferens moesta tura, merumque manu.
Umbrarumque sacer custos, tumulique sacerdos
    concinerem querula tristia verba lyra.
Nec me complexa quisquam divelleret urna,
    quin cineri moriens oscula summa darem.
15 At si, quod potius cupio, tibi fata dedissent,
    lumina formosa condere nostra manu:
tunc, mihi cum caros vultus spectare liceret,
    atque anima tecum iam fugiente loqui,
ipsa meos tumulo Manes laniata vocares,
20   inque tuo legeres ossa minuta sinu:
flebilis et longos scindens ad busta capillos,
    clamares nomen iam moritura meum.
Tum cineri, et mutae persolvens iusta favillae,
    mixta dares rutilis lilia cana rosis.

age to my bones, and may a white sheep bleat not far from the   45
tomb. Let other funerals boast of gifts from Panchaia and claim
marbles cut from the ridges of Paros. It will be enough for me if
Phyllis recalls our loves of old and plants spring roses before my
grave.   50

III. To His Mistress

No woman will be able to draw away my affection, though Venus
herself depart from the heavens and the stars. From my tender
years of boyhood you were my first flame, you will be the final
glow of my trembling old age. Once, then, the gods ratified the
compact between us, a compact not to be broken until the con-   5
cluding funeral pyre, so that, if my life were to survive your death
(but may the gods let the omen vanish into the winds!), I myself
would offer homage to the bones buried in your well-built tomb,
carrying incense and wine in my sorrowful hand. As sacred guard- 10
ian of your shade and priest of your tomb, I would sing sad notes
on the complaining lyre. Nor would anyone tear me away from
embracing your urn without my giving a last kiss to your ashes as I
died.

But if, as I prefer, the fates had granted that you close my eyes 15
with your lovely hand, then, while I could gaze at your dear face
and speak with you as my soul fled, torn by grief you would call
on my shade in the grave and collect my tiny bones in your lap.
Weeping and tearing your hair at my tomb, even on the verge of   20
death you would call out my name. Then, after granting their due
to the ashes and silent embers, you would bestow white lilies
mixed with red roses. In your grief you would yearn to spend your

25   Illic moesta dies, illic consumere noctes
          optares, nec te vinceret alter amor.
      Sed memor usque viri, canis veneranda capillis,
          adferres tremula munera cara manu.
      O mihi, dum tales tumulo reddantur honores,
30   tam lentam Lachesis scindat avara colum!
      Non ut nostra novos Arabum bibat urna liquores,
          ustus et Assyrio spiret odore cinis:
      aut ut clara mei notescat fama sepulcri,
          altaque marmoreus sidera tangat apex;
35   sed magis ut liceat longas audire querelas,
          et gerere e lacrimis serta rigata tuis.
      Tunc ego Lethaeae spatiatus in aggere ripae,
          qua nitet obtuso lumine falsa dies,
      quaque levis casiae nemus, ambrosiaeque virentis,
40   et fortunatos abluit unda greges:
      dulcia praeteritae repetens insomnia vitae,
          ostendam Elysiis tot mea dona choris.
      Felicesque animas inter felicior ipse
          excipiam plausus lata per arva novos.
45   Atque aliquis comitum, laetusque hilarisque recentes
          sparget humi flores, et mihi serta feret.
      Nec contentus eo, fidos extollet amores,
          narrabitque aliis de pietate tua.
      Sed quoniam tenerae vernant nunc laeta iuventae
50   tempora, et amplexus iungere fata sinunt,
      dulcia lascivo iungamus gaudia lecto:
          iam properat mortis panda senecta comes.
      Iam properant rugaeque graves, et serior aetas:
          nec dabitur molli ludere posse toro.
55   Interea cupidis nectamus colla lacertis:

days there, to spend your nights. No other passion would win you   25
over. But, ever mindful of your lover, worthy of respect with your
white hair, you would bring costly offerings in your trembling
hand. O, provided that such honors be granted to my grave, may
greedy Lachesis cut my all-too-slow thread, not so that my urn   30
may drink fresh perfumes from the Arabs and my burnt ashes
breathe Assyrian fragrance, or that my celebrated sepulcher grow
in fame and its marble peak touch the lofty stars, but rather that it
might hear your sustained complaints and bear garlands bedewed   35
with your tears. Then, wandering along the barrow of Lethe's
bank, where counterfeit day gleams with blunted light and where
the wave refreshes the tender plantings of marjoram and of green
ambrosia and the crowds of the blessed, as I recall the sweet   40
dreams of my bygone life I will display to the Elysian throngs my
many gifts. Among the happy souls, I myself, happier still, will re-
ceive new acclaim throughout the broad fields. And, glad and joy-
ful, someone of the company will scatter fresh flowers on the   45
ground, and bring me garlands. Not content with that, he will cel-
ebrate the faith of our love, and tell others the tale of your fidelity.

But since now the glad times of our tender youth remain green
and the fates allow us to unite in embrace, let us join in the sweet
pleasures of the lusty couch. Already bent old age, crony of death,   50
hastens. Already deep wrinkles hasten and the time that is too
late, and we won't have the chance to frolic on the soft bed. Mean-
while let us twine our necks with desiring arms. Soon the final
hour, when it wishes, will undo the two of us. Gods, see to it that   55

ultima iam solvet, cum volet, hora duos.
Dii facite, haec longos maneat spes certa per annos,
candidus et pennis omina firmet Amor.

*IV. Ad Lucinam, parturiente Cornelia Piccolominea,
Antonii Garlonii Allifarum domini coniuge*

Affer opem tenerae tandem, Lucina, puellae:
auxilio, digna est, quam tueare tuo.
Te vocat, et madidis solam suspirat ocellis,
et roseo tacitas fundit ab ore preces.
5 Illa quidem insueto languet male firma dolore,
vixque potest longae tot mala ferre morae.
At tu, diva, veni, tecumque unguenta repostae
pyxidis, et siqua est quae iuvet herba, feras.
Sic flentis miseros iuvenis compescere questus,
10 sic una poteris sorte levare duos.
Lucis adest dea magna: metum iam comprime, Garlon;
non frustra est lacrimis illa vocata tuis.
Da costum, myrrhamque focis, quaeque orbe remoto
cinnama per rubras navita vectat aquas.
15 Ipse deam venerare, sacras proiectus ad aras,
et Genio annosum saepe refunde merum.
Sed trepidi cessere metus, cessere querelae:
iam parit adventu tacta puella deae.
Iam puerum est enixa: vides, ut lumine matrem
20 exprimat? En, tenero quantus in ore decor.
Salve, parve puer, cui iam felicia rident
saecula; cui pharetram sponte remittit Amor.
Nam sive auratis humeros armare sagittis,
seu iuvet accensas sollicitare faces,
25 seu potius iactare leves pueriliter alas,
et dare neglectas post tua terga comas,

this hope rest sure for length of years, and that Love, his wings gleaming, affirm the omens.

IV. To Lucina, at the confinement of Cornelia Piccolomini, wife of Antonio Garlon, Prince of Alife

Bring at last your aid, Lucina, to a tender maid: she is worthy of being protected by your support. She invokes you and sighs for you alone with her weeping eyes, and pours forth silent prayers from her rosy lips. Her strength gone, she is feeble from unaccustomed pain and indeed can scarcely endure so many pangs from 5 the long delay. Come, goddess, come, and carry with you ointments from a casket stored away and any herb that might avail, if any there be. In this way you will be able to check the sad groans of the young man, in this way by one grant you will be able to bring relief to two. 10

The great goddess of light is near. Quell now your fear, Garlon. She has not been invoked in vain by your tears. On the hearth offer spikenard and myrrh and twigs of cinnamon that the sailor ships through the red waters from a world away. You yourself, prostrate before the holy altars, worship the goddess, and often 15 pour aged wine to your Genius.

But your anxious worries have come to an end, your laments have ended. Now, touched by the goddess's arrival, the girl gives birth. Now she has borne a son. You see how he resembles his mother in his eyes? Behold the grace spread across his tender features. Hail, tiny child, for whom now the happy ages smile, for 20 whom Love willingly foregoes his quiver. For whether it should please you to equip your shoulders with gilded arrows or to stir the flames of your torches, whether instead, like a boy, to flap your nimble wings and to toss your unkempt locks behind your back, 25 who would not consider you reared in the valleys of Paphos or the

quis te non Paphiis eductum vallibus, aut quis
    Idaliae puerum non putet esse deae?
Vive, precor, blandumque oculis ridere parenti
30   assuesce, et dulces disce movere iocos.

V. Ad Iulium senensem, exulem

Cum mihi languentes dolor oppugnaret ocellos,
    cogeret et tristi solvere verba sono:
ingratos inter gemitus, moestasque querelas
    allata est manibus litera missa tuis.
5 Inspexi, agnovique tuas, mea numina, Musas,
    Pieriosque haustus, Castaliumque decus.
Poscis ut iratum placent mea carmina Phoebum,
    et flectant duras ad tua vota Deas.
Non hoc ingenium, non haec facundia nostra est:
10   i, precor, atque alio flumine pelle sitim.
Ille mihi faciles iampridem denegat aures,
    et vetat argutae tangere fila lyrae.
Nec mihi iam solito latices de fonte ministrat,
    nec docet optatos Calliopea choros.
15 Quid petis extinctam dilapso a torre favillam?
    Quid miser a nostro vulnere quaeris opem?
Iam tibi felici decurrunt carmina vena,
    et rapit ad patrium te tua Musa decus.
Ipsa mihi visa est, te lamentante, Thalia
20   ingemere, et tristi Delius ore queri:
qualis Strimonias olim cum fleret ad undas
    Orpheus indignis vocibus Eurydicen:
qui cantu Ismarii gelidis in rupibus Haemi
    adtonuit quercus, adtonuitque feras,
25 saxaque Bistoniis deduxit montibus, et te
    currentem adstrictis, Hebre, repressit aquis.

child of the Idalian goddess? Live on, I pray, and grow accustomed
to smile gently on your mother with your eyes, and learn to enjoy
the sweetness of play.   30

V. To Giulio of Siena, exile

When grief was assaulting my enfeebled eyes and forcing me to
loose words of sadness, amid my unhappy groans and sad laments,
a letter was delivered, sent by your hands. I have examined and
recognized your Muses, my divinities, and draughts from Pieria
and Castalian grace. You ask that my songs calm an angry Apollo   5
and incline the pitiless goddesses toward your prayers. This talent,
this eloquence isn't mine. Be on your way, I pray, and quench your
thirst at another stream. For a long time the one you speak of has   10
denied me open ears and forbidden me to touch the strings of the
melodious lyre. Calliope no longer either furnishes waters to me
from her usual source or teaches the dances I have desired. What
do you seek from a torch that has lapsed into dead embers? Why,   15
poor creature, do you call for help from my hurt?

  Your songs yet issue from thriving store, and your Muse still
tugs you to your ancestral glory. While you were sorrowing,
Thalia herself seemed to me to keen, and the Delian to lament in
sad voice, as when long ago Orpheus, by the waves of the   20
Strymon, wept for Eurydice with outraged cries. Amid the chill
rocks of Ismarian Haemus he spellbound the oaks, spellbound the
beasts with his song. He drew down rocks from the Bistonian
mountains, and brought your flow to a stop, Hebrus, by checking   25
your waters.

Scilicet egregios semper Fortuna poetas
    tanget, et ancipiti deprimet usque rota?
Neve sit extremos tantum submotus ad axes
30   ille, Tomitana qui iacet exul humo:
te quoque nunc rigidi premit inclementia fati,
    longius et patria cogit abesse domo.
Sed nisi per magnos quaeratur fama labores,
    omnis in ardentes est abitura rogos.
35 Sic pius Aeneas, sic stirps Laërtis Ulysses
    maius post cineres emeruere decus.
Sic quoque sublatis Tirynthius undique monstris
    visit ab Oetaea regna paterna pyra.
Et te, crede mihi, tot saeva incommoda passum
40   virtus sublimi ducet in astra via.

VI. In funere Sarri Brancatii Lucretia uxor

'Ergo importunae ruperunt stamina Parcae,
    stamina lanifica tam bene ducta colo?
Ergo ego, quae fueram tali modo nupta marito,
    frigida nunc tristi conqueror in thalamo?
5 Quique his dignus erat vitam exhalasse labellis,
    occidit externis advena litoribus?
Felices nimium, fortunataeque sorores,
    quae datis aeternis tura Sabaea focis.
O utinam numquam amplexus, numquam oscula nossem,
10   essem pars vestri nempe ego parva chori.
Care vir, audaci nimium confise iuventae,
    et nimium lacrimis umbra gemenda meis:
quis te tam densos immittere corpus in hostes
    iussit? An ad pugnam non satis unus erat?
15 Me miseram, non ulla tuae te cura puellae,
    non subiit moestae certa ruina domus.

Must we think that fortune will always strike eminent poets
and ever bring them low with the hazards of her wheel? Lest the
only one relegated to the farthest poles be that famous man who
lies an exile in the ground of Tomis, the sternness of unrelenting   30
fate now humiliates you also, and compels you to dwell a far dis-
tance from the home of your fathers. But unless fame be sought
through mighty efforts, it will completely vanish in the flames of
the funeral pyre. So pious Aeneas, so Ulysses, scion of Laërtes,
earned greater acclaim after their deaths. So also the Tirynthian,   35
once he had rid the world of monsters, saw the realm of his father
after the pyre on Oeta. Believe me, after you have endured so
many harsh troubles, Virtue will lead you on its lofty pathway to
the stars.   40

VI. His wife Lucretia speaks of the death of Sarro Brancacci

"Is it true, then, that the relentless Parcae have broken your
threads, threads drawn so well from the spinner's distaff? Is it so,
then, that I, who had just now been married to such a husband,
utter my lament, now cold in my sad marriage-chamber? Has he
died, he who was worthy of breathing forth his life upon these
lips, a stranger on foreign shores? O sisters, fully happy and   5
blessed by fortune, who offer incense from Saba on undying altars,
would that I had never known his embraces, never his kisses: I
would surely be a small part of your chorus.   10

"Dear husband, who trusted too much in the boldness of your
youth, and shade, too much to be wept by my tears, who gave you
the order to plunge your body into the mass of foes? Was not sin-
gle combat sufficient? Wretched me, no thought of your girl oc-
curred to you, nor of the sure ruin of your mournful house. It was   15
your custom to take an oath on our blessed nuptial rites, on the

Tu mihi per sanctos solitus iurare hymenaeos,
    per non laedendi foedera coniugii,
te non immemorem carae fore coniugis umquam,
20   etsi Lethaeus tingeret ora liquor.
Quin ipsa admonui, ne sic violentus in arma
    irrueres: eheu quo, violente, ruis?
Quo raperis? Quo iam nostri tibi cura recessit?
    An potes uxoris non meminisse tuae?
25 Vix equidem credo, quamvis heu credere cogar,
    tam cito pectoribus me cecidisse tuis.
Sed cecidi: sic sors tulit impia, nullaque pro me
    vota salutares demeruere deos.
Hectora sic coniux, sic coniux flevit Achillem,
30   sic misera extinctum Laodamia virum.
Nunc mea virginitas, quando inlibata remansit,
    servetur cineri non violanda tuo.'

VII. *Ad divum Iacobum Picenum*

Sancte senex, quem nec sceleris contagia nostri,
    nec pessum vitiis saecla dedere suis,
aequasti magnos qui paupertate triumphos,
    tantus amor niveae simplicitatis erat.
5 Silva tibi sedes, viridique e cespite lectus,
    explebant mensas amnis, et herba tuas.
Talis erat priscis victus mortalibus olim,
    sed priscis tantum vivere cura fuit.
At te diversos naturae expendere casus
10   iuvit, et instantes divum aperire metus.
Submotumque oculis animo percurrere caelum:
    quasque tenes sedes, mente adiisse prius,
noscere praeterea cunctarum exordia rerum,
    quod vix humanae conditionis erat.

compact of our sacrosanct marriage, that you would never forget
your dear wife, though the water of Lethe moistened your lips. In- 20
deed I myself warned you not to rush to arms with such violence:
alas, man of violence, where are you rushing? Toward what place
are you carried away? Whither has your thought of me now van-
ished? Can you have no memory of your wife? Myself I can
scarcely believe, though, alas, I am compelled to believe, that I fell 25
so swiftly from your heart. But I have fallen. Such my wrongful
destiny has brought about, and no prayers on his behalf have won
the favor of saving gods. Thus his wife wept for Hector, his wife
wept for Achilles, thus wretched Laodamia for her dead husband.
Now let my virginity, since it remained intact, be preserved, never 30
to be violated, for your ashes."

VII. To San Giacomo Piceno

Holy old man, whom neither the taint of our sin nor the times
have ruined by their faults, who found poverty the equal of great
triumphs — so great was your love of snow-white simplicity — the
woods were your dwelling, your bed was of green sod, the stream 5
and grass supplied your meals. Once upon a time such was the life
of ancient man, but for the ancients the only care was to stay alive.
But it pleased you to weigh the differing accidents of nature, and
to expound the fearsome presences of the gods, to explore in your 10
mind a heaven far removed from our eyes and to approach ahead
of time in your thought the abode you now possess, to learn, be-
sides, the origins of all things — something scarcely available to our
human lot. Great the task: how in the first beginning of the bur-

15 Magnum opus, ut prima surgentis origine mundi,
  omnia sint senis edita luciferis:
 utque Pater sancta demum cessare quiete
  perfecto artifices iusserit orbe manus.
 His addis cultusque pios, ritusque verendos,
20 cunctaque legifero tradita sacra duci;
 quaeque suis castae saeclis cecinere Sibyllae,
  quaeque sacer vatum spiritus ore refert:
 sidereos partus, demissaque pignora caelo,
  atque inopes cunas, stramineumque torum,
25 speratumque diu terris, caeloque probatum
  verum hominem, verum mente, animoque Deum,
 hinc et supplicium infandum, atque opprobria mortis,
  claraque de Stygia ducta tropaea domo:
 denique ut ad patrem populo spectante suorum
30 cesserit, igniferis praesideatque locis:
 quantaque nos maneant promissae gaudia vitae:
  quantaque venturae gloria lucis erit.
 Miremur, tibi si placidi penetrale Tonantis,
  et patet immensi regia clara poli,
35 cum tantum his superas meritis sit scandere in arces,
  qua plaga securum lactea monstrat iter?
 Scilicet inde datur terras spectare iacentes,
  et circumfusi brachia curva maris,
 solis et ardentes radios, lunaeque recursus,
40 qualiter et pacta stent elementa fide:
 nec minus aeternis niteant ut sidera flammis:
  et peragant varias noxque, diesque vices.
 Felix, qui nostras potuisti linquere curas,
  et procul humanas despicere illecebras.
45 Felices, qui te colles videre loquentem,
  quaeque tibi gratos praebuit herba toros:
 quaeque arbor, rupesve sacra te fovit in umbra,

geoning universe everything was brought forth in six days, and 15
how the Father, after the world was finished, commanded his skill-
ful hands at last to stop in holy rest. To this you add the pious
offices and worshipful rites, and all the holy duties handed down
to the law-giving leader, and what the chaste Sibyls sang to their 20
generations, and what the Holy Spirit tells through the mouths of
the prophets, the birth in the stars and pledge sent down from the
sky, the meager cradle and bed of straw, true man, true God in
mind and soul, long awaited on earth, commended in heaven, then 25
the unspeakable torture and shame of death, and the bright tro-
phies borne from the Stygian dwelling, finally how, with a crowd
of his followers looking on, he departed to his Father and reigns in
the fire-bearing regions, and what great joys await us in the prom- 30
ised life and what great glory there will be in the light to come.

Should we marvel at how the sanctuary of the serene
Thunderer and the bright palace of the enormous sky lie open for
you, since only for these merits is it possible to scale the lofty cita-
dels where the Milky Way offers a safe pathway? For sure it is 35
granted you from there to behold the earth lying below, and the
curving arms of the embracing sea, and the burning rays of the
sun, and the moon's returning courses, and how the elements per-
sist in trusted assurance, and also how the stars glimmer with un- 40
dying fires, and how night and day accomplish their changes.

Happy you who were able to abandon our concerns, and from
afar to look down on the temptations of mankind. Happy the hills
that beheld you preaching, and the grass that furnished you with 45
pleasing couches, and the tree or crag that cherished you in its
holy shade, and the urn that now holds your ashes. Indeed,

et quae nunc Manes continet urna tuos.
Nam licet incultis fuerit tibi vita sub antris,
50   nunc pedibus data sunt astra terenda tuis.
Attamen o dic, sancte pater, dic, addite caelo
    gloria, dic, patriae fama, decusque tuae:
ecquid te solitis mulcet sapientia chartis,
    mollis ubi Elysium concitat aura nemus?
55 An iuvat aurata meditantem carmina canna,
    nectere purpurea tempora cana rosa?
An mage virgineis sedet invigilare choreis:
    cum deceat caelo, quicquid in orbe libet?
An potius, toto superum spectante senatu,
60   diluis aethereo crimina nostra foro?
Denique quicquid agis, nitidi novus incola caeli,
    pectoribus nostris non leve numen eris.

VIII. Ad Petrum de Roccaforti,
maximum regis Galliarum cancellarium

Quod pectus tibi forte, quod ardua pectoris arx est,
    quod forti dignum pectore nomen habes,
quod leges sua iura tenent te vindice, quodque
    omnia virtuti pervia facta tuae:
5 autumni sedem, chelasque Astraea reliqui,
    advenique tuos, noster alumne, lares.
In cunis ego te, si nescis, sedula fovi;
    reptasti gremio sarcina grata meo.
Ipsa tuos finxi mores, animumque, manusque:
10   ingeniumque sagax, iudiciumque dedi.
Hinc nostri cultusque frequens, optandaque rerum
    cognitio, hinc fidei nomina tanta tuae.
Ad te igitur duplices subnixo poplite palmas,
    insuetis tendo sollicitata malis.

though your life was passed beneath rough caves, now it is the
stars that are granted for your feet to tread.   50

Nevertheless tell us, tell us, holy father, glory added to heaven,
tell us, fame and ornament of your fatherland: does wisdom
soothe you with her accustomed pages, where the soft breeze stirs
the grove of Elysium? Or is it your pleasure, as you ponder songs
on your gilded reed, to wreathe your graying temples with the pur-   55
ple rose? Or rather is it your determination to keep watch at the
dances of virgins, since what gives you pleasure on earth is suitable
for heaven? Or instead, while the whole senate of supernal powers
looks on, are you annulling our sins in the celestial forum? In   60
short, whatever your concern, new denizen of gleaming heaven, in
our hearts you will be an august divinity.

VIII. To Pierre de Rochefort, Grand Chancellor of the King of France

"Because your heart is stalwart, because your heart's citadel is tow-
ering, because you bear a name worthy of a stalwart heart, because
laws preserve their rights through your championship, because all
deeds are accessible to your virtue, I, Astraea, have abandoned my   5
autumnal setting and the Claws, and have arrived at your house,
my protégé. I myself, in case you don't know, eagerly cherished you
even in the cradle. You snuggled, a pleasing burden in my lap. I
fashioned your character, your intelligence, your skills. I gave you
keen wit and judgment. From this comes your continuous worship   10
of us, your welcome understanding of existence, from this the
great repute of your loyalty. And so, beset by unprecedented trou-
bles, on bended knee I stretch forth both my palms to you.

15   Ne patiare meas Latio languescere vires:
      pendet ab auxilio spes mea tota tuo.
    Deprimor audaces inter derisa ministros,
      nec fas ingenuum tollere ad astra caput.
    Quodque diu partum est virtute, et fortibus armis
20   imperium, foedae servit avaritiae.
    Nec mirum, vestro tantum cum distet ab orbe,
      terraque censura sit procul illa tua.
    Quis credat? Tectis cives pelluntur avitis,
      adrogat iniustas dum sibi fiscus opes.
25   Fiscus opes miserorum: hoc est, heu, parcere victis?
      Hoc est Ausonio reddere iura solo?
    Cogitur infelix alienas ire per oras
      nobilitas, patriis exspoliata bonis.
    Culpaturque fides domino servata priori,
30   et maris, et terrae non labefacta minis.
    Scilicet est crimen duram contemnere mortem,
      scilicet est reges crimen amare suos.
    O bene fortunae memores, quicumque superbas
      gentibus a victis abstinuere manus.
35   Nam quamvis saevos illectet praeda tyrannos:
      magnanimos reges gloria sola iuvat.
    Delentur nullos hominum benefacta per annos;
      quaque licet faciunt nos ratione Deos.
    At siquis serae spernit praeconia famae,
40   quercubus alpinis adnumerare potes.
    Ergo tu, regem cui fas lenire potentem,
      da desideriis vela secunda meis.
    Effice, iustitiae soliti reddantur honores;
      dignus es altricem qui tueare tuam:
45   sed soror ut nostros aequet Clementia fasces:
      qua sine, dura nimis, difficilisque vocer.
    O decus, o lapsi spes constantissima saecli,

"Do not allow my strength to waste away in Latium. All my   15
hope hangs on your help. An object of ridicule, I am humbled
amid presumptuous ministers, nor do I have the right to raise my
noble head to the stars. The realm that long ago was won by cour-
age and brave arms is a slave to foul avarice. And no wonder, since   20
it is so distant from your region and that land is far from your
oversight. Who would believe it? Citizens are driven from their
ancestral dwellings while the public treasury lays claim to unjust
riches. The riches of the downtrodden as the treasury: alas, is this
to spare the conquered? Is this to restore rights to the soil of   25
Ausonia? The unfortunate nobility, plundered of its fathers'
wealth, is driven to make its way through foreign lands. Loyalty
maintained for a former master, unshaken by threats on sea or on
land, suffers blame. It is seen as a crime to despise merciless death,   30
seen a crime to love one's kings! O duly mindful of fortune are
those who have held off haughty hands from conquered peoples!
For although booty attracts savage tyrants, glory alone brings plea-   35
sure to great-souled kings. No stretch of years blots out man's no-
ble deeds. In every possible way they make us gods. If anyone
scorns the plaudits of late reputation, you can number him among
Alpine oaks!   40

"And so you, whose right it is to turn a powerful king toward
leniency, grant favorable sailing to my desires. See to it that her
accustomed honors are restored to Justice—you are worthy to
protect your nurse—but also that our sister Clemency, without
whom I might be called too unyielding and intractable, shares
equally in our power. O our glory, O securest hope of our fallen   45

o vir fortuna fortior ipse tua.
Sic tibi contingat Solyma de gente triumphum,
50   captaque per nostros signa videre duces.
Sic Rhodanum Nilo spectes dare iura subacto:
    perque Araris ripas plurima laurus eat.
Hoc ego te, mecum hoc Phoebus, doctaeque Sorores,
    hoc pietas, hoc ius nobilitasque rogant.

IX. Ioviani Pontani de studiis suis et libris

Qui primus patrios potuit liquisse penates,
    et maris, et longae taedia ferre viae,
quem non moesta domus, quem non revocare parentes,
    non potuit fusis blanda puella comis;
5   impius, et scopulis, et duro robore natus,
    atque inter tigres editus ille fuit.
Non mihi circumstat solidum praecordia ferrum,
    nec riget in nostro pectore dura silex,
ut possim dulcesque lares, limenque puellae
10   linquere, et ignoto quaerere in orbe domum.
Sed Phoebi sacros cogor lustrare recessus,
    vocalemque undam, Thespiadumque choros:
ut fugiam nigras supremo in funere flammas,
    et volitem populi docta per ora mei.
15   Meque inter claros attollat fama poetas,
    nec rapiat nomen nigra favilla meum;
et nostro celebrata superbiat umbra sepulcro,
    spernat et e Pariis marmora caesa iugis:
non tamen ut magni tumulum tentare Maronis
20   audeat, aut tantum speret habere decus.
Sed quis tam niveis vellat mea colla lacertis?
    Quis vetet optato membra fovere sinu?
An tanti fuerit sacro Parnassus hiatu,

age, O hero yourself stronger than your fortune, may it thus befall you to see a triumph over the people of Jerusalem and their standards seized by our captains. Thus may you behold the Rhône 50 prescribing laws for the conquered Nile, and many a laurel making its way along the banks of the Saône. This do I ask of you, this Phoebus and the learned Sisters along with me, this, piety, this, justice and nobility."

IX. *On the pursuits and books of Gioviano Pontano*

The man who was capable of leaving behind his ancestral home and withstanding the trials of the sea and of the long road, whom neither his house in mourning, nor his parents, nor his charming girl, her hair streaming, could call back: impious was he, sprung from crags and hard oak, and born from among tigers. No rigid 5 iron surrounds my heart, no hard flint stiffens in my breast, so that I could leave behind my sweet household gods and the threshold of my girl, and seek an abode in an unknown world. I 10 am constrained to haunt the holy retreats of Phoebus, the articulate spring and the dances of the Thespian sisters, so that I might escape the black flames of my final obsequies and gain flight through the learned lips of my people, that my renown might raise me to the company of famous poets, and the black ash not snatch 15 away my reputation, that my eminent shade might grow prideful within the tomb and scorn marble cut from the ridges of Paros, though not that it should dare to challenge the sepulcher of mighty Maro or hope to possess such great glory. 20

But who could tear my neck from your snow-bright arms? Who might forbid me to warm my limbs in your longed-for bosom? Will Parnassus with its holy ravine have been worth

perque suas passim templa habitata deas,
25   ut tibi sit nitidos lacrimis corrumpere ocellos,
      discessumque fleas, cara puella, meum?
    Ah pereat, quicumque leves sectatur honores,
      et sequitur famae nomina vana suae.
    Tecum ego nocturnis dubitem cessare choreis?
30   Tecum ego conspersa gaudia inire rosa?
    Deductumque levi crinem perfundere amomo?
      Et noctem insolitis ducere blanditiis?
    Scilicet et Turcas Pontanus in aequora classes,
      Alfonsi et fortes ducat in arma manus,
35   qui nunc nascentis canit incunabula mundi,
      aureaque aetherea sidera fixa domo;
    utque imbres, lapidesque pluant, ut nubibus ignes
      exsiliant, salsas ut mare volvat aquas;
    Hesperidumque hortos, excussaque poma draconi,
40   rusticaque ad primos munera missa toros,
    delicias, Lepidina, tuas, resonansque vicissim
      pastorum argutis carmen arundinibus:
    qualiter et fulvis radiet Sertorius armis,
      et Pompeianus proelia tentet eques:
45   audeat arguto neu quis contendere versu,
      ille vel aeterno digna Marone sonat.
    Te pater irriguis audit Sebethus in antris,
      iurgia ad ingratas dum iacis ipse fores.
    Inde vocas sacrum festas Hymenaeon ad aras,
50   optati referens foedera coniugii:
    utque tuis primum surgens complexibus uxor,
      visa sit erepta virginitate queri.
    Felix, qui fidos expertus coniugis ignes,
      vidisti sobolis pignora certa tuae:
55   naeniolasque rudes cecinisti, et blanda parentis
      oscula, et ad cunas murmura nata suas.

enough, and the shrines everywhere occupied by their goddesses, for you to mar your shimmering eyes with tears and weep, dear 25 girl, for my departure? Ah, may he perish who pursues insubstantial honors and follows after the hollow celebrations of his own renown. Should I hesitate to dally with you in nightlong dances, to enter on delights with you, at the scattering of a rose, to pour your 30 cascading hair with delicate perfume and to draw out the night with unaccustomed pleasures?

Certainly let Pontano draw the Turkish armadas into the seas and the brave squadrons of Alfonso into the fight, Pontano, who now is singing of the infancy of the newborn world, and the 35 golden stars secured in their celestial abode, and how showers and meteorites rain, how fires leap forth from clouds, how the sea rolls salty waves, and the gardens of the Hesperides, and the apples shaken from the dragon, and primitive gifts bestowed on the first marriages, and the song of shepherds re-echoing in turn your plea- 40 sures, Lepidina, on clear-voiced reeds, and how Sertorius shines in panoply of gold and how Pompey's cavalry undertakes its battles. Let no one dare vie with him in clear verse: he sings what is wor- 45 thy even of undying Maro.

Father Sebeto gives ear in his dewy caves while you hurl curses against unresponsive doors. Then you call holy Hymenaeus to the festive altars, telling of the compact of longed-for marriage, and 50 how your wife, rising for the first time from your embraces, appeared to lament the taking of her virginity. Happy you, having experienced the faithful passion of your wife, for beholding the sure guarantees of your offspring: you have sung simple lullabies, and their parent's loving kisses, and the cooings at their cradles. 55

Felix excultum torsit quae Fannia vatem,
    quaeque illi regnum Cinnama subripuit.
Quamvis dissidii leges patiantur amaras,
60   spectabunt cineres nomen habere suos.
Eridani post haec sed te quis credat ad amnem
    populea canas fronde ligasse comas?
Et Stellam cecinisse, atque impendisse querelas,
    spectandos cum iam vix daret illa pedes:
65 Baianosque sinus, myrtetaque cognita Nymphis,
    clausaque sulfureis antra recurva iugis:
tum superum laudem, mutisque incisa sepulcris
    nomina, collapsos et reparare rogos:
denique Pindaricosque modos, resonantia plectra,
70   et Methymnaeae fila novasse lyrae.
Cum tamen interea motus, atque agmina regum,
    bellaque Campanae discutis historiae.
Quin et iucundo distringis saecula morsu,
    dum vafer in Stygio disputat amne Charon.
75 Varronisque tui, Nigidique exempla secutus,
    grammaticae haud spretas incipis ire vias.
Carminis hinc numeros nostris depromis ab ausis,
    dignatus pueri verba referre senex.
Quid loquar, ut sacros Mariani exhauriat amnes
80   Aegidius, verum dum canit ore deum?
Aut apta ingratos taxet sub imagine mores
    qui super infusas spernit Asellus aquas?
Te iuvenesque, senesque colunt praecepta ferentem,
    Parthenope spreto quae Cicerone legit:
85 ex adytis quicquid divum sapientia pandit,
    et, Stagira, tui dogmata firma senis.
Quid deceat fortemque virum, quae principis artes,
    largificas praestet quae dare dona manus:
parendi leges quae sint, legesque loquendi:

Happy the Fannia who turned the attention of the refined poet,
and the Cinnama who seized mastery from her. Although they en-
dure the bitter rules of separation, they will behold the reputation
that death brings.   60

But who would believe that after this, by the river Po, you
bound your graying hair with poplar leaves and sang of Stella, and
wasted your laments, since soon she scarcely proffered her feet for
view; and you celebrated the bays at Baiae and its myrtle groves
appreciated by the Nymphs, and its sinuous caves enclosed by sul-   65
furous slopes; then you sang praise of the saints, reviving names
inscribed on silent graves, and pyres fallen in, and at last restored
life to Pindar's measures, his reechoing plectra, and the strings of
the Methymnaean lyre, while in the meantime you also investi-   70
gated the stratagems and armies of kings, and the wars in Cam-
pania's history?

Likewise you challenge your times with light-hearted satire
while artful Charon carries on his debates by the river Styx, and,
following the lead of your Varro and Nigidius, you begin to travel 75
the honored avenues of grammar. Next you bring out the mea-
sures of poetry from the store of our attempts, an ancient deigning
to repeat the words of a child. Why should I tell how Aegidius
drinks up the holy streams of Mariano while from his lips he sings
of the true God, or of how the Ass, who scorns the waters poured 80
over him, censures ungrateful conduct under a suitable guise?
Both young and old revere you as you convey the teachings that
Parthenope reads when Cicero is scorned. Whatever wisdom dis-
closes from the shrines of the gods, and, Stagira, the steady princi- 85
ples of your old man, and what befits a hero, the qualities of a
prince, to give what gifts makes hands generous, what are the rules
for obedience and the rules for conversation, so that the eloquent

90 edat ut argutos lingua diserta sales.
  Quid fortuna homini, quid det prudentia, quantum
    immanes animos incitus ardor agat;
  magnanimique viri quae sint ad singula partes,
    sive colat pacem, seu fera bella gerat.
95 Nec fugis astrorum causas aperire latentes,
    et Ptolemaeaei fata reposta poli.
  Salve, sancte senex, vatum quem rite parentem
    praefecit terris Delius Ausoniis;
  non te Lethaeae carpent oblivia ripae,
100 nec totum in cineres vertet avara dies.
  Nec tibi plebeio ponetur in aggere bustum;
    Niliacas dabitur vincere Pyramidas.
  Quid tibi victrices exspectas, Umbria, palmas?
    Moenibus has patriae rettulit ille meae.
105 Ille suis longum studiis, et laude fruatur;
    me iuvet in dominae consenuisse sinu.

X. Ad Ioannem Sangrium Patricium Neapolitanum,
de suo immaturo obitu

  Si me saevus Amor patriis pateretur in oris
    vivere, vel saltem matre vidente mori,
  ut quae vix uno nunc sunt ingesta libello,
    essent illa suis continuata locis:
5 forsitan immites potuissem temnere Parcas,
    ductaque de pulla tristia pensa colo.
  Nec me plebeio ferret Libitina sepulcro,
    aut raperet nomen nigra favilla meum.
  Nunc cogor dulcesque lacus, et amoena virecta,
10 Pieridumque sacros destituisse choros:
  nec pote, quae primis effudit Musa sub annis,
    emendaturo subdere iudicio.

tongue may voice its trenchant wit, what fortune, what prudence   90
grants a man, how far the quickening of passion can drive brutish
spirits, what is the constitution, detail by detail, of a great-souled
person, whether he cultivates peace or wages fierce wars. Nor do
you avoid explaining the hidden rationale of the stars and the ar-
cane destiny of the Ptolemaic universe.   95

Hail, blessed old man whom the Delian has appointed father of
poets in the land of Ausonia. The forgetfulness of Lethe's bank
will not hold you in its grasp nor will greedy time wholly turn you
to ashes. Nor will your tomb lie within a common mound, but it   100
will be granted to surpass the pyramids of the Nile. Umbria, why
are you waiting for your palms of victory? He has returned them
to the walls of my fatherland. May he long enjoy his pursuits and
his praise. Let my pleasure be to grow old in the lap of my mis-   105
tress.

X. To Giovanni di Sangro, Patrician of Naples, on his own untimely death

If fierce Love had allowed me to survive in the land of my fathers,
or at least to meet death as my mother looked on, so that the proj-
ects, which are now thrust into scarcely a single volume, might be
pursued in their own setting, perhaps I could have scorned the
pitiless Parcae and the sad threads drawn from their dark distaff.   5
Libitina would not place me in a common tomb nor would the
black ash snatch away my name. Now I am compelled to leave be-
hind both the sweet pools, and the lovely stretches of green, and
the holy dances of the Pierian Muses, nor can I submit for your   10
correction and judgment what my Muse poured forth in my young
years. So, alas, so is young grain mowed down in its furrows, so

Sic heu, sic, tenerae sulcis resecantur aristae,
    implumes nido sic rapiuntur aves.
15 Pro superi, tenues ibit Syncerus in auras?
    Nec poterit nigri vincere fata rogi?
At tu, quandoquidem Nemesis iubet, optime Sangri,
    nec fas est homini vincere posse deam,
accipe concussae tabulas, atque arma carinae,
20   naufragiique mei collige relliquias.
Errantesque cie quocumque in litore Manes,
    taliaque in tumulo carmina caede meo:
Actius hic iaceo: spes mecum extincta quiescit:
    solus de nostro funere restat Amor.

XI. In maledicos detractores

Quid ruis in sacros temeraria turba poetas?
    Saevaque mordaci proelia dente moves?
Desine sacrilega convicia fundere lingua,
    desine: pro populo stat Deus ipse suo.
5 Quis novus in furias armat dolor? ite profani,
    ite, nec immeritas conscelerate deas.
An monet hoc Stygiis immersus Scuccha lacunis,
    dum flens Eumenidum verbera torta timet?
Illum olim tinctae iuverunt felle sagittae;
10   nunc miserum facti poenitet usque sui.
Parcite tam cari Manes violare parentis,
    per stupra, et talos, per cyathosque rogo.
Ars sua quemque iuvet: non vos Helicona subire,
    non fas virginei polluere amnis aquam.
15 Scilicet hanc sumpto Ioviani Musa cothurno
    hauriat, et magno digna Marone sonet.
Cui comes intactae lustrans sacraria silvae
    Altilius, docto pectore carmen hiet.

unfledged birds are snatched from the nest. Gods above, will
Syncerus disappear into thin air, and will he not be able to over-   15
come the destiny of the black pyre?

But you, excellent Sangro, since Nemesis gives the order and it
is not right for a man to prevail over a goddess, receive these
planks and tackle from my stricken vessel. Gather up what is left
after my shipwreck, and invoke my spirit as it wanders on what-   20
ever shore, and carve on my tomb such verses:

Here, I, Actius, lie. My hope rests extinguished with me.
Only Love remains after our death.

XI. *Against detractors speaking ill*

Rash throng, why do you descend upon sacred poets and enter
into fierce battles with biting tooth? Stop spreading slander with
your cursed tongues, stop: God himself takes his stand on behalf
of his people. What fresh resentment mobilizes you into frenzy?
Off with you, impious creatures, off with you: do not pollute the   5
undeserving goddesses. Does not Scuccha, sunk in the ponds of
Styx, give warning of this, while he trembles weeping at the
Eumenides' twisted whip? Once arrows dipped in gall gave him
pleasure; now the wretch forever regrets his action. Cease to pro-   10
fane the shade of such a dear parent with debauchery and gaming
and drinking at the grave.

Let his own artistry please each man. It is not right for you to
approach Helicon, not right to corrupt the water of the Virgins'
stream. Certainly the Muse of Gioviano may drink of it, after she
has donned the buskin, and sing matters worthy of great Maro.   15
His comrade, Altilio, haunting the shrines of the virginal woods,
may pour out song from his learned breast. Likewise Compater,

Nec minus et Musae repetens monimenta iocosae
20   Compater, argutos ingerat ore sales.
Elysiusque hedera comptus florente capillos,
    rara, sed Aoniis concinat apta choris.
Extendatque armis titulos Aquivivus avitos,
    et doceat nostras cernere castra deas.
25 Ipse suae referat Cabanilius ardua Troiae
    moenia, et antiquos, Appula regna, lares.
Quique velut tenera surgit novus arbore ramus
    Corvinus, quavis aure probanda canat.
Et qui Pieriis resonat non ultimus antris
30   Albinus, referat principis acta sui.
Tu quoque quid cessas doctis deflere querelis
    excidium patriae, culte Marulle, tuae?
Quique tot egregias animas, tot clara virorum
    ingenia enixu format, alitque suo,
35 nectat honorata Maius sua dicta corona,
    tamque pias ferulas regia sceptra vocet.
Quin et rite suos Genio Chariteus honores
    praebeat, et festas concinat ante dapes.
Aelius at blandae fretus dulcedine linguae,
40   facunda totos conterat arte dies.
Nec te iam pudeat venturo ostendere saeclo
    eloquii vires, Scala diserte, tui.
Certent Socraticis Zenonis scripta libellis,
    cuius apis vernos intulit ore favos.
45 At tu Castaliis non inficiande choreis,
    Castalidos, Carbo, nunc cane regna tuae.
Te quoque, quem gemina mulcet sapientia lingua,
    Parde, iuvet studiis invigilare tuis.
Atque alii, quorum doctas it fama per aures,
50   extremo properent vincere fata die.

recalling the productions of his happy Muse, may give vent to his
clear-voiced wit. And Elisio, his hair arranged with blossoming 20
ivy, can sing what is exquisite and suitable for the dances of Aonia.
And Acquaviva through feats of arms can expand the reputation
of his ancestors, and teach the camp to recognize our goddesses.
Cabanilla himself can tell of the steep ramparts of Troia and of 25
your ancient dwellings, realms of Apulia. Corvino, growing like a
new bough on a delicate tree, sings what any ear should applaud.
Albino, not last to set the Pierian caves to reecho, can tell of the
deeds of his prince. And you also, refined Marullo: are you slow to 30
mourn the ruin of your fatherland in learned laments? And Maio,
who shapes so many outstanding spirits, so many exceptional tal-
ents, and nourishes them by his own efforts, may entwine his
words with a well-deserved crown and call his dutiful rods kingly 35
scepters. Likewise Cariteo may duly present his respects to his
Genius and sing before solemn banquets. Elia also, relying on the
sweetness of his winning tongue, may exhaust whole days with his
eloquent art. Nor, articulate Scala, should it shame you to demon- 40
strate now the force of your eloquence to a future generation. Let
the writings of Zeno, in whose mouth a bee has placed the honey
of spring, vie with the volumes of Socrates. You too, Carbone,
never to be disowned by the Castalian choruses, sing now of the 45
realm of your own Castalian muse. May it be your pleasure also,
Pardo, whom wisdom beguiles in two tongues, to stay wakeful
over your studies. Let others whose reputation makes its way
through learned ears hasten on their final day to win victory over
death. 50

Nos quoque, si magnus non aversatur Apollo,
　　cantemus Nymphas, capripedesque Deos.
Nam bene Thespiacas, livor licet audiat, undas
　　novimus, et dextro pressimus antra pede.
55　At vos incautis sociis aconita parate,
　　et furtis miseras exstimulate domos:
Oedipodique modo, thalamos foedate paternos,
　　si modo dat certum vulgus habere patrem;
nocturnisque dolis agitate, et caedibus urbem,
60　　perque fora infestam reddite, perque vias.
Haec studia, has artes primis didicistis ab annis,
　　non Aganippaeae tangere fila lyrae.
Nam neque Calliope vobis, nec dexter Apollo
　　Permessi sanctos exhibuere lacus;
65　dira sed Alecto gemina comitata sorore
　　pocula coenoso de Phlegethonte tulit.
Nimirum hinc nigro mores, et carmina tabo
　　pallent, et foedo livor in ore sedet.
Fallor, an hos nobis misit gravis Aetna Cyclopas,
70　　mitis et hanc sentis tu quoque terra luem?
Heu, mea Parthenope, quae te contagia laedunt?
　　Talia tu numquam gignere monstra soles.
Dii patrii, quorum monitis huc advena classis
　　appulit, Euboicas constituitque domos,
75　litoribus talem nostris avertite pestem,
　　moenia felici si posuistis ave.
Vosque umbrae insontes, quas iam letale venenum
　　ante diem Stygias ire coegit aquas,
ultrices huc ferte faces, fumoque sequaci
80　　authores vestrae sollicitate necis.

As for us, if mighty Apollo does not turn away, let us also sing
the Nymphs and the goat-footed gods. For even though envy give
ear, we too have come to know well the waves of Thespiae and
have trodden its caves with nimble foot. But you, make ready poi-
son for your comrades unaware, and provoke wretched homes 55
with your thievery. Like Oedipus, befoul your father's marriage
chambers, that is if people grant that you have known a father. Set
the city on edge with robbery and murder by night, and render it
open to threat in its squares and in its streets. You have learned 60
these pursuits, these trades from your first years, not how to touch
the strings of Aganippe's lyre. For neither Calliope nor propitious
Apollo has shown you the holy pools of Permessus. But the Fury
Alecto, accompanied by her twin sister, has brought you goblets of 65
muddy Phlegethon. Doubtless as a result, your character and your
poetry discolor from black decay, and envy sits on your foul
features. Am I mistaken or has brooding Etna sent us these
Cyclopes, and do you also, my gentle land, feel this pestilence?
Alas, my Parthenope, what plagues are doing you harm? You are 70
never in the habit of bearing such monsters. Gods of our fathers,
by whose counsel the foreigner directed his fleet to this place and
established Euboean dwellings, turn aside such disease from our
shores, if you founded our walls under a happy omen. And you, 75
guiltless shades, whom their deadly poison has now forced to go to
the waters of the Styx before your time, bring here avenging
torches and with pursuing smoke harass the instigators of your
death. And you, O Muses, surest divinities of poets, divinities 80

Et vos o vatum certissima numina, Musae,
    numina carminibus non violanda meis,
parcite, si vestras nunc primum laesimus aures:
    iusta lacessita sumpsimus arma manu.

Liber Secundus

I. Ad Alfonsum Ferdinandi filium Aragonium Siciliae regem

Alfonse, invicto laus accessure parenti,
    Hesperios inter non leve nomen avos,
quid me laudatos Parnassi mittis ad amnes?
    Obruitur largo flumine nostra sitis.
5   Gloria Virgilio est, currus atque arma referre;
    Nasonis medio fata in amore mori.
Battiaden docti sectatur Musa Properti.
    Flaccus Pindaricos dividit aure modos.
Passeris exequias fracto canit ore Catullus.
10   Tu Nemesim laudas, culte Tibulle, tuam.
Omnia non uno desudant esseda campo:
    noster in exiguo tramite currit equus.
Si me Castalia docuisset Phoebus in umbra,
    oraque Gorgonea nostra rigasset aqua,
15 meque vel Aeschyleo donasset Musa cothurno,
    et foret in nostro grandior ore sonus,
non ego Phasiacae canerem certamina pubis,
    aequora non prima sollicitata rate,
non coniuratos subvertere Pergama reges,
20   non Troiae profugos post duo lustra deos,

never to be defiled by our songs, grant us pardon, if now for the first time we have strained your ears. Our hand has been assailed, and we take up arms.

Book II

I. To Alfonso of Aragon, son of Ferdinando, king of Sicily

Alfonso, glory soon to be added to your invincible father, no slight name among your Hesperian forbears, why are you directing me to the honored springs of Parnassus? Our thirst is drowned by the stream's expanse. It is Virgil's glory to tell of chariots and weapons. It is Naso's doom to die in love's midst. The muse of learned 5 Propertius follows Battus's offspring. Flaccus distinguishes Pindar's measures with his ear. With broken voice Catullus sings the death of a sparrow. Elegant Tibullus, you praise your Nemesis. Not all chariots compete on a single course. My horse runs on a 10 narrow path. If Phoebus had taught me in the shade of Castalia and bedewed my lips with the Gorgon's water, and the Muse had bestowed on me the buskin of Aeschylus and a more exalted 15 sound abided on my lips, I would not sing of the challenges of the youth of Phasis, not of waters troubled by the first bark, nor of the kings who conspired to overthrow Pergama, nor of the gods of Troy, exiled after ten years, nor the battle-ranks at Thebes, the 20

Thebanasve acies, fratrumque immitia bella,
    saevaque discordi funera rapta pyra.
Teque, tuosque meo celebrarem carmine, nec me
    pignore tam grato dulce gravaret onus.
25 Nam canerem victosque duces Hispanaque regna
    horridaque a proavis bella peracta tuis.
Demissumque genus antiqua ab origine regum,
    quantaque magnanimi gesta feruntur avi,
dum Libyae tractus, veteres Carthaginis arces,
30   Lotophagum dites et populatur agros,
reginae accitu mox Itala regna secutus,
    Chalcidicasque arces, Parthenopenque subit.
Sed quoniam instabiles animos muliebria versant
    pectora, suspectos deserit ille lares,
35 ac patriae petit arva suae, nec longa moratus
    ultores rursum ducit in arma deos;
obsessamque intrat Nymphis comitantibus urbem,
    qua per operta vagus labitur antra liquor.
Aurea quin illo dicunt sub rege fuisse
40   saecula; felices qui meruere frui.
Quid patris invictas acies, quid concita dicam
    classica per campos, Daunia terra, tuos;
disiectosque duces, populataque castra, neque ullis
    clara magis regum proelia temporibus?
45 O mihi supremos si Parca indulserit annos,
    quanta canam, quantus vox mea plausus erit!
Tunc ego Maeonios ausim perrumpere fontes,
    saevaque terribili bella tonare tuba.
Utque alios sileam, tua fortia facta referrem,
50   proveherentque animos tot monumenta meos:
ut puer extremas regni percurreris oras,
    lustratis referens praemia litoribus:
et male pacatos sedaveris ante tumultus,

pitiless wars of brothers and fierce corpses snatched from discord's pyre, I would celebrate you and your people in my song, nor, with such a happy assurance, would the sweet burden lie heavy on me.

I would sing of generals defeated, and the realms of Spain, and 25 dread wars brought to completion by your ancestors, a line descended from an ancient race of kings, and the mighty deeds which are told of your high-souled forefather while he lays waste the reaches of Libya, the ancient citadels of Carthage and the opulent fields of the Lotophagi. Pursuing the realms of Italy at the 30 summons of the queen, he enters the Chalcidican citadels and Parthenope. But since the hearts of women change their fickle minds, he departs from her untrustworthy domain and seeks out the fields of his fatherland and, without lengthy delay, leads again 35 his avenging gods to arms. With his companion Nymphs he enters the city he had besieged where wandering water glides through hidden caverns. Indeed they say that, while he was king, the golden age existed: happy those who deserved to enjoy it. Why 40 should I tell of the undefeated armies of your father, of trumpets blaring throughout your plains, land of Daunia, of leaders routed, camps plundered, battles, more famous than in any regal age? O, if the Parca looks favorably on my final years, what great events will 45 I sing, how much applause will my voice form! Then I might dare to invade the springs of Maeonia and thunder forth savage wars on dread trumpet. To pass by others in silence, I would tell of your brave deeds, and your record of achievement would stimulate my thoughts: how as a boy you scoured the farthest extent of your 50 kingdom, bringing back plunder from the shores you surveyed, how you put smoldering revolts to rest before driving the enemy

quam patriis hostes finibus expuleris.
55   Primus honos, forti defensos milite Locros
      servasse, et muros, urbs Meliboea, tuos.
    Necnon Marte pari summas Caulonis in arces
      venisse, inque suo templa sacrata iugo,
    templa deae, vastis late quae praesidet undis,
60   una Iovis coniux fida, sororque Iovis.
    Testis Crathis erit, testes Sybaritides undae,
      oraque, quae fluctus prospicit Ionios.
    Adde, quod Etruscos oppleveris agmine campos,
      et tibi captivis fluxerit Arnus aquis;
65   totque pharetratas, Turcarum corpora, turmas
      Ausoniis dederis Manibus inferias.
    Gratia dis Italis, praerupta Ceraunia, et arces
      Buthroti, nostras pertimuere minas,
    captivumque ducem, fractosque aspeximus arcus,
70   detulit huc domita quos tua classis aqua.
    Hinc Ligurum furias, compressaque iurgia ferro,
      Gallicaque in partes oppida versa duas.
    Ipse ego quae vidi, referam: scit Tuscula tellus,
      quaeque cadit summo lympha Aniena iugo.
75   Nam duce te, Latios ferro dum subruis agros,
      tempora militiae prima fuere meae.
    Bis Nomentanas, bis magni Tiburis arces
      vidimus ad nostros proiecere arma pedes:
    cum iam sit media trepidatum pene Subura,
80   et Capitolino vota parata Iovi.
    Nec semel, ut fatear, Collinae ad limina portae
      fregimus, armatos reppulimusque duces.
    Parce tamen, veneranda Parens, si iusta secutus
      signa sub Alfonso: rex erat ille meus.
85   Lanuvium infelix, fatis contraria nostris
      terra, potes certas tu variasse vices.

from their fatherland. Your first honor was to have saved the
Locrians by the defense of your brave soldiery, and your walls,   55
Meliboean city, and also with equal military skill to have reached
the loftiest citadels of Caulon and the blessed temples on its ridge,
temples of the goddess whose rule is wide over the expansive
waves, at once Jupiter's faithful wife and sister of Jupiter. Crathis   60
will be witness, the waves of Sybaris witnesses, and the shore that
gazes on the Ionian floods. Add that you filled the Etruscan fields
with your army and for you the Arno flowed with its waters cap-
tive, that you presented so many quivered squadrons, Turkish
corpses, as funeral offerings to Ausonian ghosts. As favor to the   65
gods of Italy, the cliffs of Ceraunia and citadels of Buthrotum have
cowered before our threats. We have seen their leader taken cap-
tive and their bows broken that your fleet bore here over a subju-
gated sea. After this the madness of the Ligurians and disputes   70
quelled by the sword, and the towns of Gaul divided into two fac-
tions. I will tell what I myself have seen: the land of Tusculum knows
and the water of the Anio that falls from its topmost slope. For
under your leadership, while you were crushing the fields of Latium
with the sword, I experienced military service for the first time.   75
Twice we have seen the citadels of Nomentum, twice, of great Tivoli,
cast their weapons before our feet, when there was terror almost in
the heart of the Subura and prayers were readied for Capitoline
Jupiter. Not just once, to speak out, have we broken and repelled   80
armed leaders at the threshold of the Colline Gate. Nevertheless
grant me pardon, venerable Mother, if I followed beneath
Alfonso's just standards: he was my king. Unfortunate Lanuvium,
land opposed to what was fated for us, you have the ability to   85

Nam quod ad hostiles flexit Victoria partes:
    fortunae magis hoc, quam fuit artis, opus.
Ille sed Eridani ripas non fractus in altas
90   contendens, carae regna sororis adit:
metatusque locum castris, Insubria passim
    fudit, et Euganeis agmina missa iugis.
Dicite io, populi: turmas spectastis ovantes,
    et per victrices foedera iuncta manus.
95 Ipse quoque haud sileat quos cedere Farfarus hostes
    risit, et exutum vertere terga ducem.
Heus ubi nunc, Roberte, tuae vocesque, minaeque,
    Campani peteres cum tibi iura soli?
Iam nostros reges, iam sternere cuncta parabas;
100   nunc fuga degeneres arguit ecce metus.
Hortarisque tuos dimittere signa maniplos.
    Heu pudor, et longae praemia militiae.
Hos tamen ille pius, quamvis diversa secutos,
    Alfonsus miti fovit, et auxit ope.
105 Macte animo custosque hominum, macte optime regum,
    Ausoniae tu sol, tu pater unus ades.
Quid memorem pacisque artes, bellique labores,
    perpetuumque animi tempus in omne decus?
Sed me formosae deterrent iussa puellae,
110   ne possim tantis invigilare choris:
et vetat asper Amor dulces contemnere curas,
    cogit et inviso subdere colla iugo.
Nec prosunt lacrimae, nec verba precantia mortem:
    ille suas in me concutit usque faces.
115 Quare si nostri veniet tibi nuncia leti
    fama, triumphales iam prope siste rotas;
atque haec ad cineres moerens effare sepultos:
    saevitia dominae rapte poeta iaces.

change your certain lot. For the fact that Victory shifted to the side of the enemy was more the result of fortune than of skill. But he, uncowed, marching against the lofty banks of the Po, reached the realm of his dear sister, and, after measuring out his encamp- 90 ment, he routed the whole of Insubria and the battalions sent from the Euganean Hills. Shout "Bravo," O peoples: you have seen the rejoicing throngs and treaties forged through his victori- ous hands. Also let Farfarus cry out. He laughed to see the enemy retreating and their leader, stripped of his arms, turning tail. Alas, 95 Robert, where now are your shouts and your threats, when you were seeking for yourself rights over the Campanian territory? Just now you were preparing to lay low our princes, to lay everything low. Look now: your flight betrays your contemptible fears, and 100 you urge your troops to abandon their standards—alas, the shame!—and the booty from a lengthy campaign. But Alfonso, pious as he is, comforted them, though their allegiance lay else- where, and encouraged them with kindly aid. Hail for your cour- age, guardian of mankind, hail, best of kings: you alone are the 105 sun of Ausonia, you alone the father. Why should I recall your arts of peace and your efforts in war, your unceasing grace of mind on every occasion? But the dictates of a lovely girl prevent me from being able to spend the night hours on such choruses. And 110 harsh Love forbids me to despise sweet cares, and compels me to lower my neck under a hateful yoke. Tears are no help, nor words that pray for death. He ever shakes his torches against me. So if Rumor telling of my death reaches you, halt then your triumphal 115 chariot nearby and in sorrow speak these words to my buried ashes:

Poet, here you lie, carried off by the harshness of your mistress.

II. *In festo die divi Nazarii martyris,*
qui poetae natalis est

Ecce mihi totum lux exspectata per annum
  iam redit, Aoniae, serta novate, deae.
Haec me vitales genitum produxit in auras,
  iussit et erectum tollere ad astra caput.
5 Nunc mihi purpureis aram cumulate hyacinthis:
  cingite et intexta limina nostra rosa.
Sic etenim coluisse decet geniumque, laresque:
  ferte coronato tura, merumque foco.
Tuque apio innexos dudum acceptura poetas,
10 splendida solemnes instrue mensa dapes.
Hic mihi puniceo Pontani Musa cothurno
  incipiet posito carmen hiare mero:
naturaeque vias, tenerique exordia mundi
  proferet, et certa cuncta obitura die.
15 Crassus at aeterno frondis redimitus honore,
  solvat Pieriis ora rigata modis;
et mihi Linternumque vetus, placidumque Petrinum,
  ostendatque atavi regna opulenta mei:
regna male ad seros heu perventura nepotes,
20 dum versat varias sors inimica vices.
Altiliusque novos superis laturus honores,
  Pindarica feriat carmina docta lyra.
Sfortiadum mox dicat, Aragoniosque hymenaeos:
  iure quibus cantus aequet, Homere, tuos.
25 Nec gemat exilium Spartani Musa Marulli,
  ventura ad nostras ingeniosa dapes:
verba sed antiqui reddat, numerosque Lucreti:
  dum magnis divos laudibus accumulat.
Adde tuos, Puderice, sales, adde inclyta patris
30 eloquia, adde animo tot bona parta tuo.

II. On the feast day of San Nazario, martyr,
the birthday of the poet

See how my day, awaited through the whole year, now returns.
Renew the garlands, goddesses of Aonia. This brought me forth,
newborn into the breezes of life, and ordered me to raise my head
aloft to the stars. Heap up, now, my altar with purple hyacinths
and swathe my threshold with a weaving of roses. For in this way   5
it is fitting to worship genius and lares: bring incense and wine for
the festooned hearth. And you, gleaming board, soon to receive
poets crowned with parsley, provide the customary banquet.   10

   Here, after the wine is set in place, the Muse of Pontano, in
crimson buskin, will begin to sing for me her song. She will recite
the ways of nature and the beginnings of the fragile earth, and
everything destined to pass away on an appointed day. But let
Crasso, garlanded with leafage's undying glory, open his lips,   15
sprinkled with the measures of Pieria, and display for me both an-
cient Linternum and quiet Petrinum and my rich ancestral realms,
realms, alas, scarcely destined to reach later descendants, since
hostile fate works her motley changes. And let Altilio, sure to   20
bring fresh honors to the gods, strike learned songs on Pindar's
lyre. Let him soon sing the wedding of the sons of Sforza and the
Aragonese with which, Homer, he may justly match your songs.
Let the talented Muse of Spartan Marullo not mourn for her exile   25
as she prepares to arrive at our feast, but let her recite the words
and measures of ancient Lucretius while he heaps the gods with
great praises. Add your wit, Poderico, add the famous declama-
tions of your father, add the many gifts bestowed on your mind.
Count up the pleasantries and writings of Panormita, and the   30

Iamque Panhormitae lusus, et scripta recense,
  et Iovianaeae tempora amicitiae.
Hos inter meritis rediens Aquivivus ab armis,
  prodat honoratae praemia militiae:
35 atque chori princeps docti argumenta Plutarchi,
  cumque suis referat dogmata principiis.
Ipse autem haud dubitet Cabanilius acta referre
  vel sua, vel magno iuncta parentis avo.
Nec Phoebo minus ipse suo, quam Marte probatus,
40 Phocaico pexas tingat in amne comas.
Tu quoque, quem iuvenem veneror, dulcissime Garlon,
  incipe iam docta plectra movere manu:
Allifasque tuas mihi concine, dum vaga Lunam
  sidera per tacitum nocte sequuntur iter.
45 Talibus auspiciis geniales ducere coenas,
  Thespiadumque modis concelebrare iuvat.

III. Calendis Ianuariis ad Fuscum

Exoritur lux alma, caput sol detegit aureum,
  qui toties nostros exhilaravit avos.
Exoritur: redit ecce anni melioris origo.
  Quisquis ades, sancta concipe voce preces.
5 Cingantur de more sacris fastigia templis,
  quae vaga Sebethi Nais ab amne legit.
Ipse sui Ianus praepandat limina templi,
  cui geminum liquido stillet odore caput.
Illius et castas fument pia tura per aras:
10 atque focos supra stet, videatque suos.
Nunciet et tibi, Fusce, novos virtutis honores.
  Iam reor haec animum vota fovere tuum.
Nec magis optaris, quas Lydius amnis arenas,

span of his friendship with Gioviano. In their midst let Acquaviva, returning from glorious feats of arms, proclaim the tributes of rewarded military service, and, as chief of the assembly, let him proclaim the theses of learned Plutarch and his doctrines with their principles. Nor should Cavaniglia hesitate to report either his own 35 deeds or those of his father in union with his noble grandfather. No less applauded by Phoebus than by his Mars, he himself should dip his well-groomed locks in the stream of Phocis. You 40 also, sweetest Garlon, youth whom I revere, begin now to move the plectrum with skilled hand, sing to me now your Allifae, while the wandering stars at night follow the Moon on her silent path. With such omens it gives me pleasure to conduct my genius's feast 45 and to rejoice according to the measures of the Muses.

III. On the first of January, to Fuscus

The kindly light is rising. The Sun, which so often brought cheer to our ancestors, reveals his golden head. It rises: see, the start of a better year returns. You, whoever is at hand: frame prayers with hallowed voice. According to custom let the pediments of the blessed temples be girded with wreaths that the wandering Naiad 5 plucks from the stream of Sebeto. Let Janus himself open wide the entrance to his temple, his double head dripping with a flow of perfume. Let holy incense also smoke on his pure altars, and let him stand and watch over their hearth. Let him also declare new 10 honors for your virtue, Fusco. It is my belief that your mind now cherishes these hopes. Nor would you rather wish for the sands that the Lydian river, that the proud water of the tawny Tagus

quas volvit flavi lympha superba Tagi.
15 Nec magis uberibus quicquid sibi colligit arvis
      Medus, et assiduo sole perustus Arabs.
    Iusta precor: Latiis utinam discedat ab oris
      hostis, et indecori victus oberret equo.
    Victus Hydruntinas cogatur linquere terras,
20   et plangat nostram sanguinolentus humum.
    Haec veniet lux, Fusce, tuis laetissima votis,
      cum pax optatas ducet in urbe moras.

IV. In morum candidam

Nunc, Erato, virides capiti subnecte corymbos,
    profer et auratae fila canora lyrae.
Arboris umbriferae casus referamus acerbos.
    Non erat haec nostro fabula nota solo.
5 Audiat, et molli cantantes protegat umbra
    ipsa [lac.]
    Olim Baianis fuerat pulcherrima silvis
      Naias, errantes figere docta feras.
    Quam liquidus clausis Lucrinus saepe sub antris
10   optavit lateri iungere posse suo.
    Nec semel illius pharetram laudavit, et arcum
      pastorum incultis fistula carminibus.
    Testes Cumaeae, testes Linternides undae,
      sanctaque Gauranae numina Hamadryades,
15 illam Silvanos, Panasque odisse bicornes,
      et quoscumque colit silva, nemusque deos.
    Sed quid fata parant? solitis Morinna redibat
      montibus—hoc illi nomen, et omen erat—
    cum subita caelum texit caligine nimbus,
20   et multa canam grandine fecit humum.
    Illa hiemem fugiens, diversa per arva cucurrit,

rolls, nor rather whatever the Mede gathers from his fertile fields
and the Arab, scorched by the unrelenting sun.   15

My prayer is just: would that the enemy withdraw from the
Latin shores and wander away defeated, with his inglorious horse.
Defeated, let him be compelled to abandon the territory of
Otranto and, bloodied, let him bewail our ground. Fusco, this day   20
will arrive, most happy from your prayers, when peace will happily
extend its duration in the city.

IV. On the white mulberry

Weave now, Erato, fresh ivy-berries for my head and fetch the re-
sounding strings of your gilded lyre. Let us tell the bitter misfor-
tunes of a shady tree. This story was not known in our land. Let
[. . .] hear, and may she herself safeguard us as we sing in her soft
shade [. . .] Once upon a time in the woods of Baiae there lived   5
the loveliest of Naiads, skilled at shooting wandering beasts of the
wild, and limpid Lucrinus in confines of his caves yearned to be
able to clasp her to his side. Not just once did the shepherds' pipe   10
praise her quiver and her bow in uncouth strains. Cumae was wit-
ness, the water-nymphs of Linternum were witnesses, and the
Hamadryades, holy presences of Monte Gauro, that she hated the
Silvanuses and the twin-horned Pans and whatever gods were   15
worshipped by forest and grove. But what do the Fates have in the
offing? Morinna (this was her name as well as her omen) was re-
turning from her accustomed mountains when a storm cloud
shrouded the sky in sudden darkness, and whitened the ground
with a covering of hail. As she fled the blizzard, she ran through   20
one field after another, her head covered with garlands, her head

tecta caput sertis, grandine tecta caput.
Vallis erat prope sulfureos male pervia montes,
    candida quam Graio nomine signat humus.
25 Hanc super excisis pendebat cautibus antrum,
    agricolum hirsutis nota domus gregibus.
Pugnantes huc forte coegerat impiger hircos
    semideusque caper, semicaperque deus.
Quem procul ut vidit nymphe, sic pectore toto
30   insequitur, tales et iacit ore sonos:
'Quo properas, ah dura, measque ingrata querelas
    despicis? Aspectus ne fuge, nympha, meos.
Mecum capreolos, mecum venabere damas:
    parebit iussis hoc pecus omne tuis.
35 Nil est, quod fugias: mihi, crede, recentia semper
    pocula de niveo fagina lacte madent.
Semper picta rosis, semper contexta ligustris
    de nostro poteris munera ferre sinu.'
Dixit; at illa volans celeres praevertitur auras,
40   imbre nihil motos impediente gradus.
Iamque petens tristesque lacus, sterilemque paludem,
    consitaque arbustis non minus arva novis,
aspicit exesi longe sub faucibus antri
    obscurum caeco pulvere noctis iter.
45 Huc, tamquam in latebras se coniicit; haud minus ille
    insequitur praedae tractus amore suae.
Iamque patens caelum rursus, solemque videbat,
    liquerat et montem post sua terga cavum:
dextra pontus erat, praeruptaque saxa sinistra:
50   et iam defessam, iamque premebat amans.
Protinus exclamans, 'Fer opem mihi, Delia,' dixit:
    oraque supremo diriguere sono.
Attulit auxilium nymphae dea, seque vocanti
    praebuit; illa cadens sponte recumbit humi,

covered with hail. There was a barely passable valley near the sul-
furous mountains, known in Greek by the name "white earth."
Above this was perched a cave where the cliffs were hollowed out,
a well-known shelter for the farmers' shaggy flocks. Hither by   25
chance the energetic half-god goat, and half-goat god, had herded
his butting he-goats. When the nymph spied him from afar, he
pursued her with his whole heart, and hurled out such sounds
from his lips: "Where are you rushing, pitiless creature? Do you   30
ungratefully despise my groans? Nymph, do not flee the sight of
me. Together with me you will hunt roebuck, with me deer. This
whole flock will obey your commands. There is nothing that you
should flee. Trust me: my newly made cups of beech are always   35
brimming with snowy milk. You will be able to receive from our
lap gifts always decorated with roses, always woven with privets."

He spoke, but she surpassed the swift breezes as she flew, while
the hail slowed not at all the rush of her pace. Seeking now the   40
gloomy lakes and barren marsh, along with fields planted with
strange trees, afar off, underneath the entrance mouth of the hol-
low cave, she spied a path dim in the night's black dust. Here she
thrust herself for a hiding-place. Nonetheless he followed,   45
charmed by love of his prey. And now she saw again the open sky
and the sun: she had left the mountain cavern behind her back.
The sea was to her right, sheer cliffs on her left, and now, even
now, the lover was pressing hard upon the exhausted girl. Crying   50
out at once she said: "Grant me help, Delia." Her lips froze in
their last utterance. The goddess brought aid to the nymph. She
heeded her suppliant. The nymph, falling of her own accord, lay
on the ground. And suddenly she became a tree (earlier genera-

55 fitque arbor subito: morum dixere priores,
    et de Morinna nil nisi nomen habet.
Pes in radicem, in frondes ivere capilli,
    et quae nunc cortex, caerula vestis erat.
Brachia sunt rami; sed quae nitidissima poma,
60   quas male vitasti, nympha, fuere nives.
Flevit Misenus, mutatam flevit Avernus,
    fontibus et calidis ingemuere deae.
Quin etiam flevere suis Sebethides antris
    Naiades, et passis Parthenopaea comis.
65 Sed tamen ante alios lacrimas in stipite fudit
    Faunus, et haec tristes addit ad inferias.
'Inter silvicolas o non ignota sorores,
    nunc morus, duris candida corticibus
vive diu, et nostros semper tege fronde capillos,
70   cedat ut ipsa tuis pinus acuta comis.
Tu numquam miserae maculabere sanguine Thysbes,
    immemor heu fati ne videare tui.
Tu, nec fata negant, niveis uberrima pomis,
    his olim stabis frondea limitibus;
75 et circum puerique canent, facilesque puellae,
    ducentes festos ad tua sacra choros.'
Hactenus insigni cecinit testudine Musa:
    Aoniasque volans laeta revisit aquas.

V. Ad Bacchum

Bacche bimater ades: sic sint tibi nexa corymbis
    cornua, sic nitidis pendeat uva comis.
Seu te nunc Thebae, seu te nunc Ismarus horrens,
    sive habet umbrosis Naxos amica iugis.
5 Huc, pater, huc propera frondenti candide thyrso,
    huc potius gressus dirige, Bacche, tuos.

tions called it Morus) and kept nothing of Morinna except the 55
name. Her foot grew into a root, her hair into leaves, and what is
now bark was her dark clothing. Her arms are branches, but what
are now shimmering berries were the hail-drops which, Nymph,
you barely escaped. 60

Misenus wept, Avernus wept for the changed girl, and the god-
desses in their warm springs mourned. Indeed even the Naiads of
Sebeto wept in their grottoes and Parthenopea, her hair out-
spread. But even so Faunus, more than the others, poured out his
tears on the trunk, and added this to the sad obsequies: "Not un- 65
known among the sisters who cherish the woods, now Morus,
white with hard bark, may you live long and always cover our locks
with your foliage so that the needled pine herself yields to your
leaves. You, alas, in case you seem unmindful of your fate, will 70
never be spotted with the blood of pitiable Thisbe. You—and the
fates do not refuse it—within these precincts will one day stand
leafy, richly abundant with snow-white fruit, and around about
both the youths and the indulgent girls will sing, as they perform 75
celebratory dances at your rites."

Thus sang the Muse on her splendid shell and in joyous flight
revisited the Aonian waters.

V. To Bacchus

Be present, Bacchus of two mothers: so may your horns be woven
with berries of ivy. So may a grape cluster hang from your gleam-
ing locks. Whether now Thebes possesses you, whether now
dread Ismarus, or friendly Naxos with shady ridges, hasten here,
father, here, bright with your leafy thyrsus. Here, rather, Bacchus, 5
direct your steps. But now put aside your *palla* and your painted

Sed pallam iam pone gravem, pictosque cothurnos,
　　et musto teneros tu quoque tinge pedes.
Tecum etiam Dryadesque deae, Satyrique bicornes
10　　adsint, et calamos, concavaque aera sonent,
raucaque subductis percurrant tympana palmis,
　　Bassaridum fusis turba verenda comis.
Quas male festinans Silenus pone sequatur,
　　et procul, ut maneant, subsideantque, roget.
15　Tum secum auriti fatum deploret aselli,
　　incedet ferula dum titubante senex.
At deus hortorum, cui vertice fixa rubenti
　　canna tremit, saevas falce repellat aves.
In medio crater caelato maximus auro,
20　　spumet inexhaustum, Lesbia dona, merum:
et circum de more tuas cava tibia laudes
　　intonet, appositas concelebretque dapes.
Ipse ego perque vias urbis, perque omnia passim
　　compita, perpetuo sacra colenda feram.
25　Ipse gigantaeo referam memorata triumpho
　　nomina, et evantes, orgia laeta, choros,
nec sileam fuscas acies, Gangetica regna,
　　gestaque odoratis proelia litoribus.
Mox thalamus, Ariadna, tuos, taedasque iugales,
30　　quaeque nitet medio fixa corona polo.
Iamque pios ritus, indictaque sacra frequentans,
　　instituam virgas fronde virente tegi;
incedamque tuas vates tam magnus ad aras,
　　quam nec Virgilius, quam nec Homerus erat.
35　Tu mihi, sancte pater, mordaces exime curas,
　　nubilaque annoso pectora solve mero.
Tu mihi securos adige in praecordia somnos:
　　afflatuque iuva lumina fessa tuo.
Scimus enim, quantos ineunte aetate labores

buskins, and also dye your tender feet with must. Let the goddess Dryads and twin-horned Satyrs also be present with you, and let them sound the pipes and the hollow bronze, and let the awe-in- 10 spiring troop of Bassarids, with streaming hair stroke the hoarse timbrels with upraised hands. Let Silenus, barely keeping pace, follow them from behind and from a distance beg them to pause and wait. Then let the old man, while he approaches with totter- ing cane, lament the death of his long-eared donkey. Now let the 15 god of gardens, with trembling reed perched on his ruddy pate, ward off fierce birds with his sickle. In their midst let an enormous mixing bowl of graven gold, a gift from Lesbos, foam with limit- less wine, and roundabout let the hollow flute resound your accus- 20 tomed praises and herald the festive board.

I myself will carry your rites everywhere, to be celebrated con- tinuously, both through the streets of the city and through the crossroads. I will tell of your notable repute from the triumph over the giants, the choruses shouting "Evhoi," your joyous mysteries. 25 Nor shall I remain silent about the swarthy ranks, the realms of the Ganges, and battles waged on aromatic shores, then, Ariadne, your wedding chamber and bridal torches, and the gleaming crown, stationed in the center of the sky. And now celebrating 30 your holy ceremonies and the proclamation of your rituals, I will command that staves be covered with green leaves, and I will make my progress to your altars, as grand a bard as was neither Virgil nor Homer.

Holy father, take away from me biting cares, clear my breast's 35 gloom with unmixed wine. Urge untroubled sleep upon my heart and strengthen my exhausted eyes with your inspiration. For we know what great troubles you withstood, as your life began, what

40   pertuleris, quantos fulminis igne metus.
     Infelix Semele, quid munera poscis amantem,
        quae tibi, quae nato sunt nocitura tuo?
     Posce Iovem, quae digna tuis sint praemia votis,
        posce: feres votis praemia digna tuis.
45 Non tibi silvicolum proles de plebe deorum,
        sed cui sint Phoebus, Mercuriusque pares;
     sed quam Saturnus non dedignetur ab alto
        noscere; quam laeto Iupiter ore probet.
     Salve, cara patri soboles, mitissime divum,
50   salve, hominum requies, laetitiaeque parens:
     et faciles, si iusta peto, mihi prospice Musas,
        et me pacato numine dexter adi.

VI. Ad Ludovicum Montaltum Syracusanum,
Caroli Caesaris Scrini magistrum

   Mons altus nomen clarum tibi, sive nivosis
      nascenti dederit fertilis Aetna iugis,
   seu lustrata vagis Nebrodis saxa Napaeis,
      sive Dionaeo numine clarus Eryx:
5   seu quod Olympiaco reptaris vertice, teque
      pertulerit placido blanda Arethusa sinu,
   nobile frondoso defluxit nomen Olympo,
      Elei referens sacra vetusta Iovis.
   Seu mage quod celsas puer exuperaveris Alpes,
10   dum patet in laudes Belgica terra tuas,
   oceanique petis non explorata Britanni
      murmura, nec canae Tethyos antra times;
   exhaustos praeferret ut illa aetate labores,
      aeria nomen venit ab Alpe tibi.
15 Quicquid id est, quicumque huius tibi nominis auctor
      mons, et inaccessi verticis asperitas:

great fears from the thunderbolt's fire. Unfortunate Semele, why   40
of your lover do you demand gifts which are to bring harm both to
you and to your son? Demand of Jupiter gifts that are worthy of
your prayers. Demand: you will gain gifts worthy of your prayers.
Not for you an offspring from the rank and file of woods-dwelling
gods, but one to whom Phoebus and Mercury are equals, whom   45
Saturn does not disdain to recognize from on high, whom Jupiter
can approve with happy countenance. Hail, dear offspring of your
father, most gentle of gods, hail, repose of mankind, begetter of
joy. If my request is righteous, see that my Muses are indulgent   50
and come propitiously to me, with your godhead at peace.

VI. *To Ludovico Montalto of Syracuse,*
Chancellor of the Emperor Charles

Mons Altus is your illustrious name, whether Etna, prolific with
snowy ridges, gave it to you at birth, whether the crags of the
Nebrodes, roamed by Napaeans, or Eryx, famous for the worship
of Dione, or because your crawling began on the peak at Olympia
and gentle Arethusa carried you in her kindly bosom, your name   5
has derived from leafy Olympus, recalling the holy rituals of Elean
Jupiter. Or rather because as a boy you crossed the lofty Alps,
while the territory of the Belgae lay open to your praises and you   10
pursued the unexplored roar of the ocean of the Britanni, and did
not fear the caves of foam-capped Tethys. To proclaim the trials
you underwent at that age, your name came from the soaring Alp.
   Whatever the case, whichever mountain and jagged, unap-
proachable peak was the source of this name of yours, it beheld   15
not character, not accomplishments, but the sharpness of a tower-

non mores, non facta, sed altae mentis acumen
   vidit, et ingenii praevia signa tui.
Nam licet ipse animo nubes, et sidera vincas,
20   cunctaque sint sensu pene minora tuo:
   non te per duros aditus, rupesve fragosas,
     sed per floriferum vallis adimus iter,
vallis, perpetuo quam vestit gramine rivus,
    et quam vicini litoris aura fovet.
25 Hoc est, hoc, mihi crede, deos aequare merendo;
    hoc est aeterni sceptra tenere Iovis.
Cetera mortales inter peritura labores
    desere, et hoc unum vita sequatur opus.

VII. Ad Iunianum Maium praeceptorem

Dum tibi Baianae spectantur ab aequore nymphae,
    stagnaque vicinis hospita litoribus:
qua vetus Herculeos perduxit semita tauros,
    longius excluso concita claustra mari;
5 quaque iacet Baulos inter lucumque Sibyllae,
    et Prochytae rectum per iuga tendit iter:
nos hic, ut nosti, durae parere puellae
    cogimur, et tristes ducere in urbe moras.
Nec tamen aut studiis animum intendisse severis,
10   aut prodest sanctas excoluisse deas.
Cumque tot unanimes dederint mihi fata sodales,
    auxilium nemo est, qui mihi rite ferat.
Instat saevus Amor, reficitque in cote sagittas,
    nec patitur presso colla movere iugo.
15 Et licet assiduis tabescant pectora curis:
    quaerimus, unde queant tanta venire mala.
Atque utinam tristes Lachesis mihi finiat annos,
    claudat et aetatis tempora dura meae:

ing mind and the tokens heralding your talent. For though you
yourself surpass the clouds and the stars in intellect, and nearly all
things are secondary to your judgement, we approach you not   20
through forbidding passages or rugged escarpments but through a
valley's flower-rich path, a valley which a stream forever clothes
with grass and which the breeze from the nearby shore cherishes.
This, this, trust me, is to equal the gods in merit, this is to hold   25
the scepter of immortal Jupiter. Forego other transient matters
among human ambitions. Let your life pursue only this effort.

VII. *To his teacher, Giuniano Maio*

While the Nymphs of Baiae are in your view from the water and
the welcoming lakes at the nearby shore, where the age-old path
led along the bulls of Hercules, a barrier lashed for a distance by
the shut-out sea, where lies the road between Bauli and the Sibyl's
grove, and is bound straight for the ridges of Prochyta: here, as   5
you know, I am compelled to obey a harsh girl and drearily to con-
tinue lingering in the city. It still does no good to have devoted
one's mind to stern studies or to have worshipped the holy god-
desses. And although fate gave me so many like-minded friends,   10
there is no one to bring me help, as one might expect. Savage Love
is in pursuit: he repairs his arrows on a whetstone and does not al-
low me to move my neck under his heavy yoke. And although my
heart wastes away from unremitting anxiety, I ask from where   15
such evils can come. Would that Lachesis might put an end to my
troubled years and terminate my life's hard times, or that some re-

aut aliquis, saevi quae sit medicina furoris,
20   non vanus nostra cantet in aure deus!
Sed iam laurigeris cessant oracula Delphis:
    mutaque Cumaeae virginis antra silent.
Nec Pan Maenalia reddit responsa sub umbra,
    nocte licet pastor viscera libet ovis.
25 Nec mihi Chaonias spes est audire columbas;
    cornigerumque pudet fata referre Iovem.
Oblitasque loqui iampridem Graecia quercus
    mirata est posito conticuisse deo.
At tibi venturos, Mai, praedicere casus
30   fas est, et mites consuluisse deos.
Nec tantum aut arae fumos, aut nuntia sentis
    fulgura, sed Stygiis somnia missa locis,
somnia quae miseram perturbant saepe quietem,
    dum mens incertis pendet imaginibus.
35 O quoties per te vanum posuisse timorem
    me memini, et laetos continuasse dies.
O quoties, trepidus cum non spernenda putarem,
    in nostrum cavi damna futura caput.
Saepe meae tibi cum narrassem visa puellae,
40   dixisti, certos haud procul esse metus.
Saepe illam madidos lustrare in flumine crines
    iussisti, et misto solvere farra sale.
Quod si olim terris talem te fata dedissent,
    sprevisset Tuscos Martia Roma viros.
45 Nam te quis melius calidas deprendere fibras,
    consulere aerias aut potuisset aves?
Illa triumphatum regeret nunc legibus orbem,
    nec foret in cineres obruta pene suos.
Nec fera vidisset Cannensis funera pugnae,
50   aut aquilas Parthos tam male ferre duces.
Scipiadum patriis habitarent sedibus umbrae,

liable god might intone in my ear a remedy for my savage passion.
But now the oracles withdraw from laurel-rich Delphi, and the   20
mute caves of the Cumaean virgin remain still. Pan gives back no
answers under the shade of Maenalus, though by night the shep-
herd offers him the entrails of a sheep. I have no hope of listening
to the doves of Chaonia and it shames horned Jupiter to announce   25
the future, and Greece has marveled that its oak trees, for a long
time now forgetful of speaking, have grown silent, with their god
abandoned.

   But it is right for you, Maio, to prophesy events to come and to
seek advice from propitious gods. You draw your feelings not only   30
from either altar smoke or foreboding thunderbolts but also
through dreams sent from the land of the Styx, dreams which of-
ten trouble our wretched sleep when our mind is disturbed by per-
plexing visions. O how many times I recall that, because of you, I
discarded empty fear and prolonged my days of happiness. O how   35
many times, when in my fear I considered them not to be disre-
garded, I was on guard against injuries looming over my life. Of-
ten, when I recounted to you night-visions of my girl, you replied
that sure fears were quite near at hand. Often you ordered her to   40
cleanse her dripping hair in a stream and to grind up wheat mixed
with salt. But if once upon a time fate had given such as you to the
world, Mars's Rome would have scorned the men of Etruria, for
who better than you could have scrutinized warm innards or ob-   45
served the flights of birds. She would still be ruling with laws the
world she had conquered and would not be nearly smothered in
her own ashes. Nor would she have seen the cruel deaths at the
battle of Cannae nor her legions able so poorly to withstand the
Parthian leaders. The shades of the Scipiades would rest in their   50
ancestral dwellings nor would the soil of Spain bury such great

tanta nec Hispanum conderet ossa solum.
Te duce, veridicae patuissent scripta Sibyllae,
    non intellecto quae nocuere deo.
55 Fortunate deum interpres, quem sidera norunt,
    cui superum mentes explicuisse licet:
non te letali tetigit puer improbus arcu,
    quamvis et dominos implicet ille deos.
Nec tibi securos rumpunt suspiria somnos,
60   fallaces Veneris despicis insidias.
At nos incertis caeci iactamur in undis:
    ducimus et nullo tempora consilio.
Et quisquam mihi nunc longos optaverit annos,
    cum videat vitae taedia tanta meae?
65 Non me Sisyphio superent impulsa labore
    saxa, nec infernis dolia adacta vadis.
Et Tityi rostro cedet mihi vultur obunco,
    pomaque Lethaeis risa sub arboribus.
Vos igitur, qui me victum iam fletis, amici,
70   sic mea compositis caedite busta notis:
Actius hic situs est; cineres gaudete sepulti.
    Iam vaga post obitus umbra dolore vacat.

VIII. In dominae natalem, ad Iunonem

Iunoni fer sacra, novas lege, musa, coronas:
    natalis dominae iam mihi festus adest.
Ipsa sed in primis solemnes indue cultus,
    et mihi purpurea tempora cinge rosa.
5 Utque aliquid gratas divae meditemur ad aras,
    affer inauratae garrula plectra lyrae.
Tu quoque, vita, tuos auro subnecte capillos,
    plurimaque in niveo pectore gemma micet.
Haec mihi te, mea lux, seros promisit in annos,

bones. With your direction the writings of the truth-telling Sibyl would have been clear, which have done harm when the god was not understood. Blessed explainer of the gods, whom the stars recognize, to whom it is permitted to expound the thoughts of the   55
celestial beings: the shameless boy hasn't touched you with his deadly bow though he embroils even the princely gods. No sighs shatter your carefree sleep; you scorn Venus's treacherous snares. But in my blindness I am tossed on unsure waves and pass my   60
time without guidance. Would anyone now wish me length of days when he sees the great weariness of my life? Rocks pushed by the effort of a Sisyphus would not surpass me, nor wine vessels   65
dipped into the underworld's waters. Tityus's vulture with its hooked beak will give place to me, and the fruit scoffed at under the trees of Lethe.

Therefore you, friends who now weep for me in defeat, carve thus my tomb in well-worked letters: 70

Actius here is laid to rest. Rejoice, buried ashes.
Now after death his wandering shade is free of grief.

VIII. *On the birthday of his mistress, to Juno*

Bring sacrifice, gather fresh garlands, Muse, for Juno: the celebration of my mistress's birthday is now at hand. But first do you yourself don festive garb and gird my temples with the purple rose. And that we might devise something for the goddess for her pleasing altars, bring along the chattering plectrum of your gilded lyre.   5
You, too, my life, bind your hair with gold and let many a jewel sparkle on your snowy breast: this day, my light, pledged you to me into our advanced years, this day directed that you be assuredly

221

10   haec mihi te certam iussit habere dies.
     Quanta mihi hac primum fulserunt gaudia luce,
         quantus in hoc uno tempore venit honos!
     O mihi Erythraeis merito signanda lapillis;
         o mihi delicias inter habenda meas.
15   Quisquis ades, bona verba, et laetos edite cantus,
         libaque de Siculo dulcia melle date.
     Alba mihi vestis nullo violata veneno
         adsit, et in geminos defluat apta pedes.
     Ante aram viridi texant umbracula quercu
20   formosis Dryades, rustica turba, comis.
     Phoebus odorata circum tegat atria lauro;
         at myrto duplices tu, Cytherea, fores.
     Ipsa Arabum merces Nyseia turba ministret:
         Lenaeusque ferat Naxia vina pater.
25   Omnia sint laetis operata ex ordine sacris,
         et caelum niveis constrepat alitibus.
     Magna parens Iuno, centum comitata ministris,
         huc ades, et votis annue, diva, meis.
     Vos quoque per vacuum quae luditis aera, nymphae,
30   cingite felici nubila summa choro,
     scilicet eventus haec sint bona signa futuri:
         haec eadem plenae nuntia laetitiae.
     Ipse ego vestra sequar iucundo gaudia plausu,
         et peragam varios ore, manuque modos,
35   quin etiam sertis, et ture calentibus aris,
         excipiam sancta numina vestra die.
     At tu, Natalis, nullos non fauste per annos,
         semper honorata luce serenus eas.
     Quodque opto, innumeras (si quid prece posse putamur)
40   Cumaeae vincas vatis Olympiadas.

mine. What great joys first shone for me on this day, what great 10
honor came to me at this special time! O day deservedly to be
marked by me with Erythraean jewels! O day to be considered by
me among my delights. Whoever is at hand, utter propitious
words and joyous songs. Offer cakes sweetened with Sicilian 15
honey. Let me have a white garment stained by no poisons, and let
it flow neatly onto both my feet. Let the rustic throng of Dryads,
their hair comely, weave sunshades from oak's greenery. Let Phoe- 20
bus cover the forecourts roundabout with fragrant laurel, but you,
Cytherea, the double entrance-doors with myrtle. Let the Nysaean
throng supply the wares of the Arabs and let father Lenaeus bring
the wines of Naxos. Let everything be carried out in due order at
the happy rites, and let the sky resound with snow-white birds. 25
Great mother Juno, be present here, attended by a hundred ser-
vants, and, goddess, grant approval to my prayers. You also,
nymphs, who make merry amid the empty air, surround the top-
most clouds with your happy band. Let these for sure be good 30
omens of what lies ahead, let them also be harbingers of abundant
happiness. I myself will follow your rejoicing with glad applause,
and perform a medley of measures with song and gesture. Indeed
on the holy day I'll also receive your divinities with garlands and
with altars warm with incense. But you, Natal Spirit, favorable 35
through the years, may you always make your unclouded way on
this honored day. What I desire—if we believe that anything can
happen through prayer—is that you surpass the countless Olym-
piads of the Cumaean seer. 40

IX. *Ad ruinas Cumarum urbis vetustissimae*

Hic, ubi Cumaeae surgebant inclyta famae
    moenia, Tyrrheni gloria prima maris,
longinquis quo saepe hospes properabat ab oris,
    visurus tripodas, Delie magne, tuos,
5 et vagus antiquos intrabat navita portus,
    quaerens Daedaleae conscia signa fugae:
(credere quis quondam potuit, dum fata manebant?)
    nunc silva agrestes occulit alta feras.
Atque ubi fatidicae latuere arcana Sibyllae,
10   nunc claudit saturas vespere pastor oves.
Quaeque prius sanctos cogebat curia patres,
    serpentum facta est alituumque domus.
Plenaque tot passim generosis atria ceris,
    ipsa sua tandem subruta mole iacent.
15 Calcanturque olim sacris onerata tropaeis
    limina: distractos et tegit herba deos.
Tot decora, artificumque manus, tot nota sepulcra,
    totque pios cineres una ruina premit.
Et iam intra solasque domos, disiectaque passim
20   culmina setigeros advena figit apros.
Nec tamen hoc Graiis cecinit deus ipse carinis:
    praevia nec lato missa columba mari.
Et querimur, cito si nostrae data tempora vitae
    diffugiunt? Urbes mors violenta rapit.
25 Atque utinam mea me fallant oracula vatem,
    vanus et a longa posteritate ferar:
nec tu semper eris, quae septem amplecteris arces:
    nec tu, quae mediis aemula surgis aquis.
Et te (quis putet hoc?) altrix mea, durus arator
30   vertet, et: 'Urbs,' dicet, 'haec quoque clara fuit.'

IX. *To the ruins of Cumae, most ancient of cities*

Here where rose the famed walls of Cumaean renown, chief glory
of the Tyrrhenian Sea, where often a traveler from distant shores
hastened to behold your tripod, great Delian, and the roaming
sailor entered your ancient harbors, in search of traces evoking 5
Daedalus's flight: now (who could have believed it then, while its
destiny remained firm?) a lofty forest hides beasts of the wild, and
where the sanctuary of the prophetic Sibyl lay hidden now a shep-
herd in the evening pens his well-fed sheep. The council-hall that 10
of old marshaled the venerable fathers has become the dwelling of
snakes and birds. The entrance-rooms, filled everywhere with so
many ancestral masks of wax, themselves in the end lie over-
whelmed by their own mass, and the thresholds once freighted
with sacred trophies are trampled upon, and grass covers the shat- 15
tered images of gods. A single downfall lies heavy on so many
graceful objects, the work of artisans, so many well-known tombs
and so many holy burials. And now, in the middle of empty dwell-
ings and roof-beams scattered everywhere, a stranger shoots bris-
tling boars. 20

Nevertheless the god himself did not prophesy this to the
Greek ships, nor did the dove sent ahead over the wide sea. And
do we complain if the span of time allotted our life flees away? De-
structive death grasps cities. Would that my oracles might deceive
me, their prophet, and I be considered false by the future far 25
ahead: neither will you exist forever, who hold seven hills in your
embrace, nor you who rise up in rivalry from the waters' midst.
And you (who might believe this?), my nurse, a harsh ploughman
will turn over and he will say: "This city also was famous." Fate 30

Fata trahunt homines; fatis urgentibus, urbes,
 et quodcumque vides, auferet ipsa dies.

X. Mala Punica

Quid miser externas perquiris navita gentes?
 Et tam longinquo gurgite quaeris opes?
Nec te ventorumque minas, pelagique procellas,
 nec piget ignotae damna subire viae?
5 Aspice, quam tenui velemus cortice gemmas.
 Iam tibi, quicquid habent litora rubra, damus.
Seu vis purpureos roseo fulgore hyacinthos:
 infensam Baccho sive amethyston amas;
ardentes seu quae torres imitantur, et ignes:
10 seu mage diluto lumine chrysolithos.
Sed rude divitias extollit vulgus inanes,
 nec meminit, quantis sit caput inde malis.
Divitiae fera bella viris, letumque tulerunt.
 Nam prius aeterna pace vigebat humus.
15 Divitiis natoque pater, natusque parente
 caeditur, et caro fratre verenda soror.
Nec tantum saevae tractant aconita novercae,
 sed iugulat partus mater avara suos.
Adde, quod et gemmae solo fulgore probantur,
20 adscitusque illis quaeritur arte decor.
At nobis natura oculos tardare tuentes,
 et dedit, arenti pellere ab ore sitim.
Nec nostrae populos armant in proelia gemmae,
 nec suadent magnos clam violare deos.
25 Sed semper placidis visunt convivia mensis:
 stant ubi iucundo pocula plena mero.
Illic nos tenerae vir porrigit ipse puellae,
 porrigit et cupido fida puella viro.

carries men along. Under the pressure of fate time itself will take
away cities and whatever you see.

X. Punic apples

"Why, wretched sailor, are you seeking out foreign peoples and
searching for wealth in far distant waters? Aren't you troubled by
threatening winds and storms at sea, and by enduring the losses of
travel through the unknown? Look at with how thin a cover we
cloak our jewels: we present you, here and now, with whatever the   5
red shores possess, whether you desire sapphires radiant with a
rose's gleam, or you love the amethyst inimical to Bacchus, or
those that resemble burning brands and fires, or topaz instead,
with its attenuated light. But the uncouth mob exalts empty   10
riches, nor does it remember what great evils spring from their
source. Riches have brought fierce wars and death to mankind, for
in time past earth flourished with enduring peace. On account of
riches father is slain by son and son by father, and sister must be   15
dreaded by dear brother. Not only do harsh stepmothers handle
aconite, but a greedy mother murders her offspring. Add that jew-
els gain favor only by their gleam; their beauty is achieved through
the accession of art. But nature has granted us to slow the eyes'   20
gaze and to drive thirst from the parched mouth. Our jewels do
not arm peoples for battle nor urge them to profane the mighty
gods in secret, but they always attend banquets whose tables are
tranquil, where goblets stand brimming with delicious wine.   25
There the lover himself holds us out to his tender girl and the
faithful girl toward her eager lover. We are the work of peace and

Pacis opus sumus, et pacati munus amoris,
30   quod capit a Satyro Nais amata suo.
Nec temere, infernis cum nos libasset in hortis,
    noluit ad matrem nata redire suam.
Nos quoque, dum Libycos errat Pomona per agros,
    obstupuit pleno fracta rubere sinu;
35 ac rarum mirata decus, mirata liquorem,
    in sua de patrio transtulit arva solo.
Ergo Puniceae laus haec, et gloria silvae,
    vincere gemmiferi lucida dona maris;
pallentique graves depellere corpore morbos,
40   aegraque Paeoniis ora levare modis.
Quod nec Erythraei praestabunt litora ponti,
    non opibus pollens Indica terra suis.
Tu vero, duplici fulgent cui tempora lauro,
    militiae et sacri dux, Aquivive, chori:
45 accipe nos, laudum contentus luce tuarum,
    muneraque invisae despice luxuriae,
et seu carminibus, seu delassaberis armis,
    diluat exundans haec tibi gemma sitim.

Liber Tertius

I. Ad Fredericum Ferdinandi filium
Aragonium Siciliae regem

Ergo ego fallaci tantum servire puellae
    natus, et adverso semper amore queri?
Nec me Pieria spectabit Phoebus in umbra
    inter certantes carmina ferre choros?
5 Qua densos Helicon saltus, collesque virentes

the gift of peaceful love that a beloved Naiad takes from her Satyr. Nor was it without reason that, when she had tasted us in the gardens of the underworld, the daughter had no wish to return to her mother. While she was roaming through the fields of Libya, Pomona halted in astonishment that we were red in our full hollow, and, in admiration of our rare beauty, in admiration of our juice, she carried us across from our paternal soil to her own land. As a result this praise and boast of the Punic grove surpasses the glittering gifts of the jewel-bearing sea; it drives away heavy diseases from the wan body, and refreshes the features of the ill by the means of Paeon, something which neither the shores of the Erythraean sea will surpass nor the region of India, renowned for its resources.

"But you, Acquaviva, whose brow gleams with double laurel, leader of warriors and of the holy troop, happy in the brilliance of your praise, welcome us and scorn the gifts of odious excess, and, whether you will be exhausted from poetry or arms, let this gushing jewel quench your thirst."

Book III

I. To Federico of Aragon, son of Ferdinando, king of Aragonese Sicily

Was I born then only to be slave to a deceitful girl and ever to complain about love's hostility? Will not Phoebus behold me in the Pierian shade, voicing my songs among vying choirs, where Helicon spreads out her thick woodland and verdant slopes, and

pandit, et Aonidum perluit antra liquor,
dispositaeque iugis intexunt serta puellae,
    pendentesque sonant per cava saxa lyrae.
Iam libet intactis haurire e fontibus undam,
10   et lustrare sacrum, qua via nulla, nemus.
Ardua sunt tentanda; novas en, carmina, vires
    sumite: per durum gloria anhelat iter.
Nunc opus est alia crinem compescere fronde:
    nil mihi cum sertis, Bacche iocose, tuis.
15 Ipse audax virides Parnasi in vertice lauros
    decerpam, aut silvis, Pinde canore, tuis.
Ipse lyram nullo percussam pollicis ictu
    suspendam ex humeris, praemia rara, meis.
Non ego nunc molles meditor lascivus amores,
20   nec iacio ad surdas carmina blanda fores.
Maior ad heroos me sublevat aura cothurnos:
    maior et in nostro personat ore deus.
Laetus ades, Federice, tuas ex ordine laudes
    exequar: auspiciis fama petenda tuis.
25 Nam quamquam antiquis regum bene fulta triumphis
    stat domus, et tantis se tibi iactat avis,
maiorum tua non titulis innixa recumbit
    gloria, nec priscis gestis imaginibus:
sed certat magnos virtus anteire parentes,
30   aeternum et vera laude parare decus.
Nec tua facta olim titulo breve marmor habebit:
    immensum magni carminis illud opus.
Seu te quis teneris puerum miratus ab annis,
    aetatis referat tempora prima tuae:
35 seu casus rerum varios, durosque labores,
    exhausta et saevo proelia Marte canat.
Egressum vixdum cunis Aeneia nutrix
    sensit, et adventu mota repente tuo est:

streams bathe the grottoes of the Aonides, and the maidens, ar-
rayed on the ridges, weave garlands, and their hanging lyres re-
sound through the hollow of the rocks? Now it is my pleasure to
quaff water from untouched springs and to roam the sacred, path-
less grove. I must assay the heights. So seize new strength, my   10
songs. It is a difficult road along which glory pants. Now I must
bind my hair with a different foliage. I have no concern with your
garlands, playful Bacchus. Boldly I myself will pluck green laurel
on the crest of Parnassus or in your forests, resonant Pindus. I   15
myself will hang from my shoulders a lyre—rare reward—never
touched by the thumb's stroke. I give no sportive thought now to
soft loves nor hurl my seductive songs at deaf doors. A mightier   20
breeze is wafting me toward the buskins of epic, and a mightier
god resounds upon my lips. Be joyously at hand, Federico: I will
recount your praises in order. My fame is to be sought under your
auspices, for, although your house stands well bolstered by its
kings' victories of old, and boasts to you of such great ancestors, 25
your glory does not rest supported by the reputations of your fore-
bears, nor do you exult in ancient portraits, but your virtue strives
to surpass your great origin and to acquire undying honor from
praise that is true. Nor will it be a small marble that someday lists 30
your deeds in its inscription. That is the huge undertaking of an
expansive poem: whether someone who has admired your youth
from its tender years tells of the first stages of your life, or sings of
the changing circumstances of your affairs, and your hard efforts,
and battles fought to the end with savage Mars.   35

When Aeneas's nurse felt that you had scarcely left the cradle
and was suddenly roused by your arrival, after praying three times

terque deos venerata, caput ter substulit urna,
40   et tandem Phrygio lingua voluta sono est:
'En iterum, Sol magne, meae post diruta Troiae
    Pergama, post Latios spes mihi surgit avos.
Hac aetate vagi quondam per prata Scamandri,
    Aenean vidi ludere saepe meum.
45 Nec tu maior eras, cum iam post fata Creusae
    reptares gremio, pulcher Iule, meo;
certaresque iocis curas mihi demere aniles,
    deducens blandas nostra per ora manus.
His tamen auspiciis Albanae ad sidera turres
50   crevere, et rerum maxima Roma caput,
hinc Decios, Fabiosque, hinc pectora dura Catones
    vidimus, et fasces, Brute severe, tuos.
Vidimus et ductos non uno ex hoste triumphos,
    auctaque Iuleis stemmata Caesaribus.
55 Ingredere o, felixque subi pede nostra secundo
    moenia, propensos et venerare deos.
Ingredere, Antiphatae pollens tibi regia servit,
    et Laestrygonio limina tuta metu.
Sit Iove Creta potens; sint clari ab Apolline Delphi;
60   laudet Amyclaeos Taenaris ora duces:
Alciden, Bacchumque ferant ad sidera Thebae:
    terra rudimentis nostra beata tuis.
Nam te, dum rapidos arcet de finibus hostes,
    ardua magnanimus misit in arma pater.
65 Auspice te, nostrae nullis incursibus arces
    succumbent nullis litora nostra minis.
Sed bene habet, cessere metus, cessere pericla:
    barbarus hostiles ad sua vertit equos.
Iam iuga, iam lati respirant undique campi:
70   nec tuba veliferas concitat ulla rates.
Tu tamen ad patrios revocabere victor honores,

to the gods, she three times raised her head from the urn, and at last her voice rolled forth in Phrygian tones: "Mighty Sun, behold, 40 after the destruction of the Pergama of my Troy, after the ancestry of Latium, my hope arises again. At this age I once often saw my Aeneas playing through the meadows of the meandering Scamander. Nor were you older, handsome Iulus, when, after the death of Creusa, you then wriggled in my lap, and when with your playful- 45 ness you struggled to rid me of my old woman's worries, caressing my features with your soothing hands. Under these auspices the towers of Alba stretched to the skies, and mightiest Rome became the world's head. After this we saw the Decii, and Fabii, after this 50 the Catos, sturdy of heart, and your fasces, stern Brutus. We have seen triumphs led over many an enemy and lineage enhanced by the Julian Caesars. Make your way in, and, blessed by fortune, en- ter our walls with favorable tread, and offer prayers to benign 55 gods. Make your way in: the powerful court of Antiphates does you service and our thresholds are safe from fear of the Laestrigonians.

"Let Crete gain its power from Jupiter. Let Delphi be famous because of Apollo. Let the Taenarian region praise the leaders from Amyclae. Let Thebes raise Alcides and Bacchus to the stars. 60 Our land is blessed because of your first beginnings. For your great-souled father, when he was warding off the fierce foe from his frontier, sped you into the tasks of arms. Under your auspices our castles yield to no onslaughts, our shores to no threats. But it 65 is well: fears have departed, dangers departed; the barbarian turns his aggressive cavalry toward his own territory. Now the mountain ridges, now the wide plains everywhere about breathe again, nor does any trumpet rouse sail-bearing ships to action. Nevertheless 70 in victory you will be called back to receive the honors of your fa-

maternosque sinus, Parthenopenque petes.
Mox Salentinos ibis metator in agros,
    qua secat Oebalia culta Galesus aqua.
75 Sed quo livor edax non irruis? Ecce repente
    fata iubent longas te procul ire vias;
Romanumque patrem, sacrasque invisere sedes,
    in primis magnos promeruisse deos.
Tum pontes arcusque ducum, delubra, viasque,
80   cumque suis cernes structa theatra foris.
Interea Vaticanas numerare per aedes
    tot signa artificum, tot monumenta licet.
Mox Veios, veteresque Umbros, fortesque Sabinos
    transgresso, Adriacum stat superare latus,
85 Aemiliaeque domos, Apenninumque nivalem,
    et Phaetontaeo proxima regna Pado.
Quis sumptus, Leonora, tuos, quis publica dicat
    munera, Atestinis edita principibus?
Iam veteres superas, dives Ferraria, ludos,
90   aurea dum celeri praemia ponis equo,
effigiesque deum, spectandaque signa per aras
    extruis, et variis pegmata celsa locis.
Quis rursum Venetae miracula proferat urbis?
    Una instar magni quae simul orbis habet.
95 Una Italum Regina, altae pulcherrima Romae
    aemula, quae terris, quae dominaris aquis,
tu tibi vel reges cives facis, o decus, o lux
    Ausoniae, per quam libera turba sumus;
per quam barbaries nobis non imperat, et sol
100   exoriens nostro clarius orbe micat.
Proxima sunt, Gonsaga, tuae spectacula terrae,
    donaque per magnos ante parata duces.
Mantua queis, largoque exsultat Mincius ore,
    ausus spumiferum tollere ad astra caput.

therland; you will seek out your maternal bays and Parthenope.
Soon you will make your way to delimit the territory of the
Salentini where the Galaesus cuts through plough-land with its
Oebalian flow. But where, biting Envy, do you not rush in? Be- 75
hold, suddenly fate orders you to take a long expedition afar, to
visit the Father in Rome and the Holy See, above all to win the fa-
vor of the mighty gods. Then you will behold bridges, leaders'
arches, shrines, streets, theaters built with their own rows of seats.
Then throughout the Vatican palace you can catalogue so many 80
sculptors' statues, so many monuments. Then, when you have
traveled beyond Veii, the ancient Umbrians and brave Sabines,
your purpose is to pass by the Adriatic coast, the dwellings of
Aemilia, the snowy Apennine , and the realms next to Phaeton's 85
Po. Who could tell of your extravagance, who of your public dis-
plays, Leonora, sprung from princes of Este? Wealthy Ferrara, you
now surpass the games of antiquity, when you place golden prizes
for the swift horse, and rear likenesses of the saints, and statues, 90
worthy of admiration, for your altars, and lofty scaffolding in vari-
ous locales. Who could proclaim yet again the marvels of the city
of Venice that she alone, like a grand universe, possesses all at
once. Sole queen of the Italians, most beautiful rival of lofty
Rome, whose domain is the lands, the seas, you make even your 95
kings citizens, O grace, O light of Ausonia, you because of whom
we are a free people, because of whom barbarism doesn't lord it
over us, and the rising Sun gleams more brightly on our world.
Next are the sights of your territory, Gonzaga, and the gifts al- 100
ready won by the hands of eminent dukes. You are mighty, Man-
tua, and the Mincio glories in its broad mouth, having dared to
raise its foaming source to the stars, Mincio, pleasant shrine of im-

105 Mincius aeterni sacrum geniale Maronis,
      cui cedit flavo lucidus amne Meles.
    Hinc populos, Ticine, tuos spectare licebit,
      dictaque lanigerae moenia pelle suis,
    Taurinosque altasque Alpes Poeninaque castra
110   et Rhodanum et ripas, magne Lemanne, tuas.
    Inde per immensum lati spatiabere campi;
      ostendit sacrum mons ubi Iura nemus.
    Et veteres felix custodit Claudius arces,
      Claudius aeternae conciliator opis.
115 Hic formidatas acies, ipsumque videbis
      elatum longa prosperitate ducem.
    Finitimis dum bella parat, tibique arma, virosque
      commendans, magni ius dabit imperii.
    Nimirum ingeniumque sagax miratus, et artes,
120   quaeque dabis mentis plurima signa tuae.
    Quapropter mediis generum te deligit armis,
      pollicitus natae spemque, torumque suae.
    Ac velut Oenomai currus, astumque secutus,
      eludet pacti foedera coniugii.
125 Sed male ut Oenomao currus cessere, dolique,
      perfidiae poenas sic ferus iste luet.
    Ter victus, ter iam castris exutus ab hoste,
      postremo miseram corruet ante diem.
    Nam deiectus equo, fossaque inventus in alta,
130   obscoenam turpi sanguine tinget humum.
    Nec iam erit, extremos funus qui curet ad ignes,
      non lapis, incisis qui tegat ossa notis.
    Tu celsus, tu sublimis, tu victor honorem
      accipies, tibi quem Gallia tota dabit,
135 bisque tuis referet superatos Lingonas armis,
      ductaque bis pulsos signa per Helvetios:
    praeterea quantum populorum Mosa coercet,

mortal Maro: the clear Meles with its tawny flow yields to you. 105
From here it will become possible, Ticino, to see your peoples and
the walls named from the skin of a wool-bearing sow, the Taurini
and the lofty Alps and the Pennine forts, and the Rhône and your
banks, mighty Lemannus. From there you will range through the 110
wide plain's vastness where Mount Jura displays her holy forest,
and fortunate Charles watches over his ancient citadels, Charles,
mediator of immortal aid. Here you will behold his dreaded ar-
mies and the duke himself, exalted from the length of his success. 115
While he is readying war against his neighbors, entrusting both
his weaponry and his soldiers to you, he will grant you jurisdiction
over a grand command, in his wisdom doubtless admiring both
your intelligence and your skill as well as the many examples of
your wisdom that you will display. And so, in the midst of his 120
warfare, he chooses you for son-in-law, having promised the pros-
pects and the marriage-bed of his daughter. But imitating the
chariot and the cunning of Oenomaus, he will evade the terms of
the marriage agreement. Yet just as his chariot and his deceitful-
ness turned out badly for Oenomaus, so that savage will pay the 125
penalty for his treachery. Thrice defeated, thrice stripped of his
camp by the enemy, he will in the end fall before his wretched
time is due. For, thrown from his horse and found in a deep ditch,
he will make the ground filthy with his corrupt blood. Nor will 130
there then be anyone to care for his corpse at the final flames, no
stone with graven characters to cover his bones. You exalted, you
imposing, you the conqueror, will accept the honor which all
France will bestow on you: she will tell of the Lingones twice over-
come by your forces, and of your standards borne through the 135
twice-defeated Helvetii along with whatever tribes the Meuse en-

quantum caerulea Rhenus inundat aqua.
Atque erit is nostrae gentis vigor, omnia credi
140   ut possit iusto succubuisse metu.
Hic ego te, laudesque tuas, fortissime Iuli,
    non sileam, et valida proelia gesta manu.
Quem titulis Aquiviva domus praelustribus ornat,
    mortalesque inter, semideosque locat.
145 Et iam militiae moles tibi creditur omnis,
    omnia sub leges allicis ipse tuas.
At te patrato, iuvenum pulcherrime, bello,
    tempus erat patriis dona tulisse deis,
mendacisque simul fastus, odiumque tyranni
150   cum prope defenso deseruisse solo.
Eia age, rumpe moras, invisaque castra relinque,
    fidaque magnanimi limina regis adi.
Cui vel ad Oceani fines tot litora parent,
    iuraque dant sceptri Celtica regna sui.
155 Hic tibi felices taedas, certosque hymenaeos
    expediet, tutas et simul addet opes.
Testis erit Liger, Arvernis qui fusus ab antris
    libera devexum per loca findit iter.
Interea patrem, Campanaque tecta revise,
160   debitaque auspiciis, hei mihi, regna tuis,
debita, sed fatis cito iam cessura malignis,
    evertet tantas cum ferus hostis opes.
Dii maris Etrusci, per quos Tyberinus, et Arnus,
    Macraque caeruleis iungitur altus aquis,
165 dum redit in patriam iuvenis, tot honoribus auctus.
    Candida felici solvite vela noto.
Vosque citae puppes iussum properate per aequor:
    fata dabunt istas saepe iterare vias:
nec semel hos tractus, Ligurumque videbitis oras,
170   aut Vari infaustum fluminis hospitium,

closes, whatever the Rhine washes with its sea-blue flow. And such
will be the strength of our people that everything can be believed
to have yielded before rightful fear.   140

"At this point, bravest Giulio, I will not pass by in silence your
praises and the battles waged by your strength of hand. The house
of Acquaviva adorns you with conspicuous distinctions and places
you between mortals and demigods. And now the whole weight of
the campaign is entrusted to you; you yourself win over everything   145
to your allegiance.

"But, with the war brought to completion, it was time for you,
handsomest of youths, to bring gifts to your fathers' gods, and to
abandon at the same time the haughtiness and hatred of the lying
tyrant, along with the land you had lately defended. Come now,   150
break off delays, and leave the loathed camp and approach the
faithful threshold of the high-souled king whom so many shores
obey, even to the Ocean's bounds, and on whom the Celtic lands
bestow the rights of their rule. He will make ready for you the joy-
ous torches and the certainty of marriage hymns, and will add as- 155
sured wealth as well. The Loire will be witness, which, gushing
from Arvernian caverns, cuts its sloping way through unbarred
fields. Meanwhile revisit your father and your Campanian dwell-
ings, and the kingdoms—woe is me—owed to your authority,   160
owed, but already destined to yield to evil fate, when a barbarous
foe will overturn such great dominion.

"Gods of the Etruscan Sea, through whom Tiber, and Arno,
and deep Magra are joined to your blue waters, while the youth,
furnished with so many honors, is returning to his fatherland,
with favoring south wind release his glimmering sails. And you,   165
speedy vessels, hasten over the ordained waters: fate will allow
you often to retrace these routes: not just once will you see these
reaches, and the shores of the Ligurians, and the ill-starred wel-
come of the river Var, the bays with ramparts of cliffs, the   170

vallatosque sinus scopulis, Toroentia claustra,
 et sparsas mediis Stoechadas aequoribus:
denique Phocaicosque sinus, Marioque refossum
 litus, et antiquae moenia Massiliae.
175 Donec fatales Turonum accedere muros
 permittant vestro fata sinistra duci.
Ah Liger, ah nimium lacrimis urgende meorum,
 qualia spectabis flumine busta tuo!
Busta, quibus magni ponant diademata reges,
180 grataque solemni flore parentet humus.
Atque aliquis Latio veniens novus hospes ab orbe,
 portet honoratas munus ad inferias,
et dicat: "Federice, tuorum hic meta laborum
 haesit; habet nostros haec brevis urna deos."'

II. Ad Cassandram Marchesiam
quod pueritiam egerit in Picentinis

Est Picentinos inter pulcherrima montes
 vallis: habet patrios hic pia turba deos.
Quam super hinc caelo surgens Cerretia rupes
 pendet, at huic nomen Cerrea silva dedit.
5 Parte alia sacra respondent saxa Tebennae,
 quique rigens Merulae nomine gaudet apex.
Et circum nigra late nemus accubat umbra,
 plurima qua riguis effluit unda iugis,
semiferi, si vera canunt, domus horrida Fauni;
10 convectant avidae quo sua lustra ferae.
Accipit hic tergo formosum bucula taurum;
 accipit immundum sima capella marem.
Mille tori Dryadum, Satyrorum mille recessus,
 antraque silvicolae grata latebra deae.
15 Vivula nomen aquae, tenuique Subuncula rivo,

Toroentian harborage, the Stoechades scattered in the midst of the
sea, finally the Phocaian harbor, the shore rechanneled by Marius
and the fortifications of ancient Marseilles, until his unfortunate
fates allow your leader to approach the fatal walls of the Turones.
Alas, Loire, alas, to be overburdened by the tears of my people,   175
what tombs will you behold from your stream, tombs on which
mighty kings place their crowns and the kindly earth makes
offering of ritual flowers. Some new guest coming from the world   180
of Latium might bring a gift for the honored dead and might say:
'Federico, here remains the end of your sufferings. This little urn
possesses our gods.'"

II. To Cassandra Marchese:
That he passed his childhood among the Picentini

There lies a most beautiful valley amid the Picentine mountains:
here a devoted people has its ancestral gods. Above it, rising on
this side to heaven, hangs the cliff of Cerretia (a forest of oaks has
given this its name). The holy rocks of Tebenna form a balance on
the other side, and the severe crag that rejoices in the name   5
Merula. Roundabout broods a broad forest with black shade,
where a bounteous stream flows from well-watered slopes. This, if
they tell the truth, is the dread dwelling of the half-wild Faunus,
where greedy beasts gather in their lairs. Here the heifer receives   10
on her back the handsome bull, the snub-nosed she-goat receives
her squalid male. A thousand couches for Dryads, a thousand
hideaways for Satyrs, and caves, happy retreats for the goddess
who cherishes the woods. The water is called Vivula, and there is
Subuncula, with its slender flow, and the one that burbles, named   15

et quae de gelida grandine dicta sonat.
Huc mea me primis genitrix dum gestat ab annis,
  deducens caro nupta novella patri,
adtulit indigenis secum sua munera divis,
20   in primis docto florea serta gregi.
Grex erat Aonidum, coetu comitata sororum
  ipsa sui princeps Calliopea chori.
Delius argutis carmen partitus alumnis
  flectebat faciles ad sua plectra manus.
25 Atque hic me sacro perlustravere liquore,
  cura quibus nostrae prima salutis erat.
Tum lotum media puerum statuere chorea,
  et circumfusis obstrepuere sonis.
Denique praecinctumque hederis, et virgine lauru,
30   ad citharam dulces edocuere modos.
Tantus erat laetis avium concentus in agris,
  ut posses ipsos dicere adesse deos.
Venerat omne genus pecudum, genus omne ferarum,
  atque illa festum luce habuere diem.
35 Tunc ego pastorum numero, silvestria primum
  tentavi calamis sibila disparibus.
Deductumque levi carmen modulatus in umbra,
  innumeros pavi lata per arva greges.
Androgeumque, Opicumque, et rustica sacra secutus,
40   commovi lacrimis mox pia saxa meis,
dum tumulum carae, dum festinata parentis
  fata cano, gemitus dum, Melisaee, tuos.
Ac tacitas per operta vias rimatus, et antra
  inspecto, et variis flumina nata locis.
45 Mox maiora vocant me numina, scilicet alti
  incessere animum sacra verenda Dei,
sacra Dei Regisque hominum, Dominique Deorum,
  primaevum sanctae religionis opus;

after "frozen hail." When from my early years my mother, a young
bride, carried me here, leading me to her dear father, she brought
her gifts with her for the native gods, above all garlands of flowers
for the learned flock. The flock was of the Aonian Muses. Accom- 20
panied by a throng of sisters Calliope herself was the leader of her
chorus. The Delian, after sharing the song with his melodious
protégées, was bending supple fingers to his lyre. And here they,
whose chief concern was my wellbeing, purified me with blessed
water. Then in the middle of their troop they placed the boy they 25
had washed, and shrilled with a roundel of sound. Finally they
taught him, garlanded with ivy and virgin laurel, sweet measures
for the lyre. In the joyous fields there was such great harmony of 30
birds that you could say that the gods themselves were at hand.
Every type of farm animal, every type of wild beast, had come, and
on that day held festival. Then, among the crowd of shepherds, for 35
the first time I attempted sylvan whistlings on uneven reeds and,
after I had sounded a fine-spun song in the slight shade, I fed
countless sheep across the broad pastures. After being in thrall to
Androgeos and Opicus and rural rites, I soon moved the holy
rocks with my tears when I sang of the grave, the hurried doom, 40
of my mother, when of your lamentations, Melisaeus. And, after I
had explored silent paths through hidden places, I cast my gaze
upon caves and streams from manifold sources. Soon greater
Powers summon me. Nothing less than the awe-inspiring holiness 45
of God on high entered my mind, the holiness of God, both the
King of men and the Lord of Gods, our blessed religion's original

nuncius aethereis ut venerit aliger astris,
50   dona ferens castae Virginis in gremium.
Quid referam caulasque ovium, lususque canentum
     pastorum, et reges, Arsacis ora, tuos?
Nec minus haec inter piscandi concitus egit
     ardor in aequoreos mittere lina sinus,
55 fallacesque cibos vacuis includere nassis,
     atque hamo undivagos sollicitare greges,
quandoquidem salsas descendi ego primus ad undas,
     ausus inexpertis reddere verba sonis.
Quid referam mollesque elegos, miserabile carmen,
60   et superis laudes non sine ture datas,
quaeque aliis lusi numeris, dum seria tracto,
     dum spargo varios per mea dicta sales?
Multaque praeterea, dilectae grata puellae,
     adscisco antiquis rursus Etrusca modis.
65 Ut sileam nunc impensos tot regibus annos,
     tot data belligerae tempora militiae,
et sileam vexata malis mea corpora morbis,
     vixque Machaonia restituenda manu.
Adde graves populique fugas, procerumque ruinas,
70   inflicta et miseris urbibus exilia.
Ipse per infestos tecum, Federice, labores
     multa adii terra, multa pericla mari.
Tuscorumque vadis, Ligurumque exercitus undis,
     postremo litus Massiliense subii.
75 Iam Rhodanum, Volcasque feros, Vocontiaque arva
     legimus, et fines, Belgica terra, tuos.
Bisque pruinosas cursu superavimus Alpes:
     bis metas magni vidimus Oceani.
Atque hic te tandem deflevimus, optime regum,
80   quantum Hecube natos fleverat ipsa suos;
quantum discissis fratres Cassandra capillis,

244

achievement: how the winged messenger came from the ether's
stars, carrying gifts for the lap of the chaste Virgin. Why should I   50
tell of the sheepfolds, and the sporting of shepherds at song, and
your kings, realm of Arsaces? Likewise along with these matters
an excited passion for fishing drove me to launch my nets into the
sea's bays, to hide deceitful bait in weels, to tempt wave-wandering   55
schools with the hook, since I was the first to make my way down
to the salt waters, having dared to render words in untried melo-
dies. Why should I also tell of soft elegies, song of lament, and of
praises, graced with incense, given to the gods, and what I played   60
in other meters, while I was dealing with serious matters, while I
was strewing my words with assorted wit? Furthermore I adapt
again to ancient meters many Tuscan matters, pleasing to my be-
loved mistress. Let me now remain silent about so many years de-
voted to kings or so much time granted to wartime soldiering, and   65
be silent about my body pestered with evil diseases and scarcely to
be brought back to health by the hand of Machaon. Add the peo-
ple's burdensome banishments, the disasters of princes, exiles im-
posed on pitiable cities.   70

   I myself, in the course of dangerous trials, approached with
you, Federico, many perils on land, many on sea. Driven along the
Tyrrhenian shoals and the waters of the Ligurians, finally I neared
the shore at Marseilles. Now we skirt the Rhône, the fierce Volcae,
the fields of the Vocontii, and your territory, land of the Belgae.   75
Twice in our route we climbed the frosty Alps, twice we saw the
bounds of the mighty Ocean. And here, at the last, we wept for
you, best of kings, as much as Hecuba herself wept for her chil-
dren, as much as Cassandra, her tresses torn, for her brothers, and   80

Andromacheque sui dum legit ossa viri.
O fatum infelix, o sors male fida, quid illic
    egimus? o tristi mersa carina loco.
85 Cum nullum interea frugis genus imbre, vel aestu
    redderet ingenio Musa vocata meo.
Et iam miramur, longo si pressa labore
    amisit vires parvula vena suas?
Ipse deum simul, atque hominum celebrator Homerus
90   deficeret, nedum segnis, inersque lyra.
Deficeret pater ipse, et carminis auctor Apollo,
    Pegasidum sacras qui tenet unus aquas.
Ergo, tanta meae cum sint dispendia vitae
    facta, potes nostram quisque dolere vicem,
95 quod non ingenio, quod non profecimus arte,
    quod mea sit longo mens prope victa situ:
quod mala subrepens imos ceu pestis in artus
    irruerit, fracto corpore, segnities;
nec pote iam lapsae studium revocare iuventae,
100   ingenii cum sit tanta ruina mei.
Tu saltem, bona posteritas, ignosce dolori,
    qui facit, ut spreto sit mea fama loco:
Musarum spolierque bonis, et nomine claro
    vatis, et haec ultro credar habere mala.
105 Prosit, amicitiae sanctum per saecula nomen
    servasse, et firmam regibus usque fidem.
Vosque vel ignavo, vel tardo parcite, amici,
    cui Natura suas dura negarit opes;
dum tamen ambitione mala, atque libidine turpi,
110   et caream invisae crimine avaritiae.
Tu quoque vel fessae testis, Cassandra, senectae,
    quam manet arbitrium funeris omne mei,
compositos tumulo cineres, atque ossa piato,
    neu pigeat vati solvere iusta tuo.

Andromache when she collected the bones of her husband. O un-
fortunate fate! O trustless fortune! What did we do there? O my
bark, overwhelmed in a place of sadness, since in the meantime my
Muse, though I summoned her, gave my wit back no type of fruit,
whether during the time of rain or of heat. And now are we aston-   85
ished if my minuscule talent, burdened by length of suffering, has
lost its strength? Homer himself, bringer of glory at once to gods
and to men, would falter, not to mention his sluggish, feeble lyre.
Apollo, himself the father and source of song, who alone lays   90
claim to the sacred waters of the Pegasides, would falter. There-
fore, since such great losses have occurred in my life, each of you
can grieve at my plight: that I have gained fulfillment neither in
talent nor in skill, that my intelligence is nearly overcome by long   95
stagnation, that evil sloth has made its onslaught since my body
has been broken, creeping like a disease into my inmost limbs.
Nor is it possible now to summon back the zest of my fleeting
youth since so great is the collapse of my talent. Good people of   100
the future, you at least pardon the sorrow that makes my reputa-
tion lie in a place of scorn, and me, bereft of the Muses' posses-
sions and of the famous name of poet, and believed to possess
these evils of my own volition. Let it be in my favor that through
the ages I have ever kept holy the name of friendship and un-   105
shaken the loyalty to my kings. And you, friends, spare a man ei-
ther slothful or slow to whom hard Nature has denied her sup-
port, provided that nevertheless I lack evil self-interest, and base
lust, and the charge of hateful greed. Cassandra, you also as wit-   110
ness even of my weary old age, in whose hands lies wholly the su-
pervision of my last rites, deal devoutly with my ashes, collected
for the grave, and with my bones. Have no regret to pay what is

115 Parce tamen scisso seu me, mea vita, capillo,
   sive: sed heu prohibet dicere plura dolor.

III. Deos nemorum invocat in extruenda domo

Dii nemorum salvete: ego vos de rupe propinqua,
   de summis patriae moenibus aspicio;
aspicio, venerorque; cavae mihi plaudite valles,
   garrula vicinis perstrepat aura iugis.
5 Vos quoque perque focos felicia dicite cives,
   verba, per intectas flore decente vias.
Victima solemnes eat inspectanda per aras,
   turbaque Palladia fronde revincta comas.
Mosque ut ab antiquae repetatur origine Romae,
10   exterior forda cum bove taurus aret.
Ac prius infosso tectum quam cingere sulco
   incipimus, iustos ture piate deos
nulla per obductum decurrant nubila caelum:
   candidaque augustum concinat omen avis.
15 Exsurgat paries, ventos qui pellat, et imbres,
   qui multa circum luce serenus eat.
Adsit dispositis series concinna columnis,
   quaeque ornet medias crebra fenestra fores.
Ipse biceps primo custos in limine Ianus
20   occurrat laetis obvius hospitibus.
Protinus a dextra sacrae, mea turba, sorores
   cingant virgineis atria prima choris.
A laeva nitidis stratum Pythona sagittis
   miretur posita Cynthius ipse lyra.
25 Aedibus in mediis parvi sinus amphitheatri,
   visendas regum praebeat historias.
Ac primum triplici sese defendat ab hoste
   Fernandus rapido iam metuendus equo.

248

due to your poet. Nevertheless, my life, spare your torn tresses
or—but sorrow forbids me to say more.   115

III. He invokes woodland gods at the building of his house

Hail, gods of the woodland: I am watching you from a nearby
rock, from the topmost ramparts of my fathers' city. I watch and I
revere. Grant me your applause, valley hollows. A chattering
breeze rustles through the neighboring ridges. You also, fellow citi-
zens: speak words of good omen by your hearths and along your   5
streets mantled with fitting flowers. May a victim worthy of admi-
ration make its way past the ceremonial altars and the throng with
its hair bound by the foliage of Pallas. So that a custom from the
beginning of ancient Rome may be renewed, let a bull, on the far
side of a pregnant cow, be set to ploughing. Before we start to en- 10
circle the house by digging a furrow, propitiate the appropriate
gods with incense. Let no clouds traverse a darkened sky, and let a
white bird sing an auspicious omen. To keep wind and rain at bay
let the wall rise, making a glad circuit in a flood of light. Let there 15
be columns positioned in elegant array and many a window to
grace the central doors. Let two-headed guardian Janus himself be
present at the outer threshold to greet happy guests. Immediately   20
on the right let my throng, the holy sisters, encircle the first court-
yard with their virginal dancing. On the left let Cynthius himself,
with his lyre set aside, marvel at Python, laid low by his gleaming
arrows.

At the dwelling's center let the bow of a small amphitheater
present to view the histories of our kings. First let Ferdinando, an 25
object of terror now on his rushing steed, defend himself from the

Alfonsusque pharetratas, dira agmina, gentes
30   cogat Hydruntinis cedere litoribus.
Tum iuvenis ex ipse, et regum insignibus auctus
    Alpinos adigat linquere castra duces.
Postremo Federicus, avito laetus honore,
    Dalmaticas grandi classe refringat opes.
35 Infestosque deos, metuendaque iura minatus,
    indicat nato bella gerenda suo.
Hic bene conveniens membris variantibus ordo
    adspiciat celebres e regione situs.
Exedrae, existique, tablinum, hypocausta, diaetae,
40   et quae privatis usibus apta velim.
Atque aliae occasus, aliae vertantur in ortus,
    quaeque habeant Boream, quaeque inhibere Notum.
Iungantur longis quadrata, obliqua rotundis:
    et capiat structos plurima cella toros.
45 O studiis placitura meis, o mille per artes
    otia Pieriis nostra iuvanda modis.
Hic ego tranquillo transmittam tempora cursu;
    dum veniat fatis mitior hora meis.
Viximus aerumnas inter, lacrimosaque regum
50   funera; nunc patria iam licet urbe frui,
ut quod tot curae, tot detraxere labores,
    restituat vati Parthenopea suo.

triple foe. Let Alfonso compel the quivered races, dread battle-
lines, to withdraw from the Hydruntine shores. Then let the   30
youth, himself a king and ennobled by the regalia of kings, force
the Alpine leaders to abandon their camps. Finally let Federico, re-
joicing in his ancestral glory, shatter Dalmatia's resources with his
enormous fleet. After holding out the menace of hostile gods and
fearsome obligations, let him outline for his son the wars that he   35
will have to fight.

At this point let the sequence, nicely harmonious in its distinc-
tive parts, command a direct view of its celebrated site. Let there
be open bays, colonnades, a tablinum, heated baths, summer-
houses, and things that I would want, suitable for an individual's
needs. And let some face west, other east, let some suffer Boreas,   40
some keep off Notus. Let the square be connected to the linear,
the slanting to the round: and let most chambers contain well-
appointed couches. O leisure, mine, ready to commend my stud-
ies, to be delighted by Pierian measures through a thousand arts: 45
here I will pass the time in calm voyage until a gentler moment
may approach my destiny. I have lived among troubles and the sor-
rowful deaths of kings. Now at last I am allowed to enjoy my na-
tive city, so that what so many trials, so many tribulations, have   50
taken away, Parthenopea might restore to her poet.

EPIGRAMMATON

Liber Primus

I. *Ad Federicum regem*

Scribendi studium mihi tu, Federice, dedisti,
    ingenium ad laudes dum trahis omne tuas.
Ecce, suburbanum rus et nova praedia donas:
    fecisti vatem; nunc facis agricolam.

II. *Ad villam Mergillinam*

Rupis o sacrae pelagique custos,
villa, Nympharum domus et propinquae
Doridos, regum decus una quondam
    deliciaeque,

5   nunc meis tantum requies Camoenis,
urbis invisas quoties querelas
et parum fidos popularis aurae
    linquimus aestus,

tu mihi solos nemorum recessus
10   das et haerentes per opaca laurus
saxa; tu fontes Aganippidumque
    antra recludis.

Nam simul tete repeto tuasque
sedulus mecum veneror Napaeas,
15   colle, Mergillina, tuo repente
    Pegasis unda

effluit, de qua chorus ipse Phoebi
et chori Phoebus pater atque princeps

EPIGRAMS

Book I

I. To King Federico

Federico, you have given me my zeal for letters, since you draw all talent to your praises. See: you give me land on the edge of the city, and a new estate. You made me a poet. Now you make me a farmer.

II. To his villa at Mergellina

O villa, guardian of the blessed cliff and of the sea, home of the Nymphs and of nearby Doris, once the ornament as well as the delight of kings, now only the place of rest for my Camoenae, whenever we leave behind the odious squabbles of the city and un- 5 trustworthy passions of the people's whim: you grant me the groves' solitary retreats and laurels clinging among shadowy rocks. You open out the fountains and grottoes of the Aganippides. For 10 as soon as I revisit you and by myself eagerly worship your Napaeans, suddenly from your hill, Mergellina, flows the water of Pegasus from which Phoebus's chorus itself and Phoebus, the cho- 15 rus's father and leader, strive now to lure more streams for me as I

nititur plures mihi iam canenti
20   ducere rivos.
Ergo tu nobis Helicon et udae
Phocidos saltus hederisque opacum
Thespiae rupis nemus, et canoro
    vertice Pindus.
25 I, puer: blandi comitem laboris
affer e prima citharam columna;
affer et flores; procul omnis a me
    cura recedat.
Principis nostri decus atque laudes
30 fama per latas spatiata terras
evehat, qua Sol oriens cadensque
    frena retorquet,
quaque non notos populos et urbes
damnat aeternis Helice pruinis,
35 quaque ferventis cumulos arenae
    dissipat Auster.
Ille crescentes veneratus annos
vatis, antiquum referentis ortum
stirpis et clarum genus et potentum
40   nomen avorum,
contulit larga numerosa dextra
dona et ignavae stimulos iuventae
addidit, silvas et amica Musis
    otia praebens.

III. Calendae Maii

Maius adest; da serta, puer. Sic sancta vetustas
    instituit; prisci sic docuere patres.
Iunge hederam violis; myrtum subtexe ligustris;
    alba verecundis lilia pinge rosis.
5 Fundat inexhaustos mihi decolor Indus odores,

sing. And so you are our Helicon and glades of moist Phocis, our   20
forest of the Thespian rock, shadowy with ivy, and Pindus with its
echoing peak. Go, boy: from the first pillar fetch away the lyre,   25
companion of my sweet toil. Fetch also flowers. May all trouble
withdraw far from me. May Fame, who has traveled earth's
breadth, carry the glory and praise of our prince where the rising   30
and setting Sun turns his reins, where Helice condemns unknown
peoples and cities to everlasting frost and where Auster scatters   35
heaps of burning sand. Doing honor to the burgeoning years of
his bard, who tells of the ancient origin of his family, his famous
race, and the repute of his powerful forebears, he bestowed abun-   40
dant gifts with his generous right hand, and applied goads to
youth's sloth, granting woods and leisure, friendly to the Muses.

III. The Kalends of May

May is here. Give me garlands, boy. Thus hallowed antiquity or-
dained, thus taught our fathers of old. Bind ivy and violets. Weave
myrtle with privets. Paint white lilies with blushing roses. Let the
swarthy Indian pour for me an undiminished flow of perfume, and   5

255

et fluat Assyrio sparsa liquore coma.
Grandia fumoso spument crystalla Lyaeo,
    et bibat in calices lapsa corona meos.
Post obitum non ulla mihi carchesia ponet
10   Aeacus; infernis non vitet uva iugis.
Heu vanum mortale genus, quid gaudia differs?
    Falle diem: mediis mors venit atra iocis.

IV. *In tumulum Ladislai regis*

Miraris niveis pendentia saxa columnis,
    hospes, et hunc, acri qui sedet altus equo?
Quid si animos roburque ducis praeclaraque nosses
    pectora et invictas dura per arma manus?
5 Hic Capitolinis deiecit sedibus hostem
    eisque triumphata victor ab urbe redit
Italiamque omnem belle concussit et armis
    intulit Etrusco signa tremenda mari.
Neve foret Latio tantum diademate felix,
10   ante suos vidit Gallica sceptra pedes.
Cumque rebellantem pressisset pontibus Arnum,
    mors vetuit sextam claudere Olympiadem.
I nunc, regna para fastusque adtolle superbos:
    mors etiam magnos obruit atra deos.

V. *Ad Federicum regem*

Clausa quod effossis erumpunt ossa sepulcris
    et reserant veteres putria saxa rogos,
nimirum tanto cupiunt sub principe manes
    vivere et ad nutus umbra vocata venit.
5 Utque decet, longo mansuras tempore sedes
    spondent et regnis otia laeta tuis.
Quaeque diu ambiguis tecum Fortuna vagata est

let my locks drip from a sprinkling of Assyrian balm. Let massive goblets froth with smoked Lyaeus, and let the wreath, slid into my cups, drink deep. After death, Aeacus will place no tumblers before me. The grape doesn't flourish on the underworld's slopes. Alas, foolish race of mortals, why do you postpone your joys? De- 10 ceive the day: black death arrives in the midst of our pleasures.

IV. To the tomb of King Ladislas

Visitor, do you wonder at the carvings perched on snow-white columns, and at him who sits high on his spirited horse? What if you were to experience the duke's energy and strength, his noble heart and hands, invincible throughout hard wars? He hurled the enemy from his station on the Capitolium, and twice returned victorious 5 after triumphing over the city. He shook all of Italy with war and weaponry, and bore his fearful standards on the Etruscan Sea. And lest he be fortunate only with Latium's crown, he saw before his feet Gaul's scepters. When he had been laying siege to the re- 10 bellious Arno at its bridges, death forbade him to close out his sixth Olympiad. Go now, procure realms, extol grandeur and pride: black death overwhelms even mighty gods.

V. To King Federico

Given that imprisoned bones leap forth from graves dug up and moldering rocks unlock ancient pyres, no wonder the ghosts desire to live under so great a prince, and the shade arrives when summoned at your command. As is suitable, they promise that your 5 residence and happy leisure will remain in your kingdom for many a day. Fortune long roamed with you on uncertain feet. Here she

passibus, hic certa stat bene nixa rota.
Sume animos, Federice: tuis hic meta periclis
10   haeret. Habent Manes et pia busta fidem.

VI. Ad Ninam

Sexcentas, Nina, da, precor, roganti
sed tantum mihi basiationes:
non quas dent bene filiae parenti,
nec quas dent bene fratribus sorores,
5   sed quas nupta rogata det marito,
et quas det iuveni puella caro.
Iuvat me mora longa basiorum,
ne me tam cito deserat voluptas.
Nolo marmora muta, nolo pictos
10   dearum, Nina, basiare vultus,
sed totam cupio tenere linguam,
insertam humidulis meis labellis,
hanc et sugere morsiunculasque
molles adiicere et columbulorum
15   in morem teneros inire lusus,
ac blandum simul excitare murmur.
Haec sunt suavia dulciora melle
Hyblaeo et Siculae liquore cannae.
Haec sola ambrosiaeque nectarisque
20   succos fundere, sola habere possunt.
Quae si contigerint mihi tuisque
admovere sinas manum papillis,
quis tunc divitias, quis aurum et omnes
assis me putet aestimare reges?
25   Iam non maluerim mihi beatas
Aurorae Venerisque habere noctes,
non Hebes thalamos beatiores,

stands firm, well supported by her steady wheel. Take heart, Federico. Here rests the turning point to your dangers. The ghosts and holy tombs have faith. 10

VI. To Nina

Nina, I pray, when I ask give me, but only me, six hundred kisses, not the sort that daughters may appropriately give their father, nor which sisters might appropriately give brothers, but which a bride when asked might give her husband, and which a girl might give 5 to a dear young man. A long lingering over kisses gratifies me, lest pleasure abandon me so quickly. I don't want to kiss silent statues. Nina, I don't want to kiss the painted features of goddesses, but I 10 yearn to grip your whole tongue, thrust between my wet little lips, and to suck it, to add soft little nibbles, and, like small doves, to engage in tender sport, and at the same time to arouse a soothing 15 murmur. These kisses are sweeter than the honey of Hybla and than the syrup of Sicilian sugarcane. These alone are able to pour forth, are able to lay claim to, the juices of ambrosia and of nectar. If these fall to my lot and you allow me to touch your breasts, who 20 would then think that I value wealth, that I value gold and a multitude of kings, as worth a penny? I would not now prefer to possess the happy nights of Aurora and of Venus, not the still happier 25

non si deserat haec suum maritum,
non si me roget usquequaque, non si
30 aeternam mihi spondeat iuventam.

VII. De natali Altilii vatis

Musarum lux alma, meus cui tura quotannis,
    cui rite Altilius fundit in igne merum,
accipe servatos hiberno frigore flores,
    quaeque madent Siculis annua liba favis.
5 Quandoquidem magnum Latio rarumque dedisti
    pignus et Aoniis non leve nomen aquis.
At tu, sic tristes numquam experiare tenebras;
    sic Phoebi nitido semper honore mices:
fausta, precor, longos tamen exspectata per annos,
10   Altilioque tuo concolor usque redi.

VIII. Ad Federicum regem

Hibernas tibi pampineis cum vitibus uvas
    mittimus, o regni gloria honosque tui.
Praela vacant; riget omnis ager; spumantia tandem
    musta silent; mensis est tamen uva tuis.
5 Iam pater Autumnus vernantia lilia mittet,
    talia si medio frigore bruma dedit.

IX. De expeditione Alfonsi regis

Venturos olim Romana ad moenia Turcas
    dixerunt vates: credite; vera canunt.
Scilicet Alphonsum Turcas in bella trahentem
    exspectas fatis anxia Roma tuis.
5 Pone metum; vincet, sed te meliora manebunt
    imperia: Alphonso principe maior eris.

bedchamber of Hebe, not if she were to abandon her husband, not
if she were to ask me over and over, not if she were to promise me
undying youth.   30

VII. On the birthday of the poet Altilio

Gracious day of the Muses, on which my Altilio annually offers
due incense, on which he offers wine in the fire, receive flowers
preserved from winter's chill, and yearly cakes dripping with Sicil-
ian honey. The reason is that you have given a great and excep-
tional pledge to Latium, and no small repute to the waters of   5
Aonia. May you never experience evening's sadness, may you al-
ways glow with the bright glory of Phoebus: awaited through the
length of years, return propitious, I pray, and ever in harmony
with your Altilio.   10

VIII. To King Federico

O glory and honor of your kingdom, we send to you winter grapes
along with the vines' shoots. The winepresses are empty. Every
field is impervious. The frothing of the must at last grows silent.
Nevertheless there are grapes for your table. Soon father Autumn
will send lilies touched by spring, if winter has bestowed such   5
things in the midst of its chill.

IX. On the expedition of King Alfonso

Seers have said that one day the Turks would come to the walls of
Rome. Believe me: they sing the truth. Certainly, Rome, in worry
about your future you await Alfonso as he draws the Turks into
war. Set your fear aside. He will win. Yet better realms will be in
store for you. You will be the greater with Alfonso as your prince.   5

X. In tumulum Laurae puellae

Et lacrimas etiam superi tibi, Laura, dedissent,
    fas etiam superos si lacrimare foret.
Quod potuit tamen, auratas Puer ille sagittas
    fregit, et exstinctas moesta Erycina faces.
5 Sed quamvis homines tangant tua fata deosque,
    nulli flebilior quam mihi, vita, iaces.
Felices animae, quibus is comes ipsa per umbras,
    et datur Elysium sic habitare nemus.

XI. De partu Nisaeae, Charitei coniugis

Dum parit et longas iterat Nisaea querelas,
    scinditur incerta seditione polus.
Pierides puerum, Charites optare puellam:
    his Venus, ast illis docta Minerva favet.
5 Adstat amans Veneri Mavors Phoebusque Minervae,
    magnanimusque aequa Iupiter aure sedet,
cum subito aurato surgit Puer improbus arcu,
    et caelum notis territat omne minis.
Adsensere metu superi. Pater ipse deorum
10 risit, et Aonias iussit abire deas.
Exsultat palma Venus, et nascente puella
    augentur Charites, Cypria turba, deae.

XII. Ad Federicum regem

Edicto nuper cum tu, rex magne, caveres,
    audaci ne quis stringeret arma manu,
deposuisse tuum vel primus diceris ensem
    et monstrasse palam primus inerme latus.
5 Quid maius populisve tuis, Federice, vel urbi
    accidere huic nostrae per tua dona potest?

X. On the grave of the girl Laura

If it were proper for the gods also to weep, the gods would also have shed tears for you, Laura. Nevertheless the well-known Boy broke his gilded arrows — something that he was able to do — and sad Erycina her smothered torches. But, although your doom touches men and gods, you lie, my life, mourned by no one more 5 than by me. Happy the spirits with whom you make your way as companion through the shades, and to whom it is granted to dwell thus in the grove of Elysium.

XI. On the birthing of Nisaea, wife of Cariteo

While Nisaea is giving birth and repeating her drawn-out moans, the heavens are divided by undecided discord. The Pierides yearn for a boy, the Charites, for a girl. Venus supports these, but learned Minerva those. Her lover Mavors is allied with Venus, and Phoebus with Minerva. Great-souled Jupiter is sitting by with un- 5 prejudiced ear when suddenly the naughty Boy with the gilded bow stands up, and all the firmament is frightened by his well-known threats. The dwellers aloft came to agreement out of fear. The father of the gods himself smiled, and ordered the Aonian goddesses to depart. Venus takes pride in her victory, and at the 10 girl's birth the number of goddess Graces, the Cyprian's throng, is increased.

XII. To King Federico

Great king, when by edict you recently stipulated that no one un-sheathe weapons with bold hand, you were said even to have been the first to have laid down your sword, and the first to have dis-played openly your flank unarmed. What greater event can there be either for your populace, Federico, or for this city of ours, 5 through your gifts? After our enemies have been conquered, amid

Post domitos hostes, inter tot commoda pacis,
  contigit exemplis vivere posse tuis.
Publica nimirum res tunc sibi constat et aequum
10 imperium, cum rex, quod iubet, ipse facit.

XIII. De emendatione Catulli ad Iovianum

Doctus ab Elysia redeat si valle Catullus,
  ingratosque trahat Lesbia sola choros,
non tam mendosi moerebit damna libelli,
  gestiet officio quam, Ioviane, tuo.
5 Ille tibi amplexus atque oscula grata referret,
  mallet et hos numeros quam meminisse suos.

XIV. De Caesare Borgia

Qui modo prostratos iactaret cornibus ursos,
  in latebras taurus concitus ecce fugit.
Nec latebras putat esse satis sibi. Tibride toto
  cingitur et notis vix bene fidit aquis.
5 Terruerat montes mugitibus; obvia nunc est
  et facilis cuivis praeda sine arte capi.
Sed tamen id magnum: nuper potuisse vel ursos
  sternere, nunc omnes posse timere feras.
Ne tibi, Roma, novae desint spectacula pompae,
10 amphitheatrales reddit arena iocos.

XV. Ad eundem, dum ab Ursinis premeretur

O taure, praesens qui fugis periculum,
(nam te nec odio taediove tam bonas
sprevisse silvas, tam bonos putem lacus)
dic, quis propinqua nubibus tibi iuga
5 molestus invidet? Iuga illa iam tuis

so many advantages of peace, we have been allowed to be able to
live in accordance with your model. For certain, a republic is har-
monious, and an empire just, when the king himself acts according
to his orders.   10

XIII. On the correction of Catullus, to Gioviano Pontano

If learned Catullus were to return from the vale of Elysium, and
Lesbia alone were to lead behind her her thankless throngs, he will
not so much bewail the losses in his blemished little book as he
will exult in your service, Gioviano. He will bestow on you em-
braces and appreciative kisses. And he would rather remember   5
these verses than his own.

XIV. On Cesare Borgia

The bull, who just now was tossing exhausted bears with his
horns —watch!—shaken, he has fled into hiding. Nor does he
think that the hiding-place is enough for him. He is surrounded
by the whole Tiber, and scarcely trusts with confidence its famous
waters. He had terrified the hills with his roars. Now he is vulner-
able, and anyone's easy prey for the taking without stratagem. But   5
nevertheless, this is the important point: he was recently able to
lay low even bears; now he can fear every beast. Rome, lest you
lack displays for a new parade, the arena again gives sports for the
amphitheatre.   10

XV. To the same, when he was hard-pressed by the Orsini

O bull, who flees the looming danger (for I wouldn't think that
you scorned such handsome woods, such handsome lakes, out of
hatred or boredom), tell me: what annoying person begrudges you
the ridges that neighbor the clouds, those ridges for which you
struggled with your horns and conquered with your battles? Who   5

sudata cornibus tuisque proeliis
devicta? Quis saltus et amnium uberes
cursus torosque marginum virentium?
Quis uda rivis prata? Quis recondita
10 nemora? Quis umbras sibilantium arborum
male advocatus abstulit tibi deus?
Non amplius videbis, ah miser, miser,
amata regna; non videbis amplius
tuos amores; non licebit, heu, tibi
15 posthac cubanti sub genistulis tuis
mollive fulto niveum amaraco latus
audire voces ruminantium gregum;
meridianum non inire somnulum.
Quae nunc adibis tesqua? Quae petes loca,
20 miselle taure? Quas subibis ilices?
Ubi myricae? Ubi virentis arbuti
iucunda sedes? Ubi salicta et omnibus
eheu iuvenca praeferenda pascuis?
Iuvenca, solos quae relicta ad aggeres
25 Padi sonantis, heu malum sororibus
omen, dolentes inter orba populos
te te requirit, te reflagitans suum
implet querelis nemus, et usque mugiens
modo huc, modo illuc furit, amore perdita.
30 Omnia peragrat arva; lustrat omnia
num qua bisulcae signa cernat ungulae:
quaerit per alta montium cacumina;
quaerit per ima vallium cubilia,
memor locorum, non tamen sui memor.
35 Te mane primo, te rubente vespero
luget, nec illam Luna cum recurreret
caelo, nec atrae noctis alma sidera
videre dormientem; abire flumina,

begrudges the glades, and the fertile courses of rivers, and resting-
places along their greening banks? Who the meadows wet from
streams? Who the sequestered groves? What god, poorly invoked,
has wrested from you the shade of rustling trees? Ah, poor, poor   10
creature, you will no longer see your beloved kingdom, you will no
longer see your loves. Hereafter, alas, you will no longer be al-
lowed to recline under your broom plants or, with your snowy   15
flank pillowed on soft marjoram, to listen to the lowing of rumi-
nating flocks, or to take a noontime nap. What wilderness will you
now approach? What spots will you seek, poor little bull? What
ilexes will you go beneath? Where are the tamarisks? Where a   20
happy setting of green arbute? Where osiers, and a heifer, ah, to
be preferred to all the pastures? The heifer, abandoned at the
lonely banks of the roaring Po—alas, an ill omen for her sisters—
bereft, among the grieving throngs, seeks you, you. Demanding   25
you who are hers, she fills the grove with her groans, and, bellow-
ing continuously, she raves now here, now there, at her wit's end
from love. She scours, she combs all the fields, all, where she   30
might notice the traces of a cloven hoof. She searches through the
lofty crests of mountains. She searches through the lowest lairs of
valleys. Not giving a thought to herself, she has the landscape in
mind. You she mourns at break of day, you, when the evening red-
dens, nor has the Moon, as she runs her course through the heav-   35
ens, nor have the kindly stars of the black night seen her taking
sleep. She beholds the streams disappear, the Sun disappear, ev-

abire Solem, abire cernit omnia;
40   at ipsa moestam sola non abit domum,
humi recumbens, strata sub nudo aethere.
Hanc et puellae nemorum et ipse corniger
Silvanus adspicit; hanc bubulcus intuens,
miser bubulcus, nec iuvare eam valens,
45   tantum, quod unicum in malis refugium habet,
suspirat, ingemit, deum invocat fidem,
iratus ursis, quod coegerint procul
abire silvis albulum iuvenculum,
et tam venustam clamitare buculam.

XVI. *In gemmam suam*

Haec, mihi quae roseos iussit sordere hyacinthos
   et nitet articulis unica gemma meis,
cuius in exiguo ductor stat Troicus orbe
   Anchisesque senex Ascaniusque puer:
5   quis credat? Veteres inter neglecta ruinas
   et vili latuit semisepulta solo.
Tu tamen obrueras, nec te, Sinuessa, pudebat
   hoc decus heu terris occuluisse tuis.
Scilicet Aenean natumque patremque gerentem,
10   ignibus ereptos obrueresque deos?
Parcere debueras, cui iam pia flamma pepercit,
   nec te tam turpi dedecorare nota.
Et dubitem Belgasque feros rigidosque Britannos
   hac comite, ignotos et penetrare sinus?
15   Haec est Iliacos pietas spectata per ignes,
   cum verita est profugos laedere flamma deos.

erything disappear, but she herself, in her loneliness, does not de- 40
part for her sad home, reclining on the ground, stretched under
the naked sky. Both the nymphs of the woods and horn-bearing
Silvanus himself spy her. The plowman, the unhappy plowman,
watching her, wanting the strength to help her, sighs, groans, in-
vokes the gods' assurance — the only recourse he has in his trou-
bles — angered at the bears because they have compelled the little 45
white baby ox to depart far from the woods, and so charming a lit-
tle heifer to make such an outcry.

XVI. *On his gem*

This gem, which has commanded me to scorn the rose-red hya-
cinths and, one of a kind, gleams on my fingers, on whose tiny
round stands the Trojan leader and the old man Anchises and the
boy Ascanius: who can believe it? It lay hidden, ignored among
the ancient ruins and half-buried in the worthless ground. You 5
had indeed covered it up, Sinuessa, nor were you ashamed, alas, to
have concealed this jewel in your earth. Would you really cover up
Aeneas, bearing his son and his father, and the gods snatched
from the flames? You should have spared the one already spared 10
by the righteous flame, and not disgrace yourself with such an ugly
mark of shame. Would I hesitate, with this as companion, to con-
front the fierce Belgae, and stern Britanni, and seas unknown?
This is the piety beheld amid the flames of Troy, when the fire 15
feared to harm the gods set for exile.

XVII. De Venere et Marte

Dum Venus armatum complectitur obvia Martem,
    distrinxit teneram fibula adunca manum.
Sensit, et ante Iovem ridens ait aemula Pallas:
    'Bella iterum gessit cum Diomede soror.'

XVIII. De Endymione et Luna

Spreverat hirsutas pascentem Pana capellas
    candida nocturnis quae dea fertur equis.
At postquam niveae conspexit munera lanae,
    posthabuit notas Endymionis oves.
5 Qui simul ac tristes somno inclinarat ocellos,
    'Mors haec, mors,' inquit, 'non mihi somnus erit.'

XIX. De Ferdinando iuniore

Corniger aesculea Faunus recubabat in umbra,
    cum prope latrantes sensit adesse canes.
Mox iuvenem superis similem, divinaque tela
    conspiciens, trepido sic movet ora sono:
5 'Seu Mars, sive alto Phoebus descendis Olympo,
    iam iam linquo omnes te veniente feras.'

XX. De Poggio Florentino historico

Dum patriam laudat, damnat dum Poggius hostem,
    nec malus est civis, nec bonus historicus.

XXI. De Bartholomaeo Platina

Ingenia et mores vitasque obitusque notasse
    pontificum argutae lex fuit historiae.

XVII. On Venus and Mars

While Venus was holding armor-clad Mars in close embrace, a hooked brooch scratched her tender hand. Her rival Pallas noticed and, all smiles, addressed Jupiter: "My sister has been making war again with Diomedes."

XVIII. On Endymion and the Moon

The bright goddess, who is charioted along by the horses of night, had scorned Pan as he fed his shaggy goats. But after she saw his gifts of snowy wool, she disdained the familiar sheep of Endymion. And he, as soon as he had lowered his poor sad eyes in   5
sleep, says: "This will be my death, my death, not sleep."

XIX. On Ferdinand the Younger

Horned Faunus was reclining under the shade of an oak when he noticed that barking dogs were near at hand. Soon catching sight of a youth like to the immortals and of spears worthy of a god, he speaks thus with awe-struck voice: "Whether, Mars or Phoebus, you come down from lofty Olympus: now, now, at your arrival I   5
forego all wild creatures."

XX. On Poggio of Florence, historian

When Poggio praises his country, when he excoriates its enemy, he is neither a bad citizen nor a good historian.

XXI. On Bartolomeo Platina

Noting the talents and habits, the lives and deaths, of the popes was the principle of your clever history. But after this you deal

Tu tamen hinc lautae tractas pulmenta culinae:
    hoc, Platina, est ipsos pascere pontifices.

XXII. De Diana et Ferdinando II

Errabat Diana suis immista puellis,
    cum procul ecce mei conspicit ora ducis
atque ait: 'Huc, Nymphae, concedite; namque propinquat,
    qui regat in saevas certius arma feras.'

XXIII. De mane et vespere

Sol iubet exoriens, Faunos, Dryadasque puellas
    quaerere et herboso ducere monte choros.
Declivis, vitreas suadet descendere ad undas
    Doridaque et lusus, o Galatea, tuos.
5 Causa patet: quia, sublimes cum tendit in arces,
    nos quoque per saltus et iuga summa rapit,
cum vero Hesperios petit imae Thetyos amnes,
    exemplo ad fontes nos vocat ipse suo.
Hinc adeo natura hominum loca mane requirit
10   ardua; caeruleis vespere gaudet aquis.

XXIV. De Vulturno et puero regio

Miramur tacitis Vulturnum currere lymphis,
    et tardos dura compede ferre pedes.
At magis occulto mirabimur urier igni,
    et puerum tota nocte vocare suum.
5 Tunc etiam, formose puer, vaga flumina torques?
    An fuerit reges perdomuisse parum?
Quin etiam combure deos, dominoque deorum
    arma move, et pulso da Ganymede merum.

with savories of a luxurious kitchen. This means, Platina, to feed
the popes themselves.

XXII. On Diana and Ferdinand II

Diana was roaming, thronged about by her damsels, when from a
distance — look! — she sees the features of my prince and says:
"Withdraw over here, Nymphs, for he approaches who with more
assurance directs his weapons against beasts of the wild."

XXIII. On morning and evening

The sun at its rising commands the Fauni and Dryad maidens to
go on a quest, and to lead dances on the grassy mountainside. As
it sets, it urges them to make their way down to the glassy waves,
to Doris and to your sporting, O Galatea. The reason is clear: be-
cause, when he aims toward the steep heights, he seizes us as well   5
through glades and topmost ridges, but when he seeks out the
Hesperian streams of Thetis in her depths, by his own example he
summons us to the waters. Hence it is that man's nature in its
morning goes in search of lofty realms, in its evening it takes plea-
sure in the blue-green sea.   10

XXIV. On the Volturno and the royal boy

We are astonished that the Volturno runs with silent flow, and
moves his feet slowed by an unyielding shackle. But we will be the
more astonished that he is burned with a hidden fire, and all night
long calls out for his boy. Beautiful boy, are you even still torturing
the wandering waters? Was it not enough to have subjugated   5
kings? Yes: consume even the gods with fire, and take up arms
against the lord of the gods. Yes: pour the wine, now that
Ganymede is displaced.

XXV. In Quintium

Clara tibi videor scripsisse epigrammata, Quinti.
　　Sunt, fateor: medio scripsimus illa die.
Tu latebras obscurus amas, quia lumine nullo
　　atque intempesta scribere nocte soles.

XXVI. De Mercurio et Amore

Dum comes aligero Cyllenius iret Amori
　　aliger, incauto subripuit faculas.
Deprenso tum fure, manum referebat ad arcum,
　　sed non inventa risit Amor pharetra.

XXVII. In tumulum Hannibalis

Hannibal huc victas secum Carthaginis arces
　　transtulit; haec ambos terra Libyssa tegit.

XXVIII. De Venere et Iunone

Confidit nimium iaculo dum pulcher Adonis,
　　inguina setosus candida rupit aper.
Accurrit miseranda Venus, tum nupta Tonantis:
　　'Quid gemit haec? Nullo Mars meus ictus apro est.'

XXIX. In Fabianum

Esse tibi sapiens et vir, Fabiane, videris,
　　at mihi nec sapiens, nec, Fabiane, vir es.

XXV. *Against Quinzio*

I seem to you to have written brilliant epigrams, Quinzio. So they are, I agree. I wrote them during the middle of the day. In your obscurity you love hiding-places, since with no light you are accustomed to write in the darkness of night.

XXVI. *On Mercury and Love*

While the winged Cyllenian was companioning winged Amor on a journey, he snatched his torches from unsuspecting Amor. After the thief had been caught, Amor was putting hand to bow, but he had to smile when he couldn't find his quiver.

XXVII. *On the grave of Hannibal*

Hannibal has brought with him to this spot the conquered citadels of Carthage. This land of Libya shrouds both.

XXVIII. *On Venus and Juno*

When beautiful Adonis placed too much faith in his javelin, a bristly boar broke open his pale white groin. In pitiable state Venus runs to help. Then the wife of the Thunderer: "What is she groaning about? My Mars hasn't been stricken by any boar."

XXIX. *Against Fabiano*

Fabiano, you seem to yourself to be wise and manly, but, Fabiano, to me you are neither wise nor manly.

XXX. *De praetore praeside deside*

Ait nefastas esse nundinas praetor.
  Fari recusat: quid nefastius dicas?

XXXI. *Atramentum scriptorium*

Ferrum putre situ spumanti fervet aceto,
  mandet ut aeternis scripta voluminibus.
Scilicet hoc illud, vatum volitare per ora;
  hoc est, Pyramidas vincere, Nile, tuas.
5   Infelix fatum! Sanies rubiginis ergo
  eripit inviso nomina nostra rogo?

XXXII. *Ad Federicum regem*

Ne tibi non aliquid Iani misisse Calendis
  arguar aut laetam non celebrasse diem,
mittimus hibernis servatas mensibus uvas,
  insuper et faustas addimus ore preces,
5   ut tibi qui nitido cum Sole renascitur annus,
  felici redeat candidus usque pede.

XXXIII. *In Mancinum*

Qui ferro fratres, stupro, Mancine, sorores
  fas violare putat: quid putat esse nefas?

XXXIV. *Tumulus Maximillae*

Hic hic siste, precor, gradum, viator.
Hoc sub marmore Maximilla clausa est.
Quacum frigiduli iacent Amores

XXX. On a praetor as lazy protector

A praetor proclaims that workdays are unfit for business. He refuses to speak in judgment. What more unspeakable thing could you say?

XXXI. Ink for writing

Iron, flaking from rust, boils in frothing vinegar that it might commit writings to ever-enduring books. This is certainly, as they say, to take wing through the voices of poets! Nile, this is to surpass your Pyramids! Unfortunate fate! So the juice of rust snatches our   5
reputations from the hateful pyre?

XXXII. To King Federico

Lest I be accused of not having sent you anything on Janus's Kalends, or of not commemorating the happy day, we send grapes saved for the winter months, and with them we also utter prayers of good omen: that the year that is reborn with the gleaming Sun,   5
for you ever return shining with fortunate tread.

XXXIII. Against Mancinus

The man who considers it right to violate his brother with the sword, his sisters with debauchery: what does he consider to be wrong, Mancinus?

XXXIV. The grave of Massimilla

Traveler, here, pause here on your way. Massimilla is confined under this marble. With her lie, all shivering, Amours and Pleas-

et Lusus Veneresque Gratiaeque.
5 Hanc illi miserae severa Clotho
pro dulci thalamo domum paravit.
Has matri dedit, has patri querelas
pro plausa choreisque nuptiarum.
Quid firmum tibi, quid putes, viator,
10 mansurum inviolabile aut perenne,
si quae deliciae iuvenculorum
et decus fuerat puellularum,
nunc eheu iacet ecce Maximilla,
luctus perpetuus iuvenculorum,
15 aeternae et lacrimae puellularum?

XXXV. *De mirabili urbe Venetiis*

Viderat Hadriacis Venetam Neptunus in undis
    stare urbem et toto ponere iura mari:
'Nunc mihi Tarpeias quantumvis, Iupiter, arces
    obiice, et illa tui moenia Martis,' ait.
5 'Si pelago Tybrim praefers, urbem adspice utramque:
    illam homines dices, hanc posuisse deos.'

XXXVI. *De Alphonso duce Calabriae*

Alphonsus magnum dum traiicit Apenninum
    castraque non solita primus in Alpe locat,
armorum sonitus galeasque aerataque tela
    silvarum dominae pertimuere deae.
5 Nec minus occultas Satyri petiere latebras,
    assueti imbelles ante videre feras,
spectaruntque procul celsa de rupe silentes,
    agmina dum et magnos cogeret ille duces.
Atque aliquis signa adspiciens, miratur et inquit:
10 'Imperium vobis urbis et orbis erit.'

antries and Venuses and Graces. Instead of a sweet marriage
chamber this abode harsh Clotho readied for her in her sorrow.
Instead of the applause and merriment of a wedding, she offered 5
these laments to her mother, these to her father. Traveler, what,
think you, is steadfast for you, what sure to remain imperishable
or ever enduring, if she, who was the delight of the young lads and 10
the grace of the damsels, now, alas, lies — behold Massimilla! —
an eternal sadness for the young lads and perpetual tears for the
damsels? 15

XXXV. On the marvelous city of Venice

Neptune had seen the city of Venice, steady in Adriatic waters,
and extending laws to the whole sea. He speaks: "Challenge me
now, Jupiter, as much as you like, with the Tarpeian citadel and
those walls of your Mars. If you prefer the Tiber to the sea, cast
your eye on both cities. You will say that men built that one, the 5
gods this."

XXXVI. On Alfonso, Duke of Calabria

While Alfonso crosses the mighty Apennines and establishes his
camp for the first time on an unfamiliar Alp, the goddess-mis-
tresses of the woods were terrified by the reverberation of weap-
onry and by helmets and javelins of brass. The Satyrs, formerly
used to facing pacific beasts, also sought their hidden lairs. In si- 5
lence they watched in the distance from a lofty crag while he mar-
shaled his forces and mighty chieftains. Someone is awestruck as
he beholds the standards, and says: "Yours will be the ruling
power of the city and of the world." 10

XXXVII. De Innocentio VIII pontifice maximo

Innocuo priscos aequum est debere Quirites:
  progenie exhaustam restituit patriam.

XXXVIII. Ad Venerem

Quid mihi te facilem blandis promittis ocellis,
  si miserum sic post uris, acerba Venus?
Non decet hoc superos: aut te mihi fronte serena
  concilia, aut torvo lumine bella move.

XXXIX. De Galla

Omnes, quos scripsi, versus vult Galla videre:
  mittam ego, pro libris si mihi labra dabit.

XL. De Vetustino

Emit sepulcro praedium Vetustinus,
  sed quod futuros non sequatur heredes,
  iratus aeque mortuisque vivisque.
  Scribique curat grandibus notis, demens,
  VIGINTI. IN. AGRO. IN. FRONTE. TER. PEDES. OCTO.
5 Habitat sub urbe scandulis tribus tectus,
  ne pensione degravetur aut sumptu.
  Dormite grabato, quo nec ipse iam vellet
  dormire cimex, nec lacerta, nec sorex.
10 Cenat per hortos alliumque caepasque
  et salgamorum iure lividos caules
  vel, siquid optat unctius sibi poni,
  piscatur ipsis in paludibus ranas
  aut e cloaca colligit meras sordes,
15 putrem palumbum, mortuumve caponem.

XXXVII. On Innocent VIII, pontifex maximus

It is right that the ancient Quirites are in debt to an innocent man: he restored their bereft fatherland with his offspring.

XXXVIII. To Venus

Why, cruel Venus, do you promise, with your lovely soft eyes, to be accommodating to me, if thereafter you burn me thus in my misery? This does not befit the gods above. Either endear yourself to me with unclouded brow or with grim glance declare war.

XXXIX. On Galla

Galla wishes to see all the poems that I have written. Send them I will, if she will give me her lips in return for my library.

XL. On Vetustino

Vexed impartially at both the dead and the living, Vetustino has purchased property for his grave that, however, will not come to his future heirs. In his folly he has it written in block letters: TWENTY FEET IN LENGTH; IN BREADTH TWENTY-FOUR. He 5 dwells on the outskirts of the city, sheltered by three shingles, lest he be weighted down by debt or expense. He sleeps on a pallet upon which not even a bedbug, or a lizard, or a shrewmouse would now wish to sleep. In his vegetable garden he dines on garlic and onions and the stems of pickles blackened in their juice. 10 Or, if he wants to be served richer food, he goes fishing for frogs right in the swamps, or from the sewer gathers absolute dregs, a rotting pigeon or dead chicken. He also swallows the muddy sedi- 15

Et doliorum turbidam bibit faecem,
tamquam Falernum consulare vel Chium,
Opimianae quod refuderint cellae.
Nec iam profestis hoc, sed Idibus tantum
20   sacrisque potat ferculis Calendarum.
Et mane veste currit anxius rapta
ad architectos marmorumque sectores,
ut de sepulcro conserat novas lites.
Quos iam misellos pessimis modis mulctat:
25   ducit, reducit, distrahit, rapit, vexat,
per angiportus viculosque clivosque
et per ruinas urbis et per anfractus;
monstrat theatra porticusque priscorum
arcusque claris principum sacros armis;
30   hinc et deorum templa et obrutas thermas
et quidquid altis fornicum subest clivis.
Nec iam Favissas linquit, et nigros Manes,
demum trecentis cum laboribus fractos
et aestuantes pariter et fame siccos
35   vix officinae post meridiem reddit
iam feriatae vectibusque adhuc clausae;
culpat coronas zophorumque permutat,
spiras reformat, et scapos columnarum,
et nunc Etruscas, nunc Corinthias mavult,
40   nunc Doricarum laudat ordinem tantum:
guttas, triglyphos, taenias, toros, plinthos.
Quid cum columnis nunc tibi, Vetustine,
aut cum voluta, Ionicisve pulvinis?
Dormi, miselle: sat diu laborasti;
45   cenare fessos et aliquando permitte.
Aut, si sepulcri cura te coquit tanta,
cadaver istud vel Gemoniis conde.

ment of jars, as if it were Falernian with a consul's date, or Chian, which the cellars of Opimius might have poured forth. Nor does he guzzle this on ordinary days but only on the Ides and with the holy dishes on the Kalends. In the morning he grabs his cloak and rushes worriedly to the architects and marble cutters to argue afresh about his grave. He then punishes the poor souls in the worst ways. He leads them out and back, he perplexes them, tugs at them, irks them, through alleyways, and hamlets, and slopes, through the ruins and windings of the city. He points out theatres and porticoes of the ancients, and arches dedicated to the famed weaponry of princes; after this also the temples of the gods, and baths in a state of collapse, and whatever lurks under vaults' lofty inclines, nor does he omit the Favissae and the dark Manes. At last, after midday he reluctantly returns them, broken from three hundred trials, sweating and equally dry from hunger, to their workshop, already closed for the day and shut tight with bars. He finds fault with the cornice, changes and reshapes the swirls of the frieze and the shafts of the columns. Now he prefers Etruscan, now Corinthian, now he praises only their Doric order, guttae, triglyphs, fillets, mouldings, plinths. What concern have you now, Vetustino, with columns or with volutes or the ridges of Ionic capitals? Sleep, poor little creature. You've struggled enough, and for quite awhile. Allow the worn-out folk to have a meal from time to time. Or, if such worry about your grave puts you in a stew, as a possibility give over that corpse of yours to the Gemoniae.

XLI. *In tumulum Neaerae*

Quae voces? Charitum. Quae circum pompa? Neaerae.
    Unde odor hic? Cineri tura ministrat Amor.
Unde pyra? Ex pharetra. Quinam struxere? Lepores.
    Ast haec illacrimans quae legit ossa? Venus.
5   Fortunate lapis, tumuloque beatior omni!
    Tu tegis in terris siquid honoris erat.

XLII. *De Hybla*

Hybla, mei quondam dulcissima cura Marulli,
    Hybla, suburbano nuper humata solo,
accipe quae multo promuntur verba dolore,
    accipe de lacrimis humida serta meis.
5   Te rosa, te violae, te mollis amaracus ornet;
    te pia suspenso pondere velet humus.
Et tibi, quod rarae possunt sperare puellae,
    contingant vatis carmina docta tui.

XLIII. *De Aufidio*

Dum caput Aufidio tractat chirurgus, et ipsum
    altius exquirit, quo videat cerebrum,
ingemit Aufidius. 'Quid me, chirurge, fatigas?
    Cum subii rixam, non habui cerebrum.'

XLIV. *Ad Alphonsum*

Qui prius Herculeae sensit leo vulnera clavae,
    hic, Alphonse, tuos corruet ante pedes.
Quaeque viret nostras quercus passura secures,
    deseret immundos fulmine tacta sues.
5   Victa dabit Bellona manus; Pax arva reviset.

XLI. To the tomb of Neaera

"Whose voices?" "The Graces'." "What cortège at hand?"
"Neaera's." "Whence this aroma?" "Love furnishes incense to the
ashes." "The source of the pyre?" "From his quiver." "Who built
it?" "The Charms." "But who is this person in tears collecting the
bones?" "Venus." Exceptional stone, more blessed than every
tomb. You shroud whatever nobility there was on earth.   5

XLII. On Hybla

Hybla, once the sweetest concern of my Marullo, Hybla, recently
buried in the earth outside the city, receive the words that are in-
spired by my enormous grief, receive the garlands damp from my
tears. Let the rose, let the violets, let the soft marjoram bedeck
you. Let the respectful ground cloak you with lightened weight.   5
And may the learned songs of your poet make their way to you—
an event for which only exceptional girls can hope.

XLIII. On Aufidius

While the surgeon attends to Aufidius's head and delves into it
quite deeply to see his brain, Aufidius groans aloud: "Why are you
picking at me, surgeon? When I got into that fight, I didn't have a
brain."

XLIV. To Alfonso

The very lion, who once upon a time felt the bashings of the club
of Hercules, will collapse before your feet, Alfonso. The oak tree,
which flourishes only to endure our ax-blows, will abandon his
grimy pigs when gashed by your thunderbolt. Conquered Bellona
will be your slave. Peace will reclaim the fields. With Mars at   5

Claudentur dirae Marte sedente fores.
Tunc pia Parthenope laetos tibi ducet honores;
    per fora, per vicos otia vulgus aget.
Sebethosque pater, fluviis metuendus Etruscis,
10   aurea caeruleum tollet ad astra caput.

XLV. In Lydam

Cum dixi medio tibi macram algere sub aestu,
    non dixi fluvium, Lyda. Quid ergo? Cutem.

XLVI. In Ollum

Omnia facturum te dicis, nil facis, Olle.
    Nihil mirum: levius dicere, quam facere est.

XLVII. Ad Rufum

Tamquam prisca mihi saxoque inventa vetusto
    disticha, Rufe, soles saepe referre tua.
Stultum adeo me, Rufe, putas? Ego tam mala credam
    carmina Romano marmore posse legi?
5 Archemoro longos adfingis Nestoris annos;
    Andromaches puerum Laomedonta vocas.
Desine mentiri Pyliam Phrygiamque senectam.
    Sint vetera haec aliis, mi nova semper erunt.

XLVIII. De Cyparisso puero

Flerat adhuc moerens cervo Cyparissus adempto,
    cum sua conspexit cortice membra tegi.
Delius exclamat: 'Quid nostro, silva, dolore
    crescis? Tu Daphnen, tu Cyparisson habes.'

rest, his dread doors will be closed. Then holy Parthenope will sponsor happy celebrations for you, and through the squares and streets the people will hold holiday. Father Sebeto, object of terror to Etruscan streams, will lift his gray-blue head to the golden stars.   10

XLV. Against Lyda

"When I said to you that something thin remained chill during sweltering heat, I wasn't speaking of the river, Lyda." "So what was it?" "Your skin."

XLVI. Against Ollus

You say that you will do everything. You do nothing, Ollus. Nothing strange: it is easier to say than to do.

XLVII. To Rufus

Rufus, you are often accustomed to recite for me your distichs as if they were ancient and discovered on a hoary rock. Rufus, do you think that I am stupid enough to believe that such hideous verses could be read on a Roman marble? You ascribe Nestor's length of years to Archemorus, and you call Andromache's son Laomedon.   5 Stop telling lies about Pylian and Phrygian old age. Let these be ancient to others. They will always be new to me.

XLVIII. On the boy Cyparissus

Cyparissus had been still in tears, mourning for his lost stag, when he noticed that his limbs were covered with bark. The Delian shouts: "O woods, why are you expanding at the expense of my sorrow? You have Daphne, you have Cyparissus."

XLIX. De Harmosyne

Harmosynen quisquis seu vir seu femina vidit,
    deperit: anne oculos Actius unus habet?

L. De Iucundo architecto

Iucundus geminos fecit tibi, Sequana, pontes:
    iure tuum potes hunc dicere pontificem.

LI. De Aenea et Didone

Immemor ah miserae cur ensem linquis Elisae,
    nate dea? Profugas non gravat ille rates.
Anne parum fuerat causam dare mortis acerbae,
    ni ferrum fugiens tu quoque triste dares?
5 Tolle precor, tumidas tecum hoc, iam tolle per undas.
    Discessu, satis est, si perit illa tuo.

LII. In Caecilianum

Si tibi per genium fas est iurare Minervae,
    per Veneris flavas, Caeciliane, comas,
nec iubar excipitur Solis, nec cornua Phoebes,
    nec Capitolini crura caputque patris,
5 cur mihi tu ventrem, cur intestina deorum,
    Hispana tactus religione, sonas?
Non pudet heu caelum rebus foedare pudendis?
    An credis magnos haec quoque habere deos?

LIII. Ad Marinum Caracciolum

O dulce ac lepidum, Marine, factum,
    dignum perpetuo ioco atque risu,
    dignum versiculis facetiisque,

XLIX. On Harmosyne

Whether man or woman, whoever sees Harmosyne, dies of love.
Or does Actius alone have eyes?

L. On Giocondo, the architect

Giocondo made two bridges for you, Seine. Rightly you can call
him your Bridge-Builder.

LI. On Aeneas and Dido

Alas, offspring of a goddess, in your forgetfulness why are you
leaving behind your sword for lovesick Elisa? It adds no weight to
your exiled vessels. Was it insufficient to supply the cause of her
bitter death without also giving her the grim sword as you fled?
Take it with you, I pray, take it now through the roiling waves. It   5
is enough if she perishes because of your departure.

LII. Against Caecilianus

If it is appropriate for you, Caecilianus, to swear by the intelli-
gence of Minerva, by Venus's blond locks, nor are the Sun's rays
exempt, nor the horns of Phoebe, nor the legs and head of the
Capitoline father: tainted by Hispanic superstition, why do you
call out in my presence upon the belly, upon the innards of the
gods? Aren't you ashamed, my oh my, to befoul heaven with   5
shameful matters? Do you believe that the great gods actually pos-
sess these things?

LIII. To Marino Caracciolo

O sweet and charming situation, Marino, worthy of unceas-
ing laughter and amusement, worthy of our ditties and our skill,

nec non et salibus, Marine, nostris.
5 Ille maximus urbis imperator
Caesar Borgia, Borgia ille Caesar,
Caesar patris ocellus et sororis,
fratrum blanditiae, quies, voluptas,
Montis pupulus ille Vaticani,
10 ille inquam dominae urbis inquinator
Caesar Borgia, Borgia ille Caesar,
moechus ille sororis atque adulter,
fratrum pernicies, lues, sepulcrum,
montis bellua tetra Vaticani,
15 quingentas modo qui voravit urbes
imbutus scelere et malis rapinis,
urbes sub ducibus suis quietas,
quascumque aut Latium ferax virorum
aut Campania pinguis aut per alta
20 divisi iuga continent Sabini,
hisque ingessit Ariminum, Pisaurum,
Urbinum, Populoniamque magnam,
Camertes pariter, Forumque Livi,
Cornelique Forum Faventiamque,
25 et quantum Aemiliae est Etruriaeque,
quantum circuitu hinc et inde longo
Neptuni lavat aestuantis unda:
at nunc quis neget esse opus deorum?
Dum vecors animi impotente morbo,
30 quaerit plura, nec est potis misellus
explere ingluviem periculosam?
Ecce evomit, o Iovem facetum!
O pulchram Nemesim! O venusta fata!
Verum scilicet id, Marine, verum est,
35 quod dici solet; en fides probat nunc:
fortunam si avide vorare pergas,

Marino, as well as of our wit: that all-powerful Emperor of the
city, Cesare Borgia, that Borgia Caesar, Cesare, the apple of his   5
father's eye, and his sister's, the charm, the serenity, the pleasure
of his brothers, that dear little boy of the Vatican Mount, that
polluter—I say—of the mistress of cities, Cesare Borgia, that   10
Borgia Caesar, that defiler and adulterer of his sister, the ruin, dis-
ease, and doom of his brothers, abominable beast of the Vatican
Mount, who, not long ago, tainted with crime and with the evils
of pillage, swallowed five hundred cities, cities at peace in the   15
hands of their own leaders—all those that either populous Latium
or fertile Campania or the Sabini, separated by their lofty ridges,
contain—and along with these ate up Ariminum, Pisaurum,   20
Urbinum, expansive Populonia, Camertes likewise, and Forum
Livi and Forum Corneli and Faventia, everything in Aemilia and
in Etruria, everything that the wave of swirling Neptune in its ex-   25
tensive round washes on this side and that. But now who would
deny that this is the work of the gods? Out of his mind by an un-
controllable disease, while he seeks more, he isn't able, poor little
creature, to satisfy his dangerous maw.   30

Look, look: he's vomiting! O witty Jupiter! O gorgeous Neme-
sis! O delightful outcome! It's true, Marino, the old saying is true.
See! Experience now confirms what is regularly said. If you're in a   35
hurry greedily to gobble up your fortune, you're bound to have in-

eandem male concoquas necesse est.
Et iure evomere hunc putemus ipsum,
qui tantum miser hausit oppidorum.
40 Ast id omne, quod hausit, oppidorum,
quod quinque assiduis voravit annis,
imbutus scelere et malis rapinis,
scis quot evomuit diebus? Uno.
O lucem niveam! O Iovem facetum!
45 O pulchram Nemesim! O venusta fata!
O dulce ac lepidum, Marine, factum!

LIV. De Caesare Borgia

'Aut nihil aut Caesar' vult dici Borgia: quid ni,
cum simul et Caesar possit et esse nihil?

LV. Ad eundum

Omnia vincebas; sperabas omnia, Caesar.
Omnia deficiunt; incipis esse nihil.

LVI. Dies genialis

Aureli, perfunde meis unguenta capillis,
tu super et vernas sparge, Nearche, rosas.
Sed prius aestivum ramis defendite solem
et viridi mollem sternite fronde torum.
5 Non plumae, non picta iuvant me stragula, nec quae
pavonis vario sponda colore nitet.
Larga coronata disponite pocula mensa,
Setino et gelidas adsociate nives
certatimque leves potanti inducite somnos.
10 Sic iuvat aetatis ducere fila meae.
An scimus miseri, quid lux ventura minetur?
Vivamus: mortem fallere nemo potest.

digestion. As a result we should consider that the poor creature who has wolfed down so many towns deserves to vomit. But do you know how many days it took him to vomit all those towns which he wolfed down, which he, tainted with crime and with the 40
evils of plunder, swallowed over five busy, busy years? One! O day white as snow! O witty Jupiter! O gorgeous Nemesis! O delightful outcome! O sweet and charming situation, Marino. 45

LIV. On Cesare Borgia

Borgia wishes as his title: "Either nothing or Caesar." Why not, since he *can* be at once Caesar and nothing?

LV. To the same

You were conquering everything, you were hoping for everything, Cesare. Everything is passing away. You begin to be nothing.

LVI. Birthday

Aurelius, pour unguents on my locks, and you, Nearchus, scatter as well spring roses. But first ward off the summer sun with branches, and spread a soft couch with green foliage. Neither feathers nor embroidered coverlets please me nor a sofa that glim- 5
mers with a peacock's dappled hue. Place wide goblets on the gar-landed table. Mingle the chill of snow with the Setian. Vie in con-veying easy sleep as I drink. So it pleases me to draw out my life's 10
threads. Poor wretches, do we foresee what the morrow's light threatens? Let us live. No one can deceive death.

LVII. Ad amicam

Da mihi tu, mea lux, tot basia rapta petenti,
  quot dederat vati Lesbia blanda suo.
Sed quid pauca peto, petiit si pauca Catullus
  basia: pauca quidem, si numerentur, erunt.
5 Da mihi, quot caelum stellas, quot litus arenas,
  silvaeque quot frondes, gramina campus habet;
aere quot volucres, quot sunt et in aequore pisces;
  quot nova Cecropiae mella tuentur apes.
Haec mihi si dederis, spernam mensasque deorum,
10 et Ganymedea pocula sumpta manu.

LVIII. Ad Bassum de Phyllide

Cum de cathedra, Basse, surgeret nuper
  mammosa Phyllis, tunica mollis, ut saepe
  his accidit, qui obesulas habent clunes,
  intravit illuc, unde prodeunt aurae,
5 quae de Sabaeis messibus nihil spirant.
  Quod ut animadvertit dicaculus quidam,
  urbaniorem ut se faceret, ait ridens:
  'Meus, Phylli, quisnam mordicus tenet vestem?
  Vorabit hanc, ni praecaves.' Ad hunc Phyllis,
10 'Immo,' inquit, 'ut scias, sibi labra abstergit.
  Accede, pupe, basiare te nam vult.'

LIX. Ad Vesbiam

Adspice, quam variis distringar, Vesbia, curis;
  uror, et heu nostro manat ab igne liquor.
Sum Nilus sumque Aetna simul; restinguite flammam,
  o lacrimae, lacrimas ebibe, flamma, meas.

294

LVII. *To his mistress*

My light, grant me in my desire as many kisses snatched from you as charming Lesbia had given to her poet. But why do I seek only a few kisses, if Catullus sought only a few? They will indeed be few, if they are countable. Grant me as many as the heavens have stars, as the shore sands, as the woods leaves, as the field grass, as 5 many as there are birds in the air, as many as fish in the sea, as many as fresh honey-combs that Cecropean bees guard. If you will grant me these, I'll scorn the banquets of the gods and goblets taken from the hand of Ganymede. 10

LVIII. *To Bassus on Phyllis*

Bassus, when bosomy Phyllis got up just now from her chair, her soft dress, as so often happens to those with over-plump buttocks, entered the spot whence come breezes wafting nothing of the harvest of Saba. When a certain smart aleck noticed this, in order to 5 promote himself as quite the wit, he said with a laugh: "Good heavens, Phyllis, who is that clutching your dress in his bite? He will gobble it up, if you don't watch out." To this Phyllis says: "On the contrary, in case you want to know: he's wiping his lips. Draw 10 near, my boy. He wants to kiss you."

LIX. *To Vesbia*

Behold, Vesbia, with what a mixture of tribulations I'm torn apart. I am ablaze, and, alas, moisture drips from my flames. I am, at once, the Nile, at once, Etna. Quench my fire, O tears. Drink up my tears, O fire.

LX. Ad Aeglen

Si tibi sum Phoebus, si sum tibi Iupiter, Aegle,
    cur tu non Daphne sis mihi, non Danae?

LXI. Ad Pulicianum

Ait nescio quis Pulicianus,
    ni pulex mage sit vocandus hic, qui
    unus grammaticus, sed his minutis
    vel longe inferior minutiorque est,
5   divinum sibi passerem Catulli
    haudquaquam bene passerem sonare;
    nec iam id esse quod autument legentes,
    sed quod versiculis parum pudicis
    ludens innuat ipse Martialis:
10 *Da mi basia, sed Catulliana:*
    quae si tot fuerint, quos ille dicit.
    Donabo tibi passerem Catulli.
    Ut sit, quod puero poeta possit
    post longas dare basiationes,
15 quod salvo nequeat pudore dici.
    Proh, dii, quam vafer es, Puliciane:
    solus qui bene calleas poetas!
Nimirum, et quod ab omnibus probetur,
    mutandum quoque suspicaris illud,
20 quod nunc illepidumque et infacetum
    mendosis Epigrammaton libellis
    insulse legit imperita turba:
    Sic forsan tener ausus est Catullus
    magno mittere passerem Maroni:
25 cum sit simpliciusque rectiusque
    mitti, dicere, mentulam Maroni.

LX. To Aegle

If I am Phoebus to you, Aegle, if I am Jupiter to you, why might you not be Daphne to me, why not Danaë?

LXI. To Poliziano

A certain Pulicianus — unless he should be called a flea instead; he's a nonpareil scholar, but far lesser and tinier than these tiny ones — says that the immortal sparrow of Catullus doesn't ring at 5 all well as sparrow, nor is it in fact what readers allege but what Martial jokingly hints at in his none-too-chaste little verses: "Give me kisses, but of the Catullan sort: If there are as many of these as 10 he says, I will give you Catullus's sparrow." This is to say: what the poet can give the boy after long bouts of kissing, what cannot be uttered with chastity intact. Ye gods, Pulicianus, how clever 15 you are, since you alone have wise insight into poets!

Doubtless (and this would gain everyone's approval) you suspect that should also be changed which, now charmless and ill-wrought, in a blemished little book of epigrams, the untutored 20 crowd reads in its foolishness: "So perhaps delicate Catullus dared to send his Sparrow to mighty Maro." How much more straightforward and to the point to say that his prick is sent to Maro. 25

Sed quid vos, Aganippides, puellae,
ridetis? Meus hic Pulicianus
tam bellum sibi passerem Catulli
30   intra viscera habere concupiscit.

LXII. De eodem

Vanas gigantum iras et impetus graves
  miratur aliquis audiens mortalium,
  ausumque caelo vincula inferre irrita
  saevum Typhoea, cum iugosum Pelion
5   adderet Olympo, matre nec Terra satum
  agnosceret se se; impium donec pater
  iratus ardenti igne sustulit caput,
  ut par erat: nam quis petat sanus deos?
  At nunc quis hoc, quis hoc ferat mortalium?
10   Iners, pusillus, unus heu pulex ciet
  turmas, cohortes, copias, manipulos
  muscarum et altos scandere adparat toros
  heroum, opacis qui sub umbris arborum
  strati ac perenni flore subfulti caput,
15   ducunt quietem perpetem, aeternam, optimam;
  nec nostra curant dicta vel facta amplius,
  ut qui beatos incolant tuti locos;
  et nomen alta in arce sacrarint suum,
  functi periclis et malis laboribus;
20   cunctasque Fortunae improbae calcent minas,
  ne dum pusilli pulicis morsus leves.
  At tu, moleste, amare, vesane, impie
  pulex, inepti concitator agminis,
  quo proripis te? Quo vocas muscarias
25   istas phalanges? Quo volatiles globos
  impellis audax? I procul, miser, miser,

Why, girls of Aganippe, are you chuckling? This Pulicianus of mine
lusts to have Catullus's ever-so-charming sparrow within his insides.   30

LXII. On the same

Any human being is amazed when hearing of the fruitless wrath
and the weighty onslaughts of the Giants, and of fierce Typhoeus
who dared in vain to threaten heaven with chains, when he was
trying to add Pelion's ridges to Olympus, and he did not recognize
that he was the child of mother Earth—until the wrathful father   5
in blazing fire did away with his cursed head. As was only correct:
who in his right mind would go after the gods? But now who on
earth, who on earth would put up with this? A single weakling,
minuscule, flea—can you bear it?—stirs up squadrons, battalions,   10
troops, maniples, of flies, and readies itself to clamber onto the
couches of heroes who, stretched under the trees' darkening shade
and with heads pillowed on everlasting flowers, share in an ex-
traordinary peace that endures forever. Furthermore, they care nei-   15
ther for our words or our deeds, safely dwelling, as they do, in the
places of the blest. In their lofty citadel they have exalted their re-
pute earned through perils and the evils of suffering. They stamp
on all the threats of outrageous Fortune, to say nothing of the cur-   20
sory bites of a teeny flea. But you, flea that you are, annoying, bit-
ter, crazed, accursed, instigator of a stupid army, where are you
rushing? Where are you summoning your army of fleas? Where in
your boldness are you driving your airy swarms? Off with you, you   25
criminal, way off, poor, poor creature: go to the devil. It is quite

i, criminose, maximam in malam crucem.
Haud fas quietas Manium sedes deum
muscas subire pulicumque copias.
30   Nil hic negotii vel tibi vel pessimis
tuis maniplis: quid moraris, impie?
Abi profundam in noctem et ultimum Chaos.
Speranda certe gloria hic nulla est tibi.
Quos dii probavere semel, hos semper probant.

LXIII. Actaeon Marmoreus

Viderat Idaeo nudas in vertice divas
    Phryx Paris, et dixit: 'Vincis utramque, Venus.'
At si, Gargaphiis quam nos male vidimus undis,
    vidisset, poterat dicere: 'Cede, Venus.'

LXIV. Orpheo respicienti

Hoc fuit, infelix, et adhuc heu respicis, Orpheu,
    quod te, quod miseram perdidit Eurydicen.

LXV. Echo loquitur

Vidi, arsi, flevi, tristemque (heu fata!) repulsum
    spreta tuli: sum nunc vox, sonus, aura, nihil.

LXVI. Eadem iocatur

Cum facie caream, quaeris, cur dicar imago.
    Cum tua verba sequar, dic, ubi lingua mea est?

LXVII. In malum librum

Si sapis, hospes, abi; miserum neu tange libellum.
    Non hic Maeoniden Virgiliumve leges,

wrong for flies and troops of fleas to approach the calm dwellings
of the Spirits of the dead. There is no business here either for you
or your vile maniples. Why are you lingering, cursed creature?   30
Off, down into the depths of night and the farthest Chaos! For
surely here you should have no aspirations for renown. Those
whom the gods have approved once, these they approve forever.

LXIII. A marble Actaeon

Phrygian Paris had beheld the naked goddesses on the crest of
Ida, and said: "Venus, you surpass the other two." But if he had
beheld her whom I myself, to my misfortune, saw by the waters of
Gargaphie, he would have said: "Give place, Venus."

LXIV. On Orpheus looking back

This it was, unfortunate Orpheus—and still, alas, you are looking
back—that destroyed you, that destroyed poor Eurydice.

LXV. Echo speaks

I beheld, I burned, I wept, and, scorned, I endured sad rejection
(woeful destiny!). Now I am voice, sound, breeze, nothing.

LXVI. She also makes a jest

Since I lack a face, you ask why I am called an image. Since I
mimic your words, tell me: where is my tongue?

LXVII. Against a bad book

If you are wise, stranger, take your leave. Don't touch the wretched
little book. You won't read here a Maeonides or a Virgil, but the

sed foedas Bavii chartas et olentia Maevi
    carmina, Romani dedecus eloquii.
5 Quid dubitas sacros incendia poscere lucos,
    abnuerit liquidas si dare Phoebus aquas?

Liber Secundus

I. Ad Federicum regem

Cum vehor picta vacuus phaselo
et modo septos iaculis echinos,
nunc bene haerentes scopulis laboro
    vellere conchas,
5 tange vocales, studiosa, chordas,
Musa, et auratum moderare plectrum:
pauca de multis referamus acta
    regis amati,
qualis herboso spatiata campo
10 virgo, iam matris decus et voluptas,
nectit e solis violis coronam,
    cetera linquens.
Hic ubi veras imitata turres
tot simul pinnis niveisque tectis
15 rupe Mergillina sedens, propinquum
    spectat in aequor,
adsit ex imo Galatea fundo,
nil timens saevos Polyphemi amores;
nec mihi durum refluens canenti
20   obstrepat unda.
Sic licet magnus trepidasque turmas
fregerit primis Federicus ausis,

foul pages of Bavius and the stinking songs of Mavius, the disgrace of Roman eloquence. Why do you hesitate to ask the sacred groves for fire, if Apollo refuses to offer his clear streams? 5

Book II

I. To King Federico

While I sail at my ease on my dappled skiff, and struggle now to pluck sea-urchins, encircled with spears, now conches, sticking fast to their rocks, pluck your sounding strings, my zealous Muse, and 5 guide your golden plectrum. Let us report a few of the many deeds of our beloved king, as a maiden, strolling on a grassy field, already the grace and delight of her mother, weaves a garland only 10 from violets, leaving all others aside. Here where Mergellina, emulating real towers, with its multitudes of merlons and shimmering rooftops, perches on its rock, gazing over the nearby sea, let 15 Galatea appear from the depths below, in no fear of Polyphemus's brusque advances. Nor let the wave, in its thudding flow, roar against my song. Although mighty Federico in his initial exploits 20 routed the trembling throngs, when as a youth he made his way to

cum puer celsas penetravit Alpes
    saxaque Rheni;
25 texerit latis pelagus carinis,
    Dalmatum dites populatus urbes;
    senserit presso prope fulminantem
        ore Timavus;
    cinxerit sacra meritum corona
30 et caput; Gallos quoniam feroces
    contudit, totas revocarit Orci ex
        faucibus urbes:
    nil tamen maius, nihil egit umquam
    fortius quam quod titubante regno,
35 cum sibi sceptrum et diadema posset
        sumere tutus,
    coniugem caram propriosque natos
    liquit et fidas lacrimas clientum,
    fratris heu pulsam sobolem secutus
40   per mare vastum.
    Ergo nunc illi moderator alti
    aetheris, cui sunt pia facta curae,
    regium frontis decus et negatos
        addit honores.
45 O Fides, rarum placidumque numen,
    o mihi nullis reticenda saeclis,
    te te ego aeternum prece victimisque
        pronus adorem.

II. *De Andrea Matthaeo Aquivivo*

Cernis, ut exsultet patriis Aquivivus in armis
    duraque spumanti frena relaxet equo?
Quis mites illum Permessi hausisse liquores
    credat et imbelles excoluisse lyras?

304

the lofty Alps and the rocks of the Rhine; though he covered the
sea with broad ships, laying waste the rich cities of the Dalmatae;
though the Timavo, its mouth blocked, felt his thundering near to   25
hand; though he has also girded his deserving head with a holy
crown; though, since he crushed the wild Galli, he has summoned
whole cities back from the jaws of Orcus: nevertheless he has ac-   30
complished nothing greater, nothing braver, than, with his king-
dom tottering, when in safety he could assume to himself the
scepter and diadem, that he left his dear wife and his own children 35
and the tears of his faithful dependants to follow over the wide
sea the wrongly exiled offspring of his brother. Now, therefore, the 40
ruler of the lofty sky, who cares about pious deeds, adds the
adornment of kingship to his brow and the honors hitherto de-
nied. O Faith, divinity peerless and serene, never to be held in si- 45
lence by me as the generations pass, you it is, you, that I should
ever worship in obeisance with prayer and offerings.

II. On Andrea Matteo Acquaviva

Do you witness how Acquaviva triumphs in the weapons of his
ancestors and loosens the tough reins from his frothing horse?
Who could believe that he has quaffed the waters of the
Permessus and cultivated the unwarlike lyre? Snow-white plumes

5   Consurgunt niveae fulgenti in casside cristae,
      at clypeus torvo Gorgonis ore tumet.
   Macte animo, rigidum Musas qui stringere ferrum,
      qui Martem doctos cogis amare choros.
   Haec ducis est virtus, non uni insistere palmae,
10   sed nomen factis quaerere, et ingeniis.

III. In Bubonem

Nam quis te, inepte bubo, tam stolidus furor
   adegit importunum inire proelium
   isto indecenti rostro et alis luridis?
   Quid bellicosae volucris, insulse, asperos
5   lacessis ungues? Desine, miser, dum licet,
   ne dormientis excites somnum tuo
   cum maximo, ut par est, malo ac clade ultima.
   Sed pervenire vis in ora vulgi, et hac
   via cupis, sceleste, fieri notior?
10 Non assequere, nec profecto tam bono
   fruere fato. An hoc pudendo sanguine
   se tingat aquila, fulminum et caeli immemor?
   Ponenda honestae mortis haec spes est tibi.

IV. Ad Mathonem

Ut mandem victura meis tua nomina chartis,
   dicis amicitiam te, Matho, velle meam.
Et tibi semper in ore duces, quos Graius Homerus,
   quos noster Latia vexit in astra tuba.
5   Dumque ego sum tanti te iudice, venit ab horto
   cum donis olitor bisve semelve tuus,
scilicet aeterni pretium mihi grande daturus
   nominis et fidae pignus amicitiae.
O Matho, quam felix et amico et vate reperto es,

rise on his gleaming helmet, but his shield swells with the   5
Gorgon's fierce features. Take pride in your spirit, you who compel
the Muses to draw from its sheathe an unbending sword, their
learned choirs to be enamored of Mars. This is a duke's excellence:
not to settle for a single reward but to seek repute with deeds and
with talent.   10

III. Against an owl

What madness so brutish drove you, foolish owl, to start a mis-
guided fight, with that ugly beak of yours and yellowed wings?
Why, stupid soul, do you challenge the sharp claws of a bird made
for warfare? Lay off while you can, poor thing, lest you waken him   5
from sleep to your own enormous misfortune — it's only proper —
and disaster in the end. Is it your wish to make your way via the
lips of the hoi polloi? Is this the manner, scoundrel, by which you
yearn to become more the talk of the town? You won't succeed.
Assuredly you won't enjoy such a happy fate. Would the eagle, for-   10
getful of thunderbolts and the heavens, dye himself in this loath-
some blood? You should abandon this hope of a noble death.

IV. To Matho

You say, Matho, that you wish for my friendship, that I might en-
trust your reputation to my pages so it will never die, and that the
leaders are always on your lips whom Greek Homer, whom our
poet with his Latian trumpet carried to the stars. While I remain
so valuable in your opinion, your gardener came once or twice   5
from the vegetable patch with gifts, clearly so as to render me great
thanks for your undying reputation, and a guarantee of friend-
ship's trust. O Matho, how fortunate you are to have discovered
both friend and bard, how fortunate in your vegetable patch and

10 quam felix horto muneribusque tuis,
  si quod diis genitis vix tot peperere labores,
    id tibi lactucae prototomique dabunt.

V. De patria Homeri

Smyrna, Rhodos, Colophon, Salamin, Ios, Argos, Athenae,
  cedite iam: caelum patria Maeonidae est.

VI. De luna et pane

Effudit longas Tegeaea in rupe querelas
  Pan, captus forma, candida Luna, tua.
Cumque levi calamos cera coniungeret, addit:
  'Praedata es sensus tu quoque, canna, meos.'

VII. In tumulum Amaranthae

Hic Amarantha iacet, quae, si fas vera fateri,
  aut Veneri similis vel Venus ipsa fuit.

VIII. Ad Ferrandum regem

Ex ferro nomen tibi sit licet, aurea condis
  saecula: nam sub te principe nemo metit.

IX. De Summontii pietate

Excitat obstrictas tumulis Summontius umbras,
  impleat ut sanctae munus amicitiae.
Utque prius vivos, sic et post fata sodales
  observat, tristes et sedet ante rogos.
5 Nec tantum violas cineri ac bene olentia ponit
  serta, sed et lacrimis irrigat ossa piis.
Parva loquor. Cultis reparat monumenta libellis,

its offerings, if, what so many valorous deeds have scarcely created   10
for the offspring of the gods, lettuce and greens will produce for
you.

V. On Homer's fatherland

Smyrna, Rhodes, Colophon, Salamis, Ios, Argos, Athens: give
way, now. Heaven is the fatherland of the Maeonid.

VI. On the Moon and Pan

Charmed by your beauty, crystal Moon, Pan poured forth lament
upon lament at the rocks of Tegea. And when he joined the reeds
together with a thin layer of wax, he added: "Reed-pipe, you also
stole my wits."

VII. To the grave of Amarantha

Here lies Amarantha who, if it is right to pronounce the truth,
was either akin to Venus, or was Venus herself.

VIII. To King Ferrante

Though your name comes from iron, you establish an age of gold.
For with you as prince, no one reaps.

IX. On Summonte's piety

Summonte summons forth shades imprisoned in their graves that
he might fulfill the duty of holy friendship. As he formerly tended
to his comrades in life, so he cares for them after their death, and
sits before their sad pyres. He not only places violets and sweet-
smelling garlands by their ashes, he also moistens their bones with   5
his pious tears. I tell of small matters. He restores their tombs

cum possint longam saxa timere diem.
At tu, vivaci quae fulcis nomina fama,
10   poscenti gratas, Musa, repende vices,
ut quoniam dulces optat sic vivere amicos,
vivat, et in libris sit sacer ille meis.

X. De Venere et Diana

Incultam adspiciens silvis Cytherea Dianam,
    risit, et, 'An tendes retia semper?' ait.
Cui dea casta: 'Feris cur non ego retia tendam,
    tendere si potuit vir tuus illa tibi?'

XI. Ad Aeglen

Absentem quaeris, praesentem despicis, Aegle.
    Non redamas, sed me vis in amore mori.

XII. De Venere et Priapo

Tractabat clypeum Marti placitura Dione
    saevaque feminea sumserat arma manu.
'Pone, Dea,' exclamat petulanti voce Priapus,
    'pone! Decent istas haec magis arma manus.'

XIII. In Gelliam

Quem tu nunc patruum, nunc patrem, Gellia, dicis,
    hic tibi nec patruus, Gellia, nec pater est.

XIV. In Flaccum

Non largitur opes, et vult epigrammata Flaccus.
    Iure suo haec poscit; vult sibi verba dari.

through learned tomes, since stones can fear time's lengthening. But you, Muse, who support reputations by long-lived fame, give joyful recompense in response to my plea, so that, since he desires   10 his dear friends to survive in this way, he may also live on and be blessed in my books.

X. On Venus and Diana

The Cytherean, spying unkempt Diana in the woods, laughed and said "Will you forever stretch your nets?" To whom the virgin goddess: "Why shouldn't I stretch nets for beasts, if your husband was able to stretch them for you?"

XI. To Aegle

You ask for me, Aegle, when I'm away, and you scorn me when I'm here. You don't return my love, but you wish me to die in love.

XII. On Venus and Priapus

To please Mars, Dione was wielding a shield and had grabbed fierce weapons in her lady-like hand. "Put them down, goddess," shouts Priapus in his wanton voice. "Put them down. This is the equipment that more befits those hands of yours."

XIII. Against Gellia

He whom you now call uncle, now father, Gellia, is neither your uncle nor your father, Gellia.

XIV. Against Flaccus

Flaccus doesn't pay out money, but wants epigrams. His request for them is legitimate. He wants to hoodwink himself.

XV. De Peto Compatre

Petus deliciae tuae, Dione,
    uni cui Charitum sales beatos,
    cui fontes dederas facetiarum
    ac risus simul eleganter omnes,
5   Petus mortuus est tuus, Dione,
    Petus Compater usque ad astra notus,
    qui puro niveae colore mentis
    vincebat nitidissimos olores,
    cui de lacteolis tuis papillis
10   donarunt violas Iocusque Amorque;
    donavit teneram Thalia myrtum.
    Mox promens citharam decentiorem,
    versus addidit eruditiores.
    O saevae nimium malaeque Parcae,
15   vestros non potuit tenere fusos
    Petus; qui rapidas domare tigres,
    qui duras potuit movere quercus,
    vestras non potuit colos morari.
    Sic, sic occidis heu, miselle Pete,
20   nec te Pierides tuae, nec ipsa
    quae te per Paphon et Cnidon virentem,
    per colles Amathuntios vocavit,
    fatis eripuere tam malignis.
    At non unanimes tui sodales,
25   quos tu pectore tam pio colebas,
    quos tristes obitu tuo relinquis,
    hoc duro tibi defuere casu.
    Quin me trans Ligerim ferosque Celtas
    lustrantem Morinum pigras paludes,
30   dum quaero Oceani ultimos recessus,
    veris nuntius obruit querelis.

XV. On Peto Compatre

Dione, Peto, your delight, to whom alone in your elegance you had given the blissful wit of the Graces, to whom the sources of droll-ery along with every giggle, your Peto is dead, Dione, Peto 5 Compatre, known all the way to the stars. He surpassed the most gleaming swans in the unblemished shimmer of his snow-bright mind. Laughter and Love gave him violets from your milky breasts. Thalia gave him tender myrtle. Soon offering a more 10 graceful lyre, she added verses more learned. O Parcae, too harsh, too evil, Peto wasn't able to halt your spindles. He who could tame 15 rampaging tigers and set hard oaks in motion wasn't able to delay your distaffs. Thus, poor little Peto, thus, alas, you die. Neither your Pierides nor she herself, who called you through Paphos and 20 green Cnidos, through the hills of Amathus, snatched you from fates so baleful. But your like-minded comrades, whom you cher-ished with a devoted heart, whom you abandon in sadness at your 25 death, did not fail you at this harsh fate. Yes, and a message with its woeful truths overwhelmed even me, as, past the Loire and the wild Celtae, I surveyed the sluggish swamps of the Morini in search of the Ocean's farthest bays. So, what obsequies could I 30 offer you, my friend, I, the wandering traveler so far from beauti-

Ergo quid tibi tam vagus viator,
cui nec pulchra Neapolis, nec alti
colles Pausilypi, nec ipse adesset
35   Sebethos pater aut pater Vesevus,
inferre exsequiarum, amice, possem?
Rupem, quam vagus hinc et inde Nereus
alterna veniens retundit unda,
accessi, et procul angulo in supremo
40   stans supra pelagi alluentis aestus,
manes terque quaterque convocavi.
Hic fudi lacrimas amariores;
hic vici gemitus vel unus omnes,
omnes et simul omnium querelas.
45   Mox, quamvis cineri tuo decentem
Pontanus tumulum pararit ac te
cognatas veneretur inter umbras,
quamvis et diuturnius sepulcrum,
quod nec saecula vincere ipsa possint,
50   divinis paret excitare chartis,
nostrum non tibi qualecumque munus
inter frigora solitudinesque
cessavit, nec honore te supremo
fraudavi miser. Hoc scit ipsa Tethys;
55   scit late Oceani unda Gallicani.
Stant arae tibi, stat videnda nautis
terreni tumuli pusilla moles,
et buxus super et dicata quercus
(nam myrtum regio illa non habebat)
60   quae iussit pietas sacrare, ut esset
naturae tibi terminus sepulcrum.

ful Naples, from the hills of lofty Posillipo, from father Sebeto
himself, from father Vesuvius? I gained a rock, which wandering   35
Nereus erodes as he approaches with successive waves on this side
and on that, and, standing afar on the topmost crest above the
swirls of the lapping sea, I summoned your shade, three and four   40
times. Here I poured forth tears of great bitterness. Here, just by
myself, I surpassed all the groans and all the laments of everyone
together. Soon, although Pontano has constructed a graceful
mound for your ashes and honored you among the shades of your   45
kin, although he is ready to raise, through his immortal writing, a
more enduring monument which the ages themselves cannot over-
whelm, our offering to you, such as it is, has never ceased, in the   50
midst of chill and lonely places, nor in my sadness did I deprive
you of your final reward. Tethys herself is aware of this. The wave
of the Gallic Ocean is aware far and wide. Altars memorialize you,   55
a tiny mass of heaped-up earth stands for sailors to see. Moreover
box and oak were consecrated to you (for that locale had no myr-
tle) — which piety has ordered us to dedicate so that nature's   60
boundary might be your tomb.

XVI. Ignes nocturni Romae

Adspicis ut picti vultus imitetur Olympi,
    certet et astriferos vincere Roma polos.
Scilicet hos, Auguste, tibi largitur honores,
    ne cupias magni tecta videre Iovis.
5 Alta coronatae iactant incendia turres
    et Vaticano fulmina Monte tonant.
Dumque palam tantos cupit ostentare paratus
    urbs nimium in laudes ambitiosa suas,
'Vivant astra,' inquit, 'summo contenta tonante,
10   pareat Augusto dummodo Roma suo.'

XVII. De tyrannis et Bruto

Cum tot Tarquinios passim consurgere cernas,
    miraris, Brutum cur ferat Italia?

XVIII. In tumulum pueri

Nate, patris matrisque amor et suprema voluptas,
    accipe quae nobis te dare par fuerat:
busta eheu tristesque notas damus, invida quando
    mors immaturo funere te rapuit.

XIX. De Hercule et Ganymede

Palluit Alcides teneri Ganymedis amore,
    et vetus amissi cesserat ardor Hylae.
'Quid linquet nobis puer hic?' ait uxor. 'Honores
    eripuit quondam; nunc rapit ecce virum.'

XVI. Night fires at Rome

You behold how Rome mimics the surface of dappled Olympus and vies to surpass the star-bearing poles. It is a fact, Augustus, that Rome bestows these honors on you so that you will have no desire to see the dwellings of mighty Jupiter. The crowned towers hurl flames aloft and lightening-bolts thunder on the Vatican 5
Mount. And when the city, extremely eager for its own glory, desires to show off publicly its grand trappings, it says: "May the stars survive, satisfied with their highest Thunderer, provided Rome stays obedient to its Augustus." 10

XVII. On the tyrants and Brutus

When you watch so many Tarquins rising up everywhere, do you wonder why Italy produces a Brutus?

XVIII. To the tomb of a youth

Child, beloved and absolute delight of your father and mother, receive what it is right for us to bestow on you. We bestow on you, alas, a tomb and a sad inscription, since envious death has snatched you away in an untimely demise.

XIX. On Hercules and Ganymede

Alcides grew pale out of delicate love for Ganymede. His old-time warmth for lost Hylas had yielded place. "What will this boy leave for me?" says his wife. "He once snatched away my preferment. Now look how he snatches my husband."

XX. *In Ufentem crapulatoren*

Non futuit, non paedicat, non irrumat Ufens:
    ista olim. Quid nunc? Aut vomit aut comedit.

XXI. *In degenerantem*

Nomen avi, non facta refers. Diceris ab illo
    alter, sed iuvenis tu, precor; ille senex.

XXII. *De Iove et cupidine*

De Veneris nato questa est Dictynna Tonanti,
    quod nimis ille puer promptus ad arma foret.
Tum pater accito ostendens grave fulmen Amori,
    'Hoc tibi, saeve puer, spicula franget,' ait.
5 Cui lascivus Amor motis haec reddidit alis:
    'Quid si iterum posito fulmine cycnus eris?'

XXIII. *In Riccium*

Aegrotat sedis vitio, et male Riccius audit.
    Quid, si esset surdis Riccius auriculis?

XXIV. *De Danae et Iove*

Formosam Danaen munibat ahenea turris,
    et satis hoc vanus credidit esse pater.
Indoluit, tenerae miseratus fata puellae
    Iupiter, et subito factus amator, ait:
5 'Ergo arcere potes natam divisque virisque,
    at si non arces imbribus, imber ero.'

XX. *Against Ufens the drunkard*

Ufens doesn't fuck, doesn't sodomize, doesn't suck. That's what he did back then. What about now? He pukes or chews.

XXI. *Against a degenerate*

You hand on the name, not the deeds, of your grandfather. You will be called a second he, but—attend!—you are the youth, he the old man.

XXII. *On Jupiter and Cupid*

Dictynna complained to the Thunderer about the offspring of Venus, because that child was all too ready with his weapons. Then the father, after he had summoned Amor, showed him the weighty thunderbolt and said: "Impetuous child, this will break your darts." Lusty Amor, his wings aflutter, replied to him in these words: "What if you will be a swan again, after you've laid aside   5 the thunderbolt?"

XXIII. *Against Riccius*

Riccius suffers from an ulcer on his bottom, and he has a bad reputation. What if Riccius were deaf in both ears?

XXIV. *On Danaë and Jupiter*

A tower of bronze imprisoned beautiful Danaë, and her foolish father believed that this was sufficient. Jupiter was distressed. After he had pitied the tender girl's misfortune and suddenly became her lover, he said: "So you can protect your daughter away from   5 gods and men. But if you don't protect her from rain-showers, I'll be a rain-shower."

XXV. De Lucio grammatista

Noctes et noctes iterat dum Lucius, illi
  perpetuam noctem praebuit altus Arar.

XXVI. De Vulcano et Venere

Horrida caelicolis narrabat proelia Mavors
  saevaque terribili capta trophaea manu.
Quod Venus audiret, doluit Vulcanus, et, 'Heus tu,'
  inquit, 'an exspectas ut mea vincla canat?'

XXVII. De seipso

Miraris, liquidum cur non dissolvor in amnem,
  cum numquam siccas cogar habere genas?
Miror ego in tenues potius non isse favillas,
  assiduae carpant cum mea corda faces.
5 Scilicet ut misero possim superesse dolori,
  sic lacrimis flammas temperat acer Amor.

XXVIII. De Hercule et Iove

Pendebat Phrygii Tirynthius ore ministri,
  delicias magno dum facit ille Iovi.
Tum pater, 'Haud equidem favi, fortissime,' dixit,
  'formosum rapuit cum tibi Naïs Hylan.'

XXIX. De Venere et Sole

Induerat thoraca humeris galeamque decoro
  aptarat capiti, Marte iubente, Venus.
'Nil opus his,' Sol, 'Diva,' inquit, 'sumenda fuerunt,
  cum vos ferratae circuiere plagae.'

XXV. On Lucius the schoolmaster

While Lucius was repeating nights, nights, over again, the deep Saône granted him unceasing night.

XXVI. On Vulcan and Venus

Mars was telling the heaven-dwellers of dread battles and of savage trophies captured by his frightening hand. Vulcan was upset that Venus was listening and said: "Look here, are you waiting for him to sing of my chains?"

XXVII. On himself

Do you marvel that I don't melt into a pure stream, since I'm forced to have cheeks never dry? I rather marvel myself that I've not vanished into thin ash, since ever and ever torches consume my heart. So that I may actually survive my woeful suffering, fierce Love tempers his flames with tears.   5

XXVIII. On Hercules and Jupiter

The Tirynthian was hanging on the lips of the Phrygian wine-pourer while he was bestowing his favors on mighty Jupiter. Then the father said: "I did not give my approval at all, bravest of men, when the Naiad snatched beautiful Hylas from you."

XXIX. On Venus and the Sun

Under Mars's orders Venus had donned a cuirass over her shoulders and fitted a helmet to her graceful head. "You have no need, goddess," says the Sun, "to put these on, since iron nets have enmeshed you."

XXX. *Catonis tumulus*

Hic ubi Libertas magni et iacet umbra Catonis,
    quam melius poterant Caesaris ossa tegi!

XXXI. *De Venetorum signis*

Romanas Aquilae postquam liquere cohortes,
    magnanimus turmas ducit in arma Leo.

XXXII. *De Andrea Matthaeo Aquivivo, duce Hadriae*

Moesta Bituntinae duxerunt otia nymphae,
    nec Faunis solitos exhibuere choros.
Scilicet optato quidquid sine principe cernunt,
    ingratum est; tantus principis urget amor.
5 Nec satis est, positis arcum sprevisse sagittis,
    questubus et totos continuasse dies,
ast etiam nostris faciunt convicia terris
    et nos Sirenas, Lotophagosque vocant.
Vera loquor: Divae, veniam date vera loquenti:
10   non amor hic certe, sed magis invidia est.

XXXIII. *De Thelesinae crinibus*

Dum nectit flavos auro Thelesina capillos,
    contraxit radios Phoebus et erubuit.
Mox haec ad superos: 'En auro iungitur aurum:
    hoc est mortales, hoc superare deos.'

XXXIV. *In Galeatium Caracciolum*

Hippolyten, Leden, Thelesinam diligis unus.
    Dic mihi: quid tota restat in urbe boni?

XXX. On the tomb of Cato

Here, where lie Liberty and the shade of mighty Cato, how much better could the bones of Caesar be covered!

XXXI. On the flags of the Venetians

After their Eagles have abandoned the Roman battalions, the great-souled Lion leads his squadrons to arms.

XXXII. On Andrea Matteo Acquaviva, Duke of Adria

The nymphs of Bitonto have spent their leisure in sadness, nor have they shown off their usual dances to the Fauni. It is obvious that whatever they watch without the presence of their beloved prince lacks pleasure—so heavy lies their weight of affection for the prince. Nor is it sufficient to put arrows aside and scorn the 5
bow, to pass whole days in lamentation. They even hurl insults on our land, and call us Sirens and Lotophagi. I speak the truth. Goddesses, grant me pardon for speaking the truth: this surely is not love but simply envy. 10

XXXIII. On the tresses of Thelesina

While Thelesina was braiding her blond locks with gold, Phoebus contracted his rays and blushed. Forthwith this to the gods: "Behold: gold is joined to gold. This is to surpass mortals, to surpass the gods."

XXXIV. To Galeazzo Caracciolo

You alone love Hippolyte, Lede, Thelesina. Tell me: What beauty is left over in the whole city?

XXXV. In theatrum Campanum

Dicite, semidei, silvarum numina, Panes,
    et si qua adventu es nympha fugata meo:
cui licuit tantas saxorum evertere moles,
    quas iam disiectas vix nemora alta tegunt?
5 Hisne olim sueta est cuneis Campana iuventus
    amphitheatrales laeta videre iocos?
Nunc ubi tot plaususque hominum vocesque canorae,
    tot risus, tot iam gaudia, tot facies?
Scilicet heu fati leges! Rapit omnia tempus,
10 et quae sustulerat, deprimit ipsa dies.

XXXVI. De fonte Mergillines

Est mihi rivo vitreus perenni
fons arenosum prope litus, unde
saepe discedens sibi nauta rores
    haurit amicos.
5 Unicus nostris scatet ille ripis,
montis immenso sitiente tractu,
vitifer qua Pausilypus vadosum ex-
    currit in aequor.
Hunc ego vitta redimitus alba,
10 flore et aestivis veneror coronis,
cum timent amnes et hiulca saevum
    arva Leonem.
Antequam festae redeant Calendae
fortis Augusti, superantque patri
15 quattuor luces, mihi tempus omni
    dulcius aevo,
bis mihi sanctum, mihi bis vocandum,
bis celebrandum potiore cultu,

XXXV. On the Campanian theater

Tell me, demigod Pans, spirits of the woods, and you, any nymph put to flight by my arrival: who was allowed to overthrow such great masses of stones that, now scattered, the lofty woods scarcely cover? Was the joyous youth of Campania once upon a time ac- 5 customed to view the amphitheater's games from these seats? Where now are the audience's rounds of applause, their many ringing voices, where now all the laughter, all the merriment, all the spectators? It's a sad truth: the laws of fate and time's passage snatch everything away, and what the very day had raised up it 10 brings low.

XXXVI. On the fountain of Mergellina

I have near the sandy shore a glassy spring of unceasing flow from which often the departing sailor drinks friendly draughts. It alone gushes on our banks, along the hillside's huge thirsty stretch, 5 where vine-rich Posillipo runs down into the shoaly sea. Crowned with a white fillet I worship it with flowers and summer garlands, when the streams and the gaping fields live in fear of fierce Leo. 10 Before the festive Kalends of brave Augustus return, four days yet remain for the father, a moment sweeter to me than any time, twice holy to me, twice to be invoked by me, twice to be celebrated 15

duplici voto geminaque semper
20   turis acerra.
Namque ab extremo properans Eoo,
hac die primum mihi vagienti
Phoebus illuxit pariterque dias
        hausimus auras.
25 Hac et insigni peragenda ritu
sacra solemnes veniunt ad aras
Nazari, unde omnes tituli meaeque
        nomina gentis,
Nazari vastas cohibentis undas
30 aequoris saevosque domantis aestus,
quidquid et vani truculenta iussit
        ira Neronis.
O decus caeli simul et tuorum,
rite quem parva veneramur aede,
35 cui frequentandas populis futuris
        ponimus aras:
si mihi primos generis parentes,
si mihi lucem pariter dedisti
huc age, et fontem tibi dedicatum
40   saepe revise.

XXXVII. *Divo Nazario*

Natali quod, dive, tuo lucem editus hausi,
        quod tua nascenti lux mihi prima fuit,
Actius hoc riguo parvum cum fonte sacellum
        dedico; tu nutu fac rata vota tuo,
5   ut quae Sextiles lux venerit ante Calendas
        quarta, sit hic generi bis celebranda meo,
et quod solemnes revocat tua festa per aras,
        et quod natalem contigit esse meum.

with bountiful worship, with redoubled prayer, and ever with a
twin canister of incense. For, hastening from the farthest Eos, on   20
this day Phoebus first granted me his light as I wailed, and at the
same moment I drank in the bright breezes. On this day, too, the
ritual to be performed with suitable pomp occurs at the yearly al-   25
tars of Nazario: whence all the accolades and the name of my
race, of Nazario confining the vast waves of the sea and taming its
fierce swirl, and whatever the ferocious anger of foolish Nero com-   30
manded. O glory of heaven as well as of your people, whom we
duly worship in your tiny shrine, for whom we establish altars to
be thronged by crowds to come: if you gave me the first ancestors   35
of my race, if you also gave me light, come here, and often revisit
the fountain dedicated to you.   40

XXXVII. To San Nazario

Holy one, because, as I came into the world, I drank in the light
on your birthday, because your first day was mine at birth, I,
Actius, dedicate this tiny shrine with its flowing fountain. Do
please ratify the vow by your nod. So let the fourth day that ar-
rives before the Kalends of Sextilis be here twice celebrated by my   5
family, both because your feast-day bids a return to your altar's an-
nual rites, and because it happens to be my birthday.

XXXVIII. De lauro ad Neritinorum ducem

Illa deum laetis olim gestata triumphis
    claraque Phoebaeae laurus honore comae,
iampridem male culta, novos emittere ramos,
    iampridem baccas edere desierat.
5 Nunc lacrimis adiuta tuis revirescit, et omne
    frondiferum spirans implet odore nemus.
Sed nec eam lacrimae tantum iuvere perennes,
    quantum mansuro carmine quod colitur.
Hoc debent, Aquivive, duces tibi, debet et ipse
10   Phoebus, nam per te laurea silva viret.

XXXIX. In tumulum Cottae Veronensis

Sperabas tibi, docta, novum, Verona, Catullum;
    experta es duros bis viduata deos.
Nulla animum posthac res erigat, optima quando
    prima rapit celeri Parca inimica manu.
5 Quae tamen ut vidit morientis frigida Cottae
    ora, suum fassa est crimen et erubuit.

XL. In Picentem medicum

Quod noctu latras, quod sellas olfacis unus,
    da veniam, Picens, hoc canis est vitium.
Sed quia tu Cynicus vis dici et clinicus idem,
    esse idem poteris merdicus et medicus.

XLI. De Ferdinando iuniore

Si merita audieris Ferrandi, Nestora credas;
    si numeres annos, dixeris Antilochum.

XXXVIII. On the laurel, to the duke of the Neritini

That laurel, once carried in the joyous triumphs of the gods and famous as the crowning glory of Phoebus's locks, was badly tended and now for a long time had stopped sprouting new branches, now for a long time had stopped producing berries. At last, nourished by your tears, it grows green again and wafts the whole leafy grove 5 full of its perfume. But your unceasing tears didn't nourish it as much as cultivation by enduring song. This the dukes owe to you, Acquaviva, and Phoebus himself owes you. For because of you the laurel grove greens afresh. 10

XXXIX. To the tomb of Cotta from Verona

Learned Verona, you hoped for a new Catullus. Twice widowed, you have suffered the severity of the gods. Let nothing exalt your spirits hereafter, since the hostile Parca with swift hand seizes the best first. Nevertheless, when she looked at the chill features of dying Cotta, she admitted her crime and blushed. 5

XL. Against the doctor Picente

Because you alone bark at night, because you sniff at stools: pardon me, Picente. This is the defect of a dog. But, because you wish to be called Cynicus and clinician at one and the same time, you can be dunger and doctor wrapped into one.

XLI. On Ferdinando the Younger

If you gave ear to the deserts of Ferrante, you would believe him a Nestor. If you were to count up his years, you would call him an Antilochus.

XLII. *In quemdam*

Ne valeam, superi, bene si facere hic pote, quem sors
    exsilio et vinclis vexit ad imperium.
Et peream, ni cuncta evertere iam volet hic, qui
    nil meminit praeter vincula et exsilium.

XLIII. *Tumulus in quo ploratur filius unicus*

Cur heu Laetitiam falso dixere parentes,
    Tristitiam qui me dicere debuerant?
Natus erat miserae lux unica matris, ocellus
    unicus; hunc Lachesis noxia subripuit.
5   I nunc, vel Nioben confer mihi, cuius habet sors
    hoc melius, fieri saxea quod potuit.

XLIV. *In picturam*

Anna parens, cui caelestem sperare nepotem
    contigit, intactae Virginis, Anna, parens,
ut tandem te te meliori in sede locares,
    credibile est artes edidicisse novas.
5   'Scilicet obscoenae semper convicia turbae
    et scelera antiqui perpetiar domini?'
Vix haec, et medicas invadis protinus artes;
    nec mora, iam caecis lumina restituis.
Accurrunt aegri; complentur compita rhedis;
10   occupat angustas sedula turba vias.
Ecce in quo picta es, paries exscinditur, et te
    accipit hospitio nata benigna pio.
Nimirum sapis, Anna; hoc contulit ipsa senectus:
    haud aliter poteras hac caruisse domo.

XLII. Against a certain person

May I not survive, gods above, if this person can behave well whom chance has raised to rule through exile and bonds. And may I perish, if he doesn't now wish to ruin everything, he who remembers nothing except bonds and exile.

XLIII. Tomb in which an only son is mourned

Why, alas, did my parents falsely name me Laetitia who ought to have called me Tristitia? He was born the single light of his poor mother, the single apple of her eye. Baneful Lachesis snatched him away. Off with you now, or compare me with Niobe whose lot has   5 this better outcome: she was able to turn to stone.

XLIV. To a picture

Mother Anna, whose destiny it was to expect God as grandson, Anna, mother of the chaste Virgin: I'm convinced that, in order at last to find a better location for yourself, you learned new arts. "Shall I indeed forever suffer the insults of the loathsome crowd, and the villainy of my aged owner?" A moment after these words,   5 you hasten to take up the medical arts. You now restore sight to the blind in a flash. The sick hasten to you. The streets are jammed with carriages. The eager crowd crams the narrow roadways. See: the wall on which you were painted is demolished, and   10 your kindly daughter receives you in pious hospitality. Clearly you are wise, Anna. Age itself conferred this on you. Otherwise there was no way that you could have been parted from this home.

XLV. De Iunone et Ganymede

Iusserat Iliacum mensis adstare ministrum
    Iupiter, at coniux, 'Quis mihi miscet?' ait.
Ille verecundis libat crystalla labellis,
    cui dea: 'Amatori da, puer, ista tuo.'

XLVI. In Catonis laudem

Quae tegit extinctum cum Libertate Catonem,
    insultat tumulis, Caesar, arena tuis.

XLVII. De Homero in Latinum verso

Quid septem de vate sacro contenditis urbes?
    Ecce potest civem dicere Roma suum.
At vos aut nostrum, si fas, auferte Maronem,
    aut alium vobis quaerite Maeoniden.

XLVIII. In tumulum Assanii

Tu, qui disiectos artus inhumataque furtim
    Assanii occulto membra refers tumulo,
macte animi pietate. Tamen nihil irrita busti
    gloria tam claros afferet ad cineres,
5 quandoquidem voluit potius sic sparsa iacere
    quam cadere ad tristes nobilis umbra rogos.
Nunc late exigui fines egressa sepulcri,
    Eoum fama verberat Oceanum.
Contemsit dulcemque animam floremque iuventae,
10   sanguine ut agnato dedecus elueret.
Cumque hausit saevi stricto latus ense tyranni,
    laudem obitu statuit quaerere, non tumulum.
Quodque magis mirere; hilaris ridensque cruentos

XLV. On Juno and Ganymede

Jupiter had ordered the Ilian wine-pourer to take his place by the banquet tables. But his wife says: "Who is doing the mixing for me?" The boy sips the goblets with modest lips. To him the goddess: "Boy, give those to your lover."

XLVI. In praise of Cato

The sands that cover the corpse of Cato along with Liberty scoff at your grave, Caesar.

XLVII. On Homer turned into Latin

Seven cities, why do you vie for the holy bard? See how Rome can call him her citizen. But you, either abscond with our Maro, if it is right, or seek another Maeonides for yourselves.

XLVIII. To the tomb of Assanio

You, who secretly convey the dismembered body and unburied limbs of Assanio to an out-of-the-way tomb, rejoice in the nobility of your spirit. Nevertheless, the vain honor of a grave will add nothing to ashes so famous, since the honorable shade wished to lie thus scattered rather than to sink down amid a pyre's sadness. 5 Now, having escaped far beyond the limits of a tiny tomb, his reputation storms the breadth of the Eoan Ocean. He scorned his sweet life and his youth in flower that he might wash away disgrace from a relative's blood. When he drew his sword and 10 drained the tyrant's side with blood, he decided to seek praise with death, not a tomb. Something you might wonder at still more: cheerful and smiling he endured the sight of the bloody knives of

carnificis cultros cernere sustinuit.
15 Dissimulet patriam; taceat nomenque genusque:
    qui facit hoc, dicit se Lacedaemonium.

XLIX. *In tumulum Caudolae*

Heu quae te rigidi rapuit vis effera fati;
    quis matri miserae tot peperit lacrimas,
flos veterum, Caudola, virum? Tibi moesta sepulcrum
    illa dedit, tristes Actius hos titulos;
5 hos titulos, qui te nigras descendere ad umbras,
    obduci Stygia non patiantur aqua.
Tempora miretur quivis sua; talis Achilles,
    talis, cum caderet, Martius Hector erat.
I, precor, i nullos non durature per annos,
10   Nestoreos qui iam vivere dignus eras.

L. *De Iove et amore*

Iupiter infractos iactat dum saepe gigantes,
    et sibi servati dat decus omne poli:
sic est, inquit Amor; namque hoc mugire solebas
    tunc quoque, cum torva fronte iuvencus eras.

LI. *Hymnus ad divum Nazarium*

Nazari, heu quis me tibi ad hanc supremi
litoris ripam, quis ad hos putasset
Tethyos fluctus, quis ad has daturum
    tura paludes?
5 Post tot emensos pelago labores,
tot pererratos populos, sub ipso
fine terrarum datur ecce amicum
    cernere numen.

the executioner. Let him disguise his fatherland. Let him be silent
about his name and his ancestry. The man who does an act like   15
this calls himself a Spartan.

XLIX. To the tomb of Caudola

Alas, what wild force of unbending fate tore you away? Who has
produced so many tears for your grieving mother, Caudola, flower
of ancient heroes? Actius gives you these sorrowful words, this
tomb, this sad inscription — this inscription that does not allow
you to descend to the black shades, to be overwhelmed by the wa-   5
ter of the Styx. Let each person marvel at his own circumstances.
Such was Achilles, such Mars's Hector when he fell. Go, I pray,
go. You will last many years, who were already worthy to live
Nestor's.   10

L. On Jupiter and Amor

While Jupiter boasts often about crushing giants and bestows on
himself all the glory for saving the heavens, Amor says: "So be it.
For you used to roar this way then, too, when you were a bull with
menacing brow."

LI. Hymn to San Nazario

Nazario, alas, who would have thought I would offer incense to
you at this bank of the farthest shore, to you, at these floods of
Tethys, to you, at this swamp? After so many trials that traversed
the sea, so many peoples surveyed in my wanderings, close to the   5
very bound of the earth, it is granted to me — see! — to behold

Ergo in extremis, pater alme, terris
10 barbarae norunt tua sacra gentes,
qua latus dextrum Liger aestuosis
    obiicit undis.

Iamque et Aulercos genus acre et ipsos
cernis ad te Lexovios citato
15 essedo et picta volitare flavos
    puppe Britannos.

O mihi semper geniale caeli
sidus, o famae decus omne nostrae,
auctor o idem mihi gentis et spi-
20   rabilis aurae.

Si tibi debet proavorum origo, et
sanguinis si sunt decora ulla nostri,
debet et praesens genus et futurum,
    debet et haec lux

25 sacra, quae magnum mihi prima Solem
obtulit nascenti, et inane aperti
aeris pulchrosque micantis aethrae
    tot simul ignes.

Hinc tuis per me dare grata templis
30 munera, hinc natalicias coronas
annuis suevit sociare sertis,
    dum fuit haec sors.

Nunc in ignotis vagor ecce campis,
regis heu cari exsilium secutus,
35 dum fides et fas et amor piusque
    me rapit ardor.

I, puer: buxum nemore e propinquo
collige, et si quas tibi litus offert
quercuum frondes: celebrare moestum
40   sic iuvat annum.

O, ubi dulces patriae recessus

your friendly majesty. And so, kindly father, the barbarian peoples
in the most distant lands, where the Loire opposes its right side to   10
the swirl of the waves, are acquainted with your worship. And
now you behold the Aulerci, that violent race, now the Lexovii
themselves, flying to you on speedy chariot, and the blonde
Britanni with their painted ships. O star in heaven ever benign to   15
me, O full glory of my repute, O at once the advocate of my race
and of the air I breathe: if the source of my ancestors is due to   20
you, if there is any luster to our blood, both our present and fu-
ture family is due to you, this holy day is due to you, which at my
birth first displayed to me the mighty Sun and the void of the   25
open sky as well as the countless beautiful fires of the glistening
ether. Hence, while this chance was mine, it was my custom to
present thankful offerings at your shrines, hence to associate the
wreaths of my birthday with your yearly garlands. Now see me as   30
I wander in unknown fields, in the retinue, alas, of our dear exiled
king, when loyalty and duty and affection and pious devotion hold   35
me in their grip. Go, boy: collect boxwood from the neighboring
grove and any oak leaves the shore tenders to you: it is consoling
thus to celebrate a sad year. O Sebeto, where you wash the sweet   40

abluis, Sebethe, loca illa myrto
consita; o, qui Pausilypi virentes
   det mihi citros,
45 qua tuum lambens maris unda fontem
margines parvi minuit sacelli,
nostrum opus; quo se recreet quotannis
   laeta iuventus,
quae tibi sacris operata arenis,
50 frondibus remos celeresque cymbas
ornat: et forsan mea nunc, ut olim,
   dona requirit.
Heu, pater, cur heu mihi ad institutos
non licet iam iam properare cursus?
55 Cur vetor templis et adesse ludis
   rite dicatis?
Sit satis ventos tolerasse et imbres
ac minas fatorum hominumque fraudes.
Da, pater, tecto salientem avito
60   cernere fumum.

LII. De amore fugitivo

Quaeritat huc illuc raptum sibi Cypria natum,
   ille sed ad nostri pectoris ima latet.
Me miserum, quid agam? Durus puer; aspera mater,
   et magnum in me ius altera et alter habent.
5 Si celem, video quantus deus ossa peruret;
   sin prodam, merito durior hostis erit.
Adde, quod haec non est, quae natum ad flagra reposcat,
   sed quae de nostro bella cruore velit.
Ergo istic, fugitive, late, sed parcius ure:
10   haud alio poteris tutior esse loco.

bays of my fatherland, those spots sown with myrtle, O you who might offer me the ripening citrons of Posillipo, where the wave of the sea as it licks your fountain erodes the edges of the tiny chapel 45 we built for you, where the joyous youths gain refreshment year after year, who, competing in your honor on the holy sands, decorate the oars and swift skiffs with foliage: perhaps even now, as in 50 the past, they await my rewards. Alas, alas, father: why isn't it possible for me to hurry, even now, to the races that I established? Why am I forbidden to be present at the shrines and at the duly consecrated games? Let it be enough to have withstood the winds 55 and rains along with the threats of destiny and the treachery of mankind. Grant me, father, to behold the smoke leaping above my ancestral roof.
60

LII. On Amor the fugitive

The Cyprian keeps looking hither and thither for her child snatched from her, but he is hiding at the bottom of my heart. Alas, alack, what shall I do? The boy is pitiless, the mother harsh. Both the one and the other have great dominion over me. If I should shelter him, I sense how massive a god burns through my bones. But if I were to betray him, he will rightly be a more piti- 5 less enemy. Furthermore, she is not one to take the lash to her child but to wish to do battle at the expense of our blood. Hide here, then, my fugitive, but burn me a little less. You won't ever be safer in another spot.
10

LIII. De Camilla Scalampa Mediolanensi

Fumantem ambustis olim Phaetonta quadrigis
    excepit rapidis fluctibus Eridanus.
Ecce recens, Ticine, tibi de Sole trophaeum
    erigit auratis culta Camilla comis:
5   nam deus ille tuis ausus concurrere ripis,
    maioris numen sensit adesse deae.
O fatum fluviorum! ergo nova fabula vestris
    semper erunt Nymphis aut pater, aut Phaeton.

LIV. De violante Grappina, femina praeclarissima: Dialogus Veneris et Amoris

Ven. Unde mihi has violas affers, puer? *Am.* Accipe, mater,
    quando aliud calida de nive nil potui.
Ven. De nive tu calida violas? *Am.* Perstrinxit ocellos
    candor; et ecce, nivem quod puto, pectus erat.
5   *Ven.* Mira refers: sed tela ubi sunt illa aurea? *Am.* Habebam
    cum legerem violas; nunc Violantis habet.

LV. De Morinna

Sit spectanda comis, sit pulchro corpore toto,
    sit Venus et blandas spiret ab ore rosas,
Aoniasque deas, ipsam quoque Pallada vincat
    ingenio, et dulci pectore mella fluant,
5   dum tamen ire mihi noctes Morinna quietas
    et sinat arbitrii libera iura mei.
Arsimus, et primos miseri deflevimus ignes.
    Hoc satis: extremo turpe in amore mori.

LIII. On Camilla Scalampa of Milan

The Po once received in his rushing stream Phaeton, smouldering in his charred chariot. Ticino, behold Camilla, coiffed with her golden hair, raises for you a new trophy from the Sun. For that god, after he had dared to offer challenge to your banks, felt the 5 majestic presence of a greater goddess. O destiny of streams! And so either Phaeton or father will always be a fresh tale for your Nymphs.

LIV. On Violante Grappina, most outstanding woman: Dialogue of Venus and Amor

(*Venus*) From where do you bring me these violets, boy? (*Amor*) Take them, mother, since I could bring nothing else of warm snow. (*Venus*) You, violets of warm snow? (*Amor*) Their brilliance grazed my eyes. And, look, that was a breast which I think was snow. (*Venus*) You tell something astonishing. But where are those golden arrows? (*Amor*) I had them when I was plucking the vio- 5 lets. Now Violante has them.

LV. On Morinna

Let her be remarkable for her hair, for the beauty of her entire body, let her be Venus and breathe gentle roses from her lips, let her vanquish the goddesses of Aonia and also Pallas herself with her talent, let honey flow from her sweet heart, but provided that Morinna grant me nights at peace and free control of my judg- 5 ment. I burned and, pitiable, I wept at my first fires. This is enough: to die basely in my last love.

LVI. *Ad animum suum*

Arsisti, et misera consumsit flamma medullas
    aridaque in cineres ossa abiere leves.
Flevisti, roremque oculi fudere perennem.
    Sebethus lacrimis crevit et ipse tuis.
5 Ardendi flendique igitur, quae tanta cupido est?
    O anime, exsequias disce timere tuas;
neve iterum tua damna, iterum tua funera quaeras.
    Sirenum scopulos praeteriisse iuvet.

LVII. *De Cassandra Marchesia*

Desine formosae dotes numerare puellae,
    desine iam exstinctas sollicitare faces.
Nam dum saepe comas frontemque humerosque manusque
    commemoras, proprios exstruis ipse rogos.
5 Dumque oculis Cassandra, animo Cassandra recursat,
    Cassandra heu mentis ius habet omne tuae.
Blandus Amor tacitis subrepsit in ossa venenis.
    Sic sibi vel fatum quilibet esse potest.

LVIII. *Hymnus divo Gaudioso*

Gaudete, coetus virginum,
plenas habentes lampadas;
sponsus sacras ad nuptias
venit repente: surgite.

5 Venit serenus Lucifer,
nocturna pellens sidera;
optata lux solemnibus
adest dicata gaudiis;

LVI. To his heart

You have burned. The pitiable fire has devoured your marrow. Your dry bones have passed into thin ash. You have wept. Your eyes have poured forth an unremitting flow. Even Sebeto himself has expanded from your tears. What, pray tell, is this enormous desire for burning and weeping? O my heart, learn to dread your 5 funeral; don't pursue again your undoing, again your death. Let it be pleasing to have passed by the rocks of the Sirens.

LVII. On Cassandra Marchese

Stop counting the beautiful girl's talents. Stop shaking torches now quenched. For as, over and over, you recall her hair and brow, her shoulders and hands, you're building your funeral pyre yourself. For while Cassandra haunts your eyes, haunts your mind, Cassandra, alas, has complete claim on your thoughts. Love the 5 seducer with silent poison has crept into your bones. Thus each person can even be his own doom.

LVIII. Hymn to San Gaudioso

Rejoice, bands of Virgins, holding full lamps. Rise up: the bridegroom has just arrived at the holy nuptials. Tranquil Lucifer has arrived, banishing the stars of night. The day is at hand for which 5 we've prayed, devoted to our yearly rejoicing, the bright day, on

    lux clara, qua fugans nigram
10   mundi sator caliginem,
    vestri latere gloriam
    patris diu non passus est;

    qua Gaudiosi segmina,
    tot inreperta saeculis
15   suis videnda civibus,
    dives retexit urnula.

    O ter beate et amplius,
    lapis pusille, qui tuo
    tanti verendum praesulis
20   sinu recondis pulverem.

    Praesul sed o beatior,
    clarae decus Neapolis,
    tuae benignus patriae
    fer, Gaudiose, gaudia.

25   Adsit fides et veritas;
    adsis probata castitas:
    morbos, famem, pericula
    tuis repelle moenibus.

    Ergo tibi sit gloria,
30   inseparata Trinitas,
    Verbum Paterque et Spiritus,
    qui condidistis omnia.

344

which the begetter of the world, putting black darkness to flight, 10
did not suffer the honor of your protector long to lie hidden,
where the small, precious urn discloses the remains of Gaudioso,
hidden for so many generations, to be viewed by his fellow citi- 15
zens. O thrice blessed and more, you tiny stone who enclose in
your recess the venerable dust of so great a bishop. But you, 20
Gaudioso, bishop still more blessed, O glory of famous Naples,
bring joys in kindly fashion to your fatherland. Be present, faith, 25
and truth, be present, proven chastity! Drive diseases, hunger,
dangers from your walls. So be glory to you, undivided Trinity, 30
Word, and Father, and Spirit, who created everything.

LIX. De eodem ad vesperas

Audiat surgens pariter cadensque
sol tuas laudes meritosque honores,
urbis o nostrae columen tuaeque
    gloria gentis.
5 Audiat caelum, mare, terra et aer,
annuos ritus tibi dum novamus,
dum damus flammis adolenda sacris
    tura per aras.
Huc ades, festa redimite fronde,
10 caelitum plausus choreasque linquens;
et tuam sedem, tua, Gaudiose,
    ossa revise;
ossa, quae longa tumuli sub umbra
abdita, ignaras latuere gentes;
15 nocte mox pulsa redeunt apertas
    lucis in auras.
Hic dies nobis celeber, precamur,
laetior semper redeat, nec ullos
hostium motus ferat aut maligni
20   sideris aestus.
Da tuis longam, venerande, pacem
civibus, da perpetuos honores,
da bonam mentem, superique plenos
    luminis haustus.
25 Iusta poscentes animo benignus
adiuva; iniustos moderare sensus.
Sentiant per te paruisse castis
    aethera votis.
Laus tibi, caeli pater atque princeps,
30 omnium rector simul et creator,

LIX. *On the same, at Vespers*

May the Sun, as he rises as well as when he sets, listen to your praises and due honors, O pillar of our city and splendor of your race. May the heavens listen, the sea, earth, and air, as we revive 5 your annual rites, as we offer incense for burning in the holy flames of the altars. Be present here, crowned with festive wreath, abandoning the applause and the dances of the saints in heaven, and revisit your resting place, Gaudioso, your bones, bones which, 10 hidden beneath the extended shadow of the tomb, have been concealed from the unknowing folk. With darkness put to flight, they soon return to the open breezes of light. May this festal day, we 15 pray, ever return happier for us; may it not bring any disturbance from enemies, or the tumult of a baleful star. O worshipful one, 20 grant long peace to your citizens, grant ever-enduring honors, grant sound mind and full draughts of radiance from above. In kindly fashion assist our thoughts as they demand justice, control 25 unjust feelings. Let people feel that because of you the world above lies open to chaste prayers. Praise be to you, Father and Prince of

quem fides veri studiosa Trinum
  credit et Unum.

LX. *Ad divum Nazarium*

Dive, cui vasti metuenda ponti
vis et iratae famulantur undae,
quem per et spumas gradientem et aestus
    nauta vocavit,
5   ah miser poenas pelago daturus,
cum niger circumstreperet procellis
auster, et turbata minax feriret
    sidera fluctus:
te, mihi sanctum patriumque numen,
10 te canam, gentis columen Latinae,
auream prolem patris Africani,
    Perpetuaeque
matris heu vulnus grave, dum relictis
Tibridis ripis Italoque caelo,
15 sponte trans Rhaetos iter et nivosas
    arripis Alpes;
lacte depulsus velut ille, primi
quem rapit cursus generosus ardor,
pullus, et matrem fugit et rapaces
20   transilit amnes.
Mox et ad Rhenum horribilesque tendis
Treverum gentes, animosus hospes,
morte festinans capere invidendae
    praemia palmae.
25 Hic, ubi e carae gremio parentis,
iam necis magnae comitem futurum,

348

heaven, Ruler as well as Begetter of everything whom faith, zeal- 30
ous of truth, believes Three and One.

LX. *To San Nazario*

Saint, to whom the fearsome force of the sweeping sea and the an-
gry waves are in thrall, on whom the sailor has called, as you set
your course through the foam and the swirl; he, poor creature, was
on the edge of paying a penalty to the sea, when the blasts of the 5
dark south wind roared around him, and the threatening flood
struck the stars in turmoil: you I will hymn, you, holy to me, my
ancestral divinity, jewel of the Latin race, golden offspring of your 10
father Africanus and, alas, grievous wound to your mother
Perpetua, when, leaving behind the banks of the Tiber and the
Italian sky, you pursue your willing way across the Rhaeti and the
snowy Alps. Like some newly-weaned foal, whom the spirited ex- 15
citement of his initial run seizes (he escapes from his mother and
leaps across rushing streams). A guest with spirit, you soon aim 20
for the Rhine and the dread peoples of the Treveri, hastening
through your death to claim the rewards of the enviable palm.
Here, father, is where you receive Celsus from his dear mother's
lap, soon to be the companion of your illustrious martyrdom, and 25

excipis Celsum, pater, et salubri
    perluis unda.
Perluis totas, mora nulla, et urbes;
30 undique exhaustis properatur agris;
barbaros gaudent Druidae sacrorum
    ponere ritus.
Nazari nomen meritique famam
audit, si quem Liger in remotis
35 occulit ripis refugove inundat
    Sequana cursu.
Te neque iniusti rabies Neronis,
impios iam iam minitantis ignes,
non per exsertos Anolinus urgens
40   terruit enses.
Iam voluptatum gelidaeque victor
mortis et lapsi reparator orbis
diceris, milesque peraeque Iberis
    notus et Indis.
45 Ergo speratum, genitor, triumphum
et parum factis meruisse caelum est:
aureum vultu iubar et coruscos
    fundis honores.
Salve io, magni nova lux Olympi,
50 cui per extentas operosa terras
templa tot surgunt calidisque fumant
    ignibus arae.
Nos tibi hac grata scopulorum in umbra
rite parvis aediculam columnis
55 ponimus; nos perpetuo sacramus
    munere fontem.
Accipe aestivam, nova serta, citrum, et
virgines lauros gracilesque myrtos,
quosque Mergillina tulit propinquo

you cleanse him in the healthful water. Without delay you also cleanse whole cities. People hasten from everywhere, emptying their fields. The Druids are happy to put aside practice of their 30 barbarian rites. A person heard the name and fame of Nazario's merits, even if the Loire hid him on its distant banks, or the Seine drenched him with its tidal flood. Neither the rage of unjust 35 Nero, now, even now making threats with his sacrilegious fires, nor Anolinus, at your back with swords already drawn, frightened you. A conqueror of pleasures and of chill death, and soldier 40 equally known among the Iberi and the Indi, you are called also the renewer of a fallen world. Thus, father, it seems but little for you to have deserved an expected triumph and heaven through 45 your deeds. You pour forth golden radiance and shimmering glory from your features. Hail, O hail, new light of mighty Olympus, for whom so many elaborate shrines rise up everywhere in the world, 50 and so many altars smoke with hot flames. In the pleasant shade of these rocks we duly establish for you a chapel with small columns; we dedicate the fountain as a gift forever. Receive the sum- 55 mer citron as fresh garlands, and virgin laurel, and slender myrtle, and the perfumes which Mergellina has borne on the nearby

60   litore odores.
     O mihi longos liceat per annos
       hic sacra et festos renovare ludos,
     et tuum castis sine fraude votis
     poscere numen.

LXI. De Ferdinando Havalo, piscariae principe

Admoveant iterum caelo si castra Gigantes
     hoc duce, quo Ligurum gloria fracta iacet,
cum Marte Enceladus, cum Phoebo signa Typhoeus
     conferet, ipse Havalus cum Iove bella geret.

LXII. In Nolam urbem

Infensum Musis nomen, male grata petenti
     Virgilio optatam Nola negavit aquam.
Noluit haec eadem Ioviano rustica vati
     hospitium parvae contribuisse morae:
5 idcirco nimirum hoc dicta es nomine, Nola:
     nolueris magnis quod placuisse viris.
At tibi pro scelere hoc coenosos fusa per agros
     exhausit populos Styx violenta tuos.
Iamque quid, o nullis abolenda infamia saeclis,
10   imprecer? Et caelum desit et unda tibi.

LXIII. In Lygdamum

Quaeris, Lygdame, musca cur voceris?
Nam musca es, mihi crede, tam molesta,
quam nec sunt culices gravesque fuci,
quam nec vermiculique cimicesque.
5 Unum te tamen arceat necesse est,
turdelae auxilium cacantis, ut te
non muscaria milviique caudae,

shore. O may I be allowed through an expanse of years to renew   60
your rites and festive games, and in sincerity to beseech your divinity with chaste prayers.

LXI. On Ferdinando d'Avalos, Prince of Pescara

Were the Giants to march once more against heaven with this
leader, under whom the glory of the Ligurians lies broken; when   50
Enceladus will join battle with Mars, Typhoeus with Phoebus,
d'Avalos himself will wage war with Jupiter.

LXII. Against the city of Nola

Nola, name hated by the Muses, wickedly denied to Virgil water
that he wanted in his need. This same boorish spot didn't want to
offer hospitality of short duration to the poet Giovianus. This is
doubtless the reason why you are called by this name, Nola: be-   5
cause you didn't want to gratify great men. For this crime, the de-
structive Styx, coursing through your muddy fields, swallowed up
your inhabitants. What curse can I bring down on you, you dis-
grace never to be wiped away through the ages? That you lack
both sky and water.   10

LXIII. Against Lygdamus

Lygdamus, you ask why you are called a fly? For you are a fly, be-
lieve me, as annoying as are neither gnats nor threatening drone-
bees, as neither maggots nor lice. We need only one thing to keep
you away: the help of a defecating thrush, since neither fly-swat-   5

non alae accipitrum potentiorum
avertant abigantque saevientem.

Liber Tertius

I. Mariae Garloniae Grappinae

Propago formosae arboris,
formosa virgo, quae vagos
inter orta Cupidines,
    veris lilia vincis
5 rosasque molles et croci
pulchre rubentis igneum
florem et uvidulas comas
    halantis hyacinthi.
Redisti avitos ad lares,
10 felicem ocellulis tuis
redditura Neapolim,
    caro adnixa marito.
Redisti ad optatos choros
aequalium et probos sinus
15 matris ac bene cognitum
    fratris dulcis amorem.
Quis o quis hunc albo mihi
signet diem lapillulo?
Quis Sabaea calentibus
20   addat munera flammis?
Vocanda Musarum cohors.
Huc huc benigna et abditam
barbiton cape, myrteis
    frontem vincta coronis

ters nor kite's tails nor wings of hawks in full force ward you off
and drive you hence, madman.

Book III

I. To Maria Garlonia Grappina

Offspring of a beautiful tree, beautiful virgin, born among wander-
ing Cupids, you surpass the lilies of spring and soft roses and the   5
fiery flower of the sweetly blushing crocus, the moist tresses of the
fragrant hyacinth. You have returned to the house of your ances-
tors, to make Naples happy with your little glances, supported by   10
your dear husband. You have returned to the welcome gatherings
of your friends, and to the chaste bosom of your mother, and to
the well-recognized love of your dear brother. Who, O who, might   15
mark this day for me with a white pebble? Who might add the
gifts of Sabaea to the warming flames? I must invoke the band of
Muses. And Thalia, hither, hither in kindly fashion take your lyre   20
from hiding and bind your brow with wreaths of myrtle. What are

25   Thalia: quid dignum tuo
      promis favore? Quid bonae
      voce vel fidibus student
         respondere sorores?
      Sed esse quid laetum, deae,
30   hic absque amoribus potest?
      Non movet Chione suis,
         non me Lyda, papillis.
      Procul facessant hinc malae,
      saecli pudor, libidines.
35   Mi sat est, minuat graves
         si Garlonia curas.
      Iuventa, cur me tam cito
      ludendo inepta deseris?
      Haec erat facies novis
40   non fraudanda libellis.

II. Ad Cassandram Marchesiam

Quarta Charis, decima es mihi Pieris, altera Cypris,
   Cassandra, una choris addita diva tribus.

III. Se fidem servaturum

Si post fata novos animas errare per artus
   vera docent Samii dogmata nota senis,
nec pote mens eadem mutari, seu ferus altis
   erret aper silvis, seu vaga cantet avis,
5 ipse ego, mens quoniam est uni servire puellae,
   exsurgam moestis turtur ab exequiis.

you uttering worthy of your kindliness? What are your noble sis- 25
ters eager to respond, with song or lyre? But what can be joyful
here, goddesses, without love? Chione doesn't move me, Lyda 30
doesn't move me, with her breasts. Let evil lusts, the shame of the
age, be off, far from here. It is enough for me if Garlonia lessens
my heavy cares. Foolish time of my youth, why, in your trickery, 35
do you abandon me so quickly? This face of hers should not be
cheated of fresh volumes. 40

II. To Cassandra Marchesia

You are to me the fourth Grace, the tenth Pieris, a second Cypris,
Cassandra: one goddess added to three choruses.

III. About his keeping faith

If the well-known precepts of the ancient of Samos teach the
truth — that souls after death wander through new bodies, nor can
the same mind be altered, whether as a wild boar it roams the
lofty woods or as a wandering bird it bursts into song — I myself,
since it is my mind to serve one girl, will rise up from my sad fu- 5
neral rites as a turtle-dove.

IV. *In Adrianum pontificem maximum*

Classe virisque potens, domitoque Oriente superbus,
    barbarus in Latias dux quatit arma domos.
In Vaticano noster latet; hunc tamen alto,
    Christe, vides caelo—pro dolor!—et pateris?

V. *Ad Federicum*

Litibus abstinui semper, mihi testis Apollo est,
    et Musae et studiis otia grata meis.
Nunc me nescio quis per tristia iurgia versat
    Scotius et rauci cogit ad arma fori.
5 Es fateor magnus pulsis, rex inclyte, Gallis:
    pelle etiam Scotos et mihi maior eris.

VI. *Ad Eunum*

Quicquid erat tripodum Cumis Delphisque petisti,
    discere fortunam dum cupis, Eune, tuam.
At deus: 'Extabis supra regesque ducesque,'
    veridico tandem rettulit ore tibi.
5 Tu tamen hinc vanos sumpsisti, Graecule, fastus:
    iam magni dominus, iam pater orbis eras.
Ecce crucem ascendis. Non te deus, Eune, fefellit:
    omnia sunt crepidis inferiora tuis.

VII. *Ad Porciam Branciam et Isabellam sororem*

Porcia et Isabella, venustae pignora matris,
    dicite, quis vestras non amet illecebras?
Tu quoque dic, tali cum sis dignissima partu,
    quis, Leonora, tuo nolit ab igne mori?

IV. *Against Pope Hadrian*

A barbarian leader, powerful with his fleet and his troops and haughty after conquering the East, brandishes his weapons against the houses of Latium. Our leader lurks in the Vatican. Christ, do you nevertheless see him from the lofty heavens and—how it rankles!—put up with it?

V. *To Federico*

I have always avoided strife, as Apollo is my witness; and the Muses and tranquility have been dear to my pursuits. Now a certain Scotsman or other twists me into an ugly quarrel, and drives me to adopt the weaponry of the shrill forum. I grant, glorious king, that you are mighty for repelling the Gauls. Repel the Scots 5 and you will be to me mightier still.

VI. *To Euno*

Euno, in your eagerness to learn your fortune, you have sought out all the tripods at Cumae and Delphi. The god finally replied to you with truth-telling voice: "You will stand above kings and over dukes." Just the same, you Greekling, you absorbed from this a hollow pride: you were now master, now father, of the great globe. 5 See, you climb the cross. The god didn't deceive you: everything is beneath the soles of your feet.

VII. *To Porcia Brancia and her sister Isabella*

Porcia and Isabella, offspring of a charming mother, tell me: who wouldn't fall in love with your allure? Tell me also, Leonora, since you are fully worthy of such progeny, who wouldn't wish to die from your fire? He who desires to be enflamed by the allure of the

5 Natarum illecebris, matris simul ignibus uri
      qui cupit, is mortis flagrat amore suae.
    Vita vale: in lucro est periisse. Sed hoc reliquum, mors,
      quod sinis, est ipsis vix satis exequiis.

VIII. *In Leonem X pontificem maximum*

Sacra sub extrema, si forte requiritis, hora
    cur Leo non potuit sumere: vendiderat.

IX. *Ad patriam antequam iret in exilium*

Parthenope mihi culta vale, blandissima Siren,
    atque horti valeant Hesperidesque tuae.
Mergillina vale, nostri memor, et mea flentis
    serta cape, heu, domini munera avara tui.
5 Maternae salvete umbrae, salvete paternae,
    accipite et vestris turea dona focis.
Neve nega optatos, Virgo Sebethias, amnes,
    absentique tuas det mihi somnus aquas.
Det fesso aestivas umbras sopor, et levis aura
10   fluminaque ipsa suo lene sonent strepitu.
Exilium nam sponte sequor; Fors ipsa favebit:
    fortibus haec solita est saepe et adesse viris.
Et mihi sunt comites Musae, sunt numina vatum,
    et mens laeta suis gaudet ab auspiciis.
15 Blanditurque animi constans sententia, quamvis
    exilii meritum sit satis ipsa fides.

daughters as well as by the fires of the mother burns with love of   5
his own death. Farewell, life. To die I count a plus. But, death,
what you allow to be left over is scarcely enough for the funeral
itself!

VIII. *Against Pope Leo X*

If by chance you ask why in his last hour Leo wasn't able to take
the sacraments: he had sold them.

IX. *To his fatherland before going into exile*

Parthenope, most delightful Siren, adored by me, farewell. Fare-
well your gardens and your Hesperides. Mergellina, mindful of us,
farewell. Take my garlands, the scanty gifts, alas, of your weeping
master. Hail, shades of my mother, my father's shades: receive the   5
offerings of incense at your hearth. Virgin Sebethias, do not deny
me your beloved streams; may sleep bestow your waters upon me
while I'm away. May my dreams grant me the shades of summer
when I'm tired, and may a fluttering breeze and the waters them-
selves gently murmur with their rippling. For willingly I pursue   10
exile. Destiny herself will watch over me. She has often been ac-
customed to escort brave men. The Muses are also my compan-
ions. They are the inspiration of poets. My cheerful thoughts re-
joice in happiness at the auspices. My mind's steadfast intention
soothes me, although my fidelity itself is a sufficient recompense   15
for exile.

APPENDIX I

The Triumph of Christ and the Quadriga Christi [1]

There are two separate strands of intellectual history that Sannazaro here draws upon. The first is the progress of Christ after the crucifixion visualized as a continuous triumphal procession, beginning with the Harrowing of Hell (and the release of the just from Limbo), followed by the Resurrection and the Ascension into heaven. Texts of importance from the Old Testament are *Psalms* 18 and 23.

From the New Testament we should note Matthew 27:51–2, 1. Peter 4:6, and Paul to the Ephesians 4:8–10. The apocryphal Gospel of Peter and the Gospel of Nicodemus also contain important passages (see B. Ehrman, *The New Testament and Other Early Christian Writings* [New York, 2004], 124; H. Koester, *Ancient Christian Gospels* [London, 1990], 216–8).

For medieval references see Jacopo da Varazze, *Legenda Aurea* VI and Honorius of Autun, *De Ascensione Domini* (from *Speculum Ecclesiae*, Migne *PL* 172. 955):

> Christus est sol aeternus a quo omnes chori angelorum illustrantur. . . . O quam splendida cornua haec nascens luna hodie extulit dum sol alta petens jubar aeterni fulgoris ei infudit! O quam sereno vultu in ordine suo stetit dum apostolicum chorum, qui ejus ordo extitit, et per Virginem Dei Genitricem, quae ejus typum gessit, carnem suam in capite suo, id est in Redemptore suo, in Sponso suo, in Deo suo, aethera penetrare conspexit! O qualis laeticia hodie in coelo angelis oritur dum Dei Filius, qui de palacio in carcerem pro servo, immo de patria in exilium, exul pro

exule, dirigitur, hodie cum triumpho in regnum Patris
revertitur! Unde et haec dies triumphi Dei appellatur in qua
a senatu coelestis curiae ymnidicis laudibus exceptus mortis
triumphatur, vitae auctor glorificatur.

Apud Romanos mos servabatur quod victoribus
triumphus hoc modo exhibebatur: Postquam imperator vel
consul aliquam gentem Romano imperio armis subjugasset,
et victor cum praeda remeasset, senatus ac totus populus
Romanus ei obviam festivus procedit, cum canticis et
laudibus victorem excipit; ipse purpura induitur, dyadema
cum lauro auroque contextum ei imponitur, in curru auro
gemnisque radiante, quatuor niveis equis trahentibus, Urbi
invehitur. Porro nobiles victi praecedunt currum aureis
catenis vincti. Vulgus vero captivum, vinctis manibus post
tergum, sequitur currum. Pompa etiam praedae simul ob in-
signe victoriae ducitur et sic victor cum magno tripudio
summo templo laureatus inducitur et tunc praeda populo
dividitur. (For discussion see Jacoff, *op. cit.* 75–6)

In the second Christ is carried in a chariot drawn by the four
evangelists in their symbolic guises—Luke as ox, Mark as lion,
John as eagle, and Matthew as angel.[2] In origin the scenario goes
back to Roman triumphal practice,[3] which was adopted, and
adapted, in early Christian painting for illustrations of Christ, in a
chariot, in the pose of a *triumphator*.[4]

In chronological order we must also note, first, Jerome writing,
in 394, to Paulinus of Nola (letter 53. 9, from *Sancti Eusebii
Hieronymi Epistulae*, vol. 1, ed. I. Hilberg, in *CSEL* 54 [Vienna,
1910], 462):

Mattheus, Marcus, Lucas, Iohannes, quadriga domini et ve-
rum Cherubin, quod interpretatur 'scientiae multitudo,' per
totum corpus oculati sunt, scintillae micant, discurrunt

fulgora, pedes habent rectos et in sublime tendentes, terga pennata et ubicumque volitantia. Tenent se mutuo sibique perplexi sunt et quasi rota in rota volvuntur et pergunt, quocumque eos flatus sancti spiritus dixerit.

He is followed shortly by Augustine *De Consensu Evangelistarum* (dated probably 399–400), 1. 6–7 (Migne *PL* 34. 1046–7; *CSEL* 43 [Vienna, 1904], 10). Ch. 6 discusses the figuration of the four evangelists, as drawn from the *Apocalypse*. Ch. 7. begins:

Has Domini sanctas quadrigas, quibus per orbem vectus subigit populos leni suo jugo et sarcinae levi . . . .

Writing in the ninth century, Rabanus Maurus (*De Universo* XX. 31 [Migne *PL*. III. 551]) treats the *quadrigae* in scripture as either the four Evangelists or as the Gospels or as the four principal virtues.

"By the twelfth century, discussions of the *Quadriga Domini* envisage a vehicle that differs radically from the Greco-Roman one. Four horses sometimes still draw it, but the car proper is equipped with four wheels rather than two. These four wheels now usurp the role previously played by the horses in the analogy with the Evangelists" (Jacoff, *op. cit.* 18). He quotes Honorius of Autun *Expositio in Cantica Canticorum* (Migne *PL* 172. 454): "Quadriga Christi est Evangelium; quatuor rotae sunt quatuor evangelistae."

Guillaume Durandus (c. 1230/1–1296) writes (*Rationale* 6. 67. 11):

Illi namque ferentes ramos triumphum Christi nondum completum sed tempore passionis complendum prefigurabant. . . . Ecclesia vero per talia representat triumphum Christi iam completum. . . . Quia ergo non solum ipse triumphator est, sed etiam, per ipsius gratiam et sanctificationem, triumphabunt omnes electi.[5]

Of particular importance for later literature and art is Dante's depiction (*Purgatorio* 29. 92–108) of the Chariot of the Church, drawn by a griffin (probably a figure for Christ) and accompanied on either side by the evangelists, also in their symbolic guises.

For a detailed examination of the pageant in *Purgatorio* 29 and its sources, especially in the liturgies of Advent and Palm Sunday, and in the triumphal procession that forms a salient part of the latter, see R. Martinez, "Dante's Poetics of Advent Liturgies," in *Le Culture di Dante*, M. Picone, T. Cachey, Jr., and M. Mesirca, eds, (=*Atti del quarto Seminario dantesco internazionale* [Florence, 2004]), 271–304).

For the fifteenth century we have an illustration by Vecchietta in the illuminations made by Vecchietta and Giovanni di Paolo for the *Divina Commedia*. The manuscript (now London, B. M. Yates Thompson 36) was commissioned by Alfonso V of Aragon, king of Naples, and remained in his library in Naples until it was removed to Spain in 1538. The dating is most likely 1444 (J. Pope-Hennessy, *Paradiso: The Illuminations to Dante's Divine Comedy by Giovanni di Paolo* [New York, 1993], 12 and 34; for the ascription to Vechietta instead of Priamo della Quercia see 15–6). The foot of the first page of *Paradiso* contains the initial illustration by Giovanni di Paolo. But, according to Pope-Hennessy (37), "The historiated initial, showing Christ standing in benediction in a golden chariot drawn by an eagle, flanked by the symbols of the Evangelists and with Adam and Eve beneath him, is not by Giovanni di Paolo but by the illustrator of the *Inferno* and *Purgatorio*, Vecchietta."[6] Mark and Matthew are the upper and lower figures, respectively, to the left of the griffin, John and Luke to the right. For the illustration, see Pope-Hennessy, p. 40, for a full page view; P. Brieger, M. Meiss, and C. S. Singleton, *Illuminated Manuscripts of the Divine Comedy*, 2 vols. (Princeton, 1969), vol. 2, 30b.

Illustrations of the sixth of Petrarch's *Trionfi* (written between 1356 and 1374) entitled *Triumphus aeternitatis*, showing the victory of eternity over time, also play a role. This is depicted in two engravings by the Florentine Baccio Baldini, dating from around 1463–4. The first is a full page illustration of what is usually known as the triumph of divinity, with God the Father, surrounded by the twelve apostles and drawn in a chariot by symbols of the four evangelists.[7] A further plate illustrates all six "triumphs" with the triumph of divinity occupying the lower-right position.[8] The scene is also depicted on a *cassone* from the School of Jacopo del Sellaio in the Oratorio di Sant' Ansano near Fiesole.[9]

The illustration that most exactly parallels Sannazaro's description is Titian's huge woodcut, in ten blocks, of *The Triumph of Christ* (dated by Vasari to 1508 but often put a few years later, primarily because of Titian's youth at the time[10]). Instead of God the Father it shows Christ in profile, resting on a globe, his right hand raised in blessing, drawn on a chariot by symbols of the four evangelists.[11] Though the poem was not published until 1526, Sannazaro had completed a sketch of *De Partu Virginis* by 1513 and an outline still earlier. It is therefore not impossible that he would have known and, especially given his fascination with ekphrasis as a figure as well as his love for Venice, drawn inspiration from the extraordinary masterpiece of Titian's youth as he wrote *De Partu Virginis* 2. 404–39. So, with Titian, and Sannazaro, we by-pass the late mediaeval tradition of Honorius and Dante (with the Evangelists walking by the wheels of the chariot and serving as an energizing force; and, for Dante in particular, the chariot — whatever its meaning — is riderless) and return to Jerome, Augustine and the classical tradition Christianized.

NOTES

1. I am indebted in the pages that follow to M. Jacoff, *The Horses of San Marco and the Quadriga of the Lord* (Princeton, 1993).

2. The designation comes from *Apocalypse* 4:6–8 (based on Ezekiel 1:10–1).

3. See H. S. Versnel, *Triumphus: An Inquiry into the Origin, Development and Meaning of the Roman Triumph* (Leiden, 1970); E. Künzl, *Der römische Triumph* (Munich, 1988); D. Favro, "The Street Triumphant: the Urban Impact of Roman Triumphal Parades," in Z. Celik, D. Favro and R. Ingersoll, eds., *Streets: Critical Perspectives on Public Space* (Berkeley, 1994), 151–64; R. Brilliant, "Let the Trumpets Roar! The Roman Triumph," in B. Bergmann and C. Kondoleon, eds., *The Art of Ancient Spectacle* (New Haven, 1999), 220–9. See also C. Stinger, "Roma Triumphans: Triumphs in the Thought and Ceremonies of Renaissance Rome," *Medievalia et Humanistica*, n.s. 10 (1981), 189–201.

4. The earliest depiction of Christ in a horse-drawn chariot seems to be the third century ceiling mosaic in the Mausoleum of the Julii in the necropolis under the Basilica of St. Peter. See R. Jensen, *Understanding Early Christian Art* (London and New York, 2000), 42–4 and 43, fig. 9; ibid, *Face to Face: Portraits of the Divine in Early Christianity* (Minneapolis, 2005), 146–8 and 147, fig. 66).

5. Guillelmi Duranti, *Rationale divinorum officiorum I-IV*, eds. A. Davril and T. M. Thibodeau = *Corpus Christianorum, continuatio medievalis* CXL, 3 vols. (Turnhout, 1995).

6. Since the creature's left leg is that of an animal, a griffin, with head and wings of an eagle and body of a lion, is more likely meant.

7. See A. M. Hind, *Early Italian Engraving: Part I: Florentine engravings and anonymous prints of other schools*, 2 vols. (London, 1938; repr. Liechtenstein, 1970), vol. 1, no. 23 (p. 36); vol. 2, pl. A.I.23.

8. Hind, op. cit., vol. 1, no. 24 (pp. 36–7); vol. 2, pl. A.I. 24. The latter is also illustrated in V. d'Essling and E. Müntz, *Pétrarque: Ses Études d'Art,*

Son Influence sur les Artistes . . . (Paris, 1902), facing p. 170. See also J. Phillips, *Early Florentine Designers and Engravers* (Greenwich, 1955), 60–1 and 86.

9. See d'Essling-Müntz, pl. facing p. 152.

10. But see C. Gould, "Titian" in *The Dictionary of Art* (London and New York, 1996), 42–3, who points to the lack of solid evidence for opting for a date later than Vasari's.

11. For illustrations with commentary, see R. Rosand and M. Muraro, *Titian and the Venetian Woodcut* (exh. cat., Washington, 1976), 37–54. For further commentary: E. Panofsky, *Problems in Titian* (New York, 1969), 58–63; S. Sinding-Larsen, "Titian's Triumph of Faith and the Medieval Tradition of the Glory of Christ," *Acta ad archaeologiam et artium historiam pertinentia* 6 (1975), 315–51; M. Bury, "The 'Triumph of Christ' after Titian," *Burlington Magazine* 131 (1989), 188–97; Jacoff, *op. cit.*, excursus iv: "The Lord's Quadriga in Titian's *Triumph of Faith*," 137–42.

APPENDIX II

At *DMV* 3.197–232 Sannazaro quotes, varies, and comments upon Vergil's *eclogue* 4, the so-called "Messianic Eclogue" which he condenses from sixty-three into thirty-six lines. In so doing he takes the most appropriate of ancient pastorals to his theme and reworks it to form a suitable gesture in the mouths of proto-Christian "shepherds," singing a revamped pagan song. Virtually from the time of its publication, the *puer* at the center of the poem was the subject of allegory. (The "dramatic" date of *ecl.* 4 is 40 BCE, the year of the consulship of Pollio. The date of publication was probably 37.) But it was only during the early fourth century, in Lactantius's *Divinae Institutiones* and in the *Oratio ad coetum sanctorum* of his friend Constantine the Great, that the boy was seen as a prefiguration of Christ and that, as a result, Vergil was interpreted as assuming the mantle of pagan prophet. I offer the following line by line illustration:

199: et cecinit dignas romano consule silvas.

The line varies *ecl.* 4.3 — *si canimus silvas, silvae sint consule dignae* — with the addition of *romano* to draw us back into the Roman world of 40 BCE and the consulship of Gaius Asinius Pollio.

200: An exact quotation of *ecl.* 4.4, the beginning of the poem proper.

201: magna per exactos renovantur saecula cursus.

Sannazaro draws on *ecl.* 4.5 — *magnus ab integro saeclorum nascitur ordo* — and stresses renewal rather than a new beginning.

202: scilicet haec virgo, haec sunt Saturnia regna.

Compare *ecl.* 4.6 — *iam redit et virgo, redeunt Saturnia regna*. Sannazaro records the immediacy of the events that are happening before the shepherds' eyes. The *virgo*, instead of being Erigone, also known as

Astraia (see on *DPV* 3.124; *ecl.* 1.8.5), a personification of Iustitia, becomes now the Virgin Mary who has just given birth.

203: haec nova progenies coelo descendit ab alto.

Compare *ecl.* 4.7 — *iam nova progenies caelo demittitur alto.* The continued use of *haec* extends the notion that the prophecy of *ecl.* 4 is actually now being fulfilled. The change from *demittitur* to *descendit* moves from Vergil to the language of the Creed (*descendit de caelo*) Likewise the alteration from passive to active allows the Son a creative part in opting for his Incarnation.

204–5:
progenies per quam toto gens aurea mundo
surget et in mediis palmes florebit aristis.

Compare *ecl.* 4.9 — *toto surget gens aurea mundo* — and *ecl.* 4.28: *molli paulatim flavescet campus arista.* Sannazaro stresses *progenies* by repetition and eliminates Vergil's mention of the passing of the "iron race" (*ferrea gens,* 8–9), as a further reminder that his context is as much biblical as pagan. The non-Vergilian vine-shoot combines with the Vergilian *aristis* to refer to the conjunction of bread and wine at the center of the Eucharist. Sannazaro may also wish us to remember John 15:4–6 (Christ to his disciples), especially 5 (*ego sum vitis, vos palmites*). For Mary as *palmes* see *DPV* 2.38.

206–8:
Qua duce, si qua manent sceleris vestigia nostri
irrita perpetua solvent formidine terras
et vetitum magni pandetur limen Olympi.

Line 206 varies *ecl.* 4.13 with the change from *te duce,* referring to Pollio, to *qua duce,* the *nova progenies,* Christ himself, as the leader. Line 207 repeats *ecl.* 4.14. Taken together, the lines refer to the original sin of Adam and Eve, not to some *scelus* that Vergil leaves vague (Prometheus's theft of fire is usually put forward as the crime in question). Line 208 is new with Sannazaro, though the phrase *limen Olympi* comes from Vergil's fifth *eclogue* (56). There it refers to the apotheosis of the shepherd Daphnis. Here we are to imagine man's redemption from sin through the sacrifice of Christ.

209–10:

occidet et serpens, miseros quae prima parentes

elusit portentificis imbuta venenis.

The opening of line 209 repeats the initial words of *ecl.* 4.24; otherwise the hexameters are original with Sannazaro. The snake, one of nature's generalized menaces, becomes the particular Serpent under whose guise Satan seduced Eve into eating the apple. (The phrase *portentificis venenis* comes from Ovid *M.* 14.55, describing the poisons of Scylla. So, even while departing from Vergil to give his language a Christian twist, Sannazaro makes use of a notable pagan author.)

211–3:

Tu ne deum vitam accipies divisque videbis

permistos heroas et ipse videberis illis

pacatumque reges patriis virtutibus orbem?

The lines repeat *ecl.* 4.15–7 with the following alterations: *ille* (15) becomes *tu ne*, the four verbs are changed from third to second person, and the whole is phrased as a rhetorical question. Like the uses of *haec* in lines 202–3, the apostrophe takes us directly before the Christ child, in anticipation of the powerful effect of his advent.

214–5:

Aspice felici diffusum lumine coelum

camposque fluviosque ipsasque in montibus herbas.

Sannazaro draws *aspice* (here and at line 216) from *ecl.* 4.52, otherwise the lines are original, though much influenced by Lucretius *DRN* 1.9 and 17–8. In Vergil the imperative is an address to the reader. Sannazaro, through his shepherds, further apostrophizes the child directly and in the process particularizes the natural world, now bathed in glorious light, that was left general with the preceding *orbem*. The catalogue has *ecl.* 4.51 — *terrasque tractusque maris caelumque profundum* — in the background, but Sannazaro's focus on fields, streams and grassy mountains has its own gracious specificity.

216: aspice, venturo laetentur ut omnia saeclo.

An exact quote of *ecl.* 4.52, serving as summary of the details that precede and follow.

217–20:

Ipsae lacte domum referent distenta capellae
hubera nec magnos metuent armenta leones
agnaque per gladio ibit secura nocentes
bisque superfusos servabit tincta rubores.

The first two lines are a direct quotation of *ecl.* 4.21–2. Lines 219–20, however, are a Christianized variation on *ecl.* 4.42–5 where, under the new magic dispensation, sheep in the meadows will spontaneously take on color (which is to say, in one reading, that man will no longer need corrupting dyes for making the natural unnatural, but nature herself will be the artificer of such beauty). In the mention of the double dyeing, Sannazaro is probably thinking of the sacrifice of Christ, the Lamb of God, on the Cross and of the martyrdom of those who served as "witnesses" to him. Sannazaro annotates line 3.191 with a quotation from Luke (10:3: *Ecce ego mitto vos sicut oves inter lupos*) and line 3.192 with the phrase *Virginum martyria post Christi sanguinem*. (Nash [1996], 210, refers to F-P lxxii and lxxix.) Even for lines 219–20 there are classical precedents in part. See, e.g., Ovid *M.* 2.459, as Diana speaks to her companions (*nuda superfusis tinguamus corpora lymphis*).

221–2:

Interea tibi, parve puer, munuscula prima
contingent ederaeque intermixtique corymbi.

Parve puer, in apostrophe, comes from *ecl.* 4.60, and *munuscula prima* and *ederae* from *ecl.* 4.18–9. *Corymbi*, however, is used by

Vergil only at *ecl.* 3.39. There they are also conjoined with *hedera* (*diffusos hedera vestit pallente corymbos*) as part of the decoration on a cup.

223–5:

ipsa tibi blandos fundent cunabula flores

et durae quercus sudabunt roscida mella;

mella dabunt quercus, omnis feret omnia tellus.

Line 223 repeats *ecl.* 4.23 and line 224 *ecl.* 4.30. The final phrase of 225 comes from *ecl.* 4.39. The near repetition of the first three words of 225 from the preceding lines not only emphasizes the *adynaton* (and the fact that Sannazaro omits allusion to *ecl.* 4.29) but points up the virtuoso reduction of *sudabunt* into *dabunt*.

226–30:

At postquam firmata virum te fecerit aetas

et tua iam totum notescent facta per orbem,

alter erit tum Tiphys et altera quae vehat Argo

delectos heroas; erunt etiam altera bella

atque ingens stygias ibis praedator ad undas.

Save for the first two words, line 226 repeats *ecl.* 4.37 while 228–9 iterate *ecl.* 4.34–5 exactly. Lines 227 and 230 are original with Sannazaro. The first speaks to Christ's life on earth. The second, to which Vergil's reference to the epic adventures of the Argonauts is an appropriate pagan introduction, is to Christ's Harrowing of Hell as part of his own "epic" progress of Descent, Resurrection and Ascension. (See *DPV* 1.80, 247, 363–7, and especially 387–439, together with Appendix I.) Sannazaro would also have us think of the *Apostolorum et martyrum agones*.

231–2:

Incipe, parve puer, risu cognoscere matrem,

cara dei suboles, magnum coeli incrementum.

Line 231 is borrowed entirely from *ecl.* 4.60 while line 232 is a variant of *ecl.* 4.49 — *cara deum suboles, magnum Iovis incrementum* — with the necessary changes from plural gods to singular, and from "Jupiter" to "heaven." See the similar language at *DPV* 1.146.

233–6:

Talia dum referunt pastores, avia longe

responsant nemora et voces ad sidera iactant

intonsi montes; ipsae per confraga rupes,

ipsa sonant arbusta: 'Deus, deus ille, Menalca.'

By way of epilogue Sannazaro refers to Vergil's fifth *eclogue* to which he had already alluded in line 208 (62–4): *ipsi laetitia voces ad sidera iactant / intonsi montes; ipsae iam carmina rupes, / ipsa sonant arbusta: 'deus, deus ille, Menalca!'*. Sannazaro has given his shepherds names drawn from ancient pastoral. It is therefore not inappropriate not only that his final bow here to Vergilian pastoral be extensive but also that, in echoing Vergil (in a passage about pastoral echo), he uses in apostrophe the name of the actual singer in *eclogue* 5 to whom the landscape responds. But the central point, as at 205, is that the poem deals with the death and deification of Daphnis who, through Sannazaro's metamorphic skills, has been transformed into Christ, just as pagan pastoral has become a vehicle for presenting Christian ideas.

Note on the Text

ॐ

The texts in this volume are taken from the following sources:

De partu Virginis libri III. The text is based on *Iacopo Sannazaro: De Partu Virginis*, Charles Fantazzi and Alessandro Perosa, eds., Istituto Nazionale di Studi sul Rinascimento, Studi e Testi XVII (Florence: Olschki, 1988). Readers interested in the textual history of the work and variant readings should consult this excellent edition. One change has been introduced at 2.444: *phariis* has been changed to *Pariis* (see *Il Parto della Vergine*, ed. Prandi, 60 and *ad loc.*).

De morte Christi lamentatio. Except for the changes from *penasset* to *pensasset* (63) and from *reiecturos* to *reiecturus* (83) and occasional punctuation and orthographical alterations, the text is by Carlo Vecce. See his "*Maiora Numina*. La prima poesia religiosa e la *Lamentatio* di Sannazaro," *Studi e problemi di critica testuale* 43 (1991): 49–94. The text, with notes, appears on 83–94.

Eclogae piscatoriae. The text is based on *The Piscatory Eclogues of Jacopo Sannazaro*, W. P. Mustard, ed. (Baltimore: The Johns Hopkins Press, 1914). At 3.30 I follow the reading *et* of the Aldine edition (1535) rather than *nec* as in the *editio princeps* (1526), upon which Mustard based his edition. At 4.67, following a suggestion of Monti Sabia, "Storia," 269–71, I prefer the *vincit* of the 1526 edition to the *iungit* that Mustard imported from the 1535.

Fragmentum. The text survives in three redactions, the first and third in preserved in an autograph manuscript, Vatican City, Biblioteca Apostolica Vaticana, MS Vat. lat. 3361, f. 20v and f. 61r-v, respectively. The second was the version first printed in the Aldine edition of 1535 and in all subsequent editions. All three redactions are edited in Monti Sabia, "Storia," 279–81, to whom the analysis of the redactions is owed. The text printed here follows Monti Sabia's edition of the third, unfinished redaction.

The variants of the second redaction are given below. They are given in Roman type, following the readings of the third redaction in Italic type. The second redaction places lines 37–42 after line 24, and does not identify speakers.

1. *Euploea*] Euplea

2. (line omitted in second redaction)

3. *nassis*] piscanti

7. *quam*] quam . . . *quam*] quem . . . *sorores*] puellae

11. *liquido*] medio . . . *fundo*] fluctu

12. *undisonum*] horrisonum

13. *scopulos*] templum

19. *Zephyre⟨us⟩*] Zephyraeus

24. *fletus*] cantus

26. et tempora quattuor anni (after *Ventorum domos*

27. *Nunc*] Vos

30. *mecum tandem*] tandem mecum . . . *fletus*] cantus

32. *reliqui*] refugi

36. *mecum tandem*] tandem mecum . . . *fletus*] cantus

37. *caerula*] candida

40. *Ipsa fatentur*] horrida caete

41. *Aequora*] Ut saltem miseros lacerarent dentibus artus

42. *mecum tandem*] tandem mecum . . . *fletus*] cantus

Salices. The text is based on the 1728 Amsterdam edition, 78–82.

Elegiarum libri III. Based on the 1728 Amsterdam edition, 87–176. At 2.1.48, I read *saeva* for *saevae*, and at 2.1.67, *diis* has been corrected to *dis* to preserve the meter.

Epigrammatum libri III. Based on the 1728 Amsterdam edition, 179–272.

The latter edition prints *obbiice* for *obiice* at 1.35.4, presumably *metri causa*.

In the case of the last three texts, the punctuation, spelling and capitalization have been modernized.

Notes

꿢꿢꿢

ABBREVIATIONS

Arcadia	Jacopo Sannazaro, *Arcadia*
DPV	Jacopo Sannazaro, *The Virgin Birth*
ecl.	Jacopo Sannazaro, *Piscatory Eclogues*
el.	Jacopo Sannazaro, *Elegies*
ep.	Jacopo Sannazaro, *Epigrams*
fr.	Jacopo Sannazaro, *Fragmentum*
LMC	Jacopo Sannazaro, *Lamentation on the Death of Christ*
Sal.	Jacopo Sannazaro, *The Willows*
Appian *Pun.*	Appian, *De rebus Punicis*
Apollonius Rhodius *Arg.*	Apollonius of Rhodes, *Argonautica*
Apuleius *M.*	Apuleius, *Metamorphoses*
Aratus *Phae.*	Aratus, *Phaenomena*
Aulus Gellius *NA*	Aulus Gellius, *Noctes Atticae*
Bion *Id.*	Bion, *Idylls*
Caesar *BG*	Julius Caesar, *De Bello Gallico*
Calpurnius Siculus	Calpurnius Siculus, *Eclogues*
Cassian *Coll.*	John Cassian, *Collationes*
Catullus	Catullus, *Carmina*
Cicero *ad Att.*	Cicero, *Epistolae ad Atticum*
Cicero *ad Fam.*	Cicero, *Epistolae ad familiares*
Cicero *Arat.*	Cicero, *Aratea*
Cicero *De Div.*	Cicero, *De divinatione*
Cicero *Fin.*	Cicero, *De finibus bonorum et malorum*
Cicero *in Pis.*	Cicero, *In Pisonem*
Cicero *ND*	Cicero, *De natura deorum*
Cicero *TD*	Cicero, *Tusculanae Disputationes*
Cicero *Ver.*	Cicero, *In Verrem*

Claudian *De Nupt.*	Claudian, *Epithalamium de Nuptiis Honorii Augusti*
Claudian *de raptu*	Claudian, *De raptu Proserpinae*
Diodorus Siculus	Diodorus Siculus, *Library of History*
Ennius *Ann.*	Ennius, *Annales*
Hesiod *The.*	Hesiod, *Theogony*
Homer *Il.*	Homer, *Iliad*
Homer *Od.*	Homer, *Odyssey*
Horace *c.*	Horace, *Odes*
Horace *epi.*	Horace, *Epistles*
Horace *epode*	Horace, *Epodes*
Horace *sat.*	Horace, *Satires*
Isidore *Origines*	Isidore of Seville, *Etymologies*
Juvenal *sat.*	Juvenal, *Satires*
Livy	Livy, *Ab urbe condita*
Lucan *BC*	Lucan, *Bellum civile* [*Pharsalia*]
Lucilius	Lucilius, *Fragments* (ed. Krenkel)
Lucretius *DRN*	Lucretius, *De rerum natura*
Macrobius *Sat.*	Macrobius, *Saturnalia*
Manilius *Ast.*	Manilius, *Astronomica*
Martial	Martial, *Epigrams*
Martial *Spec.*	Martial, *Liber spectaculorum*
Moschus *Id.*	Moschus, *Idylls*
Nemesianus *ecl.*	Nemesianus, *Eclogues*
Orosius *Hist.*	Orosius, *Historiae*
Ovid *AA*	Ovid, *Ars amatoria*
Ovid *Am.*	Ovid, *Amores*
Ovid *EP*	Ovid, *Epistulae ex Ponto*
Ovid *F.*	Ovid, *Fasti*
Ovid *H.*	Ovid, *Heroides*
Ovid *M.*	Ovid, *Metamorphoses*
Ovid *Med.*	Ovid, *Medicamina faciei*
Ovid *RA*	Ovid, *Remedia amoris*
Ovid *T.*	Ovid, *Tristia*
[ps.]Ovid *Hal.*	[ps.]Ovid, *Halieutica*

Plautus *Aul.*	Plautus, *Aulularia*
Plautus *Per.*	Plautus, *Persa*
Pliny *HN*	Pliny, *Natural History*
Polybius	Polybius, *Histories*
Pomponius Mela	Pomponius Mela, *De chorographia*
Propertius	Propertius, *Elegies*
Seneca *ad Marciam*	Seneca the Younger, *Ad Marciam de consolatione*
Seneca *Aga.*	Seneca the Younger, *Agamemnon*
Seneca *Apoc.*	Seneca the Younger, *Apocolocyntosis*
Seneca *HF*	Seneca the Younger, *Hercules Furens*
Seneca *Oed.*	Seneca the Younger, *Oedipus*
Seneca *Phae.*	Seneca the Younger, *Phaedra*
Seneca *Phoen.*	Seneca the Younger, *Phoenissae*
[ps.]Seneca *HO*	[ps.]Seneca the Younger, *Hercules Oetaeus*
[ps.]Seneca *Oct.*	[ps.]Seneca the Younger, *Octavia*
Servius	Servius, *Commentaries on Virgil*
Sidonius Apollinaris *ep.*	Sidonius Apollinaris, *Epistulae*
Silius *Pun.*	Silius Italicus, *Punica*
Statius *Sil.*	Statius, *Silvae*
Statius *Ach.*	Statius, *Achilleid*
Statius *The.*	Statius, *Thebaid*
Strabo	Strabo, *Geography*
Suetonius	Suetonius, *De viris illustribus*
Sulpicia	Sulpicia, *Elegies* [*Corpus Tibullianum*]
Tacitus *Germ.*	Tacitus, *Germania*
Theocritus *Id.*	Theocritus, *Idylls*
Tibullus	Tibullus, *Elegies*
[ps.]Tibullus	[ps.]Tibullus, *Elegies* [*Corpus Tibullianum*]
Valerius Flaccus *Arg.*	Valerius Flaccus, *Argonautica*
Varius Rufus	Varius Rufus, *Fragments*
Varro *LL*	Varro, *De lingua Latina*
Velleius Paterculus	Velleius Paterculus, *Roman History*
Vergil *Aen.*	Vergil, *Aeneid*
Vergil *ecl.*	Vergil, *Eclogues*

Vergil *geo.*	Vergil, *Georgics*
[ps.]Vergil *Aetna*	[ps.]Vergil *Aetna* [*Appendix Virgiliana*]
[ps.]Vergil *Cata.*	[ps.]Vergil, *Catalepton* [*Appendix Virgiliana*]
[ps.]Vergil *Ciris*	[ps.]Vergil *Ciris* [*Appendix Virgiliana*]
[ps.]Vergil *Copa*	[ps.]Vergil *Copa* [*Appendix Virgiliana*]
[ps.]Vergil *Culex*	[ps.]Vergil *Culex* [*Appendix Virgiliana*]
[ps.]Vergil *Eleg. in Maec.*	[ps.] Vergil, *Elegia in Maecenatem* [*Appendix Virgiliana*]
[ps.]Vergil *Mor.*	[ps.]Vergil, *Moretum* [*Appendix Virgiliana*]
CSEL	*Corpus scriptorum ecclesiasticorum Latinorum* (Vienna, 1866-).
DBI	*Dizionario Biografico degli Italiani* (Rome, 1960-).
F-P	Iacopo Sannazaro, *De Partu Virginis*, ed. C. Fantazzi and A. Perosa, Istituto Nazionale di Studi sul Rinascimento *Studi e Testi* XVII (Florence, 1988).
Migne *PL*	*Patrologiae cursus completus*, Series Latina, ed. J.-P. Migne (Paris, 1844–64).
OLD	*Oxford Latin Dictionary*, ed. P. G. W. Glare (Oxford, 1982).

THE VIRGIN BIRTH

First published 1526.

DEDICATORY POEM TO POPE CLEMENT VII

Meter: elegiac couplet

Pope Clement VII was born Giulio de' Medici (1479–1534), natural son of Giuliano and nephew of Lorenzo de' Medici ("il Magnifico"). He reigned as pontiff from 1523 to 1534.

7. Podalirius: Legendary physician, son of Aesculapius and grandson of Apollo.

8. Paean (Paeon) is Apollo in his role as god of healing. See also *el.* 2.10.40; *LMC* 60. The dual references play on the meaning of the pope's family name.

BOOK I

Meter: dactylic hexameter, the standard meter for epic.

2. The words *progenies coeli* are a reminder of Vergil *ecl.* 4.7, a poem to which Sannazaro will often return, in detail at 3.197–232.

3. Sannazaro uses the phrase *mortalibus aegris* also at 2.357 and 3.111. Vergil, in whose writings it occurs four times (*geo.* 1.237; *Aen.* 2.268, 10.274, 12.850), adopts it from Lucretius *DRN* 6.1, who in turn is varying Homer (*Od.* 11.19).

4. Olympus: Classical home of the gods in northern Greece, here, as frequently, standing for the Christian heaven.

6. Again Vergil is in Sannazaro's mind, this time the *Aeneid* (6.129), where the Sibyl warns Aeneas of the difficulties of a journey to the underworld (*hoc opus, hic labor est*).

7. Compare Vergil's only use of the form *evolvite* at *Aen.* 9.528, an address to Calliope and the Muses.

8. Muses: See note on *ecl.* 1.120.

13. Path: Compare Vergil *geo.* 2.477.

15. Aonia: The district of Boeotia in Greece that contains Mt. Helicon, like Mt. Parnassus, sacred to Apollo and to the Muses. See also *el.* 1.11.22, *ep.* 2.55.3.

17. Sky: Compare Vergil *Aen.* 7.138.

18. *Eoos*: i.e. Eastern or oriental (from Greek *Eos*, dawn).

19. Beginning with *tuque adeo* and extending through line 32, Sannazaro offers a series of explicit and implicit references to the opening of Vergil's first *Georgic* and in particular to its dedication to the future emperor Augustus.

20. Vergil uses the phrase *alma parens* at *Aen.* 2.591 and 664 (both of Venus) and at 10.252 (of Cybele, the Great Mother).

22. For *totidem . . . tot . . . tot* Sannazaro, in a letter to Antonio Seripando (F-P 97), refers to Vergil *Aen.* 4.183 (to which should be added 181–2). For *signa tubaeque* compare Tibullus 1.1.75.

23. Gleaming shrines: Compare Ovid. *F.* 1.637.

26. Mergellina: earlier Mergelline. See below 3.511 and on *ecl.* 1.110 and 2.3; see also on *ep.* 1.2 and 2.36 as well as 2.1.15, 2.60.59, 3.9.3.

31. With *ignarumque viae* compare Vergil *geo.* 1.41, on farmers "ignorant of the way" (*ignaros viae*) whom the poet calls on Augustus to join him in helping. The word *coeptis* ends adjacent lines in both passages (*geo.* 1.40; *DPV* 1.32).

32. Sannazaro draws the phrases *tu vatem* and *diva mone* from Vergil *Aen.* 7.41, where the poet appeals to the muse Erato for inspiration. Throughout this passage, from *alma parens* (20) to *diva*, the reference is to the Virgin Mary who becomes both Christian patron, replacing the Roman emperor, and source of inspiration. Compare also the double use of *diva* at 2.343, likewise of Mary as muse. The line's concluding words, *adlabere coeptis*, come from [ps.]Vergil *Culex* 25, a poem that Sannazaro may have considered genuine. They are addressed to an Octavius in whom Sannazaro may also have seen Augustus.

34. Tartarus (or Tartara): The infernal world. See also 1.228, 387 and 398, 3.273 and 384; *LMC* 58.

35. Tisiphone: One of the Furies. See also on *el.* 1.11.65.

40. Love: Compare Vergil *Aen.* 7.496.

41. With *Ecquis erit finis?* Sannazaro is reminding us of the words with which Jupiter begins his speech to Juno at Vergil *Aen.* 12.793: "What will now be the end, my wife?" (*Quae iam finis erit, coniunx?*). See also below on 1.151.

42. With *luent poenis . . . commissa* compare Vergil *geo.* 4.454–5 (*luis commissa . . . poenas*). The parallel implies that Christ is a type of Orpheus figure who succeeds in redeeming mankind from Hell (with *DPV* 1.44–5 compare *geo.* 4.481). See further on 244 below.

57. Vergil uses the phrase *insignis facie* twice (*Aen.* 9.336 and 583). The end of the hexameter may be an echo of the phrase *fulgentibus armis* which Vergil uses six times, likewise at the ends of lines.

59. Guardian: For the archangel Gabriel as God's emissary see Luke 1:12–38.

62. Phoenicians: Inhabitants of Phoenicia, a coastal region of ancient Syria, now largely Lebanon.

63. Jordan: The principal river of Palestine, flowing due south into the Dead Sea and separating Judaea from Galilaea. See also 3.284, 338, 413–5, 497.

64. Judaea: Roman province forming the southwestern area of ancient Palestine.

72. Dwelling: Sannazaro regularly uses the word *penates*, which to a Roman meant gods of the household, by synecdoche to describe a house or its surroundings. See also 1.185 and 271, 2.40 and 253, 3.11.

77. So on your way: Compare Vergil *geo* 1.63 and *Aen.* 2.707.

80. Styx: The principal river in the underworld, here standing for the underworld itself. See also 1.363, 3.230 and 356; *el.* 1.7.28, 1.9.74, 1.11.7 and 78; *ep.* 2.49.6, 2.62.8.

82. The other: I.e. Gabriel.

82. Zephyrs: Winds from the west. See also 2.28 and 3.465.

83. With 82–3 compare Vergil *Aen.* 5.210–7. Each context contains, or is followed by, a bird simile. With *aëra tranat* compare also *Aen.* 10.265 (*aethera tranant*), also in a bird simile.

85. Meander: River of Phrygia, famed for its windings. See also 2.144.

86. Cayster: A river in Lydia, well known for its swans. See note on 2.145.

87. Compare Vergil *Aen.* 9.563 (also in simile).

91. Idume or Idumaea (Edom): Technically the country to the south of Judaea, here standing for Judaea itself. See also Statius *Sil.* 1.6.13, 3.2.138 and 5.2.139, and, for the language, Vergil *geo.* 3.12.

93. Sibyls: Female prophetesses, the most famous of whom, for Roman mythology, was located at Cumae (see on *ecl.* 2.78). She figures in two segments of Vergil's works of particular importance to Sannazaro, the fourth *eclogue* and the sixth book of the *Aeneid*. See also *el.* 1.7.21, 2.7.5 and 53, 2.8.40, 2.9.9.

95. With *fatidici vates* compare 454 and Vergil *Aen.* 8.340.

97. At hand: Compare Ovid *M.* 1.256–7.

101. Modesty: Compare the depiction of Lavinia at *Aen.* 11.480 (*oculos deiecta decoros*).

106. With Sannazaro's use of *purpureus* to describe the radiance of youth, compare Vergil *Aen.* 1.591.

108. At 106–8 Sannazaro has in mind the appearance of Venus at Vergil *Aen.* 1.402–5.

123. At 109–23 Sannazaro is paraphrasing the annunciation (*Ave gratia plena* . . .). This and the subsequent exchange between Gabriel and Mary are described by Luke at 1:28–38.

124. Pale: Compare [ps.] Vergil *Ciris* 81.

126. Seriphos: An Aegean island, among the western Cyclades. By Micon Sannazaro probably means Myconos which lies on the eastern fringe of the same island group (see F-P lxviii and n. 33). The juxtaposition of *Micone* and *parva* is an etymological pun (see Vergil *ecl.* 7.29–30, *parvus . . . Micon*, from where Sannazaro may have drawn the island's name). Seriphos and *humilem Myconon* appear in adjacent lines at Ovid *M.* 7.463–4 and in the same line at Statius *Ach.* 1.205.

127. The phrase *nuda pedem* is used twice by Ovid, of Ariadne (*AA* 1.530) and of Medea (*M.* 7.183). In the first instance the heroine, abandoned on the island of Naxos, is soon to be visited by Bacchus. Compare Tibullus 1.3.92 (*nudato pede*) where the speaker imagines Delia awaiting his return.

127. Happy mother: Compare Statius *The.* 6.340.

131. Sannazaro is thinking of Vergil's description of Latinus on learning of the arrival of the Trojans in Latium (*obtutu tenet ora soloque immobilis haeret, Aen.* 7.250).

132. Canopus: Island and town in the western mouth of the Nile, here standing for Egypt. The phrase *dona ferens* or close variants appear on six occasions in Vergil's *Aeneid*.

134. Critics have found a connection between the simile (125–34) and the opening of Heliodorus's *Aethiopica* (1.2). (See Altamura, *Jacopo Sannazaro*, III; Sparrow, "Latin Verse," 388, n. 2; compare Kidwell, *Sannazaro*, 237, n. 49.) But the resemblance is slight. In Heliodorus we come upon the heroine Charikleia, tending her lover in the midst of a scene of carnage associated with a merchant-ship become a form of battlefield. In Sannazaro a virgin watches fearfully at the approach of a vessel that turns out only to be carrying a precious cargo. A more likely source (also mentioned by Prandi, *Il Parto*, on line 129) is Ovid *M.* 5.391–401 where we find Proserpina collecting flowers (*legendo*, 394), calling on her mother (*matrem*, 397 *bis*), her clothes torn (*vestem*, 398), displaying the grief of a virgin (*virgineum dolorem*, 401), at the approach of Dis.

140. Earth: Compare Ovid *M.* 4.368, where, as regularly, Sannazaro suppresses the sexual element in his imitation.

141. Unceasing peace: Vergil uses forms of *aeterna pax* at *Aen.* 4.99 and 12.504.

142. Citadel: Compare Ovid *Am.* 3.10.21.

145. The phrase *longe . . . exulat oris* comes from Vergil *geo.* 3. 225.

147. Fruitfulness: The words *magna incrementa* and *sobolis* are drawn from Vergil *ecl.* 4.49 (the poet's only use of *incrementum*).

151. The phrase *terminus aevi* comes from Vergil *geo.* 4.206. Sannazaro (F-P 99) offers two examples of Vergil's use of *nec iam* (*Aen.* 4.171 and 10.510). Greene, *The Descent*, 151, suggests a comparison with *Aen.* 1.278–9: *his ego nec metas rerum nec tempora pono: / imperium sine fine dedi* (I myself place no limits of power or time on them. I have given empire without end).

162. Compact: For the phrase *foedera rumpam* compare Vergil *Aen.* 8.540, 12.202.

163. See Prandi, *Il Parto*, on 163ff., for a detailed discussion of the phenomenon and its iconography.

163. The phrase *quod . . . minime . . . rere* is drawn from Vergil *Aen.* 6.97 (*quod minime reris*), also in parenthesis.

169. Unexpected joys: Compare Statius *The.* 5.711 and 10.330–1, *Sil.* 1.2.46.

172. Eyes: Compare Ovid *RA* 300.

172. Blood: Compare Propertius 2.24.37.

175. Gabriel's words, informing Mary of her cousin Elizabeth's pregnancy, are based on Luke 1:36–37.

177. The phrase *oculos ad sidera* comes from Vergil *Aen.* 2.687. Vergil varies the phrase *ad sidera tollens* on eight occasions. Compare also Ovid *M.* 1.86.

178. Dwellings: For *aurea tecta* see also Vergil *Aen.* 6.13.

183. Locks: *Nosco crines* is used by Vergil (*Aen.* 6.809) of Anchises recognizing the figure of Numa Pompilius.

192. God: Sannazaro is varying Lucretius's words on the divinity of Epicurus (*DRN* 5.8: *deus ille fuit, deus*), words that Vergil also reshapes at *ecl.* 5.64 and which Sannazaro quotes at 3.236.

196. Origins: Compare Vergil *Aen.* 2.105.

199. Utmost: Compare Vergil *Aen.* 10.100, and context (referring to Jupiter).

199. Sky: Compare Vergil *Aen.* 9.630–1.

202. Tethys: Sea-goddess and wife of Oceanus, god of the encompassing sea. She is mentioned together with Oceanus at Catullus 64.29–30. See also 2.16 and 3.491 (for Oceanus); *el.* 2.6.12; *ep.* 2.15.54, 2.51.3.

202. Amphitrite: See note on *ecl.* 1.99. Her first mention in Latin letters is at Catullus 64.11. The only appearances of the adjective *raucisonus* in classical Latin are in Lucretius (*DRN* 2.619 and 5.1084) and Catullus (64.263).

209. Plumage: Compare Cicero *Fin.* 3.18; Propertius 3.7.50 and (in conjecture) 3.13.32.

212. Euri: Winds from the east. See also 2.26 and 4.465.

217. Thunderer: See note on *ecl.* 3.70. The epithet recurs at 1.447, 2.49, 3.20 and 94; *el.* 1.7.33; *ep.* 2.16.9.

219. Fires: Compare Lucretius *DRN* 6.205 and 349; Vergil *ecl.* 6.33.

220. Sannazaro here takes us, in summary, through the conclusion of Dante's *Divina Commedia*. We move from the eighth sphere of heaven, the *stellatum* of the constellations, as described in *Paradiso* 22, to the ninth sphere, the crystalline heaven (*crystallinum*) of the primum mobile, the subject of *Paradiso* 28, to the tenth sphere of heaven, the *empyreum* of fire (*Paradiso* 30). Finally, at line 219, we are in the presence of God's love (*amor*) that brings Dante's depiction of heaven, and his poem, to a conclusion (*Paradiso* 33.145).

225. Rumor: Latin *Fama*.

225. Shades: Compare Vergil *Aen.* 4.387.

227. Yearned: Compare Ovid *H.* 21.43.

228. Tartarus: The infernal regions. See note on 1.34, and compare Vergil *Aen.* 4.243.

228. Acheron: One of the rivers of the underworld.

229. Howls: With *non laetabile murmur* compare Vergil *Aen.* 12.619 (*inlaetabile murmur*).

230. Hound: Cerberus, the three-headed dog that guarded the entrance to the underworld. See 1.460 below. The phrase *tergeminus canis* appears at Propertius 4.7.52; Ovid *AA* 3.322, and *T.* 4.7.16; Seneca *Apoc.* 7.2.

231. Triple-throated: Vergil (*Aen.* 6.417) invents the adjective *trifaucis*, in connection with Cerberus.

232. Goads him on: See Tibullus 1.5.53; Ovid *T.* 1.6.9; Silius *Pun.* 2.683 and 7.717; Juvenal *sat.* 14.84.

232. Night: Compare Tibullus 1.3.67; Vergil *Aen.* 4.26 and 6.462; Silius *Pun.* 12.132.

235. Hands: Compare Cicero *Arat.* fr. 34.415; Vergil *Aen.* 5.686 and 12.936; Lucan *BC* 4.176; Silius *Pun.* 4.409.

237. Elder: David, king of Israel, writer of psalms and messianic prophet.

237. Dark: The phrase *per opaca locorum* comes from Vergil *Aen.* 2.725.

239–41. Compare Statius *Sil.* 2.1.204–5. Grass: See note on *ecl.* 1.93 and *el.* 1.3.37.

241. Silence: Compare Statius *Sil.* 2.4.8.

242. Imagination: Compare Vergil's description of Orpheus and Musaeus at *Aen.* 6.637–78.

244. The phrase *intorquens oculos* is derived from Vergil *geo.* 4.451 (*oculos intorsit*), said of Proteus as he prepares to tell the story of Orpheus (see on 42 above). Vergil uses the form *recenset* to conclude *geo.* 4.436. Again, Christ is implicitly an Orpheus figure, now capable of successfully harrowing Hell.

245–452. David's prophetic song.

245. For *nascere* at the opening of an hexameter and the beginning of a speech, compare Vergil *ecl.* 8.17.

245. The repeated use of the apostrophe *magne puer* at lines 245 and 247 is also a reminder of Vergil *ecl.* 4.60 and 62 where the apostrophic *parve puer* is also repeated, likewise with one hexameter intervening.

246. Compare Vergil *Aen.* 3.368, 10.759, and 12.177; Ovid *M.* 14.478–9; Statius *The.* 3.119; Valerius Flaccus *Arg.* 1.247; Martial 3.44.9.

247. For Christ's harrowing of hell, see below 1. 365–7, 3. 230, and Appendix I. For further details see the entries "The Descent of Christ into Hell" and "Harrowing of Hell" in *The Oxford Dictionary of the Christian Church* (3rd ed., Oxford, 1997), 472 and 738, respectively; also the entry "Harrowing of Hell" in *Encyclopedia of Early Christianity* (2nd ed., New York, 1998), 509–11.

250. Truth-telling: Lucretius applies the adjective *veridicus* twice to Epicurus: *veridico ore* (*DRN* 6.6) and *veridicis dictis*, in connection with *pectora* (6.24).

253. Through the globe's extent: Compare Vergil *Aen.* 1.457 (*bella . . . iam fama totum vulgata per orbem*).

254. Peace: For *pax alma* see Tibullus 1.10.67.

256. Kings: The Magi, or Three Kings, briefly mentioned in the New Testament only at Matthew 2:1–12.

257. Aethiopes, dwellers in Aethiopia (modern Ethiopia), in antiquity part of what is modern Sudan, in north-central Africa. See also *el.* 1.1.49.

261. Nabathaeans: Dwellers in Nabat(h)aea in northern Arabia, known for its incense.

262. Compare Ovid *H.* 13.32 and *M.* 8.448.

263. Compare Vergil *Aen.* 5.73 (*aevi maturus*) and Statius *The.* 11.427 (*venerabilis aevo*).

265. Compare Ovid *M.* 13.542; Statius *The.* 10.364; Silius *Pun.* 12.319.

265. The story of Simeon is told at Luke 2:25–35. At 266–70 Sannazaro paraphrases his prayer of thanksgiving, the *Nunc dimittis*. For *sistit ad aras* compare Vergil *Aen.* 8.85.

270. Parcae: The Roman Fates, parallel to the Greek Moirai. See also *el.* 1.6.1; *ep.* 2.15.14, 2.39.4.

274. The slaughter of the innocents and flight into Egypt are told in Matthew 2:16–18.

274. Compare Ovid *M.* 15.379; Calpurnius Siculus 5.40.

276. Compare Statius *The.* 7.22.

277. Compare Vergil *Aen.* 3.60.

279. Compare Ovid *M.* 1.185, *T.* 2.77, *EP* 4.7.25–6.

279. Royal virgin: Compare Catullus 64.86–7 (of Ariadne).

280. Paretonian land: Technically Libya, here standing for Egypt.

281. Compare Ovid *M.* 1.770.

283. Vergil uses the phrase *verum ubi* at six moments of transition.

285. Compare Vergil *Aen* 4.553 and 5.780.

286. Compare Vergil *Aen* 2.488 and 11.832–3; Manilius *Ast.* 2.532; *Ilias Latina* 86.

290. The phrase *sera nocte* is used by Vergil at *ecl.* 8.88, *Aen.* 7.16 and 492, the first and last instances in connection with moments of yearning.

292. Compare Propertius 1.3.25; Ovid *F.* 3.185.

293. Compare Vergil *Aen.* 6.887.

294. Compare Vergil *Aen.* 12.411.

295. Lucifer: The Morning Star. See note on *ecl.* 2.86.

297. The phrase *offeret ultro* is Vergilian (*ecl.* 3.66; compare *Aen.* 2.59–61, 8.611).

299. Compare Tibullus 1.1.62.

304. The story is told at Luke 2:41–52.

305. Though Vergil twice uses *arma* with forms of *ruo* (*Aen.* 2.353 and 11.886), Sannazaro may be thinking of the question that opens Horace's seventh epode: *Quo, quo scelesti ruitis?* (Where, where are you rushing, you criminals?).

308. With *crebris ignibus* compare Vergil *Aen.* 1.90 and 11.209.

309. For *unum caput* see Vergil *Aen.* 5.815.

310. See note on *LMC* 56.

310. Unspeakable hatreds: Compare Vergil *Aen.* 5.785–6.

313. For parallels to this rhetorical question that combines bewilderment with astonishment see Vergil *Aen.* 10.670; Ovid *AA* 3.667, *M.* 9.509, *F.* 4.573 and 5.147 (on three of these occasions Ovid uses the authorial first person); Lucan *BC* 1.678.

313. Vergil, describing the treacherous Sinon, ends an hexameter with the words *post terga revinctum* (*Aen.* 2.57).

314. Compare Vergil *geo.* 2.508.

317. Compare Ovid *Am.* 3.13.13, *Ibis* 165.

319. See Ovid *Am.* 1.6.22, *H.* 16.215, *AA* 1.751, *M.* 8.85; Lucan *BC* 10.518; Martial 10.50.5.

321. Compare Vergil *geo.* 3.315.

322. The phrase *tormenti genus* is Vergilian (*Aen.* 8.487).

323. See *DPV* 2.42 and 3.496 as well as Catullus 61.77 and 62.8; Vergil *Aen.* 6.779.

324. For *truci lingua* compare Silius *Pun.* 3.305. For *convicia lingua* see Propertius 3.8.11; Ovid *M.* 11.601.

325. The phrase *parte alia* is a favorite of Vergil (*Aen.* 1.474, 8.433 and 682, 9.521 and 12.346). Its first use in a Latin ekphrasis is at Catullus 64.251.

326. Compare Vergil *geo.* 2.209.

329. Compare Statius *Sil.* 3.1.186.

330. Arms: Compare Ovid *M.* 6.279.

330. Death: With *turpatos . . . morte capillos* compare Vergil *Aen.* 10.832 (*turpantem comptos de more capillos*).

332. Compare Valerius Flaccus *Arg.* 6.552.

333. Though the phrase *non iam mater* is Vergilian (*Aen.* 11.71), the phraseology of lines 333–36 is drawn more generally from John 19 and from the opening verses of the late medieval hymn *Stabat mater*.

334. Compare Vergil *Aen.* 2.772.

335. Compare Ovid *Am.* 1.7.39, *H.* 16.121.

339. Compare Vergil *Aen.* 10.463.

341. With the words *crudelia dicit sidera . . . vocat* (339–41) compare Vergil *ecl.* 5.23 (*astra crudelia vocat*). For the triple repetition of forms of *crudelis* in proximity compare Vergil *ecl.* 8.48–50 where a *mater* (Medea) is also the subject.

341. The adjective *luctisonus* is unique, in classical Latin, to Ovid *M.* 1.732.

342. Compare Silius *Pun.* 1.388; Valerius Flaccus *Arg.* 2.211–2.

343. Kisses: Compare Ovid *M.* 4.141.

343. Wood: Compare Vergil *Aen.* 9.543–4; Ovid *Am.* 1.6.74.

345. Though individual details come from elsewhere in the *Aeneid*, Sannazaro finds his greatest inspiration here in the speech of lamentation uttered by Euryalus's mother at *Aen.* 9.481–97.

347. Storm: Compare [ps.] Ovid *Nux* 163; Statius *The.* 10.539; Silius *Pun.* 17.623.

347. Compare Ovid *M.* 4.142, part of a passage also on Sannazaro's mind as he wrote Mary's lament.

348. Vergil uses the phrase *foedavit vultus* of Hector's wraith (*Aen.* 2.286).

349. Compare Vergil *Aen.* 6.502.

350. Compare Lucan *BC* 7.171; Statius *The.* 11.123 and 348–9, 12.84; Silius *Pun.* 4.47 and 11.28; Valerius Flaccus *Arg.* 3.30; Martial 4.11.3.

351. Compare Lucretius *DRN* 3.958.

352. Compare the opening words at Vergil *Aen.* 9.481.

353. Compare *Aen.* 12.57–8.

360. Compare Ovid *M.* 9.383.

361. Compare Catullus 64.194.

363. With *nate sub umbras* compare the concluding words of Vergil's *Aeneid* (12.952): *indignata sub umbras*.

364. Compare Ovid *M.* 10.15.

367. Erebus: The Greek realm of nether darkness, metonymy for the pagan underworld of the dead, here standing for the Christian hell. See also 1.405 and 456 below, 3.59 and 385.

372. Though the description of darkness at the moment of Christ's death is biblical (Luke 23:44–49), Sannazaro is also thinking of Vergil's picture of the sun's eclipse at the murder of Julius Caesar (*geo.* 1.464–68). The use of the rare word *ferrugo* comes from *geo.* 1.467. Compare also *LMC* 24.

377. Cynthia: Diana, goddess of the moon and sister of Phoebus Apollo (the name comes from Mt. Cynthus on the island of Delos where both were born). See also *el.* 3.3.24.

377. With *vultus obnubet amictu*, compare Vergil *Aen.* 11.77 (*comas obnubit amictu*).

378. Compare Vergil *Aen.* 4.449 and 10.465.

383. Vergil adopts, and adapts, this Lucretian phrase (first used at *DRN* 1.227) at *Aen.* 6.735 and 828, and 7.771.

384. Mars: Roman god of war. See also 2.182.

385. Compare Ovid *M.* 14.409.

386. Sannazaro is referring to Matthew 24 and *Apocalypse* 10–11.

387. Compare Juvenal *sat.* 8.261–2.

389. Compare Vergil *Aen.* 8.246 (*immisso lumine*).

390. Eumenides: The Furies. Here and in what follows Sannazaro is drawing on, and varying, Vergil's list of the creatures that lurk at the entranceway to the underworld (*Aen.* 6.268–89). For *dirae facies* (389–90) see Vergil *Aen.* 2.622, and compare 8.194.

391. Phlegethon: One of the rivers of the underworld ("blazing"). With the language of 391–2 compare Vergil *Aen.* 6.415–6.

393. Dis: In Roman religion, the ruler of the underworld, often standing for the underworld itself. See also 1.456.

394. Cerastae: A horned people from the island of Cyprus, changed by Venus into bullocks. They are mentioned only by Ovid (*M.* 10.223). Elsewhere, e.g. at Propertius 3.22.27, they are a species of horned snake. Briarean: That is to say gigantic. The epithet is derived from the hundred-armed giant Briareus.

395. Centaurs: A people of Thessaly, half man, half horse (compare Lucan *BC* 6.386). Gorgons: Monstrous snake-haired women of Greek mythology. See also *ep.* 2.2.6.

396. Scyllas: See note on *Sal.* 53. Sphinxes: Monsters, originally from Egypt, part lion with the head of a human. Chimaeras: See note on *Sal.* 52.

397. Hydras: Huge mythical snakes, two of which guarded the entrances, respectively, to the underworld (*Aen.* 6.287–8) and to the area of the eternally guilty, surrounded by Phlegethon (*Aen.* 6.576).

397. Hounds: Perhaps a reference to Cerberus. See note on 230 and 460.

397. Harpies: "The Grabbers," mythical women with a female head and a bird's body. With Sannazaro's list as a whole, compare Vergil *Aen.* 6.285–9.

399. Pluto: (Greek) ruler of the underworld.

400. Horns are a standard attribute for rivers and denote their power (see, e.g., commentators on Vergil *Aen.* 8.77).

401. For the phrase *virginea lauro* compare Seneca *Aga.* 312 and context.

402. Compare Silius *Pun.* 15.230–1.

404. On the language of the shout of triumph see Varro *LL* 6.68 and commentators on Horace *epode* 9.21–3 and Tibullus 2.5.117–8.

405. Manes: Spirits of the dead.

406. For the *potestates aerias*, see Orosius *Hist.* 4.5.8, Cassian *Coll.* 8.12, and, for further details, the entry *aerius* in A. Blaise *Dictionnaire Latin-François des auteurs Chrétiens* (Turnhout, 1954).

406. Compare Vergil *Aen.* 12.180.

407. For the *quadriga Christi* see Appendix I. The "team" of the chariot consists of the four evangelists in their symbolic guises of ox (Luke), lion (Mark), eagle (John) and angel (Matthew).

408. Compare Vergil *Aen.* 7.194 and 11.251.

410. The phrase *praesepibus herbas* ends the hexameter at Vergil *geo.* 3.395.

411. Sturdy neck: Compare [ps.] Vergil *Cata.* 3.1.

412. With *formosi pecoris custodia* compare Vergil *ecl.* 5.44 (*formosi pecoris custos*).

414. Compare Vergil *geo.* 1.217 (of the constellation Taurus) and 4.371 (of the Eridanus [or Po] river).

414. Gilded bristle: Compare Calpurnius Siculus 7.65.

416. Compare Propertius 2.32.58 and Vergil's description of the features of the best cow for breeding at *geo.* 3.51–3.

418. Compare Claudian *de raptu* 1.164.

420. Compare Ovid *T.* 3.5.33.

421. Compare the description of the horse to which Turnus is likened at *Aen.* 11.497.

426. Compare Vergil *Aen.* 9.433; Statius *Ach.* 1.481.

428. The association of Jupiter's eagle with his thunderbolt is appropriate (compare, e.g., Horace *c.* 4.4.1).

434. The weaving on a *chlamys* is also the source of an ekphrasis at *Aen.* 5.250–7. (At *Aen.* 4.137 a *chlamys* has a *limbus* [border], and at 8.167 another is said to be *intertextam* [interwoven].)

434. The phrase *eois lapillis* comes from Propertius 1.15.7.

435. Vergil uses the phrase *longo ordine* at *Aen.* 2.766, 6.482 and 754, 8.722 (*longo ordine gentes*, in ekphrasis and ending the hexameter) and 11.143–44.

436. Race: Compare Vergil *Aen.* 6.580 and 648.

436. For *primordia gentis* see Ovid *H.* 17.57, *M.* 5.190; Lucan *BC* 10.177; Silius *Pun.* 1.658. Sannazaro is referring to the genealogy of Christ that opens the Gospel of Matthew (1), on whose cloak it is appropriately to be found. The most salient deportation of the Jews to Babylon (the chief city of Babylonia, and center of its empire, now largely in modern Iraq), which Matthew mentions twice, occurred in 586 after the razing of Jerusalem by Nebuchadnezzar (the "Babylonian Captivity" lasted from then until 538). Jerusalem and Babylon are often seen as antitypes for civilization and decadence, good and evil. Sannazaro's relegation of Babylon to the edge of the border of the cloak suggests its distance from Jerusalem, which in turn both adumbrates the horrors of exile from homeland and more generally looks to the symbolic differentiation between the two cities. Sannazaro uses the figure of ekphrasis on three occasions. Its appearance here reemphasizes the pictorial quality of the preceding description with its debt to visual as well as verbal art (Dante's description of the "Procession of Holy Scripture" in *Purgatorio* 29 is regularly mentioned by critics). For further detail see Appendix I.

438. *Credas* is a signpost of ekphrasis (Vergil *Aen.* 8.691). See also 2.271 and 3.31. With lines 437–8 compare Ovid *M.* 6.104 (*verum taurum, freta vera putares*).

441. Compare Ovid *M.* 8.796. The phrase *indutos spoliis* echoes Vergil *Aen.* 12.947 (*spoliis indute*).

446. Sannazaro is using language of the *Apocalypse* (21–2) to describe Heaven as a type of new Jerusalem. For a classical parallel see Ovid *H.* 15.157.

448. Sannazaro uses *lares* (Roman gods of the household often linked with the *penates*) to stand for the dwellings themselves. See also on 1.72.

449. Compare Vergil *ecl.* 5.57.

451. Compare Vergil *ecl.* 9.51–2 (*longos . . . condere soles*).

454. Seer: See above, line 12.

454. Vergil uses the phrase *aggere ripae* at *Aen.* 7.106.

456. Compare Vergil *Aen.* 2.752.

457. Megaera: One of the Furies, sister of Tisiphone.

459. Compare Vergil *Aen.* 6.401.

460. Vergil has the wording *Cerberus . . . latratu* at *Aen.* 6.417.

461. Cocytus: Along with Acheron and Phlegethon, one of the rivers of the underworld. See also 3.265; *LMC* 95.

462. Sisyphus: One of the proverbial sinners in the underworld, whose usual torture was to push uphill a stone that continually rolled back down. The language of lines 456–62 recalls Vergil *geo.* 4.481–4 and its broader context. David here is also a type of Orpheus. See above on 42 and 244. For the final phrase *saxa lacertis* compare Lucan *BC* 1.384 and 3.481.

Book II

2. Compare Vergil *Aen.* 6.50 (*adflata est numine*, of the Sibyl).

5. The phrase *cura recursat* is Vergilian (*Aen.* 1.662).

9. Compare Lucan *BC* 6.661 (*audire loquentem*). An equivalent phrase is often supplied by editors at Catullus 65.9.

14. Arctos: The constellations Ursa Major and Ursa Minor (the Great Bear and the Little Bear, both translations into Latin from the Greek), separately or together, located near the celestial north pole. See also 3.41. Mary's gleam draws analogies from heavenly bodies both seasonal and quotidian, to winter (Arcturus), and to dawn and sunrise as time progresses, within the two comparisons, from night to day.

16. Aurora: Goddess of the dawn. See also 2.126, 3.6 and 492, and on *ep.* 1.6.26.

16. Vergil speaks of *sol aureus* at *geo.* 1.232 and 4.51.

17. Compare Statius *Sil.* 3.3.129.

18. The tale of Hyacinthus's death and metamorphosis is told by Ovid at *M.* 10.152–219. With lines 17–8 compare Tibullus 1.3.61–2.

19. The phrase *purpureum ver* is Vergilian (*ecl.* 9.40, also in connection with flowers).

21. For *varios colores* see also Vergil *ecl.* 4.42 and *geo.* 1.452.

22. Compare Vergil *geo.* 1.479 (*sistunt amnes*).

23. As Vergil *geo.* 3.555.

26. Noti are winds from the south (see also *el.* 3.3.42), Euri from the east. The linkage *Eurique Notique* is also found in the singular at Vergil *Aen.* 1.85 (*Eurusque Notusque*).

27. Boreas: A north wind. See also 2.457 and *el.* 3.3.42. For the phrase *atrox Boreas* see Statius *Sil.* 3.3.96 where the adjective is applied to Eurus.

27. Vergil uses the phrase *florea rura* at *Aen.* 1.430.

28. *Zephyri* and *aur(e)is* are found together at Catullus 46.3, a poem whose first line ends in *tepores*. See also Ovid *M.* 1.107–8.

30. The phrase *ut ventum ad sedes* begins the hexameter at Vergil *Aen.* 8.362.

30. Zachariah, husband of Elizabeth and father of John the Baptist.

30. Compare Lucan *BC* 7.322; Statius *The.* 2.230.

32. Compare Lucretius *DRN* 3.834.

33. Compare Ovid *H.* 18.101.

33. Elizabeth's reaction to Mary's arrival and her speech are to be found at Luke 1:41–56. Sannazaro follows the biblical narrative from Annunciation to Visitation.

36. Compare Ovid *AA* 1.253.

45. The adjective *felix* is repeated at the same position in the hexameter at Vergil *Aen.* 4.657.

48. Compare Vergil *Aen.* 6.536.

49. For a detailed examination of Sannazaro's adaptation of the Biblical narration of Mary's *Magnificat* (Luke 1:46–55), see Nash, *The Major Latin Poems*, Appendix D (206–8).

56. Compare Vergil *Aen.* 11.556.

57. Compare Vergil's only use of the phrase *per saecula nomen* at *Aen.* 6.235.

72. Servant: Israel. The word *puerum* is juxtaposed with *Israel* in the *Magnificat* itself (Luke 1:54). See further Sannazaro's explication in a letter to Antonio Seripando (quoted in F-P 102).

79. Compare Vergil *Aen.* 1.93 (*duplicis tendens ad sidera palmas*) and 9.16; Ovid *M.* 6.368 and 9.175, *T.* 1.11.21.

82. Compare Vergil *Aen.* 5.724, 6.608 and 661.

84. David, in *Psalms* 71:6 (*descendet ut pluvia super vellus*).

85. *Isaiah* 11:1.

86. *Exodus* 3:2.

87. *Numbers* 24:17.

89. Compare Vergil *Aen.* 6.185.

94. A regular title of Mary. See, e.g., the ninth century anonymous hymn *Ave Maris Stella* and line two of the eleventh century hymn *Alma Redemptoris Mater*.

99. Compare Lucretius *DRN* 1.408; Vergil *Aen.* 3.232 and 424; Ovid *M.* 1.388; Silius *Pun.* 1.366 and 15.369. See above line 14.

105. Compare Vergil *Aen.* 7.391 where Bacchic rites are the subject.

106. *Ergo iter inceptum* appears twice in Vergil (*Aen.* 6.384, 8.90).

108. The phrase *nec mora nec requies* is found three times in Vergil (*geo.* 3.110; *Aen.* 5.458 and 12.553).

108. Gaze: Compare Ovid *M.* 10.51.

114. Compare Lucretius *DRN* 3.646; Tibullus 2.4.7; Statius *The.* 3.335.

117. Augustus: The first emperor of Rome (63 BCE-14 CE).

118. Sannazaro draws here on the prose of Suetonius (*Vita Augusti* 22) and the poetry of Vergil (*Aen.* 1.293–5) and Manilius (*Ast.* 1.922–4).

121. Luke 2:1.

124. See *ecl.* 1.99.

124. Sea: Compare Ovid *M.* 6.399; Silius *Pun.* 3.258; Valerius Flaccus *Arg.* 4.270.

125. Sannazaro's tour begins in ancient Armenia, turns southwest to Cilicia, Pamphylia and Lycia on the southern coast of Asia Minor, further west to Caria at the southwest corner of Asia Minor, then north to Mysia (with a prominent stop at Troy). He turns back in an easterly direction to Bithynia, Paphlagonia, Galatia and Cappadocia, with a momentary return to the Caucasus range in Armenia. He then moves west to Thrace and south to Greece (with special mention of the battles of Rome's civil war at Pharsalus and Philippi, as well as of Greece's role as civilizer). We move up the Ionian coast and into Italy, with a pause to contemplate imperial Rome. We then journey north and southeast through mention of the Rhine and Danube. Sannazaro next takes us west, to Gaul, and south, to Spain and Portugal. He crosses to Africa and carries us from west to east across its northern littoral. He ends in Egypt before returning our attention again north, to the arrival of the holy family in Bethlehem.

We could consider the tour Rome-oriented. Rome appears virtually at the center of the description and it is the power emanating from the capital city that controls the world that Sannazaro so vividly brings before us. Nevertheless the description's shape is a rough circle, beginning and ending in the Near East. Since we commence northeast of Palestine and end at its southwest, the ultimate focus is on Judaea and the events occurring there, from where a different form of authority will emerge, gradually to master Rome's empire.

Among Sannazaro's primary ancient sources would be three works: the *Geography* of Strabo (64/3 BCE–after 21 CE), *editio princeps*: Venice, 1516, the greatest work on geography surviving from antiquity; the three books *De chorographia* of Pomponius Mela (writing c. 43–4 CE), *editio princeps*: Milan, 1471; and books 3–6, devoted to geography and ethnography, of the *Historia Naturalis* of Pliny the Elder (23/4–79 CE), *editio princeps*: Venice, 1469. Sannazaro lists them in his letter to Antonio Seripando (F-P 93–4).

126. See note on 16 above. Aurora here stands for the East in general.

127. Niphates: In antiquity, a branch of the Taurus range, in Armenia.

128. Compare [ps.] Vergil *Cata.* 14.10. For *saxa tenent* compare Vergil *Aen* 1.139.

130. Euphrates: Central river of modern Iraq.

130. Araxes: The river Aras.

132. For *bene olentia* compare Vergil *ecl.* 2.48; [ps.] Vergil *Copa* 35; [ps.] Tibullus 3.8.17; Propertius 3.17.27; Ovid *Med.* 91.

133. Taurus: Mountain range in southern Asia Minor. Amanus: A mountain range bordering Syria and Cilicia.

134. Cilicia: Roman province in southeast Asia Minor (largely within modern Turkey) whose inhabitants in antiquity were known for their penchant for piracy. See commentators on Cicero *Ver.* 4.21; Ovid *Am.* 2.16.39; Lucan *BC* 3.228 and 9.222–3.

134. Isauria was located in Asia Minor between Pisidia and Cilicia (in modern Turkey).

135. Pamphylia. Country on the southern coast of Asia Minor, to the west of Isauria.

136. Lycaonia: Area in Asia Minor between Cilicia and Galatia.

137. Compare Vergil *geo.* 1.170 and 2.189.

137. Lycia: Country to the west of Pamphylia. Compare Vergil *Aen.* 7.721.

138. Leleges: A pre-Hellenic tribe, scattered throughout Asia Minor (mentioned by Vergil at *Aen.* 8.725).

140. Ceramon: Town on the coast of Caria.

140. Gnidos (more usually Cnidos): Town in southwest Caria, at the point of a peninsula separating the Aegean and Carpathian Seas. See also on *ep.* 2.15.21.

141. Compare Vergil *Aen.* 1.7.

143. The Mausoleum of Halicarnassus (modern Bodrum), in Caria, was the tomb of the satrap Mausolus, who reigned from 377–53 BCE. It was begun in 367 and finished after the death of his sister-wife Artemisia in 351.

146. With *pascit olores* compare Ovid *Am.* 2.6.53. For *niveos olores* see Ovid *M.* 7.379; Manilius *Ast.* 1.339; Seneca *Aga.* 678; Statius *The.* 8.675; Silius *Pun.* 7.441; Valerius Flaccus *Arg.* 6.102.

147. Cayster and Pactolus: Rivers in Lydia. The Cayster was famous for its bird life, especially swans (see 1.86 and commentators on Vergil *geo.* 1.384; Ovid *M.* 5.386–7 and *T.* 5.1.11), the Pactolus for the gold that it was supposed to carry in its sand. See Vergil *Aen.* 10.142 and on *el.* 2.3.13.

148. Hermus: Another river in Lydia flowing, like the Cayster and the Pactolus, west into the Mediterranean. See also *el.* 1.1.52.

148. Sand: Compare Juvenal *sat.* 14.300.

149. Inhabitants of Mysia in northwest Asia Minor, situated between Lydia and Bithynia.

149. Celenae: A town in Phrygia where the contest between Apollo and Marsyas was said to have occurred.

150. Rhoet(a)eum is a promontory and city near Troy on the Hellespont. See commentators on Catullus 65.7.

151. Sannazaro makes detailed mention of places near Troy in preparation for his reference to Homer's *Iliad.* Pomponius Mela (1.93) refers to Mt. Ida and Sigeum as sites for the Trojan conflict and for "the warring Achaeans" (*Achivorum . . . bellantium*). Pergama is technically the citadel of Troy whose aged king was Priam. Thetis was the mother of Achilles, "the best of the Achaeans."

152. Compare Catullus 68.97 (also of Troy); Propertius 1.22.3. The juxtaposition of *quondam* and *nunc* is a commonplace (see, e.g., Vergil *Aen.* 7.411–2).

153. Modern Dardanelles, the strait that separates the Marmara and Aegean Seas. Compare Ovid *M.* 13.407 (*longus in angustum qua clauditur Hellespontus*).

154. Compare Ovid *M.* 15.294.

155. Nereids: See *ecl.* 1.45. We find them also below, at 3.473 and 500.

155. The phrase *passis capillis* is used nine times by Ovid.

156. Reference is to the Roman *conclamatio*, lament addressed to the dead (see Servius on Vergil *Aen.* 6.218).

157. Bithynia and Pontus: Adjacent Roman provinces, bordering the modern Black Sea, in the north of Asia Minor.

158. Carambis: A town and promontory in Paphlagonia, to the east of Pontus.

159. Sinope: Greek colony in Paphlagonia, also on the southern coast of the modern Black Sea.

160. Halys: River flowing between Paphlagonia and Cappadocia, area to the southeast of Pontus.

161. Iris: Cappadocian river.

162. Thermodon: River of Pontus on the Black Sea.

162. Halybes: People living on the river Halys.

162. Cliffs: The Caucasus mountains, between the modern Black and Caspian Seas. See commentators on Vergil *ecl.* 6.42 and Propertius 2.25.14.

163. Thrace, area east of Macedonia, was regularly associated with Ares (Mars). See commentators on Homer *Il.* 13.301; Vergil *geo.* 4.462 and *Aen.* 3.13.

164. See *ecl.* 3.74. Rhodope is part of Mt. (H)aemus.

164. (H)aemus is a Thracian mountain range. See also *el.* 1.5.23.

165. Waves: Compare Ovid *EP* 2.3.21; *Ilias Latina* 916; Silius *Pun.* 3.52 and 6.200; Martial 10.85.3.

165. Macetae: People of Macedonia.

166. Axius: River in Macedonia, now the Vardar. Ancient Macedonia lay between Thrace and Thessaly.

166. Halyachmon: River flowing between Macedonia and Thessaly.

167. Compare Ovid *M.* 5.550; Lucan *BC* 4.551; Silius *Pun.* 7.48 and 10.614.

168. See Vergil *geo.* 1.490–1, where the two battlefields are merged. In reality Philippi is in eastern Macedonia while Pharsalia, the district around Pharsalus, lies in Thessaly.

169. Compare Vergil *Aen.* 4.295.

173. Compare Vergil *Aen.* 9.281.

176. Epirus is an area in northwest Greece. The treacherous promontory of Acroceraunia was actually in Illyricum to its north. See Horace *c.* 1.3.20.

176. At *Aen* 3.275 Vergil has *formidatus nautis*, of Apollo and his temple at Actium.

178. Alcinous: King of Phaeacia, Homer's island of Scheria (*Od.* 5.34 and elsewhere), known to Callimachus as Drepane, to Romans as Corcyra. It is the modern Corfù.

179. Liburni: A people of Illyria, essentially modern Croatia.

180. The Ionian Sea is between Greece and southern Italy. See Silius *Pun.* 14.73.

182. Compare Silius *Pun.* 10.217.

184. Vergil uses the phrase *feta armis* of the Trojan horse (*Aen.* 2.238).

186. Compare Lucan *BC* 3.299.

187. See Vergil *Aen.* 12.703.

188. Twin water: Probably this is Sannazaro's way of describing the Adriatic Sea (*Mare superum*), off Italy's east coast, and the Tyrrhenian or Tuscan Sea (*Mare inferum*) off its west. Compare Vergil *geo.* 2.158, varied slightly at *Aen.* 8.149.

190. Rhine: Ancient Rhenus, Germany's principal river. See also *ep.* 2.1.24.

191. Danube: Ancient Danubius or Danuvius, also known as the Hister. See also 3.342.

192. Compare Horace *epi.* 1.15.14.

193. Peuce: Island at the mouth of the Danube, treated by Statius (*Sil.* 5.2.137) as the river's wife. See also Apollonius Rhodius *Arg.* 4.309 and

Valerius Flaccus *Arg.* 8.217 and following. For the geography see Pomponius Mela 2.98 and Pliny *HN* 4.79.

195. Julius Caesar (100–44 BCE) fought the wars that conquered Gaul for Rome in 58–1, and, for those and other victories, celebrated in Rome a quadruple triumph in the fall of 46. See also *el.* 3.1.54, *ep.* 1.54.1–2. With *dignitata triumphis* compare Statius *Sil.* 3.3.171.

196. Rhône: Ancient Rhodanus. See also *ecl.* 3.18–9. Saône: Ancient Arar. See note on *ecl.* 5.115 and also *el.* 1.8.53, *ep.* 2.25.2.

197. Seine: Ancient Sequana. See also *ep.* 1.50.1 and 2.60.36.

197. Garonne: Ancient Garumna, river of southwest France.

197. Vergil has *piscoso amne* at *Aen.* 11.457.

198. Pyrenees: Mountain range separating France and Spain.

198. Compare Lucan *BC* 2.431 (of the Apennines).

199. Pillars of Hercules: The promontories that bound the modern Strait of Gibraltar. See Silius *Pun.* 1.142, 14.147, 15.643.

200. Guadiana: Ancient Anas.

201. Duria: The modern Douro river (in Portugal) or Duero (in Spain).

201. Baetis: Modern Guadalquivir. See Statius *Sil.* 2.7.34–5.

202. Ancient Tagus (also modern Tejo), chief river of Lusitania (modern Portugal) that flows west from central Spain and enters the Atlantic at modern Lisbon. See also *ecl.* 4.13 and *el.* 2.3.14. For its golden sands see commentators on Catullus 29.19; Ovid *Am.* 1.15.34 and *M.* 2.251. For the phrase *sub gurgite (h)arenam* see Ovid *M.* 15.714.

203. Ebro: Ancient Iberus. See also *ecl.* 4.10.

204. Compare Vergil *Aen.* 5.368.

205. The Gaetuli were a people of northwest Africa. See also 3.187.

206. Atlas: Mountain range in Mauretania, modern Morocco, beyond which was supposedly the island on which the Hesperides guarded their groves of golden apples. See also 3.511 and *ep.* 3.9.2, and, further, Pliny *HN* 5.6–7.

206. Huts: Compare Silius *Pun.* 17.89.

210. Massyli: People of Numidia in Africa, west and south of Carthage. See also 3.188.

213. Compare Vergil *Aen.* 12.904 (*saxum immane*), the huge rock that the hero Turnus can scarcely move.

214. Carthage: In antiquity one of the most important cities on the north coast of Africa, and Rome's archenemy during the three so-called Punic Wars of the third and second centuries BCE. Mention of Carthage also elicits a milder form of moralizing from Pomponius Mela (1.34). Compare the comments on the fall of Carthage by Scipio Aemilianus, as quoted in Diodorus Siculus 32.34 (for the narrative context see Polybius 38.22, drawn from Appian *Pun.* 132).

216. See Vergil *Aen.* 12.33 for the trials (*quantos labores*) that Turnus endures.

217. The phrase *Latio et Laurentibus arvis* is Vergilian (*Aen.* 12.24). For *Laurentibus arvis* alone compare *Aen.* 9.100; Silius *Pun.* 13.60.

219. Carthage was razed at the conclusion of the Third Punic War in 146 BCE. With *nunc* and *nomina* see Vergil *Aen.* 7.411–2 (cited above on line 152).

221. Compare the parallel language at *el.* 2.9.23–4.

222. Macae: A people of Libya.

223. Barcaei: The people of the city of Barce in Cyrenaica, the district around Cyrene in northwest Libya which, together with Crete, formed a Roman province.

223. Nasamones: Libyan people located southwest of Cyrenaica. The Nasamones are mentioned by Pliny (*HN* 5.33–4) who speaks of them as "located in the midst of the sands" (*medios inter harenas sitos*).

224. Syrtes: See note on *ecl.* 3.85.

227. Compare Vergil *Aen.* 1.528.

228. Psylli: African people located southwest of Syrtis Major. See Pliny *HN* 5.27 and 7.14.

228. Garamantes: Eastern Saharan tribe. See Pliny *HN* 5.26, 36 and 38.

229. Compare Statius *The.* 4.118.

230. Reference is to the medicinal properties of asafoetida (*laser*), drawn from the silphium plant. See Pliny *HN* 19.38–45 and commentators on Catullus 7.4.

231. Sannazaro is probably referring to the famous oracle of Jupiter at (H)ammon in Libya. See Pliny *HN* 5.49 and commentators on Catullus 7.5 and Vergil *Aen.* 4.198.

231. The (H)asbytae are linked with the Macae by Pliny (*HN* 5.34).

232. Marmarica: Technically between Cyrenaica and Egypt.

233. Meroes: Presumably the inhabitants of the island of Meroe in the upper Nile, which here stands for Egypt itself. See Pliny *HN* 5.53.

233. Nile: Ancient Nilus, the great river of Egypt. See also 3.341.

238. Compare Vergil *Aen.* 6.793.

240. Compare Vergil *geo.* 3.473, *Aen.* 1.642.

241. With *recensebat . . . numerum suorum* compare Vergil *Aen.* 6.681–2.

244. Galilee: Area in northern Palestine that forms the part of Judaea adjoining Syria (compare Pliny *HN* 5.70).

245. Carmel: Mountain (and town of the same name) near the Dead Sea in Galilaea.

246. Thabor: Mountain in Galilaea, east of Nazareth, the site of the Transfiguration.

246. Samaria: Area in northern Judaea south of Galilaea.

247. Compare [ps.] Vergil *Eleg. in Maec.* 1.134.

247. Jerusalem: Capital city of Judaea.

248. Compare Vergil *Aen.* 7.160–1.

251. The phrases *pectore fatur* (*Aen.* 2.107, 11.685, 12.888) and *imo pectore* (*Aen.* 11.377 and 840) are Vergilian.

252. Bethlehem: City south of Jerusalem.

253. The phrase *salvete penates* is Vergilian (*Aen.* 7.121) where it is also connected with *salve*.

255. Compare Manilius *Ast.* 1.605–6; Statius *The.* 11.114.

256. Jupiter is said to have been brought up on Mt. Dicte in eastern Crete. See commentators on Vergil *geo.* 2.536 and 4.152.

256. On Cretans as proverbial liars see 2.384–86 and commentators on, among numerous texts, Ovid *Am.* 3.10.19 and *AA* 1.298. St. Paul (*ad Titum* 1:12), probably drawing on Epimenides *De oraculis*, finds "Cretans always lying" (*Cretenses semper mendaces*). But the original source of the saying lies in Homer, in the tales of Odysseus (see *Od.* 14.200 and 19.172).

257. Compare Ovid *RA* 511, *M.* 14.762.

258. Dirce: The reference is to the central Greek city of Thebes, focus for the worship of Dionysus (Bacchus). There Dirce, second wife of Lycus, king of Thebes, was tied to a bull by Amphion and Zetheus, children of his first wife, Antiope, and torn apart. See [ps.] Seneca *HO* 140.

259. Ortygia: The island of Delos. See *ecl.* 3.75.

259. Latona: Mother of Apollo and Diana. Compare Vergil *Aen.* 1.502.

260. Compare Lucan *BC* 9.783; Statius *Sil.* 4.2.52, 5.1.127, 5.3.159.

262. The adjective *septemgeminus*, extant first in Catullus (11.7), is applied by Statius to the city of Rome (*Sil.* 1.2.191).

264. Compare Statius *The.* 1.457 and 6.705.

266. Compare Statius *The.* 2.41.

267. Compare Vergil *geo.* 3.200; [ps.] Vergil *Aetna* 322.

271. For *turba ingens* see Propertius 3.14.29; Martial 1.73.3–4, 9.55.3.

271. See note on 1.438.

271. Compare Lucan *BC* 3.164; Silius *Pun.* 1.584.

274. The phrase *cernere erat* (as also 3.28; compare 3.369) is Vergilian and ekphrastic (*Aen.* 6.596 and 8.676).

277. Vergil *Aen.* 3.683 (of sails).

279. Compare Ovid *H.* 12.138, *M.* 12.12; Statius *The.* 12.408.

284. With *est specus haud ingens* compare Vergil *geo.* 4.418 (*est specus ingens*, the cave of Proteus).

287. Compare [ps.] Vergil *Mor.* 20; Lucan *BC* 9.905; Valerius Flaccus *Arg.* 1.462 and 780.

289. In lines 288–9 Sannazaro is remembering *Aen.* 8.233–4, describing the surroundings of the cave of Cacus.

292. Compare Ovid *M.* 8.161.

294. Compare Vergil *Aen.* 2.632.

294. Night: Compare Vergil *geo.* 4.180.

295. Compare Lucretius *DRN* 6.309.

301. See note on 3.479.

303. With *secretos calleis* compare Vergil *Aen.* 6.443 (*secreti calles*).

306. Compare Tibullus 1.2.85; [ps.] Ovid *Nux* 177 and 179; Statius *Sil.* 2.1.29 and 3.4.101, *The.* 12.267; Martial 6.87.2.

307. *Ferre pedem* puns on the double notion of a change in topic and of the poetic "foot" that will tell of it. The phrase *qua nulla priorum* ends an hexameter at Vergil *geo.* 3.292 where the context as a whole was important to Sannazaro.

308. For *vatum vestigia* compare Horace *epi.* 2.2.80.

309. Compare Vergil *Aen.* 2.268 and, for the whole context, *Aen.* 4.522–28.

310. Compare Vergil *Aen.* 5.835.

316. Vergil has *seram . . . membra quietem* at *Aen.* 8.30, and *membra quiete* at *Aen.* 1.691 and 5.836. See also below, 338.

318. This line, the unique example of a hypermetric hexameter in Sannazaro, is modeled on Vergil *Aen.* 8.228 (see Prandi, *Il Parto, ad loc.*).

319. For *caliginis umbram* see Lucretius *DRN* 3.304; Ovid *M.* 4.455; Seneca *HF* 710.

326. As Vergil, *Aen.* 10.668.

327. Compare Vergil *Aen.* 5.627–8.

328. As Vergil *Aen.* 12.96.

329. The word *suboles* is a reminder of Vergil *ecl.* 4.49, a poem lines 19–24 of which Sannazaro also here recalls with *tellus, rideat* and *floribus*.

330. Sannazaro is drawing here on Lucretius *DRN* 1.7–8.

335. Compare Vergil *ecl.* 4.60 (*parve puer*).

336. See also 3.76 (*complexu molli*). Vergil uses the phrase *molli amplexu* at *Aen.* 8.388 of Venus and Vulcan.

338. Compare Propertius 1.14.9.

339. Vergil uses the phrase *sic memorat* at *Aen.* 1.631, 8.79 and 9.324.

345. Compare Statius *Sil.* 5.3.235.

346. Compare Vergil *Aen.* 3.658 and its variation at 4.181.

347. Compare Ovid *F.* 2.7 and 6.8.

347. Happy: See Vergil *Aen.* 11.73 (of Dido).

350. Compare Silius *Pun.* 7.57–8.

353. Compare Vergil *Aen.* 1.197.

356. Compare Statius *Sil.* 2.1.78.

357. See note on 1.3.

360. For *vere tepenti* compare Ovid *AA* 3.185.

361. Eous: The dawn star which here takes its name, by metonymy, from its rising in the East (as Vergil *geo.* 1.288, et al.). See also 1.18 and 434, 3.6.

362. Compare Calpurnius Siculus *ecl.* 5.55.

363. Compare Vergil *geo.* 3.429.

364. With *viator / horridus* compare Vergil *geo.* 4.97–8 (*viator / aridus*), also in simile.

365. Compare Ovid *F.* 1.680 and 3.728.

366. Compare Statius *Sil.* 3.3.21, 4.4.81, 5.1.33, *Ach.* 1.880.

367. At *ecl.* 6.53 Vergil uses similar language of Pasiphaë's bull.

369. Vergil so describes Venus at *Aen.* 2.591 and 664, and 10.252.

369. Compare Ovid *RA* 79.

370. With *devexi ponderis* compare Vergil *geo.* 3.524 (*devexo pondere*).

373. For the language of 372–3 compare Martial 8.14.3–4.

374. For the phrase *laxat tenebras*, see Statius *Sil.* 5.1.256 and *The.* 12.254.

374. See Lucretius *DRN* 4.341 and Vergil *geo.* 3.357.

376. Phoebus: Apollo in his role as god of the sun. See also on *ecl.* 4.43 (as well as 5.23 and fr. 7), 302 above and *DPV* 3.483.

381. *Procumbit humi bos* is found at Vergil *Aen.* 5.481.

384. The phrase *Fortunati ambo!* is used also by Vergil as an exclamation at *Aen.* 9.446. Sannazaro is thinking of this passage also at 392–96.

385. Compare Propertius 2.30.28.

386. Girl of Sidon: Europa whom Jupiter, in the guise of a bull, carried from Phoenicia to Crete. Sidon is one of the former's two principal cities.

387. Cithaeron: Mountain in southern Boeotia, associated with the worship of Bacchus. The "old man" is Silenus, one of the god's attendants regularly depicted as riding on a donkey. He is the chief protagonist of Vergil's sixth *eclogue*.

392. With *refugo fluctu* compare Lucan *BC* 1.411 (*refugis fluctibus*). See also *DPV* 3.317.

393. For *terra parens* see Vergil *Aen.* 4.178 and Ovid *M.* 1.393.

394. Compare Horace *c.* 3.30.8–9 where (also in a *dum* clause) a priest (*pontifex*) climbing the *Capitolium* of Rome is a symbol of the eternal. The phrase *templa sacerdos* ends the hexameter at Vergil *Aen.* 6.41.

400. With *Quis tibi tum . . . o genitrix, cum . . . /aspiceres,* compare Vergil *Aen.* 4.408–10 (*quis tibi tum, Dido, . . . cum . . . /prospiceres*).

406. Compare Ovid *EP* 4.8.81.

409. Hero: Joseph.

410. Compare Vergil *Aen.* 8.408.

411. Compare Vergil *Aen.* 10.257.

421. For *per sudum* see Vergil *Aen.* 8.529 and context.

424. With *attonitus . . . animi* compare Vergil *Aen.* 5.529 and 7.814.

425. Compare Ovid *M.* 8.818; *Ilias Latina* 571.

426. Compare Silius *Pun.* 17.25.

430. Compare Juvenal *sat.* 6.96.

432. Compare Silius *Pun.* 2.586–7.

434. Compare Ovid *F.* 1.177.

436. Compare Vergil *geo.* 3.175.

440. Compare Ovid *M.* 2.85 and *F.* 5.194; Statius *The.* 10.109–10.

443. Vergil uses the phrase *lacrimis obortis* on four occasions, all connected with speeches (*Aen.* 3.492, 4.30, 6.867, 11.41).

444. Paros: Island in the Aegean famous in antiquity for the quality of its marble. See also *el.* 1.2.48, 1.9.18.

445. As often in ancient authors, Phrygia and Persia are interchangeable.

446. Compare Ovid *H.* 9.127 and 13.57, *M.* 6.160.

448. Compare Vergil *geo.* 1.76.

450. Sannazaro culls the phrases *laqueata tecta* from Horace *c.* 2.16.11–2 and *regifico paratu* from Valerius Flaccus *Arg.* 2.652.

451. Compare the language of Vergil *Aen.* 6.780.

455. Calpe: One of the pillars of Hercules, Gibraltar. See above, 2.199.

457. Auster: A wind from the south.

461. Compare Vergil *Aen.* 2.358, 527 and 664.

462. Forests: Compare Seneca *Phoen.* 15.

462. Jaws: Compare *Aen.* 6.80 and 102, 7.451.

464. Vergil uses the apostrophe *decus addite divis* (*Aen.* 8.301) of Hercules.

465. In the *Aeneid* Aeneas is addressed as *nate dea* eleven times.

Book III

1. The book's opening line echoes the language of the initial lines of Vergil *Aen.* 10.

7. Hesperus: Latin Vesper, the planet Venus in its rising after sunset.

9. As Ovid, *M.* 1.251.

12. Compare Ovid *M.* 1.231.

14. Vergil has the phrase *haud mora* on eight occasions.

15. For *igne corusco* see Horace *c.* 1.34.6.

17. For *ipse sedens* compare Vergil *Aen.* 8.720 (Augustus) and 10.218 (Aeneas).

19. For *ut perhibent* see Vergil *geo.* 1.247, *Aen.* 4.179, 8.135.

19. See Vergil *Aen.* 6.556 and 9.488, and compare 6.127.

21. For *decus admirable* see Statius *Sil.* 4.6.75 (of a statue of Hercules).

22. See Ovid *M.* 6.101.

23. See Lucretius *DRN* 4.1126.

27. Compare Ovid *Am.* 2.14.11 (*generis primordia nostri*).

28. For *cernere erat* as a signpost of ekphrasis Vergil *Aen.* 6.596 and, more explicitly, 8.676.

29. Compare Vergil *Aen.* 11.301.

33. Compare Vergil *Aen.* 3.361 and 6.15.

39. Compare Vergil *Aen.* 8.440 (*huc advertite mentes*).

41. At *Aen.* 1.294 Vergil treats *impius Furor* as personification of civil war — the Roman equivalent of the results in heaven of Satan's rebellion.

41. For Arctos see 2.14. Ovid has *gelidi Triones* at *M.* 2.171. Through the combination of Arctos with Triones Sannazaro is again referring to the northern constellations variously called Ursa Major and Ursa Minor or Charles's Wain (*triones* are oxen for ploughing).

44. Compare Lucan *BC* 1.347.

46. The phrase *Quos ego* also begins one of Vergil's most famous lines (*Aen.* 1.135).

48. Compare Ovid *H.* 20.133, *F.* 2.387; Valerius Flaccus *Arg.* 1.689.

49. Compare Ovid *F.* 2.265.

51. For *graves aestus* see Catullus 68.62; for *flammati pectoris* see Silius *Pun.* 14.120.

53. As often, Sannazaro combines pagan and Christian sources. Reference to *Genesis* 3 and to the forbidden fruit of the Tree of Knowledge is

combined with allusion to Vergil's golden bough (*Aen.* 6.141 contains Vergil's only use of the adjective *auricomus*, employed here by Sannazaro).

54. Compare Vergil *geo.* 2.58 (*seros nepotes*).

58. Compare Vergil *Aen.* 10.36.

58. See Seneca *Medea* 660; *Ilias Latina* 38; Valerius Flaccus *Arg.* 4.430; Martial *Spec.* 10.3.

60. At *Aen.* 4.364 Vergil has *luminibus tacitis*.

61. Compare [ps.] Seneca *HO* 838.

62. Compare Vergil *ecl.* 1.29 and 67, *Aen.* 6.409.

63. Compare Vergil *Aen.* 2.594.

67. Compare Horace *sat.* 1.3.105.

70. Compare Silius *Pun.* 3.65.

71. The phrase *quare agite* is used by Catullus (64.372) and four times in Vergil.

71. Compare Valerius Flaccus *Arg.* 1.768.

72. The phrase *duris cautibus* is Vergilian (*geo.* 4.203; *Aen.* 4.366).

76. Compare Catullus 64.88 and Vergil *Aen.* 8.388.

77. With *hubera . . . indulgens teneris . . . labris*, Sannazaro, writing to Antonio Seripando (F-P 92), compares *teneris immulgens ubera labris* (Vergil *Aen.* 11.572).

79. Compare Statius *The.* 10.822.

83. With *plausu faventes* compare Vergil *Aen.* 5.148 (*plausu . . . faventum*), and with *celebrate faventes Aen.* 1.735 and 8.173.

85. At *ecl.* 4.23–4 Vergil uses *cunabula* in connection with the death of a snake (*serpens*).

86. Compare Ovid *M.* 4.506.

87. Vergil uses the phrase *sic placitum* at *Aen.* 1.283 where Jupiter is foretelling the future of Rome.

90. Compare Silius *Pun.* 2.517; Valerius Flaccus *Arg.* 7.255.

91. Compare Ovid *M.* 14.582.

95. With this line compare Vergil's language at *Aen.* 1.255 (*vultu . . . serenat*). Ovid uses *discussa nube* at *M.* 15.70.

104. Compare Statius *The.* 10.685.

105. Sannazaro varies the names of the cardinal virtues, Faith, Hope and Charity, with *Amor* replacing *Caritas*.

111. See note on 1.3.

112. Compare Juvenal *sat.* 6.556.

113. The Horae (Hours): Ancient goddesses of the seasons who, according to Ovid (*F.* 1.125), helped guard the gates of heaven.

115. Compare Ovid *Am.* 3.8.32.

116. Compare Vergil *Aen.* 9.725, and context.

120. Compare Ovid *M.* 8.582 and 746.

121. The Hyades ("rainers"), group of five stars in the constellation Taurus usually associated with inclement weather.

121. Boötes ("drover" of the Wain [see on 42 above]), also known as Arctophylax ("Bear-Keeper"), is the astronomical name for the Athenian Icarius, father of Erigone (Virgo), 124. She is considered as ordinarily saddened by her father's unfortunate death. They are juxtaposed at Aratus *Phae.* 136.

125. Orion: Mythical gigantic huntsman, killed by Artemis/Diana. Compare Vergil *Aen.* 3.517.

129. For *pictus sinus* compare Seneca *Oed.* 317; for *nocte coruscans* compare Vergil *geo.* 1.328.

130. Compare Vergil *Aen.* 1.588.

131. Compare Silius *Pun.* 14.594.

132. Vergil uses *durum cubile* at *Aen.* 9.715.

133. Compare Seneca *Oed.* 569–70.

134. Compare Seneca *Oed.* 532.

137. Compare Vergil *Aen.* 4.506.

141. Ovid (*F.* 3.752) has *trunco condita mella.*

142. With *deducite carmen* compare Vergil *ecl.* 6.5 (*deductum . . . carmen*).

144. The final four words of line 144 also occur in the same position at Vergil *Aen.* 2.621.

147. Here and in what follows Sannazaro is drawing on Luke 2.

149. See Vergil *ecl.* 7.46.

150. Vergil links terebinth and boxwood at *Aen.* 10.136.

153. Compare Tibullus 1.2.61.

154. Compare Silius *Pun.* 4.308.

155. For *sub rupe cavata* see also Vergil *Aen.* 1.310 and 3.229.

162. Sannazaro is here thinking of the language, and the broader context, of Catullus 64.288-9. For *ab radicibus imis* see Lucretius *DRN* 1.352; Vergil *geo.* 1.319; Ovid *M.* 15.548.

168. The myrtle, Venus's tree (see, e.g., Vergil *ecl.* 7.62), here receives its name from Idalium, town on Cyprus sacred to the goddess (see *Aen.* 1.681, 5.760, 10.52 and 86).

168. The phrase *cum baccare* is a reminder of Vergil *ecl.* 4.19.

170. Compare Vergil *Aen.* 2.147, 5.770, 8.126, 10.466.

172. At Vergil *Aen.* 5.1-2 we learn that Aeneas *medium . . . tenebat / certus iter.*

172. Divine aid: Compare Vergil's language at *Aen.* 6.368.

173. Compare Vergil *ecl.* 9.20.

174. Compare Vergil *Aen.* 4.574.

176. The phrase *venientibus offert*, at the end of the hexameter, is Vergilian (*Aen.* 6.291).

179. Compare Catullus 64.236.

182. Compare Propertius 4.1.105.

183. Compare Vergil *Aen.* 8.467.

183. Compare Vergil *Aen.* 1.395.

184. Compare Vergil *ecl.* 2.45-6.

186. Lycidas: The name comes from one of the interlocutors in Theocritus *Id.* 7, [Bion] *Id.* 2 (in *Bucolici Graeci*, ed. A. S. F. Gow [Oxford, 1952], 30), and Vergil's ninth *eclogue* as well as of Sannazaro's first *eclogue*. See below on 193.

186. Aegon: For the name see Theocritus *Id.* 4.2 and 26 as well as Vergil *ecl.* 3.2 (bis, as here) and 5.72, as well as at Sannazaro *ecl.* 3.1.

189. Bagrada: River flowing into the Mediterranean near Utica (modern Medjerda, in Tunisia). See Statius *Sil.* 4.3.91.

190. Triton: See *ecl.* 3.75.

190. Cinyps: The modern Cinifo or Wady Khahan.

192. Since Sannazaro also gives the name Lycidas to the initial protagonist of his *Piscatoria* (*Eclogae Piscatoriae*), he may want us to think here of himself and his own city, hill and bay.

194. Compare Vergil *Aen.* 5.809 and 12.218.

198. Tityrus: Vergil. The link is also made in antiquity (e.g. by Servius on *ecl.* 1.1) because of apparent self-reference in his *ecl.* 1, passim, and *ecl.* 6.4. See also *Arcadia* 12, *eclogue* line 279.

198. Song: Compare Ovid *T.* 1.7.22 and 39. With *carmen avenae* compare Vergil *ecl.* 10.51, *carmina . . . avena*.

199. The reference is to Vergil *ecl.* 4.3. From here until line 232 Sannazaro is quoting, paraphrasing, or commenting in verse on Vergil's poem. For further detail see Appendix II.

210. The word *portentificus* is apparently an Ovidian neologism (*M.* 14.55).

214. Compare Lucretius *DRN* 1.9 and context.

215. Compare Tibullus 2.5.55.

219. Compare Ovid *AA* 1.260.

227. Compare Silius *Pun.* 13.793.

232. Compare 1.146.

236. Compare Lucretius *DRN* 2.145 and 346, 5.1386; Ovid *M.* 1.479.

236. Sannazaro is here quoting Vergil *ecl.* 5.64. See note on 1.192 as well as the commentary in Appendix II.

237. Compare Statius *The.* 1.310.

238. Sannazaro combines the biblical story (Luke 2:13) with Vergilian language, drawn generously from the description of the *lusus Troiae* at *Aen.* 5.545–603.

240. Compare Vergil *Aen.* 6.589.

241. Compare Vergil *Aen.* 8.529.

242. Here Sannazaro varies Vergil's phrase *belli simulacra ciebat* (*Aen.* 5.674).

244. Compare Vergil *Aen.* 8.650.

244. Compare Vergil *Aen.* 12.592.

247. Compare Vergil *Aen.* 6.887.

253. Spear: Compare Tibullus 1.10.14; Vergil *Aen* 4.73; Ovid *M.* 6.145; [ps.] Seneca *Oct.* 703; Statius *The.* 10.101; Valerius Flaccus *Arg.* 3.486; Martial 9.100.3.

254. Goblets: Compare Martial 9.94.1.

254. Pillar: Compare Vergil *Aen.* 1.428.

255. With this line compare *Aen.* 7.34.

258. Compare Ovid *M.* 8.596; Lucan *BC* 10.327; Seneca *Phae.* 1162–3; Statius *Sil.* 3.2.78.

260. Lucretius uses the phrase *lumina solis* six times, first at *DRN* 1.5.

262. Compare Vergil *Aen.* 10.557.

264. The lake of Avernus, a short way inland off the northwest coast of the Bay of Naples, was said to be an entranceway to the underworld. Here it stands for the underworld itself. See *LMC* 110 and on *ecl.* 4.45. Ovid has the phrase *nigro Averno* at *Am.* 3.9.27.

265. For the *lacunae* of the underworld see Lucretius *DRN* 1.115.

266. The language of lines 266–71 is reminiscent of Vergil *Aen.* 8.296–301.

268. See Seneca *Phae.* 825.

275. Compare Vergil *Aen.* 7.337.

279. Compare Vergil *Aen.* 1.747 (*ingeminant plausu*).

281. Grassy couch: Compare Apuleius *M.* 5.1. For *sub antris* compare Vergil *geo.* 4.509.

282. Silent heart: Compare Lucan *BC* 1.247.282. For *venturas sortes* compare [ps.] Tibullus 3.4.5.

283. Vergil uses the adjective *caeruleus* of Proteus at *geo.* 4.388, of Tiber at *Aen.* 8.64. At *Aen.* 8.77 Vergil entitles the Tiber *regnator aquarum*.

284. For *hilari vultu* compare Ovid *T.* 5.1.40.

285. The phrase *agmina densentur* is Vergilian (*Aen.* 7.794). See also Lucan *BC* 7.221–2; Silius *Pun.* 8.516. For the names in the list that follows, Homer (*Il.* 18.39–43) mentions Glauce, Doto, Proto, Thoë, Limnorea, Pherusa and Dynamene (Dinamene). These, without Thoë and Limnorea but with the addition of Galena, also appear in Hesiod *The.* 243–8. Rhoë, Pherusa and Dinamene grace the train of Proteus at *ecl.* 4.57.

285. In Cicero Glauce ("blue-gray") is the mother of the third Diana (*ND* 3.58). Statius (*The.* 9.351) calls the Nereids the *glaucae sorores*.

286. Doto: The name of a Nereid also at Vergil *Aen.* 9.102; Valerius Flaccus *Arg.* 1.134. Proto: "First." Galena: "Still," "calm." Lamprothoë: "Brilliant."

287. With this line compare Catullus 66.81. The repetition of the adjective *nudus* finds a parallel in Vergil *geo.* 1.299. For *nudis papillis* compare Propertius 3.14.19 as well as 2.15.5, and Juvenal *sat.* 6.122.

288. Callyroe, or Callir(r)hoe ("beautifully flowing"), is also the name of a Palestinian fountain (Pliny *HN* 5.72). Bryo: "Teeming." Pherusa: "Carrying." Dinamene: "Powerful."

289. Asphaltis: "Sound," "sturdy." The Greek name for the Dead Sea was Asphaltitis (Pliny *HN* 5.71). It was known for its production of bitumen.

289. For *leves undas* compare Ovid *AA* 1.761 (of Proteus).

290. Anthis: "Flower." For the form of the sentence compare Vergil *Aen.* 4.173–4. The phrase *odoratis perfusa liquoribus* is drawn from Horace *c.* 1.5.2 (*perfusus liquidis . . . odoribus*). See also *el.* 1.1.45.

291. Fresh hues: Metonymy for flowers (as Vergil *geo.* 4.306).

293. Hyale: "Glassy." See also on *ecl.* 2.23 as well as 3.65 and 73. Ovid (*M.* 3.171) gives the name to a wood nymph. Thoë: "Swift," "nimble." Crene: "Spring."

294. Gongiste: "Murmuring." Rhoë: "Flowing." Limnoria: "Lake-girl."

295. Dryope ("oak-girl") is also the name of a wood-nymph at Vergil *Aen.* 10.551. Botane: "Grassy." Compare Ovid *Am.* 2.14.39.

296. White garments: See Ovid *Am.* 3.13.27 and *Acts* 1:10, representing, respectively, pagan and Christian religious contexts.

297. With *puniceis . . . evincta cothurnis* compare Vergil *ecl.* 7.32 (*puniceo . . . evincta coturno*). At 296–7 Sannazaro replaces Vergil's triple use of *ambae* at *geo.* 4.341–2 with triple *omnes.*

298. Urns are a standard symbol of river gods in literature and art (see also 319, *caelata in urna*). Compare Vergil *Aen.* 7.792 where, within an ekphrasis, the river Inachus is "pouring his stream from an engraved urn" (*caelata . . . amnem fundens urna*). For the association see Statius *The.* 9.410 and Silius *Pun.* 1.407. At *The.* 2.218 Inachus with his urn forms a segment of a bronze statue-group.

299. Compare Catullus 64.50.

300. Compare Horace *c.* 1.18.16 and Ovid *H.* 15.157.

301. Compare Vergil *Aen.* 4.150 of Aeneas (*egregio decus enitet ore*).

301. Gift of the gods: Compare Vergil *Aen.* 1.652.

302. Compare Lucan *BC* 6.126–7.

303. Compare Vergil *Aen.* 10.724–5.

304. With *captabant frigus in umbra* compare Vergil *ecl.* 2.8 (*umbras et frigora captant*).

305. Compare Vergil *Aen.* 8.675–7.

306. Vergil uses the phrase *laeta arva* at *Aen.* 6.744.

307. Young man: John the Baptist. See Matthew 3:4. For the language compare also Vergil *geo.* 3.383.

308. With *stans celso in* compare Vergil *Aen.* 3.527, 8.680, 10.261.

309. Compare Vergil *Aen.* 7.31 (of the Tiber). The baptism of Christ is described at Matthew 3:13–17, Mark 1:1–11, Luke 3:21–2, John 1:32–4.

310. Vergil varies the phrase *viridi in ripa* at *geo.* 3.144 and 4.121. Chosen attendants: Compare Statius *Sil.* 5.1.39.

312. Compare Sulpicia 1.12 and Ovid *M.* 10.432.

313–314. Vergil uses the phrase *ipse pater* on seven occasions. We find *signa dabant* at Vergil *geo.* 1.471 and *signa dabit* at *geo.* 1.439, both passages concerned with the death of Julius Caesar. Compare also Ovid *M.* 5.468. Cloudless heavens: Compare Vergil *geo.* 1.260 and 487, *Aen.* 3.518. Dove: See Ovid *M.* 14.597.

315. For the biblical description see Matthew 3:16 and John 1:32. For the language compare Vergil *Aen.* 8.391–2; Horace *c.* 1.34.6; Ovid *F.* 6.635; Statius *Sil.* 1.5.6–7; Silius *Pun.* 11.339.

317. For parallels see Vergil *Aen.* 8.240; Horace *c.* 1.2.13–4; Ovid *M.* 10.41–2.

318. The phrase *caelata urna* appears in Vergil's brief ekphrasis of Turnus's shield at *Aen.* 7.792.

319. Compare Ovid *M.* 2.156 and 8.24. Vergil uses *ignarus* in connection with *fata* at *Aen.* 8.730–1, and *oculos singula volvit* at *Aen* 8.618, which is to say at the conclusion of, and in the introduction to, the description of the shield of Aeneas.

320. Compare Lucretius *DRN* 5.598.

322. Compare Lucretius *DRN* 1.886.

324. Compare Vergil *geo.* 4.371 (of the Eridanus or Po river)

326. Compare Ovid *M.* 14.418–9.

327. Compare Silius *Pun.* 8.593.

330. Compare Vergil *Aen.* 2.688 (of Anchises about to address Jupiter).

331. Compare Vergil *Aen.* 12.829 (of Jupiter as *hominum rerumque repertor*).

336. For Proteus see *ecl.* 1.88. The phrase *caeruleus Proteus* occurs at Vergil *geo.* 4.388.

337. Compare Statius *The.* 1.473.

338. Compare Catullus 64.328-9, for *adveniet tibi* and the repetition of *adveniet*. There the Fates are predicting the future to Peleus and Thetis at their wedding. With *adveniet* and *properantibus* compare Ovid *M.* 9.145.

340. Signs: Compare Vergil *geo.* 1.439. Oracles: Compare Statius *The.* 9.662.

341. The epithet is drawn from Ovid (*M.* 5.187). Compare Catullus 11.7-8 (*septemgeminus . . . Nilus*).

342. The Indus and the Ganges, which presently flow through Pakistan and Bangladesh, bounded ancient India on the west and east respectively. Technically the (H)ister is the lower course of the Danube. See also 2.191. For the epithet see Ovid *EP* 1.8.11; Statius *Sil.* 5.1.89.

343. Tiber: Ancient Tybris (Tiberis, Tibris), the river of Rome. See also *el.* 3.1.163; *ep.* 1.14.3. Po: Ancient Padus, northern Italy's most important river; its Greek name was Eridanos.

349. Christ's healing of lepers is frequently mentioned by Matthew (8:1-3), Mark (1:40-1) and Luke (5:12-14, 17:12-15). For *dira lues* see Ovid *M.* 7.523 and 15.626, and often elsewhere; for *manantia tabo* compare Ovid *M.* 6.646; Silius *Pun.* 6.237, 10.542, 15.428.

351. See Matthew 8:14-5; Mark 1:29-32; Luke 4:38-9.

355. Piteous to see: Compare Vergil *Aen.* 1.111; Ovid *M.* 13.422, and often elsewhere. See Matthew 17:15; Mark 9:17-27.

357. Vergil uses the phrase *spumas aget ore* at *geo.* 3.203; for *spumas tumenteis* compare Ovid *M.* 7.263.

359. Compare Ovid *T.* 4.8.23.

361. See Luke 14:2.

362. With *non alias* compare Vergil *geo.* 1.487, and see on 314 above.

363. See Matthew 9:32-3; Mark 7:32-5; Luke 11:14.

365. Compare Lucretius *DRN* 5.610 and 6.1197–8. See Matthew 9:27 and 20:29–34; Mark 10:46–52; Luke 18:35–43; John 5:11.

366. Compare Horace *epi.* 1.9.7–8; Ovid *H.* 16.283, *RA* 359, *T.* 4.10.61.

368. Compare Ovid *EP* 2.6.27.

369. Compare *cernere erat* (2.274, 3.28). For *genua aegra trahentes* compare Vergil *Aen.* 5.468.

370. See Matthew 15:21–31, 21:14. For *firmato poplite* compare Ovid *M.* 15.223.

371. Compare Lucretius *DRN* 4.1114.

372. Compare Ovid *M.* 1.400.

373. See Matthew 8:5–13; Mark 2:3–12; Luke 5:18–25. For *validas vires* compare Vergil *Aen.* 6.833.

376. Sannazaro is paraphrasing John 5:12.

377. *Donarium* is technically a temple treasury. For *innumerae voces* compare Lucan *BC* 3.540; Statius *Sil.* 1.6.81, *The.* 7.111, 10.147.

378. Compare Ovid *M.* 2.31.

379. For *parte alia* compare 1.325, 2.22; Vergil *Aen.* 1.474, 8.433 and 682, 9.521, 12.346.

380. See Matthew 12:10–3; Mark 3:1–5; Luke 6:6–10.

381. See Matthew 9:20–2; Mark 5:22–34; Luke 8:41–8.

382. Compare Vergil *Aen.* 10.822.

383. Compare Vergil *Aen.* 12.66.

385. Compare Statius *The.* 1.163. See Matthew 8:16; Mark 1:23–7, 5:8–9; Luke 4:33–5, 6:18, 8:27–33, 11:14.

386. Compare Ovid *M.* 8.83–4.

388. The Dirae are synonymous with the Furiae (Furies). For the phraseology compare Silius *Pun.* 5.189. For *frustra clamantum* compare Ovid *M.* 11.665.

389. Lash: Compare Vergil *geo.* 3.252.

389. Hollow clouds: Compare Lucretius *DRN* 6.272; Vergil *Aen.* 1.516, 5.810, 10.636, 11.593.

391. See Matthew 9:23; Mark 1:27; Luke 7:12–5; John 11:1–44.

396. Compare Ovid *M.* 1.346, *F.* 2.439 and 3.329; Statius *The.* 10.144. Vergil's examples of the pathetic fallacy, especially *ecl.* 4.50, 5.28, and 6.28, are in the background here.

397. Compare Vergil *geo.* 3.144.

398. Compare Horace *c.* 2.5.7.

399. With *somnos / carpentem* compare Vergil *geo.* 3.435.

400. For the repeated *macte* see Silius *Pun.* 4.475.

403. Compare Vergil *Aen.* 8.72.

404. Compare Ovid *M.* 14.807.

407. Napaeans: Ordinarily nymphs of wooded valleys, here nymphs in general. See also *el.* 2.6.3, *ep.* 1.2.14 and commentators on Vergil *geo.* 4.535.

408. Compare Vergil *ecl.* 8.65.

410. Compare Vergil *geo.* 4.350.

413. Compare Ovid *M.* 6.425 and 11.285–6, *F.* 2.733, *EP* 1.9.39; Lucan *BC* 9.202, and frequently in Silius *Punica*.

415. The triple repetition of a name has several classical parallels, among them the iteration of Eurydice at Vergil *geo.* 4.525–7 (where Proteus is the narrator).

420. For Ovid alone compare *Am.* 1.3.16, 1.8.11 and 2.6.51, *H.* 18.119, *M.* 9.55 and 371, 15.361, *F.* 6.715.

425. Cyrus: King of Persia, founder of the Achaemenid dynasty and initiator of its empire. The phrase *caspia regna* comes from Vergil *Aen.* 6.798. We are meant to think of the realm of the Scythians and, by association, of the conquests of Alexander the Great.

426. For Babylon see on 1.439. Again there are strong connections with Alexander the Great. For the epithet *superba* compare Lucan *BC* 1.10.

427. Sannazaro is offering a précis of a Roman triumph, the procession of a victorious general through Rome that ended at the temple of Jupiter Optimus Maximus on the Capitoline Hill. For *scandet Capitolium* compare Horace *c.* 3.30.8–9 (see above on 2.394); for *comitante senatu* compare Ovid *EP* 4.4.41.

429. For *litora longe* compare Catullus 11.3; Vergil *Aen.* 5.23.

430. See Matthew 4:18–21. Mention of *acta* may be a covert reference to Sannazaro as Actius Syncerus. See note on *ecl.* 1.1 and 2.45.

437. See Matthew 10:1; Mark 3:15, 16:18–9; Luke 9:1. Ovid has the phrase *vipereos dentes* at *M.* 3.103, 4.573 and 7.122. Orcus: God of the underworld, here standing for the underworld as a whole. See also *LMC* 108; *ep.* 2.1.31.

441. Eumenides: Here (as at Vergil *Aen.* 6.280) another name for the Furies. Doors: Compare Vergil *Aen.* 11.890. See Matthew 16:18–9.

443. See Matthew 19:28; Luke 22:30. In Dante (*Paradiso* 24) the apostles are in the realm of the fixed stars.

445. Vergil uses the phrase *iura dabunt* at *Aen* 1.293.

447. Compare Statius *Sil.* 1.2.51.

450. Reference is to the marriage feast at Cana (John 2:1). Lenaeus (god of the wine-press) is an epithet of Bacchus. For the phrase *lenaeos latices* compare Vergil *geo.* 3.509–10. For *deum rex* compare Vergil *Aen.* 3.375 and 12.851.

452. Compare Propertius 1.6.34.

453. Vergil has the *spumantem pateram* at *Aen.* 1.739.

456. Compare Lucretius *DRN* 3.784; Vergil *geo.* 4.528.

459. Compare Valerius Flaccus *Arg.* 3.22. Lucretius uses the adjective *squamiger* on five occasions. See Luke 5:5.

461. Compare Vergil *Aen.* 3.421.

462. See Horace *c.* 1.2.11–2.

463. Vergil (*Aen.* 1.54) begins an hexameter with the phrase *imperio premet*, in a similar context.

464. Compare Ovid *M.* 11.531, *T.* 1.4.15.

465. The Cori (Cauri) were north winds (see also *ecl.* 3.59). For Christ's calming of the winds see Matthew 8:26; Mark 4:41; Luke 8:24.

466. Compare Vergil *ecl.* 6.74.

467. Ceres, Roman goddess of grain, stands here by metonymy for the bread made from it. For *miserabile vulgus* compare Vergil *Aen.* 2.798.

469. See Matthew 14:16–21; Mark 6:38–44; Luke 9:13–7; John 6:9.

471. Compare Horace *epi.* 1.19.21.

472. See Matthew 14:15; Mark 6:48; John 6:18–9.

474. Compare Statius *Sil.* 3.2.3.

474. Neptune: See note on *ecl.* 2.25.

476. Phorcus: Son of Neptune, father of the gorgon Medusa, changed into a sea-god at his death. Compare Vergil *Aen.* 5.240 and 824.

476. Glaucus: See note on *ecl.* 1.47. He appears at Vergil *Aen.* 5.823.

478. For the metaphor of writing as sailing see Vergil *geo.* 2.41 and 4.117; Horace *c.* 4.15.1–4. Sannazaro draws his direct language in part from Catullus 63.1.

479. See the language of John 20:30, 21:25.

479. Parnassus: Greek mountain, sacred to Apollo and the Muses, at the foot of which was Delphi and the spring of Castalia.

482. For the image see Vergil *geo.* 2.43–4 and *Aen.* 6.625–6. Its origin is Homer *Il.* 2.488–92. See also Ennius *Ann.* 469–70 (ed. Skutsch).

488. Compare Ovid *Ibis* 127 and Statius *The* 3.639.

492. Aurora: Compare Catullus 64.271 and the variation at Lucretius *DRN* 4.538.

493. For the adjective *auricomus* see *ecl.* 4.60 and Vergil *Aen.* 6.141, where it is a coinage.

494. For *et iam . . . tempus* compare Vergil *geo.* 2.542 where racing is a metaphor for writing.

497. Compare Ovid *H.* 19.181 and *M.* 14.4.

500. Compare Ovid *M.* 8.563.

501. Sidonian purple: See note on *ecl.* 2.37. The phrase appears at [ps.] Tibullus 3.3.18.

503. Compare Ovid *M.* 1.423.

504. Compare Vergil *Aen.* 3.534; Silius *Pun.* 4.654.

505. Compare Lucan *BC* 8.739.

507. Posillipo: See note on *ecl.* 1.13.

508. Tritons: See note on *ecl.* 1.74. Vergil also groups *Tritones* at *Aen.* 5.824. Nereus: See 2.124 and on *ecl.* 1.99. Panopea is a sea-nymph at Vergil *geo.* 1.437 and *Aen.* 5.240 and 825. Ephyre is among Cyrene's sisterhood of water nymphs at Vergil *geo.* 4.343.

509. Melite: A sea nymph at Vergil *Aen.* 5.825.

511. Mergellina: See above, 1.26, and on *ecl.* 2.3. Pontano wrote two books *De hortis Hesperidum,* dealing with the cultivation of orange and lemon trees (see Nash, *Major Latin Poems,* 203–5). For *novos flores* compare Vergil *ecl.* 9.41.

512. See Vergil *geo.* 2.125–6 for reference to Persian citrons.

513. In these concluding nine hexameters Sannazaro is thinking back to the opening eight lines of Vergil *geo.* 2 and, above all, to the concluding lines of *geo.* 4 where Parthenope (which is to say Naples), which opens Vergil's antepenultimate line, is replaced by Mergillina in the same position in *DPV. Me dulcis,* e.g., is drawn from *geo.* 4.563. Compare also the mention of *otium* here at 510 and at Vergil *geo.* 4.564. For *nectit coronam* in connection with the writing of poetry, compare Horace *c.* 1.26.7–8 and *epi.* 2.2.96; for *fronde corona,* compare Lucretius *DRN* 1.118.

LAMENTATION TO MORTALS
ON THE DEATH OF CHRIST OUR LORD

Meter: dactylic hexameter.

First published in 1526.

1. Vergil begins three hexameters with the phrase *si quando* (*geo.* 4.228; *Aen.* 3.500, 12.851).

2. The phrase *diffundere coelo* has a Lucretian ring (compare *DRN* 1.9: *nitet diffuso lumine caelum*).

3. Vergil begins eight verses with the word *certatim*.

4. Diana as goddess of the moon and sister of Apollo as Phoebus, the sun-god. See *ecl.* 3.75, 77. Vergil employs the compound adjective *noctivagus* only once, also in connection with Phoebe/Diana (*Aen.* 10.215–16: *alma . . . curru noctivago Phoebe*).

6. Pliny (*HN* 2.4.10) speaks of "those many eyes of glistening stars" (*tot stellarum illos conlucentium oculos*). Manilius (1.133) calls the starry fires "eyes of the world" (*mundi oculos*).

9. The phrase *cuncta supercilio* comes from Horace *c.* 3.1.8, where it also begins the verse. It is there applied to the power of Jupiter.

10. For the phrase *aegri mortales* see on *DPV* 1.3.

11. Sannazaro found the phrase *traiecta . . . pectora ferro*, also at the end of a hexameter, at Vergil *Aen.* 1.355 where the subject is Sychaeus, Dido's husband killed by her brother.

15. Compare Statius *The.* 11.499.

18. In verses 17–18 Sannazaro draws his language in part from Vergil *ecl.* 4.50 (*aspice convexo nutantem pondere mundum*). The anaphora of *adspicite*, at the opening of lines 11 and 14, is likewise modeled on the repetition of *aspice* that initiates *ecl.* 4.50 and 52.

21. With Sannazaro's language at 20–21 compare Vergil *ecl.* 5.22 (referring to the dead Daphnis who is also a quasi-divine shepherd) and *Aen.* 11.59 (the dead Pallas).

24. Sannazaro is thinking of Vergil's use of *ferrugo* to describe one of the reactions of the sun at the murder of Julius Caesar (*geo.* 1.467). Compare also *DPV* 1.372.

25. With *pallentia ora* compare Vergil *Aen.* 10.821–22 (*ora,/ ora . . . pallentia*), of the dying Lausus.

26. For this pagan epithet of God see on *ecl.* 3.70 and *DPV* 1.217.

27. Compare Vergil *Aen.* 4.698 (*flavum . . . vertice crinem*), at the death of Dido.

31. For the biblical description of the happenings immediately after the death of Christ see Matthew 27:52–3. Compare also Vergil *geo.* 1.486 (*resonare lupis ululantibus urbes*) and *Aen.* 4.609 (*Hecate . . . ululata per urbes*).

32. For *penates* as homes, see on *DPV* 1.72.

36. Compare *DPV* 3.281.

37. See on *ecl.* 1.74.

37. With *rauco . . . cornu* compare Vergil *Aen.* 7.615 (*aerea . . . adsensu . . . cornua rauco*).

40. The phrase *foedera mundi* appears at Lucan *BC* 1.80 and Seneca *Medea* 335 and 606.

43. The language of lines 42–3 is drawn from the opening of Lucretius *DRN* 1, especially lines 2–3 and 21.

50. The reference may be a learned allusion to Catullus 66.8, to the "lock of Berenice's hair" (*e Beroniceo vertice caesariem*) noticed gleaming brightly in the heavens by the astronomer Conon. The constellation Corona was also said to be made up of the crown, or locks, of Ariadne (see *OLD* s. v. 2).

50. With *pectus hians* compare *DPV* 1.332 (*lato patefactum pectus hiatu*).

54. The phrase *cuspidis ictum* ends the hexameter at Vergil *Aen.* 7.756 (compare also 10.484).

55. The phrase *duras cauteis* is Vergilian (*ecl.* 8.43; *Aen.* 4.366).

56. See Lucan *BC* 2.14–5 (*sit caeca futuri / mens hominum fati*), imitated by Statius at *Th.* 5.718–19. See also *DPV* 1.309–10 and the exclamation of Lucretius at *DRN* 2.14: *O miseras hominum mentes, o pectora caeca!* (O pitiable minds of men, O blind hearts!).

58. The phrase *nigra Tartara* is Vergilian (*Aen.* 6.134–35). Compare also *DPV* 1.34 and 227–28 (*tristia Tartara*).

59. The phrase *regnaque tristia*, also of the Underworld, concludes Horace's line at *c.* 3.4.46 (compare also Lucan *BC* 9.869 and Silius *Pun.* 16.270).

60. Hymn of praise to a god, usually Apollo who bears the name Paean (Paeon). See *DPV*, dedication, line 8, and compare the language at Vergil *Aen.* 6.657.

61. With *pone sequi* compare Vergil *geo.* 4.487 and *Aen.* 10.226.

64. The phrase *rerum sator* appears at Silius *Pun.* 4. 430. Compare Vergil *Aen.* 1.254 and *DPV* 1.246.

65. The phrase *moderatur habenas* at the conclusion of an hexameter appears at Manilius *Ast.* 1.668 and Statius *The.* 4.219. For variations see Lucretius *DRN* 2.1096, Varius Rufus fr. 3.1 (ed. Courtney), [ps.] Tibullus 3.7.115, Ovid *M.* 6.223 and *EP* 2.5.75, Silius *Pun.* 16.343.

66. See on *DPV* 1.391.

69. Sannazaro is drawing on the language of Vergil (*geo.* 4.205) describing the customs of bees: *tantus amor florum et generandi gloria mellis* (so great is their love of flowers and their glory in producing honey).

71. Once again Sannazaro is thinking of Vergil's fourth *eclogue* (13). See above 17–18 and on *DPV* 3.197–236.

72. Compare *DPV* 1.153–54.

79. With *pecudum fibras* compare Vergil *Aen.* 10.176 (*pecudum fibrae*).

81. Vergil has *bracchia pandit* at *Aen.* 6.282. Compare also *DPV* 1.329–30.

84. With *obtusas aures* compare Lucretius *DRN* 5.1054–55 (*auris . . . obtundere*) and Statius *Sil.* 5.1.171 (*obtunsae aures*).

85. With *infelix genus* compare Vergil *Aen.* 5.624–25 (*gens infelix*).

87. Compare *DPV* 1.384 and Vergil *Aen.* 10.503.

88. Compare Vergil *Aen.* 9.640 (Apollo *nube sedens*).

91. The phrase *contendere contra*, at the conclusion of an hexameter, is to be found at Vergil *Aen.* 5.370.

92. Vergil has the phrase *mens sibi conscia recti* (the consciousness of right) at *Aen.* 1.604.

95. See on *DPV* 1.461. For the language compare Lucretius *DRN* 1.115.

99. The adjective *trifidus* is a neologism of Ovid (*M.* 2.325). *Trifidos ignes* presumably refers to the Trinity.

100. The phrase *ad aethera palmas* is used by Ovid at *M.* 13.411 and *in aethera palmas* at *F.* 4.315.

103. With *invidiae stimulis* compare Vergil *Aen.* 11.337 (*obliqua invidia stimulisque . . . amaris*), and for *diris ultricibus* compare Vergil *Aen.* 4.610 (*Dirae ultrices*).

108. See on *DPV* 3.437.

110. See on *DPV* 3.264.

113. *Posthabitis templis* presumably announces the renunciation of pagan ways.

117. The phrase *sanctumque senatum* concludes Vergil *Aen.* 1.426.

118. Compare *DPV* 1.451. It may not be accidental that the word *stellantia* appears in Sannazaro's final line just as *stella* is the concluding word of Dante's *Divina Commedia*.

PISCATORY ECLOGUES

Meter: dactylic hexameter.

First published 1526.

I. PHYLLIS

Like his primary model, the fifth of Vergil's ten *Eclogues*, Sannazaro's poem consists formally of a dialogue between two characters, here fishermen in place of Vergil's shepherds. Sannazaro, however, departs from Vergil's pattern in two ways. The first is by giving one character, here Lycidas, the principal voice instead of allowing a generally equal balance between the two singers. The second is by maintaining the parallel subject matter—a death that has a powerful effect on the world of the singers—and its accompanying somber tone throughout the poem, without the relief from sorrow that Vergil brings through apotheosis. Lycidas is a standard name for a shepherd in Vergil's *Eclogues* (see 7.67, and 9, passim).

1–4. Sannazaro's opening (*Mirabar . . . quid*), taken from Vergil *ecl.* 1.36 where the words are also concerned with loss and lament, is equally a manifestation of his most important influence from the poetic past. Compare also Vergil *ecl.* 1.11–2 (*miror . . .*) where *undique* and *totis agris* anticipate Sannazaro's *passim*. The constancy of "evil" (*malum*, 16) in Meliboeus's situation looks ahead to Lycidas's description of the ubiquity of lament in the littoral world at the death of Phyllis. Sannazaro's *corvus* is the successor to Vergil's *cornix* (*ecl.* 9.15) in this regard. The mention of *litora* in the first verse is a reminder of the poet himself, Actius Syncerus, writer of novel piscatory eclogues (see also on *ecl.* 2.45 and 4.19; *DPV* 3.430; *el.* 1.10.23); Actius was the name given him when he became a member of the Accademia Pontaniana around 1478.

2. Vergil's only use of the noun *pabula* in his *Eclogues* occurs at 1.49 at the same position in the hexameter. There the feeders are lambs, not Sannazaro's piscatorial tunnies. The nearby use of forms of *insuetus* further urges the connection.

5. With *flebilibus . . . saxa* compare Vergil *ecl.* 10.15 (*fleverunt saxa*). The mourning of nature — a form of the pathetic fallacy — at a significant death is a motif in ancient pastoral (see, e.g., Theocritus *Id.* 1.72, Bion *Id.* 1.31–9, Moschus *Id.* 3.38–50, Vergil *ecl.* 5.25–8).

7. With *choros induceret* compare Vergil *ecl.* 5.30 (*thiasos inducere*). Propertius uses the phrase *solitos choros* at 1.20.46.

8. Phyllis: Standard girl's name in Vergilian pastoral, appearing in *ecl.* 3, 5, 7 and 10.

9. With the language of 8–9, especially *terrae / condidimus*, compare Vergil *Aen.* 5.47–9, dealing with the anniversary of the burial of Anchises. Grief for the loss of a beloved is a standard theme in classical pastoral, to be found, e.g., in Theocritus (*Id.* 1), Moschus (*Id.* 3) and Nemesianus (*ecl.* 1). But Sannazaro's primary inspiration is the fifth *eclogue* of Vergil. For Italian sources see Rosalba, *Le Egloghe*, 9 and notes 2–4.

13. Posillipo: Ancient Pausilypus ("ending pain"), spine of coastal land along the northern periphery of the Bay of Naples that separates the

city's harbor proper from the gulf of Pozzuoli (ancient Puteoli). See also *ecl.* 2.32 and 4.47; *DPV* 3.507; *ep.* 2.15.34, 2.36.7, and 2.51.43.

14. Nesis, modern Nisida, is a small island off the western point of the Capo di Posillipo, between Naples and Pozzuoli. See also *ecl.* 2.33 and 4.46; Statius *Sil.* 2.2.78 and 3.1.148.

23. The phrase *aequore mersit* at line ending is used by Vergil at *Aen.* 6.342 and 348 in connection with the watery death of Palinurus.

24. Compare the opening of Vergil *ecl.* 9.2.

25. Lycotas: Fictional name of Arethusa's husband at Propertius 4.3.1. See also Calpurnius Siculus *ecl.* 6.26 and 7.4.

26. Amyntas: Name of a shepherd in Vergil *ecl.* 2, 3, 5 and 10.

28. The adjective *tenuis* is a signpost in Vergil for the poetics of pastoral (*ecl.* 1.2, 6.8). See further on 102 below.

31. The language of lines 29–31 is drawn from Vergil *ecl.* 3.52, 5.10–12 and 9.32. Vergil employs an imperative, along with *quandoquidem* and a form of *mollis*, at *ecl.* 3.55, shortly before the commencement of an amoebaean competition.

32. The phrase *insani fluctus* occurs at Vergil *ecl.* 9.43.

33. Vergil uses the phrase *immo haec quae* at *ecl.* 9.26, and *immo haec* at *ecl.* 5.13, in parallel contexts.

35. At *ecl.* 9.59–60, Vergil ends one hexameter and begins the next with forms of *sepulcrum* and *incipio*, as does Sannazaro at 35–6. Vergil's Lycidas suggests that song might begin. Sannazaro's initiates an actual lament. *Incipiam* also begins an hexameter at *Aen.* 2.13 as Aeneas starts to tell his tale of Troy to Dido.

36. For *coniferas cupressus* see Vergil *Aen.* 3.680 (*coniferae cyparissi*).

42. For *incipe dum* in a similar context see Nemesianus *ecl.* 1.6.

42. Baiae: Modern Baia, a town on the northwestern shore of the Bay of Naples adjacent to the Lucrine lake (ancient Lacus Lucrinus), between Pozzuoli and Miseno (ancient Misenum) and its cape. Hercules is said to have built the causeway between Lacus Lucrinus and the sea (compare Propertius 1.11.1–2 and 3.18.4). See also *ecl.* 3.87 and 4.39; *el.* 1.9.65, 2.4.7,

2.7.1; Strabo 5.4.6. A resort for ancient Romans as well as in Sannazaro's day, it is the subject of Pontano's *Baiae* (see *el.* 1.9.65).

42. Milcon is the piscatory equivalent of the sheep who, at Vergil *ecl.* 10.7, serve as audience for his speaker's song.

45. Nereides: Sea-nymphs, daughters of Nereus and Doris, divinities of the sea. See also *ecl.* 2.60, 3.46, 5.13, fr. 22, and on *DPV* 2.155.

46. For the story of the fisherman Glaucus, in love with Scylla and beloved by Circe, who ate a magic herb and was changed into a sea-god, see Ovid *M.* 13.904–68 and 14.1–69. See also *ecl.* 2.53–4, 3.67; *DPV* 3.476 as well as Servius on Vergil *geo.* 1.437.

48. Sannazaro takes the phrase *novus incola ponti* from *M.* 13.904.

49. With *mutato corpore fluctus*, compare Lucretius *DRN* 3.755 (*mutato corpore flecti*). Compare also Vergil *geo.* 4.413 and [ps-]Vergil *Ciris* 527. Statius uses the phrase *feriens cauda* at *Sil.* 3.2.38.

53. With *quidve hic sperem* compare Vergil *ecl.* 2.2 (*quid speraret*).

54. For *proiectus in alga* Sannazaro is combining Vergil's depiction of the figure of Meliboeus *proiectus in antro* (*ecl.* 1.75), with that of Thyrsis *proiecta vilior alga* (*ecl.* 7.42).

56. Sannazaro may be thinking of Catullus 96.1–2: *Si quicquam mutis gratum acceptumve sepulcris / accidere a nostro, Calve, dolore potest . . .* (If anything attractive or welcome can happen to a silent grave from our grief, Calvus . . .).

59. Lucina: Roman goddess of childbirth, often synonymous with Juno.

61. Vergil juxtaposes *spes* and *requies* at *Aen.* 12.57–8, as Amata, soon to commit suicide, pronounces her dependence on Turnus.

62. With *aeternus . . . sub pectore luctus* compare Juno at Vergil *Aen.* 1.36, *aeternum servans sub pectore vulnus* (at 1.25 Vergil had already mentioned her *saevi dolores*).

66. Vergil also begins *ecl.* 7.35 with the phrase *nunc te*. There a marble statue glorifies Diana; here a stone marks the grave of Phyllis.

71. Compare Ovid *M.* 2.214 (*magnae cum moenibus urbes*).

74. Triton (or Tritons), sea-god, or gods, often in the retinue of Neptune. See also *ecl.* 3.98, 4.27, 5.80 (and passim), and fr. 21; *DPV* 3.508; *LMC* 37.

75. Compare Statius *Ach.* 1.55 whose inspiration is Vergil *Aen.* 5.822–4.

76. P. Alpers (*What is Pastoral?* [Chicago, 1996], 106) finds in these lines a source for Milton's *Lycidas*, 154–60.

78. For the juxtaposed uses of forms of *valeo*, compare Vergil *ecl.* 3.79.

80. At *ecl.* 1.42 Vergil also ends an hexameter with *quotannis*, in a context that likewise deals with numbers of altars. In these and the lines that follow, Sannazaro is drawing on Vergil *ecl.* 5.65–73. Several of the names at 84–6 appear also at *Aen.* 5.823–6. Palaemon, son of Athamas and Ino (Leucothea), was Melicerta (-es) before his metamorphosis into a sea-god (Ovid *M.* 4.481–542). See also Statius *Sil.* 3.2.39.

83. Value is important here, as well as the color contrast between red and white. Sannazaro calls attention to the number seven by its double repetition. He is heightening both the number of altars and the single repetition that he found at Vergil *ecl.* 5.65–6. For the pastoralist seven is the number of reeds in the Pan-pipe (Vergil *ecl.* 2.36) as well as of the strings on the lyre of Orpheus (Vergil *Aen.* 6.646).

84. Nisaea and Cymodoce are sea-nymphs at Vergil *Aen.* 5.826. Cymodoce and Galatea are coupled by Statius at *Sil.* 2.2.20.

86. For Panope see also *ecl.* 4.56 and *DPV* 3.508. (Panopea is the name of a sea-nymph at Vergil *geo.* 1.437, *Aen.* 5.240 and 825.)

86. Galatea: Name of a sea-nymph, daughter of Nereus and Doris, whose love for Acis and wooing by Polyphemus are the subject of Theocritus *Id.* 6 and 11. Ovid tells her tale at *M.* 13.738–897. Throughout *ecl.* 2 and at *ecl.* 5.76 and 119 her name is appropriately given to the fisherman-singer's girl. In Vergil's *Eclogues* the name belongs to a shepherd's beloved at 1 (30–1) and 3 (64, 72). It is presumably the sea-nymph Galatea who is meant at 7.37 and 9.39. See also *ep.* 1.23.4 and 2.1.17.

88. Shape-changing sea-god and seer with inspired knowledge, Proteus figures prominently in Vergil's fourth *georgic* as well as in the third book of *DPV* (334–488). According to Ovid (*M.* 11.221–56) he assisted in the

union of Peleus and Thetis, and predicted the heroic force, and fate, of their son Achilles. See also *ecl.* 3.62 and 4, title and 21.

88. For *divino pectore*, see Catullus 64.383, dealing with the Song of the Fates.

89. With *funera fleret* compare Vergil *ecl.* 5.20–1 (*funere . . . flebant*).

90. Thetis: Sea-nymph, daughter of Nereus and mother of Achilles, hero of Homer's *Iliad*.

90. With lines 84–90 compare Vergil *ecl.* 5.72–3.

91. With *at tu sive* compare Vergil *ecl.* 7.35–6 as well as Statius *Sil.* 5.3.19 (*at tu seu*).

92. Elysium: The abode in the underworld of the blessed after death. See also *el.* 1.3.42, 1.7.54; *ep.* 1.10.8, 1.13.1.

93. The waters of the underworld river Lethe were supposed to bring about forgetfulness. See also on *el.* 1.3.37.

94. With the line ending *pollice flores*, compare Vergil *Aen.* 11.68 (*pollice florem*) and Ovid *F.* 5.255.

96. With *violis pallentibus* compare Vergil *ecl.* 2.47 (*pallentis violas*), also in a list of flowers.

96. Compare Statius *Sil.* 5.3.19–27.

97. At *Aen.* 2.690 Vergil begins the hexameter with *aspice nos*, in a prayer to Jupiter.

97–98. With *numen . . . semper eris* compare Vergil *ecl.* 1.7, *erit . . . semper deus*. Sannazaro's lines may be a source for line 183 of Milton's *Lycidas*: "henceforth thou art the genius of the shore." (See *A Variorum Commentary on the Poems of John Milton* II.2, ed. A. Woodhouse and D. Bush [New York, 1972], 730.)

99. Nereus: Sea-god, father of the Nereids. See also *DPV* 3.508; *ecl.* 5.81, and fr. 10.

99. Amphitrite: Sea-goddess and wife of Neptune.

99–100. For *ut . . . sic* in a parallel context, compare Vergil *ecl.* 5.79.

101. With this line compare Vergil *ecl.* 5.42 which also introduces an epi-
taph (43–4), again a conspicuous bow to Sannazaro's principal model.

102. The phrase *tenui arundine* is Vergilian (*ecl.* 6.8), where it refers to the
"slender reed-pipe," the instrument for accompanying pastoral song, as
well as to the Callimachean stylistics of that song (compare *ecl.* 1.2, *tenui
avena*). *Tenui harundine*, the slender rod to which the fisherman ties his
line, is thus the piscatory equivalent of the shepherd's flute. The "inter-
weaving" of line and rod finds a parallel in the basket which the shepherd
weaves as he sings (Vergil *ecl.* 10.71; compare his *ecl.* 2.72), and both are
metonymies for the poet's craft.

103. Compare Vergil *ecl.* 10.2 where Lycoris might read (*legat*) the singer's
songs meant for Gallus.

104. The Sirens in myth were birds with the faces of young girls who in-
habited a group of small islands (Sirenusae, now Li Galli) off Positano
on the southern side of the peninsula that forms the southern arc of the
Bay of Naples. Their seductive voices lured sailors to their doom. Their
most famous appearance in literature is in Homer *Od.* 12.39–54 and 166–
200 (see also Vergil *Aen.* 5.864–6; Ovid mentions them in the course of
his retelling of the *Aeneid* at *M.* 14.88). See also *ecl.* 3.50, 4.60 and (with-
out being named) 75–6, 5.77; *ep.* 2.32.8, 2.56.8, 3.9.1; Statius *Sil.* 2.2.1 and
3.1.64. A monument in Naples to the Siren Parthenope is mentioned by
Strabo (5.4.7) and Pliny (*HN* 3.5.62). Her name served as one designa-
tion of the city of Naples (see commentators on Vergil *geo.* 4.564).

105. Sebeto: Stream (ancient Sebethos) that flows into the Bay of Na-
ples just east of the city's center. See also *ecl.* 5.21; *el.* 2.3.6, 2.4.63;
ep. 1.44.9, 2.15.35, 2.51.42, and 3.9.7; *Arcadia, eclogue* 12.103–11; Vergil *Aen.*
7.734; Statius *Sil.* 1.2.263.

106. With *dulce sonant* compare Tibullus 1.3.60 (the start of a pentame-
ter). The language of 106–8 has parallels at Vergil *ecl.* 5.45–7 and 81–4.

109. Pliny the Elder (*HN* 3.6.82) names a Megaris "between Posillipo
and Naples" (*inter Pausilypum et Neapolim*). Statius (*Sil.* 2.2.80) speaks, in
the context of Inarime, Prochyta, Nesis and Euploea, of a Megalia that
"strikes the curving waves as it juts out" (*ferit curvos exserta . . . fluctus*).
This may well point to the modern Castel dell'Ovo.

110. Mergelline: Modern Mergellina, western suburb of Naples near the northeastern end of Posillipo, now amalgamated with the city itself. It is the site of Sannazaro's villa, given him by his patron and friend, Federico III, King of Naples, in June of 1499, and of Santa Maria del Parto, the church that he built and in which he lies buried. See also *ecl.* 2.3; *ep.* 1.2 passim, 2.1.15, 2.36 passim, 2.60.59, 3.9.3.

111. With lines 109–11 compare the rhetoric of Vergil *ecl.* 9.30–1.

120. Muse: One of nine Greek goddesses of inspiration, who presided over the arts. They were daughters of Zeus/Jupiter and Mnemosyne (Memory). Their Roman equivalents were the Camenae. The word muse is often synonymous with poetry itself. See also *ecl.* 2.22 and 49, 3.6, 4.17 and 72, 5.19 (with note); *Sal.* 13.

120. At *ecl.* 9.67 Vergil ends his poem with an hexameter that includes both *melius* (anticipating Sannazaro's *meliora*, 120) and *canemus*, while *plura* appears in the preceding verse.

122. Prochyta ("poured forth"), modern Procida, island between the Capo di Miseno (see below) and the island of Ischia, at the northwestern tip of the Bay of Naples. See also *ecl.* 3.76 (bis), 4.35, 5.11, fr. 15; *el.* 2.7.6; Statius *Sil.* 2.2.76.

122. Miseno: Ancient Misenum, town immediately to the south of Baiae (Baia) which gives its name to Capo di Miseno, the headland at the northwestern tip of the Bay of Naples. The name Misenus comes from Vergil *Aen.* 6 where his story is told (162–74). See also *el.* 2.4.61; Statius *Sil.* 3.1.151.

123. Sannazaro draws the phrase *grandes notas* from Ovid *T.* 3.3.72.

125. With *haec carmina fecit* compare Vergil *ecl.* 1.6 (*haec otia fecit*). Vergil's Lycidas is apostrophized at *ecl.* 9.2 and 37. With the setting as a whole compare Homer *Il.* 7.85–91 (as Hubbard, "Exile," 68).

128. Vergil combines *heia* and *age* at *Aen.* 4.569 (a line also echoed at *ecl.* 4.11), and *age* with *surge* at *Aen.* 3.169, 8.59 and 10.241. He uses the word *surgamus* at *ecl.* 10.75, also the antepenultimate hexameter of his poem. As in the case of Sannazaro it signals the end of a poem and, for Vergil, the conclusion of a poetry book.

II. Galatea

For his second poem Sannazaro turns from dialogue to monologue, and for his principal prototype to Vergil's second *eclogue* that, after five introductory lines, consists of Corydon's lament for the unresponsive Alexis.

1. Lycon: The name is found in Theocritus (*Id.* 2.76 and 5.8).

1. The phrase *forte . . . consederat* is also to be found in the opening line of Vergil *ecl.* 7 and *antro* is the final word of the hexameter that initiates the narrative in his sixth *eclogue* (13).

3. Mergilline: See also *DPV* 1. 26, 3.511 and on *ecl.* 1.110.

7. With *per obscuram . . . noctem* compare *sub obscurum noctis* (Vergil *geo.* 1.478). Singing at night, an active time for the fisherman, is one of Sannazaro's variations on standard Vergilian themes. The only potential moment of nocturnal singing in the *Eclogues* occurs at 9.63–5 and it is grudging. The song of the unhappy lover in *eclogue* 8 begins as night yields to day (14–7). In Vergil's second *eclogue* the shepherd begins singing when the sun is at its height. For *meditor* and pastoral song compare Vergil *ecl.* 1.2 and 6.8.

8. The initiation of the fisherman's song looks directly to the start of Corydon's speech at Vergil *ecl.* 2.6 (*O crudelis Alexi*). On Galatea see *ecl.* 1.86. With the phrase *immitis Galatea* compare Horace *c.* 1.33.2 (*immitis Glycerae*).

10. *Scopuli* are often emblematic of the adamant or stubborn, e.g. at Horace *c.* 3.7.21. With *scopulis impegimus* compare Silius *Pun.* 12.187 (*impingitur aequor*).

11. Compare Sannazaro's language with Vergil *ecl.* 9.57–8. For the juxtaposition between nature's quiet and a lover's distraction Sannazaro may be drawing on Vergil's characterization of Dido at *Aen.* 4.522–32.

12. The rhythm and sound of this line echo those of Vergil *ecl.* 1.1.

13. Zephyr: Wind from the west. See *ecl.* 3.55; *Sal.* 21; *DPV* 2.28.

14. The rare word *conivent* is used by Lucretius (*DRN* 5.778) of eclipses of the heavenly bodies.

17. The phraseology is taken from Nemesianus *ecl.* 2.40 (*heu, heu, nulla meae tangit te cura salutis*).

18. Praxinoe and Polybotas: Names from Theocritus (*Id.* 15.1 and 10.15)

21. Aenaria: The Latin name for modern Ischia, island off the north-western tip of the Bay of Naples whose counterpart is Capri off the southern cape. Its Greek names are Pithecusa(e) and Inarime, the latter of which is used by Vergil at *Aen.* 9.716 where it is first extant (for details see *Vergil: Aeneid: Book IX*, ed. P. Hardie [Cambridge, 1994], on *Aen.* 9.715–6). See also *ecl.* 3.72–3, 4.35, fr. 15.

22. The Cam(o)enae were the Roman Muses, standing by metonymy for poetry itself. See 49 below; *Sal.* 13; *ep.* 1.2.5.

23. At Ovid *M.* 3.171, Hyale ("glassy") is a nymph in Diana's train. The name also appears at *ecl.* 3.65 and 72; *DPV* 3.293 (the name of a daughter of the river Jordan). Here Costanza d'Avalos (1460–1541), Duchess of Francavilla and sister of Alfonso d'Avalos, is most likely meant. In 1503 "she held the fortress of Ischia for four months against the blockade of a French fleet" (Mustard, *The Piscatory Eclogues*, on *ecl.* 2.23).

25. Neptune: God of the sea. See also *ecl.* 4.51; *DPV* 3.474 and 507.

28. The reed (*avena*), as at Vergil *ecl.* 1.2 and 10.51, stands as metonomy for pastoral poetry.

29. Compare Nemesianus *ecl.* 2.69 (*nostros contemnis amores*).

32. Euploea ("fair sail," an epithet of Aphrodite/Venus), small island in the Bay of Naples off the southwestern end of Posillipo (modern La Gaiola). It is also mentioned at *ecl.* 4.66 and fr. 1. Compare Statius *Sil.* 2.2.79 and 3.1.149 where it is likewise named in conjunction with Nesis (148). In the words of the Touring Club Italiano guide to *Napoli e Dintorni* (Milan, 1975), 326, the name was "dato a Venere, della quale ivi sorgeva un tempietto per implorare felice navigazione." At *Sil.* 3.1.150 Statius speaks of *Lucrina Venus*. See also on *ecl.* 3.25.

33. Nesis: See on *ecl.* 1.14.

34. The phrase *vere novo* is used by Vergil at *ecl.* 10.74 and *geo.* 1.43.

35. See commentators on Lucilius fr. 1224–5 (ed. Krenkel); Cicero *De div.* 2.33; Horace *sat.* 2.4.30 and Pliny *HN* 2.41.109 for further details on this superstition.

37. Tyre, along with Sidon, in Lebanon, was a famous source of purple dye that came from the murex (purple-fish).

39. The enumeration of potential gifts to the beloved is a standard motif in pastoral. Besides Vergil *ecl.* 2.36–43 see also Theocritus *Id.* 3.10 and 34–5, 11.40–2.

42. Melisaeus: Giovanni Pontano (1429–1503), whose regular Latin name in the Neapolitan Academy was Jovianus (Gioviano), Sannazaro's mentor and friend. See also *ecl.* 4.69; *el.* 1.9 *passim*, 1.11.15, 2.2.11, 3.2.42; *ep.* 1.13.4, 2.15.46, 2.62.3; *Arcadia* 12, *eclogue*, passim. The name here derives from Pontano's elegy for his wife Adriana entitled *Meliseus*.

43. Parallels for the consecration that Sannazaro describes are to be found at Vergil *ecl.* 2.36–8 and 5.85–6 where the passing of gifts is emblematic of the continuity of (poetic) tradition. Compare also Theocritus *Id.* 7.43 and 128–29.

43. Vergil uses the phrase *alto sub rupe canet* of a singer at *ecl.* 1.56.

45. The shepherd boasts of his abilities as a singer also at Vergil *ecl.* 2.31–3 (compare also Calpurnius Siculus *ecl.* 2.28–30). On Sannazaro's primacy in his *Piscatoria*, see also *ecl.* 4.17–20.

45. With the word *acta* Sannazaro may again be punning on his pseudonym in the Academy, Actius Syncerus. See on *ecl.* 1.1 and *ecl.* 4.17–20.

49. With *miseram . . . perdidit*, compare Vergil *geo.* 4.494 (*miseram . . . perdidit*).

50. Vergil uses doublets of *ite* at *ecl.* 1.74, 7.44 and 10.77 (twice of goats and once of bullocks), as well as at *Aen.* 9.116–7.

53. With *despicis*, compare Vergil *ecl.* 8.32.

53. Glaucus: See on *ecl.* 1.46.

55. On the boast compare Vergil *ecl.* 2.60–2.

58. See also Calpurnius Siculus *ecl.* 3.24–5.

62. With the phrase *externas trans pontum quaerere terras* compare Vergil *Aen.* 6.311–2 (*ubi frigidus annus / trans pontum fugat et terris immitit apricis*).

65. Boreas: The north wind. See also *DPV* 2.27 and 457; *el.* 3.3.42.

66. With *rigidis numquam non cana pruinis* compare Vergil *geo.* 2.376 (*frigora nec tantum cana concreta pruina*) and 4.518 (*arva . . . numquam viduata pruinis*). The challenges that heat and chill offer the happy or distraught lover are commonplaces of amatory poetry (see, e.g., Vergil *ecl.* 10.64–9 and Horace *c.* 1.22.17–22). For such extremes in a didactic context see Vergil *geo.* 3.339–83.

67. Auster: South wind. See also *DPV* 2.457.

70. The notion has an Horatian ring. Compare *c.* 2.16.18–20 and 3.1.37–40.

72. Compare the sentiments of Vergil *ecl.* 10.69.

78. Caieta, modern Gaeta, town on the southern shore of Latium between Rome and Naples. See also *ecl.* 3.29, and on *el.* 3.1.37.

78. Cuma(e), Greek Cyme (as Statius *Sil.* 4.3.65 and 5.3.168): Town on the Campanian coast fronting the Tyrrhenian Sea, just north of the Bay of Naples. It was founded by Greek colonists from Chalkis in Euboea, and famous for its Sibyl. See also *ecl.* 4.43; *el.* 2.4.13, 2.7.22, 2.9 *passim*; Statius *Sil.* 3.5.97, 4.3.24 and 115.

80. Compare Vergil's language at *Aen.* 5.165–6 (of a ship's captain to his helmsman).

82. For *scopulos infames* see Horace *c.* 1.3.20 and Statius *The.* 3.121.

83. In having the thoughts of his protagonist take a negative twist, Sannazaro turns away from his main model, Vergil's second *eclogue*, to follow Theocritus *Id.* 3.25–6, Vergil *ecl.* 8.59–60, and Calpurnius Siculus *ecl.* 3.87–8.

83. In the line immediately following the conclusion of his protagonist's speech, Sannazaro uses the same verb (*iactabat*) that Vergil gives his narrator at *ecl.* 2.5, the line preceding the beginning of Corydon's monologue—one of his final bows to the Vergilian poem that most influenced him here.

86. Lucifer is the planet Venus at her morning rising. See also *ep.* 2.58.5. In his concluding verse Sannazaro is echoing Vergil *ecl.* 8.17 as well as the concluding pentameter (94) of Tibullus 1.3: [*Aurora*] *Luciferum roseis*

candida portet equis (may bright [Dawn] on rose-red horses bring in the Day-star).

III. MOPSUS

Sannazaro here presents a third type of pastoral poem, the contest. This usually consists of an introduction followed by the antiphonal verses of two protagonists challenging each other. A judge from among the audience then pronounces the winner and awards prizes. Sannazaro would have found several examples in the poems of Theocritus and Vergil whose third and seventh *eclogues* were his primary models. Mopsus is the name of a shepherd in Vergil *ecl.* 5 and 8. Sannazaro's opening words are the same as those in Vergil *ecl.* 3.

1. Aegon: A shepherd's name in Vergil *ecl.* 3 and 5.

1. Bauli: According to Tacitus (*Ann.* 14.4) the name of a villa "washed by a curve of the sea between the promontory of Misenum and the lake at Baiae" (*quae promunturium Misenum inter et Baianum lacum flexo mari adluitur*), which is to say near the northwestern point of the Bay of Naples, between the Lucrine Lake and Capo di Miseno, modern Bacoli (see also *el.* 2.7.5).

2. The language of this line echoes Vergil *ecl.* 1.43.

3. Chromis: A shepherd at Vergil *ecl.* 6.13.

3. Iolas: Iollas is a shepherd's name in Vergil *ecl.* 2 and 3.

4. Notus: The south wind. See also *DPV* 2.26 and *el.* 3.3.42.

5. *Vacui lusistis* is derived from Horace *c.* 1.32.1–2 (*vacui . . . lusimus*).

6. The phrase *ingrata per otia* comes from Horace *c.* 1.15.3 (*ingrato . . . otio*).

7. Celadon: The name ("resounding") appears twice in Ovid (*M.* 5.144, 12.250).

8. For the *pagurus* see Pliny *HN* 9.31.97.

12. Compare Theocritus *Id.* 21.9–12.

13. Inarime: Ischia (see on *ecl.* 2.21). Sannazaro refers to the route into exile taken by him and his monarch, Federico, king of Naples since 1496

and the last of its Aragonese monarchs. They departed from Ischia, September 6, 1501, and ended at Blois on the Loire in central France. (When Federico abdicated in favor of Louis XII of France, he had been given the County of Maine in exchange for his kingdom.) See also *ecl.* 4.81–6 and 5.113–5. Federico died at Tours in November, 1504, and Sannazaro returned to Naples early the next year.

17. The rocky coast of the Ligurians: The northwestern shoreline of Italy. See also *ecl.* 5.113; *el.* 2.1.71, 3.1.169; *ep.* 2.61.2.

18. The Stoechadae are the modern Îles d'Hyères in the Mediterranean off the French coast at Toulon. See also *el.* 3.1.172.

18. Rhône: Ancient Rhodanus, central river of southern France, debouches into the Mediterranean not far to the west of Toulon. See also *el.* 1.8.51, 3.1.110, 3.2.75.

19. The name Amilcon, like Lycabas (26) and Milcon (*ecl.* 1.42), may be a synonym for Sannazaro himself.

21. But perhaps Sannazaro is also thinking of the blue war-paint associated with the Britons (compare Caesar *BG* 5.14; Propertius 2.18.31; Martial 11.53.1). See also *ecl.* 5.115, and compare Vergil *ecl.* 1.66, where the distant Britons form part of a list of possible peoples and places to receive the dispossessed Meliboeus.

23. For this practice see the discussions in Kidwell, *Sannazaro* 99, 133, 227, n. 34. Sannazaro draws his phrase *nudos per litora pisces*, from Vergil *ecl.* 1.60 (*nudos in litore pisces*). Both poems are deeply concerned with exile.

24. With *luctus renova* compare Tibullus 2.6.41 (*luctus renoventur*) and Vergil *Aen.* 2.3 (*renovare dolorem*).

25. The Lucrine lake at Baiae (Baia), separated from the sea by a narrow stretch of land. See *ecl.* 1.42; *el.* 2.7.1–4.

26. Lycabas is the name of three characters in Ovid's *Metamorphoses*: a companion of Acoetes (3.624), a companion of Phineus (5.60), and a centaur (12.302).

29. Caieta: See on *ecl.* 2.78.

30. For this phenomenon see also Strabo 3.1.5 (referring to Posidonius), Statius *Sil.* 2.7.25, Tacitus *Germ.* 45.1, and Juvenal *sat.* 14.279–80.

34. Bellovaci: A tribe of southwestern Belgium, mentioned frequently throughout Caesar's *De Bello Gallico*, whose name survives in the modern place-name Beauvais.

34. Morini: Another Belgian tribe living near the Channel coast, also mentioned frequently by Caesar (at *Aen.* 8.727 Vergil calls them "the farthest distant of men" [*extremi . . . hominum*]).

35. Tarbelli: A tribe in the extreme southwest of Aquitania whose name survives in the modern Tarbes. Tibullus uses the adjective *Tarbellus* to describe the Pyrenees at 1.7.9, in a poem written to honor his patron Messalla Corvinus's triumph over the Aquitani.

36. Loire: Ancient Liger, river of northwest France. See also *el.* 3.1.157; *ep.* 2.60.34; Caesar *BG* 7.5.4; Tibullus 1.7.12.

38. Chloris: An Horatian name, of a girl (*c.* 2.5.18) and of an old woman (*c.* 3.15.8).

38. The phrase *tu modo* opens the hexameter at Vergil *ecl.* 4.8. Likewise *si quid habes* appears at the same point in the line at Vergil *ecl.* 3.52, just before the start of the amoebaean contest.

40. Mopsus: A shepherd's name in Vergil *ecl.* 5 and 8. With *gracilem avenam* see notes to *ecl.* 1.28 and 102, and compare Vergil *ecl.* 1.2. At *ecl.* 10.71 Vergil mentions a "slender rush" (*gracili hibisco*), in an analogy between weaving and the making of poetry.

42. Compare Vergil *ecl.* 7.24.

43. With *alternos . . . versus* compare Vergil *ecl.* 7.18 (*alternis . . . versibus*). Lines 44–5 also look to 7.19–20, the introduction to a contest, while 46–8 echo the subsequent verses at 7.21–4.

45. For earlier examples of the poetic competition that follows, besides Vergil *ecl.* 3, 5, 8 and especially 7, see also Theocritus *Id.* 5–10.

47. With *Chlorida placem* compare Calpurnius Siculus *ecl.* 3.40 (*quo Phyllida carmine placem*).

49. With the phrase *nostrum sanet medicina furorem* compare Vergil *ecl.* 10.60 (*nostri medicina furoris*) and Propertius 2.1.57 (*sanat medicina dolores*).

50. Sannazaro's use of *mea cura* in apposition is based on Vergil *ecl.* 1.57 (*tua cura*) and 10.22 (*tua cura Lycoris*).

51. Nisa (Nysa): The name of a girl who scorns her shepherd-lover in Vergil *ecl.* 8 (18, 26).

53. See note on *ecl.* 1.54. Vergil uses the phrase *vilior alga* at *ecl.* 7.42 and Horace at *sat.* 2.5.8.

54. Compare Propertius 2.4.19 (*tranquillo tuta descendis flumine cumba*) and Ovid *H.* 10.65 (*ut rate felici pacata per aequora labar*).

58. For *feriant . . . procellae* see Vergil *Aen.* 1.102–3 (*procella . . . ferit*).

59. The Cori are winds from the north (see also *DPV* 3.465). With *turbentur harenae* compare Vergil *Aen.* 3.557 (*miscentur harenae*).

60. With *tremit iam terra tumultu* compare Ennius *Ann.* 309 (ed. Skutsch): *Africa terribili tremit horrida terra tumultu.*

63. Compare Tibullus 1.8.69 (*oderunt, Pholoe, moneo, fastidia divi*).

64. Pithacusae: "Land of the monkey," one of the original Greek names for Ischia. See on *ecl.* 2.21.

65. Or, reading *falsum* instead of *salsum*, "treacherous" sea.

70. Thunderer: Cult-title of Jupiter in his role as sky-god. Jupiter Tonans had a shrine on the Capitoline separate from the grand temple to Jupiter Optimus Maximus. See also *DPV* 1.217; *LMC* 26; *el.* 1.7.33; *ep.* 1.28.3, 2.16.9, 2.22.1. The island of Cyprus is in the eastern Mediterranean. Crete, Samos and Lemnos are all islands in the Aegean Sea, in its south, east and north respectively.

73. Here and in what follows Sannazaro is thinking of Vergil *ecl.* 7.53–68.

74. Gradivus: Mars, Roman god of war; Rhodope: Mountain range in Thrace (see Vergil *ecl.* 6.30 and context); Cyllene: Mountain in Arcadia where Mercury was born (see *Sal.* 31); Phoebe: Diana (see also *ep.* 1.52.3); Ortygia: Another name for the island of Delos, birthplace of Diana and

Apollo; Tritonia: Pallas Athena or, in Rome, Minerva (the name comes from Lake Triton in Libya, sacred to the goddess); Hymettus: Mountain east of Athens, here standing for Athens itself.

79. With *texendis . . . nassis vimine* compare Vergil *ecl.* 2.72 (*viminibus . . . detexere*) — an interesting merger of the pastoral and piscatory worlds.

80. Pholoe: The name of a girl in three odes of Horace and in Tibullus 1.8.

81. The phrase *contemnere ventos* is Vergilian (*geo.* 2.360 and *Aen.* 3.77, both at line endings).

85. A reference to the famous (and treacherous) sandy shoals, Syrtis Major and Minor, off the coast of Libya between Carthage and Cyrene. See Pliny *HN* 5.4.26.

86. Sinuessa: Coastal town in Latium near the border of Campania. See also *ecl.* 5.III, and on *el.* 1.1.3. Dic(ae)archus was the founder of Roman Puteoli (modern Pozzuoli) on the northwest of the Bay of Naples (as Statius *Sil.* 2.2.3 and 96 with frequent other references). See also *ecl.* 5.12. For the *p(h)ager* see Pliny *HN* 9.24.57 and 32.53.150.

87. The cliffs of Hercules: See on *ecl.* 1.42. Amalphis is modern Amalfi, situated on the Gulf of Salerno, on the south side of the peninsula that forms the southern arc of the Bay of Naples. For the *synodos* see [ps.] Ovid *Hal.* 107 and Pliny *HN* 37.67.182.

88. Parthenope: Modern Naples, said to be named for one of the Sirens buried there. See on *ecl.* 1.104. Parthenope is also mentioned at *ecl.* 4.16; *el.* 1.11.71, 2.1.32, 2.4.64, 3.1.72, 3.3.52; *ep.* 3.9.1 as well as by Vergil at *geo.* 4.564.

95. *Memini contendere* is Sannazaro's last echo of Vergil *ecl.* 7 (here 69).

96. The phrase *horrida ventosi . . . murmura ponti* is based on Vergil *ecl.* 9.57–8 (*omnes / . . . ventosi . . . murmuris aurae*).

98. Compare Theocritus *Id.* 9.25, a bow to a "piscatory" moment outside of *Id.* 21.

99. Circeio: Modern Circeo, town and mountain on the coast of Latium south of Rome. It was supposed by Vergil (*Aen.* 7.10–24) to have been the same as Aeaea, in *Odyssey* 10 the island of Circe. It was noted in an-

tiquity for its oysters (Horace *sat.* 2.4.33; Pliny *HN* 32.21.62; Juvenal *sat.* 4.140).

IV. PROTEUS

Ferdinando of Aragon (1488–1550), Duke of Calabria, son of King Federico of Aragon (1451–1504). He was for a while held a virtual prisoner in Barcelona after the fall of the House of Aragon in 1501, but became later the Viceroy of Valencia, where he was known as a patron of literature and the arts. Sannazaro's chief model in this eclogue is one of Vergil's most inventive pastorals, the sixth *eclogue.* It consists of an introduction to a patron that also is concerned with poetics. This is followed by the entrance of a third-person narrator (in Vergil's case Silenus; for Sannazaro Proteus) who enumerates a mixture of topics in a variety of styles. Among those which the two poems have in common are the apostrophizing of hapless lovers and the initiation of poets.

1. Sannazaro is making a bow to the opening of Vergil *ecl.* 4 (*Sicelides Musae, paulo maiora canamus*) which also announces a heightening of pastoral themes.

2. Crater: Name given to the Bay of Naples (Cicero *ad Att.* 2.8.2; Strabo 5.4.3 and 8).

4. Tibullus applies the epithet *caerula* to the Nereid Thetis at 1.5.46.

6. Sannazaro is here drawing on Vergil *geo.* 4.426–8.

7. Compare Statius's bow to the emperor Domitian at *The.* 1.22.

8. Pyrenees: See on *DPV* 2.198.

9. Vergil uses the phrase *dulcia arva* at *ecl.* 1.3 in a context concerned with exile.

10. Ebro: The ancient Iberus that flows from northern Spain southeast into the Mediterranean. See also *DPV* 2.203.

11. The phrase *rumpe moras* is Vergilian (*geo.* 3.43, *Aen.* 4.569, on which see also *ecl.* 1.128). Spain is ancient Hispania.

13. Modern Tagus or Tejo. See also *DPV* 2.202.

18. Lycaeus: Mountain in Arcadia mentioned many times by Vergil (first at *ecl.* 10.15). Sannazaro is referring to his *Arcadia* where it is named in

the Prologue. Compare also on *ecl.* 5.101 and the description of the piscatory eclogues at *el.* 3.2.57–8. It may not be coincidental that a parallel etymology is to be found in the names Lycidas (one of the protagonists of *ecl.* 1), Lycon (the principal character of *ecl.* 2, whose naming frames the poem), and Lycabas (*ecl.* 3.26), a clear pseudonym of Sannazaro.

19. In the phrase *deduxi primus* Sannazaro uses words in antiquity redolent of stylistics. For instance, in his great concluding "seal" poem to his first collection of odes, *c.* 3.30, Horace, addressing the muse Melpomene, can speak of himself as the "first" (*princeps*, 13) "to have led" (*deduxisse*, 14) Aeolian song to Italian measures. He reserves the word *primus* only for his originality in writing the *Epodes* (compare *epi.* 1.19.23). It is not coincidental that Vergil uses the participle *deductum* at *ecl.* 6.5 in a context that influenced Sannazaro as he wrote these lines. By the reference to his name, Actius Syncerus, in the phrase *litoream Musam* (17), Sannazaro is urging the reader to ponder his originality in the *Piscatoria*. See also on *ecl.* 1.1 as well as 2.44–5, and compare *DPV* 3.429–30.

22. Rocks of Minerva: Modern Punta Campanella, the cape that brings to an end the peninsula of Sorrento (ancient Surrentum), forming the southern arc of the Bay of Naples. It is separated from Capri by a narrow strait. See Ovid *M.* 15.709 where the *promunturium Minervae* is placed between Capri and Sorrento. Statius (*Sil.* 2.2.2) locates the villa of Pollius Felix between Sorrento and "rocks burdened by Minerva's temple" (*saxa . . . templis onerata Minervae*), and Pliny (*HN* 3.5.62) speaks of "Sorrento with its promontory of Minervae, once seat of the Sirens" (*Surrentum cum promuntorio Minervae Sirenum quondam sede*). (Strabo, 5.4.3 and 8, appropriately entitles the cape Athenaeum.) The temple's location may be suggested in the name of the town Massa Lubrense located several kilometers to the west of Sorrento, if Lubrense is a corruption of the Latin *delubrum* (temple).

22–23. *Pascentem . . . phocas* looks to Vergil *geo.* 4.395 (*pascit . . . phocas*), also of Proteus. The phrase *divino carmine* comes from Vergil *ecl.* 6.67.

24. Melanthius: The name is Theocritean (*Id.* 5.150) but originates in Homer (*Od.* 17.212 and elsewhere).

24. Phrasidamus: See Theocritus *Id.* 7.3.

25. Capri: Ancient Capreae, island in the Tyrrhenian Sea off the southern tip of the Bay of Naples. See also *ecl.* 5.77.

27. Compare Vergil *Aen.* 7.701–2 and the reaction to the song of Silenus at Vergil *ecl* 6.27–8.

29. With *cantabat ad auras* compare Vergil *ecl.* 1.56 (*canet . . . ad auras*).

30. Typhoeus: A monster, often associated with the Giants, done in by Jupiter. He is considered by Vergil (*Aen.* 9.715–6) to be buried under the island of Ischia and by Strabo (5.4.9) under that of Procida. See also *ecl.* 2.21; *ep.* 1.62.4, 2.61.3. With *terrigena . . . Typhoeus*, compare Ovid *M.* 5.325 (*terrigenam . . . Typhoea*).

34. With *partes de monte revulsas* compare Ovid *M.* 13.882 (*partem . . . e monte revulsam*).

37. Compare Vergil *geo.* 1.328.

41. In the narration that begins at line 41 Sannazaro is imitating the structure, and drawing on the lexicon, of the song of Silenus at Vergil *ecl.* 6.31–86. With *hinc* (41), *addit* (43) and the apostrophe to Pausilypus (47) Sannazaro also makes use of the language of ekphrasis so frequent in *DPV.* For *hinc* compare Vergil *Aen.* 8.635, 666, 678, 685; for forms of *addo*, *Aen.* 8.637 and 666; for apostrophe *Aen.* 8.643 and 668 (and, secondarily, *Aen.* 6.31).

41. See on *ecl.* 1.42. Hercules supposedly made the road beside the Lucrine lake so that the cattle of Geryon that he had driven from Spain could pass along the marshy ground (they are also mentioned at Vergil *Aen.* 8.203–4 and in the story of Cacus that follows).

42. Sannazaro is punning on the supposed origin of the name Pompeii from *pompa* (see Servius on Vergil *Aen.* 7.662).

43. Phoebus: Apollo, often in his role as god of the sun. See also *ecl.* 5.23 and fr. 7; *DPV* 2.302 and 376, 3.483.

43. On Cumae see on *ecl.* 2.78 and below on lines 61–2. The Cimmerii were a semi-mythical people from north of the Black Sea who were also said to dwell between Baiae and Cumae (see further Strabo 5.4.5). They were often associated with the underworld as was the nearby Lacus

Avernus (see, e.g., Pliny *HN* 3.5.61). Statius speaks of "Cimmerian gloom" (*Cimmerium chaos*) at *Sil.* 3.2.92, and Silius of *Cimmerias . . . domos* (*Pun.* 12.132).

44. Trivia: Diana of the crossroads. Vergil juxtaposes *Triviae* and *lucos* at *Aen.* 6.13.

48. Apostrophe along with the prominent appearance of the adjective *infelix* (50) helps these lines resonate with the story of Pasiphaë that Vergil has Silenus tell in the sixth *eclogue* (45–60).

54. The phrase *siste gradum* is Vergilian (*Aen.* 6.465).

56. Panope: See *DPV* 3.508 and Vergil *Aen.* 5.825. Drymo: Compare Dryope at *DPV* 3.295.

57. Cymothoe: Sea-nymph, coupled with Triton at Vergil *Aen.* 1.144, as assistant to Neptune. Rhoë: See *DPV* 3.294. Pherusa and Dinamene: See *DPV* 3.288 where they are coupled.

59. With *tum canit* Sannazaro continues his reminders of Vergil *ecl.* 6 (here of line 61).

60. For the adjective *auricomus* see *DPV* 3.493 and Vergil *Aen.* 6.141 where it qualifies the golden bough.

62. Sannazaro would have us remember here the voyage of Aeneas to Italy, especially the moment, at the end of *Aen.* 5, where the fleet passes by the rocks of the Sirens, and at the beginning of book 6 where Aeneas reaches the cave of the Sibyl and the "Chalcidican citadel" (*Chalcidica arce, Aen.* 6.17) at Cumae. The Cumaean Sibyl was supposed to have originally come from Chalkis in Euboea.

66. Euploea: See note on *ecl.* 2.32.

67. The Pharos or lighthouse is probably the light at La Gaiola, but the reference may also be to the light on Capri for which it stands by metonymy. See Statius *Sil.* 3.5.101.

68. Rocks of the Teleboans: I.e. Capri, said to have been founded by the Teleboae from Acarnania (compare Vergil *Aen.* 7.735, and Statius *Sil.* 3.5.100–1 for both the Pharos and the Teleboae). See also *ecl.* 5.77.

68. Sarnus: Modern Sarno, river that enters the Bay of Naples near Pompeii. See *Sal.* 19, 88, 91–2; *Arcadia* 12, *prosa*; Vergil *Aen.* 7.738; Strabo 4.5.8; Pliny *HN* 3.5.62. Vergil uses the phrase *pinguia culta* three times (*geo.* 4.372, *Aen.* 8.63 and 10.141).

69. The repetition of the phrase *tum canit* is a reminder of its second appearance in Vergil *ecl.* 6, this time at the start of line 64. Sannazaro's Melisaeus replaces Vergil's Gallus. As at a parallel stage in Vergil's poem we are for a moment in a world of poetry and poetics, a time when a presumed heightening of genre from pastoral to didactic is in question.

69. As at *ecl.* 2.42, Melisaeus stands for Giovanni Pontano, Sannazaro's teacher and patron (see on *ecl.* 2.42), while Corydon is Vergil.

70. The phrase *labris admoverit* is drawn from Vergil *ecl.* 3.43 (*labra admovi*).

71–2. These lines allude specifically to the opening verses of Vergil's second and eighth *eclogues*, and lines 73–4 to Pontano's *Urania* and *Meteora* (see also *el.* 1.9.36–7, 2.2.11–14).

71. The man: I.e. Vergil, as Servius on *ecl.* 2.1: *Corydonis in persona Vergilius intellegitur*.

75. *Quid referam aut* is another signpost referring to Vergil *ecl.* 6 (74, *quid loquar aut*).

75. Stabiae: Modern Castellamare di Stabia, southeast of Pompeii along the southern shore of the Bay of Naples. See also Statius *Sil.* 3.5.104.

76. Maidens: The Sirens (see on *ecl.* 1.104).

77. Vesuvius: Ancient Ves(a)evus (see also *ecl.* 5.79). Vergil describes the volcano as "the ridge of Vesaevus" (*Vesaevum iugum, geo.* 2.224), and Statius speaks of the "destructiveness of maddened Vesevus" (*insani . . . damna Vesevi, Sil.* 4.8.5, a poem published probably in 95 and therefore some sixteen years after the devastating eruption of 79 CE). Vergil perhaps, and Statius certainly, is punning on the Latin *saevus* ("fierce"). (See also Statius *Sil.* 5.3.205, published in 96 or shortly thereafter.)

79. Compare Vergil *Aen.* 8.629 (*pugnata . . . in ordine bella*).

81. The phrase *luget ademptum* is used by Ovid (*H.* 13.95; *M.* 11.273).

85. For the Loire (ancient Liger) see *ecl.* 3.36. The reference is to the exile of Federico of Aragon to France after his fall (the subject of *ecl.* 3.13–23. See also 5.113–5). Tours, where he died, September 9, 1504, is on the Loire. With the language compare Ovid *M.* 12.615–6.

86. As at *LMC* 56, Sannazaro is thinking of Lucretius's apostrophe at *DRN* 2.14: *O miseras hominum mentes, o pectora caeca!* (O pitiable minds of men! O blind hearts!).

96. With *vitreas sedes* compare Vergil *geo.* 4.350 (*vitreis sedilibus*).

V. HERPYLIS THE WITCH

The dedicatee, Cassandra Marchese, was a lady-in-waiting to Queen Giovanna, daughter of King Ferrante I and wife of King Ferdinando II (Ferrantino). See also *el.* 3.2; *ep.* 2.57 and 3.2. She replaces the unnamed dedicatee of Vergil *ecl.* 8.1–13.

Sannazaro here introduces yet another form of pastoral poem in which intercalary refrains figure prominently. Vergil's eighth *eclogue* is his primary prototype, though Theocritus *Id.* 2 is also important for both poets. It consists of an introduction followed by two expansive, essentially parallel, segments, given to two different singers. The first is a lover's lament, the second a magic ritual. Sannazaro reverses the order.

1. The phrase *vulgatos amores* is Ovidian (*M.* 4.276).

3. Dorylas: The name appears at Ovid *M.* 5.129–30, and 12.380, as well as at Calpurnius Siculus *ecl.* 2.96. Thelgon: "Enchantress" in Greek. Teleboean sea: See on *ecl.* 4.67–8. The language is drawn from Vergil *ecl.* 8.3.

5. Platamon: The name survives in the modern Via Chiatamone, at the base of the Pizzofalcone quarter in what is now central Naples, just inland from present-day Via Partenope and the Castel dell'Ovo (compare the mention of *Platamoniae excavatae . . . specus* by Pontano at *De bello Neapolitano* 6). Serapis is an allusion to the so-called Serapeum (actually the ancient town market) at Pozzuoli.

7. Pallas: Minerva. The language alludes to Vergil *ecl.* 8.6.

8. I treat *aurum et subtegmina* as an example of hendiadys. The tale of Arachne of Maeonia begins at Ovid *M.* 6.5. For gold in the materials she uses see *M.* 6.68.

9. Dryads: Wood nymphs. Compare the language of Vergil at *Aen.* 1.499–500.

15. Sannazaro's language again parallels the introduction to Vergil *ecl.* 8 (11–12). Vergil uses the phrase *non iniussa cano* at *ecl.* 6.9, also as part of a dedication. Compare Vergil's address to Lucius Alfenus Varus at *ecl.* 6.6–12.

17. With *non invitus Apollo* at the end of an hexameter, compare Vergil *geo.* 4.7 (*vocatus Apollo*).

19. Pierian maidens: A name for the Muses, from Pieria, north of Mt. Olympus in northern Greece. See also *el.* 1.5.6, 1.10.10, 1.11.29, 2.2.16, 3.1.3, 3.3.46; *ep.* 1.11.3, 2.15.20.

21. Herpylis: The name may be connected with the Greek word for thyme. Sebeto: See on *ecl.* 1.105.

22. The title Euboid means Neapolitan by metonymy with nearby Cumae, colony of Chalkis on the Greek island of Euboea. See also Statius *Sil.* 1.2.263.

23. Alcon: A shepherd at Vergil *ecl.* 5.11. The parallels between lines 17–9 and 23 suggest a complementarity between the narrating voice and Alcon.

25. Compare Vergil's description of Dido's sister Anna as *unanimam . . . sororem* (*Aen.* 4.8).

26. Compare the description of the priestess assisting Dido in Vergil *Aen.* 4.509 and 518, and of Medea in Ovid *M.* 7.183.

27. For other rare uses of the verb *submurmuro* see Augustine *Conf.* 6.9 and 8.11.

30. For *magicis sacris* see Vergil *ecl.* 8.66 and its extended context.

32. Strings are a component of the magic used by Vergil's witch at *ecl.* 8.73–5. It should also be noted that, although Sannazaro here has Vergil *ecl.* 8 in mind as background for his two songs, both the core and the concluding refrains have two variants, unlike those of his model.

33. Haemonia (Thessaly) was notorious in antiquity for its associations with magic. Compare, e.g., Lucan BC 6.480 (*Haemonium carmen*) and 486 (*Haemonias artes*).

34. With *pellere nubila caelo* compare Tibullus 1.2.49, also of a witch who *tristi depellit nubila caelo*.

38. Ovid uses the phrase *rapidae flammae* at M. 2.123.

39. Maeon: Name of a Rutulian warrior at Vergil *Aen.* 10.337.

42. Compare Vergil *ecl.* 8.78.

50. Lines 49–50 are based on two adynata. The open sea will no more become calm than pumice, proverbial symbol of dryness, will "grow fat." For the last see Plautus *Aul.* 297 and *Per.* 41–2 (to get money from an old man is like getting water from dry pumice) and for further details, see A. Otto, *Die Sprichwörter und sprichwörtlichen Redensarten der Römer* (Leipzig, 1890), 290. Compare Catullus 1.2, *arida . . . pumice*. Sannazaro is thinking back to Vergil *ecl.* 8.80 where soft mud and hard wax become their opposites as a result of magic.

58. On the "delaying" fish and its use as an ingredient in love potions see Pliny *HN* 9.41.79 (*amatoriis . . . veneficiis infamis est*) as well as 32.1.2–6 for an elaborate description of its supposed ability to delay.

60. Compare Theocritus *Id.* 2.58, Sannazaro's other main model for this poem.

65. Eoan: I.e. eastern or oriental (see on *DPV* 1.18).

65. Aegle: Name of a nymph at Vergil *ecl.* 6.20–1.

67. See Pliny *HN* 9.72.155: "Nor are there lacking dread poisons, as in the sea-slug which in the Indian sea infects even by its touch and immediately causes vomiting and looseness of the stomach" (*Nec venena cessant dira, ut in lepore qui in Indico mari etiam tactu pestilens vomitum dissolutionemque stomachi protinus creat*).

72. The phrase *pectoris aestus* also concludes an hexameter at Nemesianus *ecl.* 2.14.

76. Compare *ecl.* 2.1 and Vergil *ecl.* 7.1.

78. The phrase *alia parte* is ekphrastic. Compare Vergil *Aen.* 1.474 and 8.682 as well as *DPV* 1.325, 2.22 and 204, 3.379.

79. Ruins of Hercules: The reference is to Herculaneum on the east shore of the Bay of Naples, between Naples and Pompeii.

80. With the language of the refrain compare Ovid *M.* 13.838.

82. With *curva resonans super aequora concha* compare Vergil *Aen.* 6.171 (*cava dum personat aequora concha*). See R. G. Austin, ed., *P. Vergili Aeneidos: Liber Sextus* (Oxford, 1977), ad loc., for a list of passages where Triton puts a *concha* to use.

89. *Huc ades* is a Vergilian tag. Compare *ecl.* 2.45, 7.9, 9.39 and 43.

93. With 92–3 compare Vergil *ecl.* 9.41.

101. Maenalus: Mountain in Arcadia associated with pastoral song, here a reference to Sannazaro's *Arcadia* where it is named in the prologue (in conjunction with Mt. Lycaeus), *prosa* 9, *eclogue* 10.188. For Maenalus see also Vergil *ecl.* 8.21–61 passim, 10.15 and 55. In suggesting a parallel between Sannazaro's *Arcadia* and Vergil's *Eclogues*, the reference serves partially to differentiate the *Piscatoria* from the latter, however pervasive their influence. See also on *ecl.* 4.18 as well as *el.* 2.7.23.

101. The phrase *pendet fistula* is Vergilian (*ecl.* 7.24).

107. With Sannazaro's language here compare Vergil *ecl.* 4.58–9.

111. For Sinuessa see *ecl.* 3.86; *el.* 1.1.3; *ep.* 1.16.7. With *textas de vimine nassas* compare Vergil *geo.* 4.34 (*alvaria vimine texta*).

114. Var: Ancient Varus that enters the Mediterranean near Nice. See also *el.* 3.1.170.

115. Saône: Ancient Arar, tributary of the Rhône rising in the Vosges mountains of eastern France. See also *DPV* 2.196; *el.* 1.8.52; *ep.* 2.25.2.

115. Sannazaro is referring to his exile. See also *ecl.* 3.13–23 and 4.113–5.

118. Compare Vergil *ecl.* 1.75–6. The parallel suggests that two forms of exile merge here—the Petrarchan separation from the beloved and the poet's factual absence from Naples in 1501–5.

119. The language of 118–9 echoes that of Catullus 101.8–9, but Sannazaro is also making a final bow to Vergil *ecl.* 8 (here to line 60).

FRAGMENT OF AN ECLOGUE

This fragment of a piscatory eclogue is handed down in three drafts (see Note on the Text), separately from the other five piscatory eclogues. The second of the three drafts was the only one published, in the 1535 Aldine edition, under the title *Fragmentum eiusdem auctoris*. It may have been intended as an addition to the other five. Monti Sabia, "Storia," conjectures that it was written before the fifth eclogue (267) and that it was eventually dropped because it was a "poetic failure." It was probably Sannazaro's intention to dedicate it to Francesco Poderico, who is mentioned in line 10. The language and structure of the opening line recall the initial verse of Vergil *ecl.* 10 where an adjective and noun frame the line, where the third word is apostrophic (in Vergil's case the address is to a fountain nymph, in Sannazaro's, to an islet), and where the penultimate word is an imperative. As in the case of Vergil, Sannazaro may be signaling the end of his piscatory project, just as the opening of *eclogue* 4, perhaps half way through the collection, used allusion to Vergil to signal a new beginning.

1. Euploea: See on *ecl.* 2.32.

4. Compare the language of Ovid *M.* 7.815.

10. Poderico: Francesco Poderico (Pudericus), member of the Neapolitan Academy, supporter and critic of Sannazaro; he died in 1528, two years before Sannazaro himself. See also *el.* 2.2.29. Sannazaro compliments him by allusion, in lines 6–9, to Vergil's apostrophe to his patron Maecenas, at *geo.* 2.39–41, and, with *pars animae . . . meae*, to Horace's acknowledgement of Vergil as "half of my soul" (*animae dimidium meae, c.* 1.3.8). Poderico is a partial counterpart to Gallus in Vergil *ecl.* 10.

11. Doris: Sea-goddess, wife of Nereus and mother of the Nereids. See also *ep.* 1.2.3 and 1.23.4, as well as on *ecl.* 1.45.

12. Here Sannazaro is thinking of Vergil *Aen.* 6.172–3.

13. Lines 13–18 have much in common with Vergil *ecl.* 7.1–5. Both sets of lines anticipate an amoebaean exchange, here apparently without competition or judge. Compare Theocritus *Id.* 6. For the Lucrine lake (ancient *lacus Lucrinus*) see *ecl.* 3.25. Lucrine Venus is mentioned by Statius (*Sil.*

3.1.150). Her temple is perhaps to be identified with remains to be found between the lake and Baia.

16. The double use of *ambo* is a reminder of Vergil *ecl.* 7.4. Compare also Vergil *ecl.* 5.1–2.

22. Compare *ecl.* 5.72.

23. The two names are also linked at *ecl.* 3.80.

24. For Triton's "hollow horn" (*cava bucina*) see Ovid *M.* 1.335 and above, on *ecl.* 5.82.

25. Compare Ovid *F.* 1.117.

29. Melampos: Celebrated physician and soothsayer (see Vergil *geo.* 3.550). For his connection with hellebore see Pliny *HN* 25.21.47.

32. (H)erebus: God of darkness and son of Chaos. Chaos: The lower world imagined as a god. Erebus and Chaos appear together at Vergil *Aen.* 4.510.

37. Cymothoe: See *ecl.* 4.57. In classical mythology Clot(h)o is the Fate who spins man's destiny.

THE WILLOWS

Meter: dactylic hexameter.

First published 1526.

Traiano Cavaniglia or Cabanilla (Cabanilius in Latin), 1479–1528, Count of Montella and of Troia, protégé of King Ferdinando II (Ferrante) of Naples, member of Pontano's academy and friend of Sannazaro. See also *el.* 1.11.25, 2.2.37, and Kidwell, *Sannazaro*, 244, n. 31.

1. For the Latin expression *si vacat*, placed near the start of a poem, see Ovid *EP* 1.1.3, 3.3.1; Juvenal *sat.* 1.21.

3. Amathus: The goddess is Venus. Paphos and Amathus are towns on her island of Cyprus. For Paphos see also *el.* 1.4.27 and *ep.* 2.15.21; for Amathus, *ep.* 2.15.22.

10. Sannazaro is varying the sentiments of Catullus 50.10.

12. Greater things: Sannazaro is presumably alluding to the *Piscatoria* and *De Partu Virginis*.

13. Camenae: Roman goddesses, the equivalent of the Greek Muses, and metonymy for poetry itself. With *tenues Camoenas* compare Horace *c.* 2.16.38 (*spiritum Graiae tenuem Camenae*) where the adjective *tenuis* betokens at once personal modesty and a stylistics of restraint. See also on *ecl.* 1.120.

14. At *geo.* 2.434 Vergil links *genistae* with *salices*. Compare also *geo.* 2.12–3.

15. Satyrs: Demigods of the wilds. See also *el.* 1.2.20, 2.5.9, 2.10.30, 3.2.13; *ep.* 1.36.5. Pans: Arcadian god or gods of the countryside, usually half-man, half-goat. See 32 below, *el.* 2.4.15, 2.7.23; *ep.* 2.6 title.

16. Fauns: Usually the Roman equivalent of Pan, or Pans. See also *el.* 1.2.33, 2.4.66, 3.2.9; *ep.* 1.19.1, 1.23.1, 2.32.2. Silvanus or Silvani: Roman god or gods associated with forests and wild landscape. See also *el.* 2.4.15; *ep.* 1.15.43. Lucan connects them with Pans and Nymphs at BC 3.402–3.

17. This line is a bow to Vergil *ecl.* 2.12–3.

19. Sarnus: See *ecl.* 4.68.

22. Ovid uses the phrase *pastoria sibila* at M. 13.785.

28. Daughter of Peneus: Daphne, whose father Peneus was god of Thessaly's most important river. Daphne's pursuit by Apollo and change into a laurel tree is told by Ovid at M. 1.452–567.

29. The Nonacrian maiden is Syrinx, so named from Nonacris, mountain and district in Arcadia.

31. Cyllene: Mountain in Arcadia. See also on *ecl.* 3.74; *ep.* 1.26.1.

32. Sannazaro absorbs the anaphora of *infelix* at 29–30 from Vergil *ecl.* 6.47 and 52, and of *Pana* at 31–2 from *ecl.* 4.58–9, though the phrase *Pana deum Arcadiae* is drawn from *ecl.* 10.26.

34. Ovid recounts the story of Pan's pursuit of the nymph Syrinx and of her metamorphosis into a group of reeds at M. 1.689–712.

37. The wording of this line comes in part from Catullus 64.92–3.

43. Here Sannazaro is thinking of Vergil *ecl.* 10.8: *Non canimus surdis, respondent omnia silvae* (We do not sing to deaf ears. The woods answer everything).

48. Sannazaro is parodying the language used of keeping non-initiates from sharing in private rituals. Compare, e.g., Vergil *Aen.* 6.258.

52. To kill the hydra of Lerna was one of the labors of Hercules. Compare also *DPV* 1.397. The Chimaera was a Lycian monster, part lion, part dragon, part goat, slain by Bellerophon. See *DPV* 1.396.

53. Scylla and Charybdis were supposedly located near the modern Straits of Messina. The first was a female monster (later turned into a rock) who lured sailors to their doom (the story of her metamorphoses is told by Ovid at *M.* books 13 and 14). Charybdis was a treacherous whirlpool (see also *el.* 1.2.8). For Scylla see also *DPV* 1.396.

78. Standard epic simile to illustrate strong versus weak, violent against helpless. Compare, in Vergil *Aen.* 9 alone, 59–64 (Turnus as *lupus* from whom *agni* seek safety) and 565–6 (Turnus as a *lupus* snatching an *agnum* from its mother); Ovid *M.* 14.778 (of silent wolves).

84. The phrase *via salutis* is Vergilian (*Aen.* 6.96).

94. With the language compare Ovid *M.* 9.614–5 (Byblis of Caunus): "he doesn't bear hard flint or solid iron or adamant in his heart" (*nec rigidas silices solidumve in pectore ferrum / aut adamanta gerit*).

ELEGIES

Meter: elegiac couplet.

First published in 1535.

I.I

Lucio Crasso (Crassus), c. 1430–90, was Sannazaro's early teacher and friend (see further Kennedy, *Jacopo Sannazaro*, 12, 15, 80–2; Kidwell, *Sannazaro*, 204–5, n. 13). See also *el.* 2.2.15. Here he is traveling along the Via Appia (Appian Way) northwest of Naples (what is technically the Via Latina was miles inland). The year 1490 is presumably the *terminus ante quem* for the poem, though, if we take line 58 as a literal reference to Sannazaro's exile, the date would have to be 1501 or later.

1. The exact location of Petrinum (see also *el.* 2.2.17) is unknown, though modern Mondragone most likely marks its position. Horace (*epi.* 1.5.4–5) mentions a wine "poured between swampy Minturnae and Sinuessan Patrinum" (*diffusa palustris / inter Minturnas Sinuessanumque Petrinum*). We are therefore along the shore of the Tyrrhenian Sea, on the border between Latium and Campania that are separated by the Liris river, in one of ancient Italy's great wine-growing districts. For Sinuessa see also *ecl.* 3.86 and 5.111.

4. The field: Perhaps a reference to the famous Solfatara at Pozzuoli, but more likely to the *calidi fontes* Ovid (*M.* 15.713) places between Liternum, just north of Cumae, and the Volturnus river that he mentions along with Sinuessa at line 715.

8. The phrase *monumenta viae* is the first of a series of bows throughout the poem to the Latin elegist Tibullus, here to his elegy 1.7.57. See further *el.* 2.1.10.

18. Pales: Roman tutelary goddess of flocks and herds. See also *el.* 1.2.34.

19. The name Thyrsis, like the others that follow, comes from Vergil's *Eclogues*, in this case from the seventh.

27. Maeonides . . . Maro: Homer, who gains his name from his supposed homeland, Maeonia (eastern Lydia), and Vergil (Publius Vergilius Maro). For Homer see also *el.* 2.1.47; *ep.* 1.67.2, 2.5.2, 2.47.4. For Vergil see *el.* 1.9.19 and 46, 1.11.16, 3.1.105; *ep.* 1.61.24 and 26, 2.47.3.

29. Aeacides: Achilles, grandson of Aeacus, principal Greek hero of Homer's *Iliad*. Ulysses: Hero of Homer's *Odyssey*. See also *el.* 1.5.35.

30. Aeneas: Hero of Vergil's *Aeneid*. See also *el.* 1.5.35, 3.1.37 and 44. For Ascanius (Iulus), son of Aeneas, see also on *el.* 3.1.45.

41. The phrase *felix qui potuit* introduces one of the most famous passages in Vergil's *Georgics* (2.490). See also *el.* 1.7.43–5.

44. Venus: The goddess of love, here a metonymy for lovemaking.

45. A clear bow to Horace *c.* 1.5.2. See also *DPV* 3.290.

49. Ethiopians: Inhabitants of inland, central Africa (see also *DPV* 1.257). For "Ethiopian wool," i.e. cotton, see Pliny *HN* 19.2.13, and commentators on Vergil *geo.* 2.120.

50. The town of Sidon on the Phoenician coast was well known for its dye industry.

52. Hermus: See on *DPV* 2.148.

60. The Sabaeans, natives of Saba in Arabia Felix, were producers of incense. See also *el.* 1.6.8; *ep.* 1.58.5, 3.1.19.

73. Circe: Witch whose most famous appearance in literature is in the tenth book of Homer's *Odyssey.*

74. Haemonia: Another name for Thessaly, in northern Greece, an area notorious in antiquity for the presence of witchcraft and magic. See also *ecl.* 5.33.

1.2

Giovanni Pardo (d. after 1512), Spanish priest, minor poet and scholar, member of Pontano's academy. See also *el.* 1.11.48 and Kidwell, *Pontano,* 377, n. 99.

4. The phrase *prima corpora* is Lucretian (*DRN* 1.61 and ff.), and suggests Pardo's interest in ancient scientific texts, in particular that of Lucretius.

7. Etna: The volcano that dominates eastern Sicily. Lucretius conjoins Etna and Charybdis at *DRN* 1.722. See also *el.* 1.11.69 and on *ep.* 1.6.18.

8. Charybdis: See on *Sal.* 53.

16. Hamadryads: Wood-nymphs. See also *el.* 2.4.14.

20. Satyrs: See on *Sal.* 15.

22. The reference is probably to the pastoral idylls of the third-century BCE poet Theocritus who came from Syracuse on the south coast of Sicily (Trinacria). See [ps.] Vergil *Cata.* 9.19–20 (*carmina . . . Trinacriae iuvenis*).

32. Compare Ovid *F.* 3.670.

33. Fauns: See on *Sal.* 16.

34. A reference to Tibullus 2.5.28.

47. Panchaia was a mythical island in the Indian Ocean famous for its incense and jewels.

48. Marble quarried on the Aegean island of Paros was among the most prized in Greece. See also on *DPV* 2.444.

1.3

Throughout the poem Sannazaro draws heavily on the elegies of Propertius and Tibullus for inspiration.

30. Lachesis: The one of the three Fates who supposedly spins the thread of life's destiny. See also *el.* 2.7.17; *ep.* 2.43.4.

37. Lethe: Hell's fountain of forgetfulness. See also *el.* 1.6.20, 1.9.99, 2.7.68.

42. See on *ecl.* 1.92.

44. The phrase *lata arva* occurs four times in Ovid.

58. The phrase *candidus pennis* has a lone classical parallel at Ovid *M.* 6.96, applied there to a stork.

1.4

Antonio Diaz Garlon (d. 1546), Count of Alife, musician and friend of Sannazaro, to whom he entrusted his Latin elegies and epigrams for posthumous publication (1535). See line 11 and *el.* 2.2.41. Juno Lucina is the Roman goddess of childbirth.

14. The waters bounding Arabia, including the modern Red Sea, an area proverbial for its richness.

21. Compare Vergil *ecl.* 4.60.

28. Paphos and Idalium are towns on Cyprus, known for the worship of Aphrodite/Venus. For Paphos see also *Sal.* 3; *ep.* 2.15.21.

29. *Vive, precor* begins a line at Ovid *H.* 7.63 and *F.* 5.412; Statius *The.* 12.816.

30. Compare Vergil *ecl.* 4.62 and the context of *DPV* 2.335–7.

1.5

The addressee, Giulio of Siena, has not been identified.

6. Pieria: Area of Macedonia whose king, Pierus, fathered the Pierides, another name for the Muses. See *el.* 1.10.10, 1.11.29, 2.2.16, 3.1.3, 3.3.46; *ep.* 2.15.20.

6. The Castalian spring is on Mt. Parnassus, mountain sacred to Apollo. See also *el.* 2.1.13.

14. Calliope: Chief of the Muses, usually associated with epic poetry. See also *el.* 1.11.63, 3.2.22.

19. Thalia: Muse whose province was comedy (her name in Greek means "abundance"). See also *ep.* 2.15.11, 3.1.25.

20. Delius: Apollo, from Delos, the Aegean island of his birth (see also *el.* 1.9.98, 2.9.4, 3.2.23).

22. The story of Orpheus and Eurydice is memorably recounted by Vergil at *geo.* 4.453–527. The Strymon (modern Struma) is a river in Thrace (see *geo.* 4.508).

23. Sannazaro has merged two separate Thracian mountain ranges, Ismarus and Haemus.

26. The Hebrus is a major river in Thrace of which Bistonia is a segment.

28. For Fortune and her wheel, see commentators on Cicero *in Pis.* 22 and Tibullus 1.5.70. The best-known source for Fortune's wheel in the Renaissance was Boethius' *Consolation of Philosophy*, book 2. See also *ep.* 1.5.7–8.

30. Famous man . . . of Tomis: The Roman elegist Ovid (43 BCE–17 CE), exiled by Augustus in 8 CE to Tomis on the Black Sea.

35. Ulysses: See *el.* 1.1.29–30.

37. Tirynthian: Hercules, born at Tiryns in the Argolid, son of Zeus and Alcmene, was deified after his cremation on Mt. Oeta in Thessaly. See also *ep.* 2.28.1.

1.6

The Brancacci were a wealthy noble family with branches in Florence and Naples.

1. Parcae: Standard Roman name for the Fates (Greek Moirai). See also *DPV* 1.270; *el.* 1.10.5, 2.1.45; *ep.* 2.15.14, 2.39.4.

5. For the custom of catching the last breath of the dying, see Vergil *Aen.* 4.684–85 (with the commentary of A. S. Pease). See also Seneca *ad Marciam* 3.2.

7. Perhaps a reference to the Roman Vestal Virgins.

22. Compare Horace *epode* 7.1.

30. Laodamia's husband, Protesilaus, was notorious for being the first Greek killed at Troy. See Catullus 68.73–86 and 105, and Ovid *H.* 13.

1.7

Giacomo della Marca (Jacobus Picenus), Franciscan theologian and preacher, was born (1393) in Monteprandone and died in Naples (1476).

15. The language here directly echoes Lucretius' *DRN* (2.333), a work much on Sannazaro's mind throughout the elegy.

20. Law-giving leader: Probably Moses is meant.

21. Sibyls: See on *DPV* 1.93.

28. A reference to Christ's harrowing of Hell. The Styx is one of the Underworld's rivers. See also *el.* 1.9.74, 1.11.7 and 78, 2.7.32.

30. The Empyrean. See on *DPV* 1.218.

33. Thunderer: See on *ecl.* 3.70.

1.8

Pierre de Rochefort (d. 1507), usually referred to as Guy, Grand Chancellor of the French kings Charles VIII and Louis XII, whose forces occupied Naples for three months in 1495; he had humanist interests and was a patron of Robert Gaguin (1433–1501) and Guillaume Budé (1467–1540).

2. Sannazaro is punning on the meaning of his addressee's name, drawn from Vulgar Latin *rocca* and classical *fortis*. The poet's replacement of the usual Guy with Pierre (Latin Petrus, from *petra* [rock]) may further the wordplay.

5. Astraea, the goddess of justice, is also the Virgo of Vergil *ecl.* 4.6 and *geo.* 2.474. Her zodiacal sign, overlapping essentially with the month of September, was adjacent to that of Libra which in turn extended into that of the Claws (Scorpio). According to the myth, she abandoned the earth in response to the decadence of mankind. She will now return to honor the just Rochefort.

6. House: The Roman protective divinities of the house stand, by metonymy, for the house itself. See also *el.* 1.9.9, 2.2.7.

15. For Sannazaro in exile, Latium no doubt stands for Italy in general.

25. A direct reference to Vergil *Aen.* 6.853, further echoed at 33–4.

26. Ausonia is a Vergilian name for Italy.

40. Probably meant as an adynaton, though the proverbial hardness of oak could also qualify someone stubborn or obtuse (compare, e.g., *el.* 1.9.5).

45. The *fasces* were a bundle of rods, usually with an axe, that accompanied Roman magistrates and symbolized their office.

50. For the possibility of a contemporary crusade on the part of the French see Nash, *The Major Latin Poems*, 113.

51. Rhône: Largest river of southern France. See *ecl.* 3.18–19. The Nile is Africa's longest river, emptying into the Mediterranean at Alexandria.

52. Saône: Ancient Arar, tributary of the Rhône. See also *ecl.* 5.115; *ep.* 2.25.2. The laurel, worn by triumphing Roman generals, stands by metonymy for the triumph itself.

1.9

Giovanni Pontano (1426–1503). He was born at Cerreto near Spoleto and received his initial education at Perugia. In 1448 he left Umbria for Naples, which remained his lifelong home. He was the leading literary figure there in the last three decades of the Quattrocento and a major influence on Sannazaro. See also on *ecl.* 2.42.

12. *Thespian sisters*: The Muses, a name drawn from the town of Thespiae at the foot of Mt. Helicon, whose inspirational source was Hippocrene. For further details see on *el.* 2.1.14. See also *el.* 1.11.53, 2.2.46, 3.1.5.

14. Sannazaro is thinking of Ennius's epitaph which he would have found at Cicero *TD* 1.34. Compare also Pontano's rewriting of Catullus 1.9 (*qualecunque, quod ora per virorum*). See further Gaisser, *Catullus*, 127–29 and 173–74.

17. Sannazaro is alluding to an autobiographical moment in Propertius (4.1.63), Pontano's fellow Umbrian.

18. See note on *el.* 1.2.48, where the same final words appear.

19. *Maro*: Vergil. See on *el.* 1.1.27.

23. *Parnassus*: Mountain in Phocis on the lower slopes of which the town of Delphi, sacred to Apollo, is located. See also *el.* 2.1.3, 2.7.21, 3.1.15.

34. *Alfonso*, Duke of Calabria, later Alfonso II, King of Naples (1494–95). See *el.* 2.1.65–6, 2.3.19, 3.3.29–30; *ep.* 1.9. In 1481 Pontano joined Alfonso as his forces retook Otranto, which had fallen to the Turks. Sannazaro was probably also present for some of the action (see Kidwell, *Sannazaro*, 35).

37. The references in lines 36–7 are to Pontano's poems *Urania* and *Meteora*. See also *ecl.* 4.73–4.

39. Sannazaro is referring to *De Hortis Hesperidum*, Pontano's didactic poem on citrus trees. See also *DPV* 3.511–13.

39. Reference is to the eleventh labor of Hercules. For the guardian dragon see commentators on Vergil *Aen.* 4.484–85.

40. *Marriages*: *Toros* ("marriage-beds") here stand for marriage itself.

41. Reference to Pontano's *Lepidina* and his other eclogues.

44. Pontano's dialogue *Antonius* contains a mock-epic poem about Pompey's campaigns against Sertorius in Spain (77–71 BCE).

47. Sebeto: Ancient Sebethus. See on *ecl.* 1.105. See also *ecl.* 5.21; *el.* 2.3.6, 2.4.63; *ep.* 1.44.9, 2.15.35, 2.51.42, 2.56.4.

48. Unresponsive doors: Reference to Pontano's two books of *Parthenopeus* (*Amores*). Examples of the *paraclausithyron* (song delivered before the beloved's closed doors) can be found in Catullus and the three Augustan elegists.

49. Hymenaeus: The (Greek) wedding-refrain, personified as a god apparently not before Ovid (*H.* 11.101).

53. Pontano's *De Amore Coniugali* in three books.

55. Lullabies: The twelve *Neniae*.

58. These are characters in Pontano's *Parthenopeus* (*Amores*).

61. Po: Anciently called Eridanus by the Greeks. See also *el.* 2.1.89; *ep.* 2.53.2.

62. Poplar leaves: The poplar was particularly associated with the cult of Hercules (see commentators on Vergil *ecl.* 7.61, Horace *c.* 1.7.23, et al.) who, as participant in the voyage of the *Argo*, sailed along the Eridanus (compare Apollonius Rhodius *Arg.* 4.592–626). See also *el.* 2.1.17–18.

63. Stella: The poetic name Pontano gave to his former mistress and second wife, Stella da Argenta, from Ferrara, whom he married c. 1491 when he was at least sixty-five. She is the main subject of two books of elegies entitled *Eridanus*.

65. Baiae: See on *ecl.* 1.42. The reference is to Pontano's *Hendecasyllaborum Libri* (*Poemata Baiarum*, abbreviated as *Baiae*) in two books (edited by R. G. Dennis [Cambridge, Mass., 2006]).

67. Pontano's *De Laudibus Divinis*.

68. Pontano's *Tumuli*.

69. Pindar: Greek lyric poet (c. 518-c. 446 BCE). See also *el.* 2.1.8, 2.2.22. Pontano's lyric poetry was collected in *Lyra*.

70. Methymna was a city on Lesbos, famous as the birthplace of the citharode Arion.

72. A reference to Pontano's six book *De Bello Neapolitano* which deals with the fighting between Ferdinando II and John II of Anjou, Duke of Lorraine.

74. See on *DPV* 1.80. The reference is to Pontano's satiric dialogue, *Charon*, named for the ferryman of souls across the Styx in classical mythology.

75. Marcus Terentius Varro (116–27 BCE) was Rome's most famous polymath of the late Republican and early Augustan eras; Publius Nigidius Figulus (d. 45 BCE) was another Republican scholar with a particular interest in grammar. Sannazaro is referring to Pontano's *De Aspiratione* in two books.

77. Sannazaro is making a modest bow to his own share in Pontano's dialogue *Actius*.

79. The opening words of this line (*quid loquar*) are an echo of Vergil *ecl.* 6.74, part of the catalogue of the songs of Silenus.

79. Marianus refers to Mariano da Gennazzano, Vicar General of the Augustinians prior to Giles, and a famous preacher. For details see F. X. Martin, *Friar, Reformer, and Renaissance Scholar: The Life and Work of Giles of Viterbo, 1469–1532*, ed. J. E. Rotelle (Villanova, 1992), especially 15–17, 37–40.

80. On Egidio (Giles), Augustinian monk, bishop of Viterbo and cardinal (*c.* 1465–1532) see J. O'Malley, *Giles of Viterbo on Church and Reform: A Study in Renaissance Thought* (Leiden, 1968), and the references in Kidwell, *Pontano*, 404, n. 216, and, ibid., *Sannazaro*, 120 and 154–5. He gave his name to Pontanus's dialogue *Aegidius*.

82. A reference to Pontanus's dialogue *Asinus*, subtitled "On Ingratitude" by Summonte, its first editor (see Kidwell, *Pontano*, 193). For Summonte see on *ep.* 2.9.

84. Parthenope: Naples. See also *el.* 2.1.32, 2.4.64, 3.3.52, and *ecl.* 3.88. Cicero: Great Roman author and statesman (106–43 BCE).

86. Stagira: Birthplace of Aristotle in northern Greece.

87. Lines 87–94 deal, in order, with Pontano's treatises *De fortitudine, De principe, De liberalitate, De oboedientia, De sermone, De fortuna, De prudentia, De immanitate,* and *De magnanimitate.*

96. Ptolemy (Claudius Ptolemaeus, fl. 140 CE), scholar of the motions of the heavenly bodies. Pontano translated, and wrote a commentary upon, a work dubiously ascribed to Ptolemy known in Latin as *Centum Sententiae* (*Commentationes super centum sententiis Ptolemaei*) or *Centiloquium.*

102. The Egyptian pyramids were proverbial for endurance (see Horace *c.* 3.30.2).

103. Sannazaro is referring to the Roman elegist Sextus Propertius (c. 50-after 16 BCE), like Pontano born in Umbria, at Asisium (modern Assisi). See also *el.* 2.1.7.

104. Instead of to Umbria Pontano's laurels will go to his adoptive city, and Sannazaro's birthplace, Naples.

1.10

Giovanni di Sangro, Neapolitan nobleman, one of the executors of Sannazaro's will.

7. Libitina: Roman goddess of funerals. Sannazaro is thinking of Horace *c.* 3.30.7.

9. The phrase *amoena virecta* ends Vergil *Aen.* 6.638 (where the word *virecta* is a coinage).

14. Vergil uses the rare adjective *implumis* at *geo.* 4.513, twelve lines after employing the phrase *in auras tenuis* (499–500), adopted by Sannazaro in the next line.

15. Syncerus: Sannazaro himself.

17. Nemesis: Greek goddess of retribution. See also *ep.* 1.53.45.

19. Sannazaro is echoing Vergil *Aen.* 1.119 (*arma virum tabulaeque et Troia gaza per undas*), but varying the meaning of *arma* from weaponry to tackle.

23. See on *ecl.* 1.1 and 2.45.

I.II

7. Scuccha has not been identified. A *scucchia* is a protruding chin.

8. Eumenides: Another name for the Furies (*Furiae*).

13. Helicon: Mountain in Boeotia, sacred to Apollo and the Muses. See also *el.* 3.1.5.

15. Gioviano: The academic name of Giovanni Pontano. See on *ecl.* 2.42 and *el.* 1.9 passim.

18. Gabriele Altilio (1440–1501), bishop of Policastro and teacher of Ferrante II. See also *el.* 2.2.21; *ep.* 1.7.2, as well as Kennedy, *Jacopo Sannazaro,* 15; Kidwell, *Pontano,* 374, n. 29; ibid., *Sannazaro,* 205, n. 20, 215, n. 6.

20. Compater: Pietro Golino (c. 1431–1501), called Il Compater or Compare, friend of Pontano and Sannazaro, and member of the Accademia Pontaniana. See also *ep.* 2.15; Kennedy, *Jacopo Sannazaro,* 15, 18, 61; Kidwell, *Pontano,* 58–9.

21. Elisio: Luigi Gallucci, whose name in the Academy was Elisio Calenzio (Elysius) (c. 1430–1502), litterateur and friend of Pontano. See Kidwell, *Pontano,* 57–8.

22. Aonia is the area of Boeotia that contains Mt. Helicon. See also *el.* 2.2.2, 2.4.78, 3.1.6, 3.2.21.

23. Andrea Matteo Acquaviva (c. 1458–1529), Marquis of Bitonto, Duke of Atri, a member of Pontano's academy, to whom Pontano dedicated *De magnanimitate.* See *el.* 2.2.33, 2.10.44, 3.1.141–6; *ep.* 2.2 passim. His father is eulogized at *el.* 3.1.141–6. See Kennedy, *Jacopo Sannazaro,* 15; Kidwell, *Pontano,* 401–2, n. 131; ibid., *Sannazaro,* 51, 120, 127.

25. Traiano Cavaniglia or Cabanilla, dedicatee of *Salices,* on whom see the headnote to that poem.

25. Troia: City in Apulia.

28. Massimo Corvino (d. 1522), Bishop of Isernia, member of Pontano's academy and a relative of the poet Cariteo (see at 37 below), later a member of the court of Leo X (see *ep.* 3.8). See *DBI* 29: 832–34.

30. Giovanni Albino (Albinus) (c. 1445-c. 1497), student of Panormita and Pontano, member of the Accademia Pontaniana, diplomat and historian. See Kidwell, *Pontano*, 373–4, n. 27; *DBI* 2: 12–13.

32. Michele Marullo (1453–1500), Greek scholar, poet and soldier, born in Sparta. He is known for *Hymni Naturales*, deeply indebted to Lucretius, whose work he emended, and for epigrams. See *el.* 2.2.25 and *ep.* 1.42.1. See also Kennedy, *Jacopo Sannazaro*, 14, 64–5; Kidwell, *Marullus*, passim.

35. Giuniano Maio (1430–93), professor of rhetoric and poetry at the University of Naples, was a tutor of Sannazaro. See Kennedy, *Jacopo Sannazaro*, 13, 15, 82–3; Kidwell, *Sannazaro*, 205, n. 14.

37. Benedetto Gareth, il Cariteo or Chariteo (c. 1450-c. 1515), from Barcelona. See also *ep.* 1.11, title, *Arcadia* 12, and, for further detail, Kennedy, *Jacopo Sannazaro*, 14–15; Kidwell, *Pontano*, 377–78, n. 99; ibid., *Sannazaro*, 208, n. 16.

39. Francesco Elia Marchese (c. 1440–1517), Neapolitan nobleman and author, relative of Cassandra Marchese. See Kidwell, *Pontano*, 59.

42. Scala has not been identified.

43. Rutilio Zenone, bishop of San Marco Argentano.

46. Girolamo Carbone (c. 1465-c. 1528). See Kidwell, *Pontano*, 399, n. 76.

47. Pardo was fluent in Spanish and Italian. See *el.* 1.2, passim.

57. Oedipus: Mythical monarch of Thebes, subject of two plays by Sophocles (*Oedipus Rex* and *Oedipus Coloneus*).

62. Aganippe: Fountain on Mt. Helicon, in Boeotia, sacred to the Muses. See *ep.* 1.2.11 and 1.61.27 as well as commentators of Vergil *ecl.* 10.12.

64. Permessus: Stream rising on Mt. Helicon. See also *ep.* 2.2.3.

65. Besides Al(l)ecto the other Furies are Megaera and Tisiphone.

66. Phlegethon: One of the rivers of the Underworld ("blazing").

69. Cyclopes: One-eyed race of giants who lived near (or, in their role as workmen for Vulcan, beneath) the Sicilian volcano Etna.

74. Euboean dwellings: The reference is to Cumae. See on *ecl.* 2.78.

2.1

Alfonso, Duke of Calabria (1448–95), son of Ferdinando (Ferrante) I, later King Alfonso II of Naples (1494–95). See also the direct or indirect references to him at *el.* 1.9.34, 2.3.19, 3.3.29–30; *ep.* 1.9, 1.36, 1.44.

2. Hesperian: Western, which in this case is to say Spanish.

6. Naso: Ovid (Publius Ovidius Naso, 43 BCE-17 CE).

7. Propertius: See on *el.* 1.9.104. Battus's offspring: Callimachus (fl. 250 BCE), Alexandrian poet and scholar, descendant, perhaps son, of Battus.

8. Flaccus: Horace (Quintus Horatius Flaccus, 65–8 BCE). Sannazaro adopts the verb *divido,* whose technical sense still remains unclear, from Horace *c.* 1.15.15.

9. Sings the death of a sparrow: Poem 3 in the Catullan corpus, though it should be noted that Catullus 2 and 3 were treated as a single poem until the first Aldine edition (1502).

10. Albius Tibullus (c. 50–19 BCE). The apostrophe *culte Tibulle* is drawn from Ovid *Am.* 1.15.28, where he appears in a list of poets that also includes Callimachus and Vergil. Nemesis is the name of the poet's mistress in his second book of elegies.

14. Gorgon's water: The fountain Hippocrene draws its name in myth from Pegasus, Bellerophon's winged steed, who created it with a blow of his hoof. The horse had been born from the severed neck of the Gorgon Medusa. See also *el.* 3.2.92.

15. Aeschylus: Athenian writer of tragedies (c. 525/4–456/5 BCE).

18. Sannazaro is referring to the epic *Argonautica* of Apollonius Rhodius (3rd century BCE). The most well known of the *Argo's* adventures took it to the Phasis, river of Colchis, where Jason met Medea.

19. Pergama: The citadel of Troy, scene of Homer's *Iliad.* See also *el.* 3.1.42.

20. The reference is to Vergil's *Aeneid,* to the second line of which *profugos* is a bow.

22. Sannazaro alludes to Statius's *Thebaid.* The abstraction *discordia* regularly connotes civil war.

30. Lotophagi: Lotus-eaters, mythical people of the coast of north Africa visited by Odysseus at the start of his wanderings (Homer *Od.* 9.82–104). See also *ep.* 2.32.8. The ancestor to whom these lines refer was probably Peter III ("the Great") of Aragon (1239–85), the most famous Aragonese monarch of the Middle Ages, a crusader who conquered Sicily and invaded the Muslim kingdom of Tunisia in 1280.

32. Chalcidican citadels and Parthenope: Cumae (see on *ecl.* 4.61) and Naples (see on *ecl.* 3.88).

40. The phrase *aurea saecula* is used by Vergil (*Aen.* 6.792–3) to describe the era of Augustus.

42. Daunia: Technically Apulia. Daunia draws its name from an eponymous king Daunus.

48. I read here *saeva* for the standard *saevae*.

56. Sannazaro is drawing on Vergil *Aen.* 3.399–402 where the seer Helenus reveals to Aeneas details of his journey from Buthrotum, on the coast of Epirus, to Italy. Locri Epizephyrii, called by Vergil Narycii, was a town on the southern coast of Italy, established by Locrians from Narycum on the Gulf of Malea. The Meliboean city refers to Petelia, supposedly founded by Philoctetes, native of Meliboea in Thessaly.

57. Caulon (Caulonia), in Bruttium, is mentioned by Vergil at *Aen.* 3.553.

61. The Crathis and Sybaris are confluent streams in Magna Graecia. The city of Sybaris stood at its river's mouth.

64. Arno: Florence's river. See also *el.* 3.1.163; *ep.* 1.4.11.

67. Ceraunia: Rocky promontory in Epirus (Vergil *geo.* 1.332, *Aen.* 3.506). See also *DPV* 2.177.

68. Buthrotum: Town on the coast of Epirus, modern Butrint, in Albania (see Vergil *Aen.* 3.293).

71. Ligurians: I.e., the Genoese. See on *ecl.* 3.17.

73. Tusculum: Town in Latium, southeast of Rome, where Cicero had a villa. From 73–86, Sannazaro is referring to Alfonso's campaign in 1485–86 against Pope Innocent VIII (see on *ep.* 1.37).

77. Nomentum: Town northeast of Rome.

77. Tivoli: Ancient Tibur, town east of Rome, on the Anio.

79. Subura: The Subura was an area in central Rome between the Viminal and Esquiline hills, notorious in antiquity for its nightlife.

80. Capitoline Jupiter: The shrine to Jupiter Optimus Maximus, facing east from the Capitoline hill over the Forum Romanum, was Rome's most famous temple.

81. Colline Gate: Gate on the northeast side of Rome, the starting point of the Via Nomentana.

85. Lanuvium: Town in the Alban Hills, southeast of Rome.

89. Po: See on *el.* 1.9.61.

91. Insubria: The capital of the ancient Insubres was Mediolanum, modern Milan.

92. Euganean Hills: A range running between Padua and Este, where Petrarch had a house at the end of his life.

95. Modern Farfa, ancient Farfarus (Ovid *M.* 14.330), probably the same as Fabaris (Vergil *Aen.* 7.715): a tributary of the Tiber in the Sabine territory.

118. The last four lines echo closely the parallel lines (75–8) in Propertius 2.1, one of the two elegies that he addresses to his patron Maecenas.

2.2

San Nazario was a first-century Christian martyr whose body was discovered around 395 by St. Ambrose in a garden outside Milan. The details of his biography adopted by Sannazaro are fabricated. (See further *The Oxford Dictionary of the Christian Church*, ed. E. A. Livingstone [Oxford, 1997], s. v. Nazarius.) He is also mentioned in, or is the subject of, *ep.* 2.36.29, 2.37 passim, 2.51 passim, 2.60 passim. The surname "Sannazaro" is derived from his name; both the feast day of the saint and the poet's birthday fell on 28 July. The poem was written in 1489: See Kidwell, *Marullus*, 156; ibid., *Sannazaro*, 50–1, 214, n. 90.

7. A *genius* in Latin is a tutelary divinity of a family or individual, worshipped especially on his birthday (see commentators on Tibullus 1.7.49). For *lares* see on *el.* 1.8.6.

11. For Giovanni Pontano see on *ecl.* 2.42 and *el.* 1.9 passim. He will recite his *Urania* (see on *el.* 1.9.35–6).

15. Crassus: The recipient of *el.* 1.1.

16. Pieria: See on *ecl.* 5.19 and *el.* 1.5.6.

17. Linternum (Liternum, modern Villa Literno), coastal town in Campania, between Sinuessa and Cumae. See also *el.* 2.4.13 and the context of *el.* 1.1.1–4.

18. Technically, *atavus* means great, great, great grandfather.

21. Altilio: See on *el.* 1.11.18. Altilius (Gabriele Altilio) wrote an *epithalamium* for the marriage, in 1488, of Gian Galeazzo Sforza (1469–94) with Isabella of Aragon (1470–1524), daughter of Alfonso II, King of Naples.

25. For Marullo (Marullus) see on *el.* 1.11.32.

27. Lucretius: Roman didactic poet (c. 95-c. 55 BCE), author of *De Rerum Natura*.

29. Poderico: See on fr. 10.

31. Panormita: Antonio Beccadelli (1394–1471) of Palermo (hence the pseudonym Panormita, from the Latin Panormus), humanist and poet, mentor of Pontano and founder of the Neapolitan academy. See Kennedy, *Jacopo Sannazaro*, 13, 16–7; Kidwell, *Pontano*, 53–63; ibid., *Sannazaro*, 209, n. 27.

32. Gioviano: Giovanni Pontano (Jovianus).

33. Andrea Matteo Acquaviva. See on *el.* 1.11.23.

35. Plutarch: Greek philosopher and biographer (c. 50-c. 120 CE).

37. Cavaniglia: See *el.* 1.11.25 and the headnote on *Sal.*

40. The stream of Phocis: The Castalian Spring. See on *el.* 1.9.23.

41. Garlon: See on *el.* 1.4, title.

43. Allifae: The Latin name for modern Alife on the Campanian river Vulturnus (modern Volturno).

2.3

The dedicatee is probably Tommaso Fusco, a jurist and poet who was a member of the Roman academy; see Nash, *The Major Latin Poems*, 129. Fuscus is also an ancient Roman surname (compare, e.g., Horace *c.* 1.22.4).

6. Sebeto: See on *ecl.* 1.105.

7. Janus: Ancient Roman god of crossings, exits and entrances (hence his representation as a head with two faces, front and back). The gates of his temple on the edge of the Roman forum were open when the city was at war, closed during peacetime (see Vergil *Aen.* 1.293–4, 7.607). He gives his name to the month of January. See also *el.* 3.3.19; *ep.* 1.32.1.

14. For the Pactolus of Lydia and the Tagus of Portugal, both considered to carry gold in their flood, see *DPV* 2.147–8 and 202, respectively.

16. Mede: I.e. Persian.

19. Otranto: Ancient Hydruntum (or Hydrus) in the heel of Italy. For Alfonso's victory there in 1481 see on *el.* 3.3.29–30, and compare *el.* 1.9.33–34.

20. Sannazaro draws his language here from Ovid *F.* 1.577–78.

2.4

1. Erato: Muse, usually of erotic poetry.

6. Baiae: See on *ecl.* 1.42.

9. Lucrinus: The god of the Lucrine lake. See on *ecl.* 3.25.

13. Cumae: See on *ecl.* 2.78. Linternum: See on *el.* 2.2.17.

14. Monte Gauro: Mountain, also named Barbaro, inland, east of Cumae.

15. Silvanuses: Roman god or gods, associated with uncultivated land and forests. See also *Sal.* 16; *ep.* 1.15.43.

24. Sannazaro is referring to the so-called *colles Leucogaei* mentioned by Pliny as located between Puteoli (Pozzuoli) and Neapolis (*HN* 18.29.114 and 35.50.174; compare 31.8.12).

38. The language of this line is drawn from Propertius 1.3.25–6.

39. Compare Vergil *Aen* 7.807 on Camilla's speed.

41. Barren marsh: A reference to Lacus Avernus (Lago Averno), to the west of Monte Gauro. See note on *ecl.* 4.45.

51. Delia: Diana, born on the island of Delos.

55. Morus: The (black) mulberry.

61. For Misenus see *ecl.* 1.122. The warm springs are probably those at nearby Puteoli (Pozzuoli).

63. Sebeto: See on *ecl.* 1.105.

64. Parthenopaea: See on *ecl.* 3.88.

66. Faunus: Roman equivalent of Pan. See on *Sal.* 16.

70. The pine-tree was sacred to Faunus.

71. Thisbe: Ovid's telling of the story of Pyramus and Thisbe (*M.* 4.55–166) is on Sannazaro's mind. In the Roman poet's version the previously white berries of the mulberry were darkened from the spurting of Pyramus's blood.

73. The phrase *niveis uberrima pomis* also ends an hexameter at *M.* 4.89.

77. The tortoise shell (*testudo*), sounding board of the lyre, standing for the instrument itself.

2.5

Propertius 3.17 is a strong influence on this elegy of Sannazaro.

1. Bacchus of two mothers: Epithet of Bacchus (e.g. Ovid *M.* 4.12), brought to birth from the hip or thigh of Jupiter after the death of his mother Semele.

3. Thebes: Chief city of Boeotia in central Greece, setting for the *Bacchae* of Euripides.

3. Ismarus: Mountain in southern Thrace.

4. Naxos: One of the central islands of the Cyclades, in the Aegean Sea, where Bacchus rescued Ariadne after her desertion by Theseus. See also *el.* 2.8.24.

7. Palla: A mantle, often associated with the performance of tragedy.

12. Bassarids: Bacchantes.

13. Silenus: Tutor and attendant of Bacchus. See also on *DPV* 2.387.

17. God of gardens: Priapus. See also *ep.* 2.12 title.

20. Lesbos: Island in the northeast Aegean.

29. Ariadne: Daughter of Minos, king of Crete.

30. Ariadne's hair was the mythical source of the constellation known as Corona Borealis.

52. The final phrase, *dexter adi*, is drawn from Vergil *Aen.* 8.302, the concluding line of the Arcadians' invocation to Hercules.

2.6

Ludovico Montalto was a noble Sicilian jurist and administrator. He was an important figure in the Naples of Charles V (1500–58), who ruled the city through a viceroy from 1516–56. The title *Scrinii magister* is the equivalent of chancellor or secretary of state.

3. Nebrodes: A Sicilian mountain range.

3. Napaeans: Nymphs of wooded valleys. See on *DPV* 3.407.

4. Eryx: Mountain at the northwest corner of Sicily.

4. Dione: Mother of Aphrodite/Venus, often standing for Venus herself. See also *ep.* 2.12.1, 2.15.1 and 5.

6. Arethusa: Nymph and her fountain at Syracuse, on the south coast of Sicily. According to myth (see Ovid *M.* 5.572–641) she was originally from Elis in the northwestern Peloponnesus. There, at Pisa, was situated the grove and shrine to Olympian Zeus where the Olympic games were celebrated. The area's first temple, ascribed to Hera, lay beneath the so-called Cronus Hill. Sannazaro seems to have confused, or melded, Olympia with Mt. Olympus, in the northeast of Greece. In classical Latin the adjective *Olympiacus* (5) refers strictly to Olympia.

11. Britanni: Inhabitants of Britain. See also *ep.* 2.51.16.

12. Tethys: See on *DPV* 1.202.

2.7

For Maio, see on *el.* 1.11.35.

1. Baiae: See on *ecl.* 1.42.

3. Sannazaro is alluding to Propertius 1.11.1–2, which mention the story that Hercules constructed the sand spit separating the Lucrine Lake from the Bay of Baiae as he herded along the cattle of Geryon.

4. Sannazaro is here thinking of Vergil *geo.* 2.161–4.

5. Bauli: See on *ecl.* 3.1.

6. Prochyta: See on *ecl.* 1.122.

17. Lachesis: See on *el.* 1.3.30.

19. The final phrase of this line comes from Vergil *ecl.* 10.60.

21. Delphi: The site of Greece's chief oracle of Apollo. See also *ep.* 3.6.1.

22. Cumaean virgin: The Sibyl. See *DPV* 1.93, *el.* 2.8.40.

23. Maenalus: Mountain in Arcadia, sacred to Pan.

25. Chaonia: District in the northwest of Epirus containing the oracular shrine of Dodona, sacred to Zeus/Jupiter, who spoke through rustling oak trees or doves (or priestesses who bore that designation).

44. The Etruscans were notorious in antiquity for their powers of divination (compare, e.g., Cicero *ND* 2.10, *ad Fam.* 6.6.3).

49. Cannae: Town in Apulia where, in 216 BCE, Hannibal defeated the Romans during the Second Punic War.

50. The reference is to the defeat of Marcus Licinius Crassus by the Parthians at Carrhae in 53 BCE when the eagles (*aquilae*), images on Roman standards and here standing by metonymy for the legions themselves, were seized by the enemy.

52. Both Gnaius Cornelius Scipio Calvus and his brother Publius Cornelius Scipio (adoptive father of Scipio Africanus) died in Spain during the Second Punic War in the year 211 BCE.

66. The reference is to two of the famous sinners, or group of sinners, in the Underworld, Sisyphus and the Danaids, whose tortures involved vain and frustrating repetition.

68. Two further punishments, of Tityus and of Tantalus (where we expect the fruit to be active instead of passive).

71. See *el.* 1.10.23, and compare [ps.] Tibullus 3.2.29.

2.8

13. Erythraean jewels: Pearls obtained from what is now the Arabian Sea. See *el.* 2.10.41 and Martial 9.2.9.

17. Poison: Sannazaro draws this image for dye from Vergil *geo.* 2.465.

22. Cytherea: Aphrodite/Venus, to whom the myrtle was sacred, born in the waters off the island of Cythera. See also *ep.* 2.10.1.

23. Nysaean: The name is drawn from Mt. Nysa, usually located in India, and birthplace of Dionysus/Bacchus. See commentators on Vergil *Aen.* 6.805 and compare Propertius 3.17.22 (*Nysaeis choris*). *Lenaeus* ("belonging to the wine-press") is a standard epithet of Bacchus. For the god's connection with the Aegean island of Naxos see Ovid *M.* 3.636–49.

24. Naxos: See on *el.* 2.5.3.

40. Cumaean seer: The Sibyl. See on *DPV* 1.93. The reference forms a nice transition to the following elegy.

2.9

For Cumae see on *ecl.* 2.78.

4. Delian: Apollo, born on the island of Delos. See on *el.* 1.5.20.

6. See Vergil *Aen.* 6.14–33 where we hear of Daedalus's dedication to Apollo of the wings that brought him from Crete to Cumae and of the temple with its decorated doors that he dedicated to the god.

9. The Sibyl's cave is described at Vergil *Aen.* 6.42–4 and by innuendo in what follows.

22. The story of a dove guiding the ship of Cumae's founders is mentioned by Velleius Paterculus (*Historiae* 1.4.1).

24. Compare the language and sentiments of *DPV* 2.220–21.

28. Rome and Venice are meant.

29. Naples is the subject. The phrase *durus arator* comes from Vergil (*geo.* 4.512) where it is a figure for death.

2.10

Punic apples are pomegranates.

8. See Pliny *HN* 37.121 and 124 for the connection between amethyst and wine.

32. Proserpina (Persephone) failed to return to the upper world, and to her mother Ceres (Demeter), after eating succulent seeds of the pomegranate in Hades. For Ovid's version of the story see *M.* 5.376–571.

33. On Pomona see Ovid *M.* 14.623–771.

40. Paeon: Apollo in his capacity as healer. See on *DPV* dedication, line 8.

44. Acquaviva: See on *el.* 1.11.23.

44. The holy troop: The Muses.

3.1

Federico of Aragon (1451–1504), son of King Ferdinando I (Ferrante), younger brother of King Alfonso II, and uncle of his predecessor King Ferdinando II (Ferrandino). He himself was king of Naples from 1496 until 1501, when he was deposed. He died an exile in France. For his biography, see *DBI* 45: 668–82. See also on *ecl.* 3.13. He is the subject of, or mentioned in, *el.* 3.2.71, 3.3.33–6; *ep.* 1.1, 1.5, 1.8, 1.12, 1.32, 2.1, 3.5.

5. Helicon: See *el.* 1.11.13.

6. Aonides: The Muses. See on *el.* 1.11.22.

10. Sannazaro is here using metaphors common in classical Latin literature for poetry-making. His language is probably closest to that of Lucretius *DRN* 1.927–8 and its elaboration at 4.1–5.

13–22. He is leaving behind lyric verse to take up a loftier epic strain appropriate to praising the deeds of Federico. For variations on this theme, often taking the form of a *recusatio*, see Propertius 2.1 and 3.9, among other poems.

15. Parnassus: See on *DPV* 3.479.

16. Pindus: Mountain in northeast Greece, associated with the Muses.

20. See on *el.* 1.9.48.

36. Mars: The god of war stands here by metonymy for war itself.

37. Reference is to the opening line of book 7 of Vergil's *Aeneid*, and to Caieta, who gave her name to the port of Caieta, now Gaeta, on the southern shore of Latium.

40. Phrygian: I.e. Trojan.

42. Pergama: The citadel of Troy.

43. Scamander: One of the rivers of Troy.

45. Creusa: Wife of Aeneas and mother of Iulus (Ascanius).

50. With lines 49–50 compare Vergil *Aen.* 1.7 and 7.602–3. Alba Longa, in the hills east of Rome, was, in most accounts, the latter's mother-city.

52. Sannazaro is here thinking of Vergil *Aen.* 6.824 and 818. Those listed are heroes of the Roman Republic. For Cato the Younger see *ep.* 2.30 and 46. For Brutus the regicide see *ep.* 2.17.

54. The patrician Roman family of the Iulii, which claimed descent from Aeneas, reached the heights of its power under Julius Caesar, great-uncle of Augustus.

55. This line, by allusion, includes a double compliment to Federico. The opening imperative, *ingredere* (repeated at 57) looks to Vergil *geo.* 1.42, referring to the implicit divinity of Augustus, while the phrase *pede secundo* is a bow to *Aen.* 8.302 and a prayer to Hercules (compare *el.* 2.5.52).

57. Antiphates was a king of the Laestrygonians (Ovid *M.* 14.234) who ruled at Formiae (modern Formia, adjacent to Gaeta). The city was said to have been founded by Lamus (see commentators on Horace *c.* 3.17.1). The passage may be a reference to Federico's successful action against a French armada off Gaeta in 1494, or more likely to his early military training near Gaeta.

60. Amyclae was a town in Laconia, near Sparta, which here is called Taenarian after the southernmost promontory of the Peloponnesus. It was the birthplace of Castor and Pollux.

61. Alcides: Hercules.

72. Parthenope: See on *ecl.* 3.88.

73. The Sal(l)entini were a tribe who inhabited the heel of Italy (at *Aen.* 3.400 Vergil mentions *Sallentinos campos*). This line refers to Vergil, *geo.* 4.125–6, mentioning the river of Tarentum and the city's mythical founder, Oebalus of Sparta. King Ferrante put Federico in charge of the territory of Bari and Otranto from 1464 to 1473, despite his youth.

75. The phrase *Livor edax* comes from Ovid *RA* 389.

77. Father in Rome: Probably Pope Sixtus IV (Francesco della Rovere [1414–84], Pope, 1471–84). In 1474 Federico was sent on a long journey through Italy to Burgundy where he was to enter into marriage negotiations with Charles the Bold, Duke of Burgundy. Federico was later sent to Rome to represent the Aragonese monarchy in 1493–94 after the crowning of Pope Alexander VI.

83. Veii: Ancient Etruscan city on the Tiber north of Rome. Umbrians: Inhabitants of Umbria, area of Italy to the north and east of Rome. Sabines: People adjoining the Latins, to the immediate northeast of Rome.

85. Aemilia: Roughly the area along the Via Aemilia, which ran between Ariminum (modern Rimini) and Placentia (modern Piacenza).

86. Po: For Phaet(h)on's connection with the ancient Padus (or Eridanus), see *ep.* 2.53.1–2, and Ovid *M.* 2.324.

87. Leonora d'Este, Duchess of Ferrara, was sister to Alfonso II and Federico III, and wife of Ercole d'Este. See also *ep.* 3.7.4. Federico was a guest of Leonora in December of 1474, during his long progress through Italy to France.

88. Ateste: Modern Este.

89. Ferrara: City in the Po valley, northeast of Bologna, seat of the Este family from the thirteenth to the sixteenth century.

94. Federico passed through Venice in January of 1475. For Sannazaro's love of Venice see *ep.* 1.35. In lines 93–4 Sannazaro is playing on the language of papal encyclicals addressed *urbi et orbi*, to the city (i.e. Rome) and to the world (see also *ep.* 1.36.10). Venice replaces Rome to become

in itself also an image of the world at large. See Kidwell, *Sannazaro*, 242, n. 5.

97. Kings: Possibly a reference to Venice's doges, or Sannazaro may be alluding to *Aeneid* 1.21 where Rome is said to have a *populum late regem belloque superbum* (a people of wide dominion and proud in war).

101. The Gonzagas were the ruling family of Mantua (modern Mantova). Federico probably passed through the town on his way to Milan in late January of 1475.

103. The Mincius (modern Mincio) flows through Mantua, birthplace of Vergil. See further *el.* 1.1.27.

106. Meles: River near Smyrna (modern Izmir), on the banks of which legend has it that Homer was born.

108. The reference is to Milan, to the west of which flows the Ticinus (modern Ticino). For the late etymology, that the name Mediolanum derives from *media lana*, see R. M. Ogilvie, *A Commentary on Livy: Books 1–5* (Oxford, 1965), 713 (on Livy 5.34.9), referring to Claudian *De Nupt.* 183; Sidonius Apollinaris *ep.* 7.17.2, line 20; Isidore *Origines* 15.1.57.

109. Taurini: A tribe that gives its name to Augusta Taurinorum, modern Turin. Federico departed from Turin in February of 1475.

109. The Pennine Alps run from Mont Blanc to Monte Rosa.

110. Rhône: Ancient Rhodanus. See on *ecl.* 3.18.

110. The modern Lac Léman (the Lake of Geneva), formed by the Rhône.

112. Jura: Mountain range in eastern France and northwest Switzerland.

113. Charles the Bold (1433–77), Duke of Burgundy. Charles was involved in wars on various fronts and Federico did not meet him until 26 September at Pont-à-Mousson. Federico with a party of 100 Neapolitan knights fought for Charles under contract at the siege of Nancy. Federico remained in Charles's service until the final breakdown of matrimonial negotiations in May of 1476.

123. Oenomaus, king of Pisa in Arcadia, killed the suitors of his daughter, Hippodameia, but was himself killed through the treachery of Pelops.

128. Charles the Bold died on 7 January 1477 in a battle outside the walls of Nancy. By this time Federico had transferred his loyalty to Charles's rival, the King of France, Louis XI, in whose court he lived for several months before returning to Italy.

135. Lingones: A people living west of the Vosges, from whom modern Langres derives its name.

136. Helvetii: A Celtic tribe occupying the western area of modern Switzerland.

137. Meuse: Ancient Mosa.

143. Giulio Acquaviva d'Aragona (d. 1481), a Neapolitan condottiere who fought in France with Federico; several members of his family were also condottieri. See also on *el.* 1.11.23. For his son, Andrea Matteo, see on *el.* 1.11.23, and son Belisario, see on *ep.* 2.38.

148. Federico returned to Naples on 21 October 1476 in a triumphal procession, bearing spoils from his wars in Burgundy.

151. Vergil uses the phrase *heia age, rumpe moras* at *Aen.* 4.569.

155. After a brief marriage with the granddaughter of King Louis XI of France, Anne of Savoy, Federico spent some time in the court of Louis XI, returning to Naples in 1482. His wife died soon after their marriage at the royal castle of Plessis, near Tours, leaving him with a daughter, Charlotte; it is her death that is seemingly alluded to at the end of the elegy.

157. Loire: See *ecl.* 3.36. The Arverni give their name to the modern Auvergne.

162. Barbarous foe: Mehmed II, the Ottoman sultan, whose forces conquered Otranto in 1480; it was recaptured by Ferdinando I in 1481.

163. Tyberinus (Tiberinus), modern Tiber. See also on *DPV* 3.343.

164. Magra: River flowing into the Ligurian Sea between Liguria and Tuscany.

166. This line repeats Propertius 1.17.26, with the change from *choro* to *noto* at the end.

169. Ligurians: See *ecl.* 3.17.

170. Var: See *ecl.* 5.114.

171. Ancient Tauroentrum (modern St. Cyr-sur-Mer), harbor town between Marseilles and Toulon.

172. Stoechades: See *ecl.* 3.18.

173. Phocaea, in Asia Minor, was the mother-city of Massilia (Marseilles). See also *el.* 2.2.74.

175. Turones: Gallic tribe that gives its name to the city of Tours, on the Loire (ancient Liger). See on *ecl.* 3.13 and 4.85.

3.2

See on *ecl.* 5, headnote, for Cassandra Marchese. This moving elegy has a brief, but striking complement in *ep.* 2.57, also addressed to her. The Picentini mountains lie some twenty-five kilometers east of Salerno. The subsequent place names are all to be found in the valley of S. Cipriano Picentino.

3. The fortress of Cerra in the valley of San Cipriano Picentino. The name is derived from *cerrus* (Italian *cerro*), the Turkey oak (*quercus cerris*).

5. Tebenna: Now called S. Maria di Tevenna.

6. Merula: Modern Monte Merola.

14. Goddess: Diana.

16. Frozen hail: Kidwell (*Sannazaro*, 11) gives this stream the modern name *Alli Grandini.*

21. Aonian Muses: See on *el.* 1.11.22.

35. Lines 35–44 refer to Sannazaro's *Arcadia* whose narrator appropriately bears the name Sincero.

36. Vergil uses the phrase *disparibus cicutis* at *ecl.* 2.36, also of pastoral song.

37. The phrase *deductum carmen* comes from Vergil *ecl.* 6.5.

39. Androgeus and Opicus: Figures prominent in *Arcadia.*

41. In the eleventh *eclogue* of *Arcadia* the poet laments the death of his mother Masella under the name Massilia.

42. Melisaeus: Giovanni Pontano. See on *ecl.* 2.42.

45. Lines 45–52 refer to *De Partu Virginis*.

52. Arsaces: The name of the first king of Parthia. Reference here is to Palestine, in particular to the three kings who may have emanated from Parthia or Persia (they are mentioned at Matthew 2:1–12). See *DPV* 1.18 and 254–6, and compare 2.454.

53. Lines 53–8 refer to the *Piscatoria* (*Eclogae Piscatoriae*). Line 57 directly echoes *ecl.* 4.19.

60. Sannazaro takes note of the three books of *Elegiae* (59–60) and the three books of *Epigrammata* (61–2).

64. Sannazaro's description of his own *Rime* (63–4) may also vicariously refer to the famous *Rime in Vita e Morte di Madonna Laura* of the Tuscan poet Petrarch (1304–74).

68. Machaon: Physician of the Greeks at Troy.

72. Compare also the descriptions, at *ecl.* 3.13–36, 4.81–6, and 5.113–5, of Sannazaro's journey into exile with King Federico.

75. Volcae: A people of Gallia Narbonensis, centered at modern Nîmes and Toulouse. The fields of the Vocontii are located near the modern Vaucluse.

76. Belgae: We are now in northern Gaul. See also *el.* 2.6.10.

78. Sannazaro refers to his journey in 1502 with King Federico, from Blois to Milan and back again.

82. Female figures in the *Iliad*: Hecuba, wife of king Priam, Cassandra their daughter, and Andromache, wife of their son Hector.

92. Pegasides: The Muses. See on *el.* 2.1.14.

97. Sannazaro is drawing his language here from Catullus 76.20–1.

3.3

8. Foliage of Pallas: Olive.

10. See Ovid *F.* 4.630–1.

19. Janus: See on *el.* 2.3.7.

24. For Apollo's slaying of Python, see Ovid *M.* 1.438–47.

28. King Ferdinando I (Ferrante) of Aragon. Triple foe: Ferdinando fought at various times against the French house of Anjou, the pope, the Venetians and the Ottoman empire.

30. Reference is to the victory, in September of 1481, of Alfonso, Duke of Calabria (later King Alfonso II), over the Turks who had held Otranto from the previous year. See also on *el.* 2.3.19 and 3.1.62.

32. Sannazaro is alluding to the reconquest of the kingdom of Naples from the French in 1495 by Ferdinando II (Ferrandino), son of Alfonso II.

34. Reference to a series of naval actions in 1483–84 on the part of Federico of Aragon against Venetian shipping and bases in the Adriatic.

36. The young son is Ferdinando, son of Federico of Aragon. He is the dedicatee of *eclogue* 4 (see headnote).

39. An *exedra* was a semicircular area with recesses, often for seats or statuary; a *xystus* is a portico regularly used for athletic exercise. In the architecture of a Roman house, the *tablinum* was a room that ran from the atrium to the peristyle, while technically the *hypocauston* is the system of hot-air conduits that heated the baths.

42. Boreas and Notus: The north and south winds, respectively.

52. Parthenopea: See on *ecl.* 3.88.

EPIGRAMS

First published in 1535.

1.1

Meter: elegiac couplet.

Federico of Aragon (1452–1504), King of Naples from 1496 to 1501 when he abdicated in favor of Louis XII of France and went into exile. See on *el.* 3.1, title. In 1499 he gave Sannazaro a villa at Mergellina, immediately to the west of the center of Naples.

4. Sannazaro draws an implicit comparison between himself and Horace by having us remember Maecenas's gift to the Augustan poet of his Sabine farm with its villa. Maecenas was also the dedicatee of Vergil's *Georgics*, concerned in part with farming.

1.2

Meter: Sapphic stanza.

For the villa, see on *ecl.* 1.110 and 2.3; also *ep.* 2.1.15, 2.36 passim, 2.60.59, 3.9.3. I follow Sannazaro's Latin spelling.

3. Doris: Sea-goddess and mother of the Nereids, standing by metonymy for the sea itself. See also *ep.* 1.23.4.

5. Cam(o)enae is a Latin designation for the Muses. See on *ecl.* 2.22.

7. Sannazaro draws the phrase *popularis aurae* from Horace *c.* 3.2.20 (it is used in the plural by Vergil at *Aen.* 6.816).

11. Aganippides: The Muses. See on *el.* 1.11.62 as well as *ep.* 1.61.27.

13. Sannazaro may be referring his readers to Catullus's use of the same phrase at 51.6, in his rendering of Sappho fr. 31. If so, Catullus's trials with Lesbia become Sannazaro's delight in Mergellina.

14. Napaeans: Valley nymphs. See on *DPV* 3.407.

16. The stream of Pegasus is Hippocrene. See on *el.* 2.1.14.

22. See on *el.* 1.9.23 and 2.2.40.

23. See on *el.* 1.9.12.

24. See on *el.* 3.1.16.

25. The phrase *I, puer* is a reminder of Horace *sat.* 1.10.92, where the address is also to a servant boy.

34. Helice: Nymph, transformed by Jupiter into the constellation Ursa Major (the Great Bear, which contains the Big Dipper). It gains its Greek name from the fact that it revolves around the North Pole. See Ovid *M.* 8.207.

36. Auster: Wind from the south. See *DPV* 2.457.

43. The phrase *amica Musis* derives from Horace *c.* 1.26.1. *Otium* is a standard prerequisite in classical poetry for the writing of both pastoral and georgic poetry.

1.3

Meter: elegiac couplet.

The Kalends are the first day of the month in the ancient Roman calendar. Calendimaggio was also a popular spring festival in many Italian cities.

5. The phrase *decolor Indus* is a reading at Propertius 4.3.10, accepted into the Oxford Classical Texts (ed. Barber [2nd ed., Oxford, 1960]; ed. Heyworth [Oxford, 2007]).

7. Smoked Lyaeus (*fumoso Lyaeo*): I.e. "smoky wine." Lyaeus ("the freer") is an epithet for the wine god Bacchus, smoky because bottles were stored near the kitchen.

10. Aeacus: After death, one of the three judges in the underworld (see commentators on Horace *c.* 2.13.22).

12. The command *falle* appears in the last line (31) of another scolion, Horace *epi.* 1.5.

12. For *atra mors* see commentators on Tibullus 1.3.4–5, and note the following *ep.* 1.4 where the phrase also appears in the poem's final line.

1.4

Meter: elegiac couplet

Ladislas of Durazzo (1376–1414), the last male of the senior Angevin line, King of Naples from 1386 until his death. He was the last ruler to aspire to create a kingdom of Italy before Charles VIII of France in 1494 (for further details see Kidwell, *Sannazaro*, 202–3, n. 9). His tomb is in the church of S. Giovanni a Carbonara, Naples.

5. Capitolium: Rome's central hill. Ladislas captured Rome and much of the Papal States between 1406 and 1414.

10. Ladislas successfully challenged Louis II, of the junior Angevin line, for control of Naples.

12. He died in 1414 at the siege of Florence (whose river is the Arno), when he would have been thirty-eight years of age. An Olympiad would ordinarily be a four year period.

1.5

Meter: elegiac couplet.

1. The phrase *effossis . . . ossa sepulcris* comes from Vergil *geo.* 1.497.

8. For the *rota Fortunae* see *el.* 1.5.27–8.

1.6

Meter: hendecasyllabic (phalaecean). It is used by Catullus in poems 5 and 7 which Sannazaro here has in mind.

18. Hybla: Town in eastern Sicily, southwest of Mt. Etna, known for the quality of its honey. See commentators on Vergil *ecl.* 1.54. See also *ep.* 1.42.1.

24. Compare Catullus 5.3.

26. Aurora was married to Tithonus, fated to grow continuously older but never to die. Venus was the goddess of love. Hebe, goddess of youth, was the wife of Hercules after the latter's divinization (see also *ep.* 2.19).

1.7

Meter: elegiac couplet.

For Altilio see on *el.* 1.11.18.

6. Aonia: Location of Mt. Helicon, one of the Muses' habitats.

1.8

Meter: elegiac couplet

1.9

Meter: elegiac couplet.

Alfonso II, King of Naples from 1494 to 95, when he abdicated. In 1480–81, as Duke of Calabria, he expelled the Turks from Otranto. Predictions of the imminent arrival of the Turks at the walls of Rome were frequent between the fall of Constantinople in 1453 and the death of Mehmed the Conqueror in 1482. See *ep.* 1.36 and 44; *el.* 1.9.34, 2.3.19 and 3.3.29–30.

1.10

Meter: elegiac couplet.

The identity of Laura is unknown.

4. Erycina: Venus, from her temple on Mount Eryx in western Sicily.

6. Sannazaro is thinking of Horace *c.* 1.24.10.

1.11

Meter: elegiac couplet.

For the background, see on *el.* 1.11.37.

3. Pierides: See on *el.* 1.5.6.

3. Charites: The Graces. Sannazaro is punning on the relation between Cariteo's Latin name, Chariteus, and Charites. See on *el.* 1.11.37.

12. Cyprian: Aphrodite/Venus had several shrines on the island of Cyprus.

1.12

Meter: elegiac couplet.

1.13

Meter: elegiac couplet.

Sannazaro may be being specific or general about Pontano's work on the text of Catullus, Latin lyric poet (c. 84-c. 54 BCE). The correction of classical authors was a favorite activity of the Accademia Pontaniana. For an example see on *el.* 1.9.14. For Pontano, see on *ecl.* 2.42.

6. The structure and, to a degree, the content of this epigram parallel those of Catullus 96, a poem with notorious textual problems.

1.14

Meter: elegiac couplet.

Cesare Borgia (1475/76–1507) was the natural son of Alexander VI (Rodrigo Borgia [1431–1503], pope, 1492–1503). See also on *ep.* 1.54.48. His position in Rome was endangered soon after the accession of Pope Julius II in 1503, who restored the influence of the Orsini. Cesare fled to Naples in 1504 where he was arrested and sent into exile in Spain. He was rumored to have had incestuous relations with his sister Lucrezia. See also *ep.* 1.15 passim, as well as 1.53–55.

1. Bull: An ox is the central figure of the Borgia coat-of-arms.

2. Bear: A reference to the Orsini family of Rome, whose name is drawn from the Italian for bear (*orso*, Latin *ursus*).

3. Tiber: Ancient Tibris (Tiberis), the river of Rome. See also *DPV* 3.343 and *el.* 3.1.163.

1.15

Meter: iambic trimeter.

17. Sannazaro is thinking of Vergil *ecl.* 6.53–4 where the bull beloved of Pasiphaë is the subject.

25. Po: Ancient Padus, Italy's most important river.

35. Sannazaro is parodying Vergil *geo.* 4.465–66, telling of Orpheus mourning for Eurydice.

43. Silvanus: Roman god of woods and uncultivated fields. See also *el.* 2.4.15.

1.16

Meter: elegiac couplet.

4. Aeneas, his father and his son, from Vergil's *Aeneid*. Sannazaro is thinking especially of events in the epic's second book.

7. On Sinuessa and Sannazaro's ancestral past, see *el.* 1.1.1–4.

11. In the *Aeneid* Vergil uses the adjective *pius* to define Aeneas' most notable characteristic. It is here reinforced by the abstract *pietas* (line 15).

13. Belgae: Inhabitants of northern Gaul. See *el.* 2.6.10, 3.2.76.

13. Britanni: Inhabitants of Britain. See *el.* 2.6.11, *ep.* 2.51.16, and especially *ecl.* 3.21 and 5.115, references suggesting that the present epigram also looks to the poet's own years of exile.

1.17

Meter: elegiac couplet.

4. A reference to the wounding of Aphrodite by Diomedes, described by Homer (*Il.* 5.330–62).

1.18

Meter: elegiac couplet.

4. Compare Vergil *geo.* 3.391–93. Macrobius (*Sat.* 5.22) says that the story, in which Pan replaces the expected Endymion, comes from Nicander.

1.19

Meter: elegiac couplet.

Ferdinando II (Ferrandino), 1467–96, son of Alfonso II and king of Naples, 1495–96. See also *ep.* 2.8 and 41.

1. See on *Sal.* 16.

1.20

Meter: elegiac couplet.

Poggio Bracciolini (1380–1459), humanist scholar, papal secretary and later Chancellor of Florence. In the latter role he composed a *History of Florence* which Sannazaro takes to task for its chauvinism.

1.21

Meter: elegiac couplet.

Bartolomeo Platina (1421–1481), c. 1477 appointed Prefect of the Vatican Library by Sixtus IV (see on ep. 1.44.2), wrote a history of the popes (edited by A. F. D'Elia in this I Tatti Renaissance Library [Cambridge, Mass., 2008]) as well as a cookbook (*De honesta voluptate et valetudine* [Rome, 1475]). For the latter see M. E. Milham, tr., *Platina on right plea-*

sure and good health (Tempe, 1998). For his own purposes Sannazaro has reversed the chronological order of publication of the two works.

4. Sannazaro is punning on Latin *pascere* (to feed but also to nurture). At John 21:15 Christ tells Peter, the first pope, to "feed my sheep" (*pasce agnos meos*).

1.22

Meter: elegiac couplet.

1.23

Meter: elegiac couplet.

4. Doris: See fr. 11.

4. Galatea: See on *ecl.* 1.86.

7. Thetis: See on *ecl.* 1.90. She stands here by metonymy for the sea itself.

1.24

Meter: elegiac couplet.

The Volturno is the ancient Vulturnus, flowing west from the Apennines, entering the Tyrrhenian Sea north of Cumae.

5. See Vergil *ecl.* 2.17 and 45.

1.25

Meter: elegiac couplet.

Quinzio has not been identified, and may not be an historical personage. Catullus addresses poems 82 and 100, also in the same meter, to a certain Quintius.

4. Sannazaro is working with a pun between *clara* (1) and *obscurus* (3), light and dark, famous and inglorious, bright and dull, that is lost in translation.

1.26

Meter: elegiac couplet.

1. Cyllenian: Mercury/Hermes, the fleet-footed messenger of the gods, who was born on the Arcadian mountain of Cyllene. One of his most famous characteristics was his bent for thievery.

1.27

Meter: elegiac couplet.

Hannibal (247–183/2 BCE) was a general who led the Carthaginians against Rome in the Second Punic War (218–201 BCE).

1.28

Meter: elegiac couplet.

4. The meaning presumably is that Mars, Venus's paramour, is still quite available.

1.29

Meter: elegiac couplet

Fabianus is the name of the addressee of four poems by Martial (3.36, 4.5, 4.24, 12.83).

1.30

Meter: elegiac couplet.

2. Sannazaro plays on the Latin adjective *nefastus* as meaning both contrary to divine law (of days) and wicked (of people). On the etymology, which the ancients derived from *fari* (to speak), see R. Maltby, *Ancient Latin Etymologies*, s. v. *fas, nefas,* and *nefasti dies*.

1.31

Meter: elegiac couplet.

Ink in the fifteenth century was made from a combination of ferrous sulfate, vinegar, gum, and water.

3. Sannazaro draws on Cicero' quotation (*TD* 1.34) of the epitaph of Ennius in which the poet uses the phrase *volito vivus per ora virum* ("I fly living through the voices of mankind"). See also *el.* 1.9.14.

4. A reference to Horace *c.* 3.30.2.

1.32

Meter: elegiac couplet.

1. Janus's Kalends: New Year's Day.

1.33

Meter: elegiac couplet.

Martial addresses two epigrams (1.43, 4.61) to a certain Mancinus who is mentioned in a third (1.37.1).

1.34

Meter: hendecasyllabic.

Though the poem is a standard sepulchral epigram, the whole is reminiscent of Catullus 3, with which it also has meter in common.

5. Clotho: One of the three Fates. See also fr. 37.

1.35

Meter: elegiac couplet.

1. Adriatic waters: The Adriatic Sea off the east coast of Italy.

3. Tarpeian: A precipice on the southwest corner of Rome's Capitoline hill, here standing by metonymy for the hill itself. It is named after Tarpeia who treacherously betrayed the fortress to the Sabines (see commentators on Livy 1.11.6). Rome was founded by Mars's offspring, Romulus and Remus.

6. For Sannazaro's love of Venice see *el.* 3.1.93–103; *ep.* 2.31. For details on the story of the city's reward for his praise, see Kidwell, *Sannazaro* 174–75, and 206, n. 28.

1.36

Meter: elegiac couplet.

Duke of Calabria: Alfonso II's title before he became King of Naples in 1494. See on *ep.* 1.9.

10. For the phrase *urbis et orbis* see on *el.* 3.1.93–4.

1.37

Meter: elegiac couplet.

Innocent VIII (Giovanni Battista Cybo [1432–92], pope, 1484–92). He inherited a bankrupt papacy owing to the refusal of Ferdinando I to pay the clerical revenues of the Neapolitan kingdom, and directed papal policy with a view to finding good marriages for his illegitimate children. See also note on *el.* 2.1.73.

1. Quirites: The technical name for citizens of Rome.

1.38

Meter: elegiac couplet.

1.39

Meter: elegiac couplet.

2. Sannazaro is punning on the aural connection between *labra* and *libris*.

1.40

Meter: choliambic (scazon).

The name comes from the Latin *vetustus* ("old").

9. Compare Catullus 23.1–2 *eqs.*

17. Falernian: Wines from the *ager Falernus* in northern Campania or from the Aegean island of Chius (Chios) were especially prized, as was a vintage bottled during the consulship of Opimius, consul in 121 BCE.

32. Favissae: Underground cellars or cisterns associated with the Capitolium.

32. Manes: The shades of the dead or their underworld abode.

47. Gemoniae: The "Steps of Groans," on the Aventine Hill in Rome, whence bodies of executed criminals were dragged down to the Tiber.

1.41

Meter: elegiac couplet.

The name Neaera appears twice in Horace (*epode* 15.11, *c.* 3.14.21) and is used of the mistress of Lygdamus in the elegies of [ps.]Tibullus, book 3.

500

1.42

Meter: elegiac couplet.

For Hybla see on *ep.* 1.6.18.

1. See on *el.* 1.11.32. Hybla was the name of the addressee's mistress.

4. A distant echo of Catullus 101.9.

1.43

Meter: elegiac couplet.

Horace gives the name Aufidius Luscus to the "praetor" at Fundi (*sat.* 1.5.34; compare 2.4.24). Aufidius Chius is an adulterer at Juvenal *sat.* 9.25 (compare Martial 5.61.10).

1.44

Meter: elegiac couplet

1. Lion: Symbol of St. Mark and thus of Venice.

1. Hercules: Referring to Ercole I d'Este (1431–1505), duke of Ferrara from 1471 until his death.

3. Oak tree: Symbol of the della Rovere family, here in particular of Sixtus IV (see on *el.* 3.1.77).

4. In 1482–4 Alfonso led the defense of Ferrara against the combined forces of Venice and of the papacy.

5. Bellona: Roman goddess of war.

6. A reference to Vergil *Aen.* 1.294.

7. Parthenope: Naples. See on *ecl.* 3.88.

9. Sebeto: See on *ecl.* 1.105.

1.45

Meter: elegiac couplet.

2. Sannazaro is punning on the derivation of the name of the river Magra (ancient Macra) from the Latin *macer* ("thin"). See on *el.* 3.1.164.

1.46

Meter: elegiac couplet.

A certain Olus is the subject of five epigrams by Martial.

1.47

Meter: elegiac couplet.

A Rufus is the addressee of two poems of Catullus (69 and 77), and Nasidienus Rufus figures prominently in Horace *sat.* 2.8. The name is common in Martial who has several epigrams on the poem's theme.

5. Nestor: Homer's epitome of ancient wisdom in the *Iliad*, who came from Pylos, in the western Peloponnesus. See also *ep.* 2.41.1, 2.49.10.

5. Archemorus: Young son of Lycurgus and Eurydice, killed by a serpent while in the charge of Hypsipyle. The story is told at length in the fourth book of Statius's *Thebaid*.

6. Andromache: Wife of Hector and mother of Astyanax.

6. Laomedon: King of Troy and father of Priam. From the evidence of all these cases Rufus hasn't mastered the myths to which his poetry refers.

7. Phrygian: I.e. Trojan.

1.48

Meter: elegiac couplet.

Ovid tells the story of Apollo and Cyparissus at *M.* 10.106–42.

3. Delian: Apollo, born on the island of Delos.

1.49

Meter: elegiac couplet.

2. Actius: Sannazaro's name in the Academy.

1.50

Meter: elegiac couplet.

The Veronese Fra Giovanni Giocondo (c. 1435–1515), Franciscan priest, antiquarian and architect (see further Kidwell, *Sannazaro*, 45–48, and

213–14, n. 74). In 1496–98 Giocondo was invited to Paris by Louis XII where he built the Pont Nôtre-Dame and the Petit Pont. Sannazaro plays on the etymology of *pontifex* (apparently from *pons* [bridge] and the root of *facio* [make]), meaning first priest, then pope.

1. Seine: Ancient Sequana. See also *ep*. 2.60.36; *DPV* 2.197.

1.51

Meter: elegiac couplet.

1. Elis(s)a is Dido's original Phoenician name.

2. Offspring of a goddess: Aeneas is so apostrophized frequently in Vergil's epic.

1.52

Meter: elegiac couplet.

The name is drawn from the Roman gens Caecilius.

1.53

Meter: hendecasyllabic.

Marino Caracciolo (1468–1538), Neapolitan nobleman and friend of Sannazaro, later a cardinal and diplomat in the service of Charles V.

4. Compare Catullus 56.1–2, and, for the language of poetry in particular, 50.4–8. Both poems are also in hendecasyllabic meter.

6. Compare Catullus 58.1–2, addressed to Lesbia, where the context also serves as commentary on Sannazaro's words.

13. Perhaps an allusion to the death (June 14, 1497) of Giovanni, Duke of Gandia, rumored to have been the victim of his brother, his rival in various sexual liaisons.

17. Sannazaro builds his poem here upon several other Catullan models, among them 29 and 56.

24. The modern names are Rimini, Pesaro, Urbino, Populonia (village, and ruins, near Piombino that still bear their ancient name), Camerino, Forlì (technically ancient Forum Livii, which will not fit the meter), Imola, Faenza.

26. The seas on either side of Italy, Tyrrhenian and Adriatic.

32. Probably a reference to the poisoning of Borgia and his father, Alexander VI, in August 1503, as a result of which Cesare lost control of the numerous cities he had acquired since 1499.

43. Perhaps a reference to the day on which Cesare's father died (August 14, 1503).

44. See on *ep.* 3.1.18 as well as commentators on Ovid *M.* 15.41.

46. The structure of this poem is drawn from the invectives of Catullus, e.g. 29 and 42 with bows to many others.

1.54

Meter: elegiac couplet.

The title comes from the name of Gaius Iulius Caesar, Roman general and politician who, through his adopted son, the future Augustus, initiated the Julio-Claudian line of emperors.

Cesare Borgia's final heraldic device had the motto *Aut Caesar aut nihil.*

1.55

Meter: elegiac couplet.

1.56

Meter: elegiac couplet.

1. An Aurelius is named in four poems of Catullus (11, 15, 16, 21).

2. Nearchus: The name of a youth at Horace *c.* 3.20.6.

8. Setian: From Setia, Latian town (modern Sezza), well-known for its wine.

1.57

Meter: elegiac couplet.

2. Compare Catullus 5 and 7.

4. By allusion Sannazaro points us to Martial 6.34, a poem that in turn refers directly to Catullus.

8. The honey of Mt. Hymettus, bordering Athens on the east, founded by Cecrops, was renowned. See also *ecl.* 3. 77.

1.58

Meter: choliambic (scazon).

Bassus is the name of several addressees in Martial's epigrams. A Caesius Bassus was a Roman lyric poet to whom Persius dedicated his sixth satire. Sannazaro may be referring specifically to the Renaissance humanist Angelo Colocci (1474–1547) whose pseudonym in the Accademia Pontaniana was Bassus.

2. Phyllis: For the name see Horace *c.* 2.4.14 and 4.11.3.

5. The harvest of Saba: Arabian incense.

1.59

Meter: elegiac couplet.

1.60

Meter: elegiac couplet.

Aegle is a nymph at Vergil *ecl.* 6.20–1.

1.61

Meter: hendecasyllabic.

Angelo Ambrogini (1454–1494) known as Poliziano or Politianus (Politian), Florentine scholar and poet. For a full interpretation of the poem that puts it in its larger literary context see Gaisser, *Catullus*, 77, 243–46, and J. Gaisser, ed., *Catullus*, Oxford Readings in Classical Studies (Oxford, 2007), Part VI (Debating the Sparrow), 305–40, especially 308–10. I have kept the Latin name here for the sake of Sannazaro's punning on the Latin word for flea (*pulex*).

8. See Catullus 16.3–4.

12. Though Sannazaro is thinking of Catullus 5 and 7, he is also quoting from Politian's *Miscellanea* 1.6 (published in 1489), where Catullus is slightly miscited, and varying Martial 11.6.14–16: *Da nunc basia, sed Catulliana: / quae si tot fuerint quot ille dixit, / donabo tibi passerem Catulli*

(Now give me kisses, but Catullan ones. If they will be as many as he said, I will give you Catullus's sparrow). In the process he is perhaps bringing to the surface an obscenity that may lurk behind Catullus's words to Lesbia, in his poems 2 and 3. But see Adams, *Latin Sexual Vocabulary*, 32–3.

26. Sannazaro directly quotes Martial (4.14.13–14), who gives a title to Catullus's *libellus* from the subject-matter of its second and third poems. Maro is Vergil (Publius Vergilius Maro). See also *ep.* 2.47.3–4; *el.* 1.1.27, 1.9.19 and 46, 1.11.16, 3.1.105.

27. See *ep.* 1.2.11.

1.62

Meter: iambic trimeter.

4. Typhoeus: See on *ecl.* 4.30.

9. Catullus 29.1 is on the poet's mind.

27. The phrase *in malam crucem* is a favorite of the Roman comic poets.

1.63

Meter: elegiac couplet.

3. Gargaphie: Fountain (and valley, of the same name) in Boeotia where Actaeon saw Diana naked and was torn apart by his hounds. See Ovid *M.* 3.156 where the story is recounted (138–252).

1.64

Meter: elegiac couplet.

For the story of Orpheus looking back at Eurydice, see Vergil *geo.* 4.491.

1.65

Meter: elegiac couplet.

1.66

Meter: elegiac couplet.

1.67

Meter: elegiac couplet.

2. Homer, whose supposed origin was Maeonia in Lydia. See also *ep.* 2.5.2, 2.47.4.

3. For Bavius and M(a)evius, see commentators on Vergil *ecl.* 3.90; for Mevius alone, Horace *epode* 10.2.

2.1

Meter: Sapphic stanza.

For Federico of Aragon, see on *el.* 3.1, passim.

17. For Galatea and her lover Polyphemus see on *ecl.* 1.86.

24. Rhine: Ancient Rhenus. See also *ep.* 2.60.21; *el.* 3.1.138; *DPV* 2.190.

26. Dalmatae: Inhabitants of Dalmatia on the east coast of the Adriatic. For Federico's naval exploits in the Adriatic, see 3.3.34.

28. Timavo: The ancient Timavus, flowing into the Gulf of Trieste.

31. Orcus: God of the Underworld, otherwise known as Dis. See also on *DPV* 3.437.

33. Nothing greater, nothing braver: France and Spain divided the Kingdom of Naples between themselves by the Treaty of Granada (1501); this treaty was recognized by a papal bull, by which Federico was also declared to be deposed. To save Naples from being sacked by troops under the command of Cesare Borgia, Federico made a truce and retired to Ischia; eventually he was sent to France, where he lived the rest of his life in honorable captivity, with Sannazaro as one of his companions.

2.2

Meter: elegiac couplet.

For Andrea Matteo Acquaviva see on *el.* 1.11.23.

3. See on *el.* 1.11.64.

6. Of the three Gorgons, the most well-known is Medusa, snake-haired monster who turned men to stone.

2.3

Meter: iambic trimeter, the meter of Catullus 4, 29 and 52.

8. See on *ep.* 1.31.3.

2.4

Meter: elegiac couplet.

Several epigrams of Martial are addressed to a Matho. It is also the name of a lawyer mocked on occasion by Juvenal (see commentators on *sat.* 1.32).

4. Our poet: Vergil.

2.5

Meter: elegiac couplet.

1. Names of cities and islands in Greece and Asia Minor.

2. See on *ep.* 1.67.2.

2.6

Meter: elegiac couplet.

1. Tegea: Town in southern Arcadia. For the tale of Pan and Luna see commentators on Vergil *geo.* 3.392–3.

3. On the story of Syrinx, pursued by Pan and turned into a group of reeds, see Ovid *M.* 1.689–712.

2.7

Meter: elegiac couplet.

2.8

Meter: elegiac couplet.

Sannazaro is punning on a connection between Latin *ferrum* ("iron") and the name of Ferrante (Ferdinando I, 1423–94; King of Naples, 1458–94), or of his grandson Ferrantino (Ferdinando II, 1469–96; King of Naples, 1494–5).

2. If the text is correct, Sannazaro may be using the verb *meto* in the sense of mow down in battle, as in Vergil *Aen.* 10.513. It is equally likely that Sannazaro is thinking of the use of iron in objects for ploughing and reaping in a non-golden age.

2.9

Meter: elegiac couplet.

Pietro Summonte (1453–1526), who in 1503 succeeded Pontano as head of the Neapolitan Academy, edited the works of Pontano after his death and published the first official edition of Sannazaro's *Arcadia* in 1504. He appears in *Arcadia* 12, both prosa and *eclogue*.

2.10

Meter: elegiac couplet.

1. Cytherean: See *el.* 2.8.22.

4. An allusion to Vulcan's means of catching Venus in adultery with Mars.

2.11

Meter: elegiac couplet.

2.12

Meter: elegiac couplet.

1. Dione: The mother of Venus, standing here for the goddess herself.

2. For the double-entendre of *arma*, especially in connection with the ithyphallic god Priapus, see Adams, *Latin Sexual Vocabulary*, 19–22.

2.13

Meter: elegiac couplet.

Sannazaro draws both the name and the theme from Catullus's Gellius poems (74, 80, 88–91, 116).

2.14

Meter: elegiac couplet.

The cognomen of the poet Horace, on which he puns at *epode* 15.12.

2. In part a play on the literal and idiomatic meanings of the phrase *verba dari*: to be given words, or to be deceived, to be lied to.

2.15

Meter: hendecasyllabic.

For Petrus Compater see on *el.* 1.11.20. Why he is called "Petus" here instead of the usual Petrus has not been explained.

1. This line alludes to Catullus 2.1, repeated at 3.4, on the death of the speaker's sparrow.

14. Parcae: See on *DPV* 1.270.

20. Pierides: See *el.* 1.5.6.

22. Paphos, Cnidos and Amathus: All three of these towns, the first (see on *Sal.* 3 and *el.* 1.4.27) and last on Cyprus (see *Sal.* 3), the second (see on *DPV* 2.140) in Caria, are sacred to Venus.

31. Sannazaro is referring to his exile in France (1501–5). For the Loire (ancient Liger) see *ep.* 2.51.11, 2.60.34; *ecl.* 3.36 and 4.85; *el.* 3.1.157; for the Morini, *ecl.* 3.34; for Ocean *ecl.* 3.20 and 4.84, *el.* 3.1.153; for the Celtae, *el.* 3.1.154.

35. All Neapolitan landmarks. For Posillipo (ancient Pausylipum) see *ecl.* 1.13; for the Sebeto (ancient Sebethos), *ecl.* 1.105; for Vesuvius (ancient Vesevus or Vesaevus), *ecl.* 4.77.

37. Nereus: See on *ecl.* 1.99.

46. Pontano: See on *ecl.* 2.41.

54. Tethys: See *DPV* 1.202.

2.16

Meter: elegiac couplet.

9. Thunderer: See on *ecl.* 3.70.

2.17

Meter: elegiac couplet.

Lucius Junius Brutus, Rome's first consul, was the assassin of its last king, Tarquinius Superbus (Tarquin the Proud). See also *el.* 3.1.52.

2.18

Meter: elegiac couplet.

2.19

Meter: elegiac couplet.

1. Alcides: Hercules, as grandson of Alceus.

2. Hylas: Youth, favored by Hercules, whom he accompanied on the expedition of the Argonauts. See also *ep.* 2.28.4.

4. After his abduction into the company of the gods, Ganymede replaced Hercules's wife, Hebe, as their cup-bearer.

2.20

Meter: elegiac couplet.

Ufens is the name of a Latin warrior, first mentioned at Vergil *Aen.* 7.745.

2.21

Meter: elegiac couplet.

2.22

Meter: elegiac couplet.

1. Dictynna: Cretan goddess, usually identified with Diana.

6. Swan: The shape assumed by Zeus/Jupiter to seduce Leda.

2.23

Meter: elegiac couplet.

Riccius has not been identified.

2. In part, a pun on the literal and idiomatic meanings of *male audire*, to hear badly or to hear ill of oneself.

2.24

Meter: elegiac couplet.

2.25

Meter: elegiac couplet.

Lucius is a Roman praenomen (perhaps most well-known as that of the hero of Apuleius's *Metamorphoses*). It is used also for one of Martial's addressees (4.55).

2. Saône: Ancient Arar. See *DPV* 2.196, *ecl.* 5.115, *el.* 1.8.53.

2.26

Meter: elegiac couplet.

2.27

Meter: elegiac couplet.

2.28

Meter: elegiac couplet.

1. Tirynthian: Hercules, as a native of Tiryns. Phrygian wine-pourer: Ganymede.

4. For the story see commentators on Theocritus *Id.* 13 and Propertius 1.20. The gist of the epigram is that, since Jupiter didn't approve when the naiad stole Hylas from Hercules, the latter shouldn't then attempt to steal Ganymede back from Jupiter.

2.29

Meter: elegiac couplet.

2.30

Meter: elegiac couplet.

Cato the Younger (Marcus Portius Cato Uticensis, 95–46 BCE) who, as a believer in the Republic, committed suicide rather than live under Caesar.

2.31

Meter: elegiac couplet.

2. See also *ep.* 1.35.

2.32

Meter: elegiac couplet.

For Acquaviva see on *el.* 1.11.23, and *ep.* 2.2.

1. Bitonto: Italian town, near the Adriatic coast, inland from Bari.

8. Sirens: See on *ecl.* 1.104.

8. Lotophagi: See on *el.* 2.1.30.

2.33

Meter: elegiac couplet.

2.34

Meter: elegiac couplet.

Galeazzo Caracciolo was a Neapolitan nobleman who helped defeat the Turks at Otranto in 1481. The statue at his tomb in S. Giovanni a Carbonara depicts him in the armor he wore at the battle.

2.35

Meter: elegiac couplet.

Sannazaro does not name the amphitheater but, given his love for local monuments from antiquity, he may mean the one whose remains are at Puteoli (Pozzuoli), or the larger and better-preserved example in S. Maria Capua Vetere.

2.36

Meter: Sapphic stanza.

See on *DPV* 1.26, *ecl.* 1.110 and 2.3 as well as *ep.* 1.2.15.

7. Posillipo: See on *ecl.* 1.13.

12. Leo: The lion, zodiacal sign whose celestial span of time is largely equivalent to the month of August, named after the emperor Augustus.

14. Father: Julius Caesar, adoptive father of Augustus, who reformed the Roman calendar in 46 BCE. See also *ep.* 1.54.1.

21. Eos: In Greek, the dawn, and by metonymy the orient. See also *ep.* 2.48.8; *DPV* 1.18, 369 and 434, 3.6; *ecl.* 5.65.

27. For San Nazario see on *el.* 2.2. Sannazaro was born (July 28, 1458) on the feast day of the saint for whom the French city of San Nazaire as well as the poet's family is named.

32. Nero: Roman emperor (37–68 CE) under whose reign (from 54 until his death) Nazarius was supposedly martyred. See also *ep.* 2.60.37.

2.37

Meter: elegiac couplet.

For San Nazario see on *el.* 2.2 and the preceding poem.

5. The fourth day before the Kalends (first) of Sextilis (August) would be July 28 (1458).

2.38

Meter: elegiac couplet.

The Neritini (Neretini) were inhabitants of Neretum, modern Nardò, in Apulia. Belisario Acquaviva (c. 1459–1528), its first duke and refounder of its Accademia del Lauro, was son of Giulio Acquaviva (see on *el.* 3.1.141) and younger brother of Andrea Matteo Acquaviva (c. 1458–1529; see *ep.* 2.2 and 32, and on *el.* 1.11.23).

2.39

Meter: elegiac couplet.

Giovanni Cotta (1480/82–1510), Latin poet and humanist, born in Verona, later a member of Pontano's academy. For further detail see Gaisser, *Pierio Valeriano*, 203–4.

2.40

Meter: elegiac couplet.

A *Picens* or *Piceno* is technically someone from Picenum, area on the east side of Italy whose central city is Ancona. Two of Martial's epigrams have an addressee with the name Picens (8.57 and 62).

3. The Cynics derived their name from the Greek word for dog.

4. The translation cannot represent the aural play on *Cynicus, clinicus* and *merdicus, medicus*.

2.41

Meter: elegiac couplet.

For Ferdinando, see on *ep.* 2.8.

1. Nestor: See on *ep.* 1.47.5.

2. Antilochus was a young son of Nestor killed at Troy. See commentators on Horace *c.* 2.9.14.

2.42

Meter: elegiac couplet.

This is an anonymous address to Pope Julius II (Giuliano Della Rovere [1443–1513], pope, 1503–13). Before becoming pontiff he had been cardinal-priest of the church of San Pietro in Vincoli (St. Peter in Chains). Hence Sannazaro's emphasis on *vincula* in lines 2 and 4, and the economic advantages that their possession implies.

2.43

Meter: elegiac couplet.

1. Laetitia: The mother's name means joyfulness. Tristitia means sadness.

4. Lachesis: One of the three Fates. See also *el.* 1.3.30.

5. After the loss of her children to the vengeance of Apollo and Diana, Niobe was turned to stone from weeping. The story is told by Ovid at *M.* 6.146–312.

2.44

Meter: elegiac couplet.

2.45

Meter: elegiac couplet.

1. Ilian: I.e. Trojan.

2. For obscene senses of *misceo* see Adams, *Latin Sexual Vocabulary*, 180–81.

2.46

Meter: elegiac couplet.

See *ep.* 2.30.

2.47

Meter: elegiac couplet.

1. Seven cities: See *ep.* 2.4.

2. Maro: Vergil (Publius Vergilius Maro). See *ep.* 1.61.24 and 26.

4. Maeonides: See *ep.* 1.67.2.

2.48

Meter: elegiac couplet.

2. Assanius: Castello in his 1928 edition of Sannazaro suggests that this is Girolamo Olgiato, one of the republican assassins of Galeazzo Sforza in 1476. According to Machiavelli's *History of Florence* (7.1), when executed for this crime at the age of 23, he was supposed to have said, with composure, *Mors acerba, fama perpetua, stabit vetus memoria facti* ("Death is bitter; repute is everlasting; the memory of the deed will remain longstanding"). As the neologism *assassinus* (from Arabic via Italian) is attested in Renaissance Latin (see René Hoven, *Lexique de la prose latine de la Renaissance*, 2nd ed. [Leiden and Boston, 2006], 48), one might consider emending *Assanio* to *assassino* if it were metrically possible and Sannazaro more tolerant of neologism.

8. Eoan: I.e. eastern, oriental. See on *DPV* 1.18.

10. A relative's blood: Machiavelli states that one motive for Olgiato's assassination of Sforza was that the latter had dishonored him "in respect to his wives or other female relatives."

16. Sannazaro may be thinking of the famous epigram of Simonides translated by Cicero (*TD* 1.42.101), and his immediately preceding description of "a certain Lacedaemonian" (*Lacedaemonius quidam*); the epigram celebrates the self-sacrifice of the Spartans at Thermopylae.

2.49

Meter: elegiac couplet.

Possibly written for the tomb of Jacopo Caldora (1369–1439), called Caudola in Latin, Neapolitan condottiere, who is buried in Sulmona in the church of Santo Spirito; or Giovanni Antonio Caldora (d. 1500), condottiere and lord of Monteodorisio. The latter belonged to the court of Ferdinando I and is known to have attended the coronation of Alfonso II of Aragon.

8. Achilles and Hector are central figures in Homer's *Iliad*. On Nestor see *ep*. 1.47.5.

2.50

Meter: elegiac couplet.

4. The reference is to Jupiter's disguise as a bull for the rape of Europa.

2.51

Meter: Sapphic stanza.

12. The town of St-Nazaire is located on the right bank of the Liger (Loire) immediately before it flows into the Atlantic. Sannazaro was no doubt there during his years of exile.

13. Aulerci: The name of several Gallic tribes.

14. Lexovii: A tribe in northern Gaul, whence the modern Lisieux.

42. Sebeto: See on *ecl*. 1.105.

43. Posillipo: See on *ecl*. 1.13.

2.52

Meter: elegiac couplet.

Sannazaro may be thinking here of the verses of Quintus Lutatius Catulus (d. 87 BCE), quoted by Aulus Gellius (*NA* 19.9.14).

1. The Cyprian: Venus.

2.53

Meter: Elegiac couplet.

Camilla Scalampa of Milan is praised for her *colte rime* in a novel (XVI) of Matteo Bandello (1485–1561).

2. In Ovid's version of the tale (*M.* 2.324), the Eridanus (modern Po) received the burned body of Phaet(h)on, who had attempted to control the chariot of his father, the Sun (i.e. Apollo). See also *el.* 3.1.86.

3. Ticino: Ancient Ticinus, which flows west of Milan and enters the Po near Pavia. See also *el.* 3.1.107.

8. The aural play on *pater* and Phaeton is impossible to convey in translation.

2.54

Meter: elegiac couplet.

Violante Grappina was mother of Maria Diaz Garlon, whose marriage is celebrated in *ep.* 3.1, and Antonio Diaz Garlon (see on *el.* 1.4 and 2.2.41). See Kidwell, *Sannazaro*, 238, n. 2.

6. Sannazaro is playing on the connection between Violante and *violae*.

2.55

Meter: elegiac couplet.

Compare *el.* 2.4.17 and 56.

3. The goddesses of Aonia: The Muses. See on *DPV* 1.15.

2.56

Meter: elegiac couplet.

4. Sebeto: See on *ecl.* 1.105.

8. The Sirens: See on *ecl.* 1.104.

2.57

Meter: elegiac couplet.

For Cassandra Marchese see on *ecl.* 5, dedication. She is also the recipient of *ep.* 3.2 and *el.* 3.2.

2.58

Meter: iambic dimeter, a meter of the Christian hymn beginning with St. Ambrose.

Saint Gaudioso was a fifth-century bishop of Naples, where his relics are preserved in catacombs under the church of Santa Maria della Sanità. His feast day is October 27.

5. Lucifer: Venus as the Morning Star.

24. Sannazaro is playing on the connection between the name Gaudiosus and the Latin word for joy (*gaudium*).

2.59

Meter: Sapphic stanza.

2.60

Meter: Sapphic stanza.

15. Rhaeti: R(h)aetia was the Roman province that embraced the eastern Alps.

22. Treveri: A tribe west of the Rhine whose center would be the modern Trier.

28. Sannazaro is referring to baptism.

34. Loire: Ancient Liger. See on *ecl* 3.36.

36. Seine: The ancient Sequana. See on *DPV* 2.197.

37. Nero: See *ep.* 2.36.32.

39. Anolinus: Prefect said to have arrested Nazarius under Nero.

44. Iberi and Indi: Peoples of the west and the east respectively.

59. Mergellina: See on *ecl.* 1.110 and 2.3.

2.61

Meter: elegiac couplet

Ferdinando (Fernando) d'Avalos (1489–1525), Marquis of Pescara, born in Naples to an important family of Spanish descent. He was the commander of Charles V's forces at the battle of Pavia (1525), where he captured Francis I of France. He died shortly thereafter of wounds he had suffered. He was the nephew of Costanza d'Avalos (see *ecl.* 2.23) and was married to the poet Vittoria Colonna. Piscaria is the medieval name of modern Pescara on the Adriatic coast of Italy.

2. Ligurians: I.e. the Genoese. See on *ecl.* 3.17.

3. Enceladus was a major protagonist in the war of the Giants against the Olympians. He is often associated with the monster Typhoeus (see on *ecl.* 4.30).

2.62

Meter: elegiac couplet.

Nola is a Campanian town northeast of Mt. Vesuvius. At lines 3 and 5 Sannazaro plays on the aural connection between the town's name and Latin *noluit* ("it didn't want") and *nolueris* ("you didn't want").

2. See Aulus Gellius *NA* 6.20.1–2. Servius also tells the story in his comment on Vergil *geo.* 2.224.

3. Jovianus: The name in the Academy of Giovanni Gioviano Pontano. See on *ecl.* 2.42.

8. The destructive Styx: Referring perhaps to the destruction caused by the eruption of Vesuvius in 79 CE.

10. I.e. air and water.

2.63

Meter: hendecasyllabic.

For the name see note to *ep.* 1.41.1.

3.1

Meter: Three lines in iambic dimeter followed by a pherecratean.

The poem celebrates the marriage of Maria Diaz Garlon, daughter of Violante Grappina (see on *ep.* 2.54), and Alfonso Sanseverino, Duke of Somma (see Kidwell, *Sannazaro*, 238, n. 2).

18. For the custom see commentators on Catullus 68.148 and 107.6.

25. Thalia: See on *el.* 1.5.19.

3.2

Meter: elegiac couplet.

See on *ecl.* 5, dedication. She is also the recipient of *ep.* 2.57 and *el.* 3.2.

3.3

Meter elegiac couplet.

2. Ancient of Samos: Pythagoras of Samos (mid- to late 6th century BCE) preached metempsychosis.

6. Doves, the birds of Venus, were proverbial for the intensity of their devotion. See commentators on Catullus 68.125–28; Martial 11.104.9, et al.

3.4

Meter: elegiac couplet.

Hadrian VI (1459–1523), born Adrian Florensz in the Netherlands, reigned as pope for 21 months (1522–23). He was widely disliked by Italian humanists who saw him as a miser and barbarian.

2. The Turkish sultan Suleiman I (the Magnificent), 1494–1566, had conquered Rhodes in December, 1522, the home of the Knights of Rhodes, later the Knights of Malta.

3.5

Meter: elegiac couplet.

4. The Scotsman has not been identified.

3.6

Meter: elegiac couplet.

Euno has not been identified.

1. Cumae and Dephi: Famous oracular sites in Italy and Greece.

3.7

Meter: elegiac couplet.

4. Leonora: See on *el.* 3.1.87.

3.8

Meter: elegiac couplet.

Leo X (Giovanni de' Medici [1475–1521], pope, 1513–21).

2. When Leo died suddenly of malaria it was widely rumored, though incorrectly, that he had not been able to take Extreme Unction, the sacrament of the dying.

3.9

Meter: elegiac couplet.

1. Parthenope: See on *ecl.* 1.104 and 3.88.

2. Hesperides: See on *DPV* 3.511.

3. Mergellina: See on *ecl.* 1.110.

7. Sebethias: Nymph of Naples's river Sebethos (Sebeto). See on *ecl.* 1.105.

11. Sannazaro is varying Aeneas's words to Dido (Vergil *Aen.* 4.361): *Italiam non sponte sequor* ("I do not make for Italy of my own will").

Bibliography

༜༜༜

TEXTS AND EDITIONS

COLLECTED WORKS

Opera omnia latine scripta, ed. Paolo Manuzio (Venice, 1535).

Opera latine scripta, ed. Jan van Broekhuizen, notes by Pieter Vlaming (Amsterdam, 1728).

Jacopo Sannazaro: Egloghe, Elegie, Odi, Epigrammi, ed. G. Castello (Milan, 1928). With notes.

Opere di Jacopo Sannazaro, ed. E. Carrara (Turin, 1952). With notes.

PISCATORY ECLOGUES

Le Egloghe Piscatorie di Jacopo Sannazaro, ed. G. Rosalba (Naples, 1908).

The Piscatory Eclogues of Jacopo Sannazaro, ed. W. P. Mustard (Baltimore, 1914). With notes.

Le ecloghe pescatorie, ed. Stelio Maria Martini (Salerno, 1995). With an Italian translation and notes.

THE VIRGIN BIRTH

De Partu Virginis, ed. A. Altamura, Studi e testi umanistici, ser. II: Testi e documenti, 2 (Naples, 1948).

De Partu Virginis, ed. C. Fantazzi and A. Perosa, Istituto Nazionale di Studi sul Rinascimento, Studi e testi XVII (Florence, 1988).

De Partu Virginis (Il Parto della Vergine), tr. G. Giolito de' Ferrari (1588), ed. with notes by S. Prandi (Rome, 2001).

LAMENTATION ON THE DEATH OF CHRIST

"Actii Synceri Sannazarii de Morte Christi Domini ad Mortales Lamentatio," ed. Carlo Vecce, in id., *"Maiora Numina"* (as below); the text, with notes, appears on 83–94.

FRAGMENT OF AN ECLOGUE

Edited by Liliana Monti Sabia in "Storia" (as below); the text appears on 279–81.

ARCADIA

Iacopo Sannazaro: Arcadia, ed. F. Erspamer (Milan, 1990).

L'Arcadie / Iacopo Sannazaro, ed. F. Erspamer, tr. with introduction and notes by Gérard Marino (Paris, 2004).

ANTHOLOGIES

Poeti Latini del Quattrocento, ed. F. Arnaldi, L. Gualdo Rosa, L. Monti Sabia (Milan, 1964). With notes. For Sannazaro see 1101–1207.

An Anthology of Neo-Latin Poetry, ed. F. J. Nichols (New Haven, 1979). For Sannazaro see 288–317 and 678–80. Latin texts with English translations.

Renaissance Latin Verse: An Anthology, ed. A. Perosa and J. Sparrow (Chapel Hill, 1979). For Sannazaro see pages 142–58.

TRANSLATIONS

Arcadia and Piscatorial Eclogues, tr. with introduction by Ralph Nash (Detroit, 1966).

An Anthology of Neo-Latin Poetry (as above).

The Major Latin Poems of Jacopo Sannazaro, tr. with commentary and selected verse translations by Ralph Nash (Detroit, 1996).

"Jacopo Sannazaro: *De Partu Virginis*, I, 91–134 (The Annunciation)," tr. D. Lattimore, in *Poemata humanistica decem = Renaissance Latin Poems*, with English translations by Friends of the Houghton Library, ed. Rodney G. Dennis (Cambridge, Mass., 1986), 22–25.

BIOGRAPHY, COMMENTARY, AND CRITICISM

Altamura, A., *L'umanismo nel mezzogiorno d'Italia* (Florence, 1941).

——— *Jacopo Sannazaro, con appendici di documenti e testi inediti*. Studi e Testi Umanistici, ser. 1: Studi di storia letteraria, 1 (Naples, 1951).

Borghini, V., *Il più nobile umanista del Rinascimento* (Turin, 1943).

Calisti, G., Il "De partu Virginis" di Iacopo Sannazaro. Saggio sul poema sacro nel Rinascimento (Città di Castello, 1926).

Cooper, H., Pastoral: Mediaeval into Renaissance (Ipswich, 1977).

Corti, M., "Sannazaro, Iacopo," in Dizionario critico della letteratura italiana, ed. V. Branca, 4 (Turin, 1986), 82–88.

D'Alessio, C., Sul 'De Partu Virginis' del Sannazaro (Florence, 1955).

Gaisser, J. H., Catullus and his Renaissance Readers (Oxford, 1993).

——Pierio Valeriano on the Ill Fortune of Learned Men (Ann Arbor, 1999).

Grant, W. L., Neo-Latin Literature and the Pastoral (Chapel Hill, 1965), especially 205–13.

Greene, T. M., The Descent from Heaven: A Study in Epic Continuity (New Haven, 1963).

Gualdo Rosa, L., "A proposito degli Epigrammi Latini del Sannazaro," in Acta Conventus Neo-Latini Amstelodamensis (12–24 August 1973), edd. P. Tuynman, G. Kuiper, and E. Kessler (Munich, 1979), 453–76.

Hall, H. M., Idylls of Fishermen: A History of the Literary Species (New York, 1912).

Heninger, S. K., Jr., "The Renaissance Perversion of Pastoral," Journal of the History of Ideas, 22 (1961): 254–61.

Hubbard, T. K., The Pipes of Pan: Intertextuality and Literary Filiation in the Pastoral Tradition from Theocritus to Milton (Ann Arbor, 1998), especially ch. 5, "Renaissance Refashionings," (247–341).

——"Exile from Arcadia: Sannazaro's Piscatory Eclogues," in Pastoral Palimpsests: Essays in the Reception of Theocritus and Virgil = Rethymnon Classical Studies, 3 (2007): 59–77.

Kennedy, W. J., Jacopo Sannazaro and the Uses of Pastoral (Hanover, 1983).

Kidwell, C., Pontano: Poet and Prime Minister (London, 1991).

——Sannazaro and Arcadia (London, 1993).

McFarlane, I. D., "Neo-Latin Literature and the Pastoral," Forum for Modern Language Studies 3 (1967): 95–114.

Monti Sabia, L., "Storia di un fallimento poetico: il Fragmentum di una Piscatoria di Iacopo Sannazaro," Vichiana n.s., 12 (1983): 255–81.

Nichols, F. J., "The Development of Neo-Latin Theory of the Pastoral in the Sixteenth Century," Humanistica Lovaniensia 18 (1969): 95–114.

Piepho, L., "The Latin and English Eclogues of Phineas Fletcher: Sannazaro's *Piscatoria* among the Britons," *Studies in Philology* 81 (1984): 461–72.

Putnam, M. C. J., "Sannazaro's Ekphrastic Vision," *Rethymnon Classical Studies* (vol. 5, 2009).

Quint, D., *Origin and Originality in Renaissance Literature* (New Haven, 1983).

Smith, N. D., "Jacopo Sannazaro's *Eclogae Piscatoriae* (1526) and the 'Pastoral Debate' in Eighteenth-Century England," *Studies in Philology* 99 (2002): 432–50.

Sparrow, J., "Latin Verse of the High Renaissance," in *Italian Renaissance Studies*, ed. E. F. Jacob (London, 1960), 354–409.

Ternaux, J. C., "Sannazaro (Jacopo) (1458–1530)," in *Centuriae Latinae*, ed. C. Nativel, Travaux d'Humanisme et Renaissance, 314 (Geneva, 1997), 711–18.

Tateo, F., "Iacobo Sannazaro" in *La letteratura italiana: storia e testi* (Bari, 1972), 3.2, 609–76.

Traina, A., "Pascoli e Sannazaro" in "Poeti latini del Quattrocento, II" in *Poeti latini (e neolatini). Note e saggi filologici.* II serie (Bologna, 1981; 2nd ed., 1991).

—— *Poeti latini (e neolatini). Note e saggi filologici*, IV serie (Bologna, 1994), 225–31.

—— "*Imitatio* Virgiliana e clausole anomale nel *De Partu Virginis* del Sannazaro," *Medioevo e umanismo* 96 (1997): 1793–99.

Vecce, C., *Gli zibaldoni di Iacopo Sannazaro* (Messina, 1998).

—— "*Maiora numina*. La prima poesia religiosa e la *Lamentatio* di Sannazaro," in *Studi e problemi di critica testuale* 43 (1991): 49–94.

—— "Multiplex hic anguis. Gli epigrammi di Sannazaro contro Poliziano," *Rinascimento* 30 (1990): 235–55.

—— *Iacopo Sannazaro in Francia* (Padua, 1988).

Zabughin, V., *Storia del Rinascimento Cristiano in Italia* (Milan, 1924).

Zumbini, B., "Dell'epica cristiana, italiana e straniera, e particolarmente dei poemi del Vida e del Sannazaro," in his *Studi di letteratura comparata* (Bologna, 1931), 39–86.

Index

❧❦❧

Lowercase roman numerals refer to page numbers in the introduction. References to Sannazaro's works are by abbreviated title, book and/or poem number, and line number (see page 379). References followed by *n* refer to notes. Line numbers in the prose translation correspond to the lines of the Latin text.

· INDEX ·

Ennius, ep.1.31.3n; *Annales*, *DPV*
  3.482n, ecl.3.60n
Envy, xvi, el.3.1.75
Eoan Ocean, ep.2.48.7
Eos, ep.2.36.20, ep.2.36.21n
Eous, *DPV* 2.36n
Ephyre, *DPV* 3.508
epic, x
Epimenides, *DPV* 2.256n
Epirus, *DPV* 2.176, *DPV* 2.176n,
  el.2.1.67n
Erato, el.2.4.1, el.2.4.1n
Erebus, *DPV* 1.367n, *DPV* 3.59,
  ecl.fr.33, ecl.fr.37n
Eridanus, ep.2.53.2n
Erigone, *DPV* 3.123
Erna, el.1.2.7n
eroticism, xix
Erycina, ep.1.10.4
Erythraea, el.2.8.12
Erythraean sea, el.2.10.41
Eryx, el.2.6.3, el.2.6.4n
Este, Ercole I d' (Duke of
  Ferrara), ep.1.44.1n
Este, Leonora d' (Duchess of
  Ferrara), el.3.1.87, el.3.1.87n
Ethiopia/Ethiopians, *DPV* 1.255,
  DPV 1.257n, el.1.1.49n,
  el.1.1.50
Etna/Aetna, el.1.2.6, el.1.11.68,
  el.1.11.69n, el.2.6.1, ep.1.59.3
Etruria, el.2.7.44, ep.1.53.25
Etruscans, el.2.1.62, el.2.7.44n
Etruscan Sea, el.3.1.162, ep.1.4.7
Euboea, el.1.11.74
Euboids, ecl.5.22

Euganean Hills, el.2.1.92,
  el.2.1.92n
eulogy, of Christian saint, xvi
Eumenides, *DPV* 1.389, *DPV*
  3.440, el.1.11.8, el.1.11.8n
Euno, ep.3.6
Euphrates, *DPV* 2.130, *DPV*
  2.130n
Euploea, ecl.fr.1, ecl.2.31, ecl.2.32n,
  ecl.4.66
Euri, *DPV* 1.212n, *DPV* 2.25, *DPV*
  2.26n, *DPV* 3.463
Europa, *DPV* 2.386n
Eurydice, el.1.5.21, ep.1.64.2

Fabiano, ep.1.29
Fabii (Roman clan), el.3.1.50
Faith, *DPV* 3.104
Falernian (wine), ep.1.40.17
Fame, ep.1.2.26
Fannia, el.1.9.57
Farfa, el.2.1.95n
Farfarus, el.2.1.94
fasces, el.1.8.45n
Fates, *DPV* 1.270n, ecl.fr.24n,
  el.1.3.30n, el.1.6.1n, el.2.4.16,
  el.2.9.30, ep.1.34.5n,
  ep.2.43.4n
Fauns, xx, el.1.2.31, ep.1.23.1,
  ep.2.32.2, *Sal.* 15–113, *Sal.* 16n
Faunus, el.2.4.64, el.3.2.9,
  ep.1.19.1
Faventia, ep.1.53.22
Favissae, ep.1.40.31
Federico III of Aragon, king, vii,
  xvii, xviii, ecl.1.110n,

Gibraltar, *DPV* 2.199n, *DPV* 2.455n

Giocondo, Fra Giovanni, xviii, ep.1.50, ep.1.50n

Giovanni, Duke of Gandia, ep.1.53.13n

Giovanni di Paolo (illuminator), 366–367 (App. 1)

Giulio of Siena, el.1.5, el.1.5n, el.3.1.141

Glaucis, ecl.2.53

Glaucus, *DPV* 3.286, *DPV* 3.476, ecl.1.46, ecl.3.67

Gnidos (Cnidos), *DPV* 2.140, *DPV* 2.140n

God the Father, x, *DPV* 1.39–81, *DPV* 3.1–88

Golino, Pietro, el.1.11.20n

Gongiste, *DPV* 3.294

Gonzaga family, el.3.1.100, el.3.1.101n

Gorgons, *DPV* 1.395, *DPV* 1.395n, el.2.1.14, ep.2.2.5, ep.2.2.6n

Grace, *DPV* 3.107, ep.3.2.1

Graces, ep.1.11.3n, ep.1.11.11, ep.1.34.3, ep.1.41.1, ep.2.15.2

Gradivus, ecl.3.74

Granada, Treaty of, ep.2.1.33n

Grappina, Maria Garlonia, ep.3.1

Grappina, Violante, ep.2.54, ep.2.54n

Greece, el.2.7.26

Guadalquivir, *DPV* 2.201n

Guadiana, *DPV* 2.198, *DPV* 2.200n

Guilelmus Durandus (the elder), *Rationale*, 365–366 (App. 1)

Hadrian VI, Pope (Adrian Florensz), xviii, ep.3.4, ep.3.4n

Haemonia, ecl.5.33, el.1.1.73

Haemus, Mount, *DPV* 2.164n, el.1.5.22, el.1.5.23n

Halyachmon, *DPV* 2.166, *DPV* 2.166n

Halybes, *DPV* 2.162, *DPV* 2.162n

Halys, *DPV* 2.159, *DPV* 2.160n

Hamadryads, el.1.2.16, el.2.4.14

Hannibal, xix, ep.1.27, ep.1.27n

Happiness, *DPV* 3.92–144

Harmosyne, ep.1.49

Harpies, *DPV* 1.397, *DPV* 1.397n

harrowing of Hell, *DPV* 1.247n, *DPV* 1.386–451, el.1.7.28n

Hasbytae, *DPV* 2.231

heaven, *DPV* 1.4n

Hebe, ep.1.6.26n

Hebrus, el.1.5.25, el.1.5.26n

Hector, el.1.6.28, ep.2.49.7

Hecuba, el.3.2.79

Helice, ep.1.2.30

Helicon, Mount, *DPV* 1.15n, el.1.11.13, el.1.11.13n, el.1.11.22n, el.1.11.62n, el.1.11.64n, el.3.1.5, ep.1.2.20, ep.1.7.38n

Heliodorus, *DPV* 1.134n

Helvetii, el.3.1.136, el.3.1.136n

Herculaneum, ecl.5.79n

Hercules, ecl.3.87, ecl.4.41, ecl.5.79, el.1.5.37n, el.1.9.39n, el.1.9.62n, el.2.7.2, ep.1.44.2, ep.2.19, ep.2.19.1n, ep.2.28, ep.2.28.1n, *Sal.* 52n

Saturn, el.2.5.46

Saturn, kingdom of, DPV 3.201

Satyrs, xx, el.1.2.20, el.2.5.9,
el.2.10.29, el.3.2.13, ep.1.36.4,
Sal. 15n, Sal. 15–113

Scala, Fulvio, el.1.11.40, el.1.11.42n

Scalampa, Camilla, ep.2.53,
ep.2.53n

School of Jacopo del Sellaio, 367
(App. 1)

Scipiades, el.2.7.50

Scipio, Publius Cornelius,
el.2.7.52n

Scipio Aemilianus, DPV 2.214n

Scipio Calvus, Gnaeus Cornelius,
el.2.7.52n

Scots, ep.3.5.5

Scuccha, el.1.11.7, el.1.11.7n

Scylla and Charybdis, Sal. 52, Sal.
53n

Scyllas, DPV 1.395

Sebethias, ep.3.9.6

Sebeto, ecl.1.105n, ecl.5.21,
el.1.9.47n, el.1.9.48, el.2.3.6,
el.2.4.63, ep.1.44.8,
ep.2.15.34, ep.2.51.40,
ep.2.56.3

Seine, DPV 2.196, DPV 2.197n,
ep.1.50.1, ep.1.50.1n,
ep.2.60.32, ep.2.60.36n

Semele, el.2.5.40

Seneca, DPV 2.318n; Ad Marciam,
el.1.6.5n; Agamemnon, DPV
1.401n, DPV 2.146n;
Apocolocyntosis, DPV 1.230n;
Medea, DPV 3.58n, LMC
40n; Oedipus, DPV 3.129n,

DPV 3.133n, DPV 3.134n;
Phaedra, DPV 3.258n, DPV
3.268n; Phoenissae, DPV
2.462n

Seneca, pseudo-: Hercules Oetaeus,
DPV 2.258n, DPV 3.61n;
Octavia, DPV 3.253n

Serapis, ecl.5.5

Seripando, Antonio, DPV 1.22n

Seriphos, DPV 1.126n, DPV 1.127

serpent, DPV 3.208–210

Sertorius, el.1.9.41

Servius, DPV 2.156n

Setian (wine), ep.1.56.7

seven (number), ecl.1.83n

Sforza, Gian Galeazzo, el.2.2.21n,
el.2.2.22

shepherds, DPV 3.133–235

Sibyl(s), DPV 1.93, DPV 1.93n,
el.1.7.20, el.2.7.4, el.2.7.22n,
el.2.7.52, el.2.8.40n, el.2.9.9

Sicily, el.2.8.15, ep.1.6.18, ep.1.7.3

Sidney, Sir Philip, viii

Sidon, DPV 2.386n, el.1.1.50n

Sigeum, DPV 2.151, DPV 2.151n

Silenus, el.2.5.12, el.2.5.13n

Silius Italicus, Punica, DPV 3.413n;
1, DPV 1.342n, DPV 1.436n,
DPV 2.99n, DPV 2.199n,
DPV 2.271n, DPV 3.298n; 2,
DPV 1.232n, DPV 2.432n,
DPV 3.90n; 3, DPV 1.324n,
DPV 2.124n, DPV 2.165n,
DPV 3.70n; 4, DPV 1.235n,
DPV 1.350n, DPV 3.154n,
DPV 3.400n, DPV 3.504n;
5, DPV 3.388n; 6, DPV

Publication of this volume has been made possible by

The Myron and Sheila Gilmore Publication Fund at I Tatti
The Robert Lehman Endowment Fund
The Jean-François Malle Scholarly Programs and Publications Fund
The Andrew W. Mellon Scholarly Publications Fund
The Craig and Barbara Smyth Fund
for Scholarly Programs and Publications
The Lila Wallace–Reader's Digest Endowment Fund
The Malcolm Wiener Fund for Scholarly Programs and Publications